A HISTORY OF THE FAMILY AS A SOCIAL AND EDUCATIONAL INSTITUTION

TEXT–BOOK SERIES

Edited by PAUL MONROE, Ph.D.

STATE AND COUNTY EDUCATIONAL REORGANIZATION.

By Ellwood P. Cubberley, Ph.D., Professor of Education, Leland Stanford Junior University.

STATE AND COUNTY SCHOOL ADMINISTRATION.

Vol. I. Text Book of Principles. *In Preparation.*
Vol. II. Source Book.

By Ellwood P. Cubberley, Ph.D., Professor of Education, Leland Stanford Junior University, and Edward C. Elliott, Ph.D., Professor of Education, University of Wisconsin.

TEXT-BOOK IN THE PRINCIPLES OF EDUCATION.

By Ernest N. Henderson, Ph.D., Professor of Education and Philosophy, Adelphi College.

PRINCIPLES OF SECONDARY EDUCATION.

By Paul Monroe, Ph.D., Professor of History of Education, Teachers College, Columbia University.

TEXT–BOOK IN THE HISTORY OF EDUCATION.

By Paul Monroe, Ph.D.

SOURCE BOOK IN THE HISTORY OF EDUCATION. For the Greek and Roman Period.

By Paul Monroe, Ph.D.

A HISTORY OF THE FAMILY AS A SOCIAL AND EDUCATIONAL INSTITUTION.

By Willystine Goodsell, Ph.D., Assistant Professor of Education, Teachers College, Columbia University.

A HISTORY OF THE FAMILY AS A SOCIAL AND EDUCATIONAL INSTITUTION

BY

WILLYSTINE GOODSELL, Ph.D.

ASSISTANT PROFESSOR OF EDUCATION, TEACHERS COLLEGE
COLUMBIA UNIVERSITY

New York
THE MACMILLAN COMPANY
1924

392.3
G62h

47,017

May 1964

Norwood Press
J. S. Cushing Co. — Berwick & Smith Co.
Norwood, Mass., U.S.A.

TABLE OF CONTENTS

CHAPTER I

CHAPTER II

THE PRIMITIVE FAMILY

CHAPTER III

THE PATRIARCHAL FAMILY: THE HEBREW TYPE

CHAPTER IV

THE PATRIARCHAL FAMILY: THE GREEK TYPE

CHAPTER V

THE PATRIARCHAL FAMILY: THE ROMAN TYPE

CHAPTER VI

THE INFLUENCE OF EARLY CHRISTIANITY UPON MARRIAGE AND FAMILY CUSTOM IN THE RO-MAN EMPIRE

CHAPTER VII

THE FAMILY IN THE MIDDLE AGES

CHAPTER VIII

THE FAMILY DURING THE RENAISSANCE

CHAPTER IX

THE ENGLISH FAMILY IN THE SEVENTEENTH AND EIGHTEENTH CENTURIES

CHAPTER X

THE FAMILY IN THE AMERICAN COLONIES

CHAPTER XI

THE INDUSTRIAL REVOLUTION AND ITS EFFECT UPON THE FAMILY

CHAPTER XII

THE FAMILY DURING THE NINETEENTH CENTURY

CHAPTER XIII

THE PRESENT SITUATION

CHAPTER XIV

CURRENT THEORIES OF REFORM

A HISTORY OF THE FAMILY AS A SOCIAL AND EDUCATIONAL INSTITUTION

A HISTORY OF THE FAMILY AS A SOCIAL AND EDUCATIONAL INSTITUTION

CHAPTER I

THE HISTORICAL STUDY OF THE FAMILY

Recency of the Historical Study of the Family. — Since the eighteenth century, when the thoughts of men once more eagerly turned to the investigation of human life and institutions as the " proper study of mankind," interest in the problems of social living has become more intense and diffused. Large numbers of intelligent men and women outside the ranks of the historians and sociologists are interested students of our present-day institutions and customs which they rightly seek to understand by tracing the slow course of their development. Historical research has thrown a flood of light upon the church, the state, economic life, law and language. One by one the institutions painfully built up through ages of coöperative social effort have been subjected to searching analysis and investigation and the fruit of these researches has been appreciatively received by an intelligent public. Only the institution of the family has, until rather recently, escaped the attention of the general student of society, although it has justly been reckoned the basis and starting point of social research by the historian and the sociologist.

The reasons for this reluctance are not far to seek. The family is the social institution closest to men's and women's hearts and associated with the tenderest and deepest experiences of their lives. Moreover, in its present monogamic form it represents to many minds in the Western world the only possible solution of the problem of wholesome sex relations, and of the proper care and maintenance of the offspring of such relationships. The family has slowly been shaped into its present form by centuries of effort; it represents society's experience and conclusions with reference to delicate problems of profound import. In consequence many thoughtful and well-meaning individuals are frankly reluctant to meddle with its adjustments. A third reason for this reluctance lies in the fact that any adequate historical study of the family must include topics such as the causes and influence of prostitution, social diseases and divorce, which society has long shrunk from discussing with frankness and in a scientific spirit. Rather has it preferred to bury these unpleasant facts and conditions out of sight in the hope that they would remain permanently out of mind. This unwillingness to discuss such questions has been united with a feeling of hostility toward social critics who proposed measures of reform at all radical in character. Thus Mrs. Parsons's thoughtful book on *The Family* met a few years ago with a storm of adverse criticism and rebuke because it rather audaciously suggested that in view of the widespread existence of prostitution, and in view of the danger of long-deferred marriages, society might find it wise to attempt the experiment of early trial marriages.[1]

Recent Interest in Problems of Family Life. — But reluctance to apply the scientific spirit and method to a study of the family has little by little been breaking down within the last decade. And here, again, the reason is not far to seek. The machinery of family life seems out of joint. Far

[1] *Op. cit.*, pp. 348–9.

from running smoothly it has forced itself upon public attention by its creaking friction until its maladjustments can no longer be ignored. The instability of the family is revealed by the marked increase in divorce among all classes and in desertion among the poor. The difficulties of family life in a congested urban population; the undoubted commercialization of vice and its effect upon family purity and integrity; the marked decline in the birth-rate, — these are a few of the problems which cry aloud to an intelligent public for solution. Little by little serious men and women have been roused to an appreciation of the fact that something is gravely wrong in the operation of the basic institution of society. This, of course, is a most hopeful sign. Attention, once aroused to the problem, has been directed toward historical studies of marriage and family customs among different races and in different periods with a view to discovering how our present conditions and laws have come about. Such careful works as Westermarck's *History of Human Marriage*, Létourneau's *Evolution of Marriage and the Family*, Howard's *History of Matrimonial Institutions* and the two studies by Mrs. Bosanquet and Mrs. Parsons on *The Family* bear witness to a genuine, if recent, awakening of social interest in the knotty questions of which they treat.

Importance of a Genetic Study of the Family. — The value and importance of an unbiassed investigation of the history of the human family lie, first, in the fact already mentioned that such study is the best preparation for an intelligent comprehension of conditions as they are. An enlightened understanding of how certain laws, customs and ideas came to be and why they are still maintained is the first step toward working out a satisfactory theory of how things ought to be. Ideals which are suggested by actual conditions, not formed in the study by speculation, are the most likely to be efficient in bringing about a better state of affairs in any problematic situation. Broad and accurate knowledge, then, must be the first step in social reform.   But there are other values attached to the historical study of the family. First, such investigation should give us a respect for facts rather than for theories about facts; secondly, it should help us to see that, although the origin of the family must be sought in animal instincts, not in ideal love, yet from this rude source has slowly come all that is pure and fine in our family life and sex relations of the present.   It is well for the student of history, as for the student of philosophy, to learn not to despise origins, but to evaluate them, as accurately as he may, in the light of history.

CHAPTER II

THE PRIMITIVE FAMILY

Definition of Terms. — At the outset of this work it becomes necessary to define the significance attached to the terms " primitive " and "family," since these have developed more than one meaning in the current usage of social writers. The word " primitive " may have reference (1) to an absolutely original state of society, or (2) it may be applied to such savage or barbarian groups as exist at the present time. In this study the term will be consistently used in the second sense. Likewise the term " family " may refer to the social unit of Western nations, comprising usually father, mother and offspring; or it may be applied, as it frequently is by anthropologists, to a much larger group tracing descent to some real or mythical ancestor and organized into clans or living in village communities. Examples of such so-called " families " are furnished by the " gens " of the Greeks and Romans and the clan of the American Indians. Even to-day the village communities among the Slavs are kinship groups and hence " families " in this sense of the term. In these villages several households of relatives live under one roof and work together in organized fashion on the farm, which is common property. Likewise all the group possessions are held in common. In the present study, however, the term " family " will be commonly employed in its more familiar usage to indicate the basic family of two generations — parents and children. Frequent reference, however, will be made to the clan, gens and village kinship group, called by a recent German writer the *Grossefamilie* (Great family).

Available Material for the Study of the Primitive Family.
— If the term " primitive " is defined strictly to mean the
original human family, the difficulties in the way of the student
are very real.   It is well-nigh impossible to collect reliable
evidence concerning the earliest forms of family life, since that
evidence is largely lacking.   Such descriptive material as
we have refers to the marriage customs of peoples who have
already proceeded some distance along the path of civilization.   This material includes (1) references to uncivilized
peoples in ancient writings, *e.g.*, in Herodotus and Strabo;
(2) travellers' accounts of family organization among present-
day savages; (3) the reports of trained investigators concerning marriage and the family among groups of barbarians
selected for special study; (4) analogies drawn from the life
of the higher animals, especially the man-like apes.   It is
hardly necessary to point out that all of these sources of knowledge except the accounts of men of scientific training should
be used with caution.   Ancient writers and modern travellers may easily fail either to observe fully and exactly or to
interpret accurately such family customs and sex relations as
they do observe.   Hence it is quite possible for social writers,
using much the same material, to form widely variant theories
on many questions concerning the family as an institution.
This is illustrated by the conflicting views of sociologists with
respect to the original form of marriage and family life.

THE SIGNIFICANCE AND ORIGIN OF MARRIAGE

Meaning of the Term " Marriage." — It is probable that
most anthropologists and social writers are in agreement
concerning the biological meaning of marriage.   The word
has reference to a union of the male and female which does
not cease with the act of procreation but persists after the
birth of offspring until the young are capable of supplying
their own essential needs.   If this view be accepted it becomes

clear at once that marriage exists among birds and some of the higher animals. Indeed birds furnish an excellent example of parental care and affection. Together the male and female share the work of nest-building; and later, while the mother sits on the eggs, the father furnishes food and protection. After the young are hatched, both share the tasks of food getting and of teaching the fledgelings to care for themselves. Apparently monogamic marriage, ending only with life, is not uncommon among birds. This is by no means the case with the higher mammals, however. Among these animals the female assumes most of the care and protection of her offspring and is even called upon at times to defend them against the attacks of the father. But the evidence of travellers shows that among the man-like apes — the orang-utan, the gorilla, and the chimpanzee — the male regularly builds a nest in a forked tree for the pregnant female and remains on guard to defend her. He also assists in the care of the young and constitutes himself their defender. Such facts make it impossible to restrict marriage, in the sense in which it is defined above, solely to human beings.

The Probable Origin of Marriage. — The previous discussion has perhaps shed some light on the question of the origin of marriage. It seems clear enough that the sexual instinct of itself could not have brought about permanent relationships between male and female. So fluctuating a desire could hardly have constituted a firm basis for family life among animals and among the cave-men, who were our original ancestors. Let it be remembered that aboriginal man in all probability had no glimmering conception of that ideal love which to-day binds men and women together in the strongest of human ties. Nor was the female's need of protection a lasting bond of union; for the female savage, like the female ape, is nearly as strong and capable of self-defence as the male. The source of marriage, then, must probably be looked for in the utter helplessness of the new-born offspring and the need of both mother and young for protection and food during a varying period. Natural selection doubtless operated to kill off those stocks in which the male refused this protection and care, and to " select " those for survival in which it was rendered. *Thus it appears that marriage has its source in the family, rather than the family in marriage.*[1] The full significance of this fact does not dawn upon us until we recall the marked decline of the birth-rate among most modern nations and reflect that the very root of the permanent union of the sexes is found in those parental duties that to-day are often repudiated with more or less deliberation and wisdom.

CONFLICTING THEORIES OF THE ORIGINAL FORM OF THE FAMILY

The Theory of Promiscuity. — At the outset we should consider a theory of sex relationships that negates the original existence of marriage and the family. This view was presented in 1861 by Bachofen, a Swiss writer, in his book called *Mutterrecht* (Mother-right). In this famous work Bachofen takes the ground that aboriginal men lived in hordes like other gregarious animals and that complete promiscuity in sex relations prevailed. Children were the charges of the group as a whole. Under such a régime of unrestricted sexual inter-course fatherhood could not be determined; consequently descent was reckoned through females, who, in the course of time, became thereby influential and even powerful. This was the period of the matriarchate when women were the ruling forces of primitive society. After long ages there developed a form of family life based on " father love " with something of the characteristics of the present monog-amous marriage. Bachofen's theory of original sex com-

[1] See Westermarck, *The History of Human Marriage*, p. 22; and Fiske, *The Meaning of Infancy, Riverside Educational Monographs*, pp. 29, 30.

munism has been widely accepted by enthusiastic followers, and has been held in modified form by social writers of considerable prominence. The Scotchman McLennan in his well-known work *Primitive Marriage* and the American Morgan in his book on *Ancient Society*, both maintain that in the beginning of human history sexual intercourse was quite unrestricted and sexual unions were transitory. Each writer then develops his own theory of the stages by which more permanent sex relationships and a crude family organization have developed. The evidence to which these writers point to support their theory is as follows: (1) A few ancient authors and some modern travellers have described savages, low in the scale of civilization, who are said to be quite promiscuous in sex relations; (2) certain savage groups at the present day have curious customs which are alleged to be survivals from a period of complete promiscuity. Such practices as " wife lending," and group marriage as it exists among certain Australian tribes to-day, are illustrations of these customs. Also the practice in some tribes of giving a bride over to the priest or medicine-man before she entered her husband's home is cited by some writers as evidence of original promiscuity in sex relations. Westermarck, in his valuable work on *Human Marriage*, has sifted this evidence very carefully and concludes (1) that no case of a people living in unrestricted sexual communism can be found to-day; (2) that the customs which point to promiscuity admit of different and more satisfactory explanations. For example, " wife lending," as found among many savage peoples, is probably traceable to their exaggerated ideas of the duty of hospitality; and the deflowering of brides by the priest might reasonably be regarded as conferring honor upon the marriage. The more the matter is investigated, the more questionable it becomes that primitive groups generally lived in a condition of absolute promiscuity, although great laxity in marital relations undoubtedly prevailed among them.

The Theory of the Patriarchal Family. — In the same year that saw the publication of Bachofen's work (1861) there appeared a book by a well-known English writer, Sir Henry Maine, which set forth a wholly different theory of original sex relationships and family organization. In this work (*Ancient Law*) the author elaborated his reasons for believing that the earliest form of family life, the germ from which all later forms have developed, was the patriarchal family as exemplified in ancient Rome. The characteristics of this type of family organization are, first, its inclusiveness. All those related by descent through common male ancestors, all persons received into the family by the ceremony of adoption, and even all slaves and servants were regarded as members of the *familia*. A second characteristic of the patriarchal family is the almost absolute authority exercised by the oldest male parent as the priest of the family in its worship of ancestors. By virtue of this priestly position he was sole administrator of the family property, and held the power of life and death over his wife, children and slaves, with few limitations. Nor did this despotic authority cease with the marriage of his sons, but was extended over their wives and children as well as themselves. A third distinguishing mark of this type of family organization is *agnation*, or the kinship system which traces relationship through males only. In the view of Sir Henry Maine the system of agnation existing among certain peoples at present, combined with the authority exercised by male heads of families over women and minor children in many parts of the world to-day, point to a period when the patriarchal family was the universal and original type.

The weakness of this theory of the original family lies in the fact that the author has failed to take note of a mass of evidence concerning savage peoples which contradicts it at several points. Very briefly this evidence goes to show that (1) the *maternal* kinship system which traces relationship through mothers only is even more widely prevalent among primitive peoples than the paternal system and traces of it may be found even among the ancient Hebrews who had developed the patriarchal family in Old Testament times; (2) the organization of the patriarchal family and its clearly defined kinship system are based upon ideas far in advance of the capacities of the primitive mind; (3) although the father among savage groups frequently exercises despotic control by reason of superior strength, this control is thrown off by his sons as soon as they are able to shift for themselves. A power grounded in brute force is hardly to be identified with the patriarchal authority of the Roman father, based as it was upon ancestor worship and exercised under more highly advanced conditions of social and industrial life than ever existed among primitive peoples. The conclusion reached by most contemporary social writers is that the patriarchal family, far from being the original social unit, is a comparatively recent development in the long history of family organization.

The Theory of Original Pair Marriage. — There remains to be considered the view of an increasing number of social investigators. This theory holds that the original form of sexual union was pair marriage — the union of one man and one woman for a period more or less transitory. The researches of Tylor, Starcke, Westermarck and others all tend to support this view, which, however, is not yet conclusively established. The arguments in its favor may be briefly summarized. First, pair marriage is occasionally found among beasts of prey, while among the manlike apes it is the more usual form. This simple family, consisting of parents and offspring, seems to be the outcome of animal experience in the intense struggle for food. It is probable that a small group can more readily obtain sustenance, where supplies are not abundant, than a numerous herd. Moreover coöperation in food getting would be far more likely to occur within a group bound together by familiar association and by the needs of helpless young than in an irresponsible horde. That such coöperation does exist among animal families has been abundantly demonstrated. Secondly, the feeling of jealousy seems too strongly rooted in the natures of men and beasts alike to make the theory of absolute promiscuity at all probable. Such a passion would tend to produce a modified form of monogamic family, even though such unions were probably transitory in character. Thirdly, polygamy and polyandry, forms of marriage held by some writers to precede monogamy, seem to be the outcome of a more advanced social and industrial organization than primitive man could have developed. For example, there is quite possibly a close connection between polygyny and the division of society into classes based on wealth or military prestige. Plurality of wives very generally adds to the social standing of the leading men in savage or barbarous tribes. Finally, for the majority of mankind pair marriage must, perforce, have been the only form of union at all possible, owing to the fact that in most countries the male and female birth-rate is nearly equal. Moreover, Westermarck has shown [1] that in cases where pair marriage does not now prevail there are evidences that it once did exist and has been superseded by a laxer form of marriage.

Relation between Family Organization and the Food Supply. — Perhaps the most obvious deduction from these conflicting views is that no one theory has been satisfactorily established. The life of primitive man is shrouded in an obscurity hard to penetrate. It is quite possible that no one type of sexual union ever prevailed over the whole earth. Rather is it reasonable to believe that the struggle for existence, reduced to its lowest terms in the struggle for food, largely determined what form of marital relationship or family life should prevail in any one locality. The close connection between family organization and the food supply

[1] *History of Human Marriage*, pp. 507–8.

seems fairly well established. The German writer Grosse, in a recent valuable study,[1] has carefully traced the forms probably assumed by the family in the hunting, pastoral and agricultural stages of civilization. The evidence goes to show that in the lowest groups which live mainly upon the produce of the hunt, eked out by seeds, fruits and shell-fish, the struggle for a livelihood is severe and a modified form of the monogamic family is the prevailing type as best suited to the conditions. When the pastoral stage is reached by certain peoples, private property in domesticated animals and rude implements has become a widespread institution and has marked effects upon the family. For, with the development of the instinct of property, wives come to be regarded as valuable assets, since they carry on crude agricultural work and perform all the productive household labor. Family organization is monogamic or polygynic, according to the wealth of the male head. If his possessions are few, monogamy is a necessity; if he has wealth in lands and cattle, he is able to purchase numerous wives who furnish him with useful offspring and add to his possessions.

In Grosse's view the agricultural stage slowly succeeds the pastoral when the population has so increased in numbers that grazing lands furnish insufficient food for the needs of men and cattle. A part of these lands is gradually cultivated with greater care and intensiveness and the returns in a steady food supply amply repay the labors of the agriculturist. The land, now coming to be regarded as the most valuable source of wealth, is held and cultivated in common as the property of the group, who divide its produce among households or individuals. Now it is no longer the simple family that constitutes the social unit, but the " Sippe " or clan which owns the land. Among many agricultural peoples the common land descends in the clan through maternal ancestors only. The reason for this probably lies in the

[1] *Die Formen der Familie und die Formen der Wirtschaft.*

fact that women were the first tillers of the soil, the inventors of agriculture; and many savage tribes, as the Iroquois, Wyandottes and Hurons in North America, recognize their rights in the land they have cultivated. The family within the clan may be monogamic or polygamic in form. This depends as before upon the ability of the male to purchase wives, since women are still looked upon as property. The households frequently contain several generations of related families and are ruled by a head who is usually, although not always, the oldest male relative. Even to-day in the Slav villages of Eastern Europe the household head apportions the work of tilling the common lands and disposes of the produce and the income with the consent of the adult members of the household.

The final stage of development recognized by Grosse is that of the higher agriculturists. At this stage industry and division of labor have so advanced that only one section of the community is devoted to agricultural pursuits. Other groups pursue a variety of industries of which crude manufacturing is most important. Among these peoples two forms of family organization may be distinguished: (1) the patriarchal family, now fully developed as in ancient Rome, China and Japan; (2) the *Sonderfamilie*, or monogamic family of two generations — parents and children — the type prevailing in the Western world at the present time. The patriarchal family no doubt existed in germ within the clan, as the Slav households above described clearly show. With the breakdown of clan organization and control, however, full power over the family (including all those related by descent through males from a common ancestor) fell into the hands of the oldest male head. The modern simple family of Western Europe and America, Grosse believes to be a later offshoot from the patriarchal family, due to an advance in economic life. As a variety of industrial pursuits developed with advance in civilization, the household was no longer held together by coöperative labor upon the family lands. Hence it was possible for the younger members of the family to break away and earn their living independently in a chosen field of industry.

Certain conclusions may be drawn from this brief summary of Grosse's theory. (1) It should be remembered that all peoples have not passed in regular order through the several stages mentioned by Grosse. Many tribes, as the Central Australians, remained in the condition of the lower or upper hunters, while the Teutonic races of Western Europe have, apparently, never developed the patriarchal family in its complete form. (2) Although it appears true that a close relation exists between the industrial conditions of a group and its family organization, this fact should not be pushed too far. The family has a psychical as well as an industrial basis. Feelings of responsibility and rudimentary affection for dependent offspring *created* the family, and these feelings, beyond question, have operated in part to maintain it. Even when the power of the clan among certain peoples became supreme and threatened the suppression of the simple family it was held together by the bonds of mutual dependence, custom and, at least in some instances, of real affection. Moreover, as Mrs. Bosanquet has pointed out,[1] the development of industry and hence of the family was dependent upon a certain degree of intellectual advancement among primitive peoples. Foresight, skill and inventiveness must have emerged and received some encouragement before the domestication of cattle and the cultivation of the soil were rendered possible. Thus many influences probably combined to maintain the family institution in any of its forms. The most that can be justly claimed for Grosse's theory is that it brings into clear light the importance of industrial conditions as an essential factor in determining family organization and the status of woman in the household.

[1] *The Family*, p. 68.

KINSHIP SYSTEMS

Very early in the history of primitive peoples there appeared a form of social organization based upon kinship other than that of the simple family. Society was divided into groups tracing descent to a real or imagined common ancestor; and from these crude divisions bound by the blood tie there developed the clan, exercising control of a political, moral and economic sort over its members. There has been much controversy among anthropologists concerning the causes which led to the kinship group and the matter remains still unsettled. Two types of kinship organization have prevailed at one time or another among different peoples all over the earth: (1) the metronymic (mother-name) system; (2) the patronymic (father-name) system.

The Metronymic System. *Causes of its Development.* — In the metronymic group kinship is traced through the mother only, the father's relationship to his offspring being sometimes entirely ignored, as among the Malay people. Various explanations have been brought forward to account for this widespread custom. McLennan [1] sees in it a proof of his theory that originally sexual relations were quite unrestricted. Thus he argues that the custom of tracing descent through mothers was rendered necessary since it was impossible to determine the father of a child in an age of sexual license. Westermarck and others, however, maintain that this theory is by no means satisfactorily proven. There are tribes living under the maternal system among whom lax sexual relations are almost unknown: whereas there are patronymic kinship groups whose marital customs reveal the utmost laxity and licentiousness. Doubtless the widespread tendency in primitive society to trace descent through females only may be in part accounted for by the close association of

[1] Cf. *Primitive Marriage*, in *Studies in Ancient History* (1886), pp. 87, 91–3.

mother and child before birth and during the latter's years of infancy and dependence. Polygyny, also, must have had its influence, since under this form of family life separate huts were built by the father for his various wives and their children. This custom would tend, of necessity, to withdraw the children from their father's influence and to strengthen the ties which bound them to their mother.

The Relative Status of Father and Mother under the Maternal System. — An important group of social writers have held the theory that the position of the father in the metronymic group was distinctly inferior to that of the mother, who was the ruling power in the household. As evidence they point to the Malay peoples, among whom it is customary for the man after marriage to visit his wife's abode only occasionally. His real home continues to be among his own people whom he assists in cultivating the family lands. The offspring of his marriage are the property of the mother's kindred and are cared for and controlled largely by their maternal uncle who is regarded as their nearest male relative. But this instance is far from typical. Where the maternal system prevails it is a general, although by no means a universal, custom for the husband to make his home among the kindred of his wife; and it is probable that in such instances his position in the household is a somewhat subordinate one. He must prove himself a good hunter and a generous provider of animal food for his wife's family. Otherwise he may be ignominiously dismissed from the household. Such was the practice among the Iroquois tribes of America. But these customs are not evidence that women under the maternal system had sufficient power and influence to establish a matriarchate. Quite often the real household head was the woman's elder brother, the uncle of her children. Moreover, even among the Iroquois, the chief political offices were held by males, although women numerically preponderated in

c

the clan councils.[1] Also it should be noted that the maternal system is likewise frequently found among peoples who have adopted the custom of removing the wife from her own kindred to the hut of the husband. In such cases, although descent is traced through the mother, property and rank sometimes descend through the father, who is the unquestioned head of his household. Such is the custom among the Fijians and many other groups of the Pacific Islanders as well as among the West Australians. These rude societies illustrate an interesting combination of the maternal and the paternal systems, that may possibly represent a transition from one to the other.

Concerning the whole vexed question of woman's status under the metronymic system the following conclusions seem fairly well established.

(1) In those instances where the husband lived and served among his wife's kindred the position of the woman was relatively high. She was protected by her male relatives from unjust divorce, from abuse and from gross overwork.

(2) On the other hand it should be remembered that the maternal kinship system does not imply that women were in supreme control of the household nor even that they held a determining voice in the management of the affairs of the kinship group or clan. This view of female supremacy or of a matriarchate has been maintained by Bachofen and other writers, but has not been satisfactorily established. On the contrary the evidence goes to show that, even when name, rank and property descended through the mother, she was not always the controlling force in the household. Rather was it the woman's oldest brother, her father, or even her husband who had the deciding voice in all important matters and who determined the training and arranged the marriages of the children.

[1] See Powell, *Wyandotte Government*, in *Smithsonian Miscellaneous Collections*, Vol. XXV, pp. 76 ff.

The Patronymic System. *Causes of its Development.* — As the name implies, the patronymic group traces kinship through males who are the dominant sex. Where this system is found, rank and property likewise descend through the father as a general custom. It would be a mistake to assume that the paternal kinship system regularly succeeded the maternal. At the present time there are peoples very low in the scale of civilization where descent is traced through the father who determines the clan or totem group of his children. This is true of the Fuegians of South America, the Todas of India and some Australian tribes. Among these rude groups there exists no evidence of a prior maternal system. One important cause of patronymic social organization may very likely be found in economic conditions. In cases where the group had come to depend largely on the produce of the hunt and where agriculture was hardly developed, or was meagre in returns, an enormous value would be placed upon the activities of the male as the chief food provider. More-over, as population increased, the struggle for food became relatively more intense and led to warfare over hunting and fishing grounds. In such a struggle for bare subsistence, the fighting qualities and superior physical strength of the men were of the utmost value to the group. It naturally followed that males gained rapidly in power and prestige at the expense of the weaker females and tended more and more to pass their name and property on to their offspring.

Another cause for the rise of the paternal kinship group lies in the relatively late discovery, among many savage tribes, of the function of the father in generation. The part played by the mother in the conception and birth of offspring is obvious enough; but an advance in intelligence was necessary before the male function was understood. With this knowledge, however, there developed a tendency to emphasize and even exaggerate the physiological tie between father and child. Westermarck [1] notes that among Australian tribes the belief is prevalent that the child owes its being to the male parent only. He quotes from Howitt the remark of an Australian native: " The man gives the child to the woman to take care of for him, and he can do what he likes with his own child." Where this notion prevailed it must have been a potent influence in the development of a patronymic social organization.

The Position of Women under the Paternal System. — This topic has already been touched upon in the previous paragraphs and need be only briefly treated here. Obviously enough the bodily structure and functions of the female put her at a tremendous disadvantage in a primitive society based upon brute strength in warfare and upon skill in trapping game. To her was assigned by nature the work of motherhood which entails not only severe physical strain, but also the care and responsibility of the nurture of helpless children. These tasks bound primitive woman to her home and its immediate environs. Upon her devolved the heavy drudgery of agriculture, which she carried on with such rude implements as the digging stick and hoe invented by herself. While she labored in the fields she often carried her youngest child strapped to her back. Under such a handicap she supplied the family with edible roots, grains and fruits to eke out the supplies of animal food furnished by the father. Such tasks must have told heavily upon the strength and energy of women in primitive societies. There is little doubt that at an earlier and even less artificial period they were much more nearly the equal of the males in physical strength as well as in the skill required in the daily hand-to-mouth struggle for food.

The custom of wife purchase, which is well-nigh universal among savage tribes, also played its part in lowering the position of woman in the family. A woman once bought

[1] *Human Marriage*, p. 106.

and paid for in cattle or other property used for barter, inevitably came to be regarded as a chattel from which the largest economic returns in labor must be wrung. This was especially true in those instances where the woman left her own family to live with her husband. To this cause of the inferior status of women should be added that of wife capture. In the almost constant warfare waged among primitive groups the lot of the conquered males was death, that of the females was capture and practical enslavement. The wives and daughters of defeated warriors became the concubines or lesser wives of their conquerors and were regarded as even more absolutely the property of the husband than his purchased wife whose kindred might well be in a position to avenge her wrongs. Doubtless polygyny of this sort is a distinct menace to the position of the head wife. The abject subjection of the captured wives tends to fall like a cloud over her and ultimately over her children. Only the widespread primitive custom of demanding from the husband the return of the purchase money in case of outrageous maltreatment of the wife, or in case of her divorce without cause, tended to keep the arbitrary power of the husband within bounds.

EXOGAMY AND ENDOGAMY

Explanation of Terms. — Among very many savage groups there exists a strong aversion to the marriage of near kin. This aversion, however, expresses itself in widely different forms. A very few groups permit sexual intercourse between father and daughter; whereas the horror of cohabitation between mother and son is well-nigh universal. Again, a limited number of tribes do not forbid the marriage of brothers and sisters, while viewing with genuine disapproval any sexual relations between parents and children. On the other hand, by far the larger number of tribes not only condemn sexual relations between blood relatives, but forbid marriages between members of the same clan, or totem group. As these clans may be metronymic or patronymic, this restriction, of course, would prevent marriage between maternal or paternal relatives as the case might be, even to the most remote degrees of kinship, but would make it possible for a man to marry a near relative of his father's or mother's clan on the ground that no kinship tie exists between them. The case of Abraham, who espoused his half-sister Sarah (his father's daughter by another wife than his mother), is a well-known instance of this apparent inconsistency. Probably in those early days the Hebrews still traced kinship through mothers, and thus Sarah was not in the same kinship group as her half-brother Abraham. The custom of marrying outside the clan or tribe is called *exogamy*. The custom of marrying within the group is called *endogamy*.

Causes for Rise of Exogamy. — Numerous explanations have been offered by anthropologists to account for the existence of exogamy. McLennan, in the work on *Primitive Marriage* already cited, holds that it was the outgrowth of a widespread custom of female infanticide which forced primitive groups to prey upon each other for wives. In time the practice of seeking a wife outside the clan or tribe would gain all the tremendous sanction of custom. Westermarck, however, has pointed out some serious flaws in this theory.

(1) Female infanticide has, apparently, never been a universal custom and is sometimes not found among very primitive peoples, *e.g.*, the Yahgans of Tierra del Fuego. (2) Even if female infanticide were general enough to force men to seek wives outside the tribe, that would not prevent men within the clan from marrying such females as were permitted to live and grow up. The theory, then, does not account for the widespread *prohibition of marriage within the clan or totem group* that is so characteristic of exogamy. Westermarck's own explanation of the rise of exogamy [1] is that the custom is the expression of an innate aversion, on the

[1] Cf. *Human Marriage*, chs. XIV, XV.

part of people closely associated from childhood, to sexual intercourse with each other. This aversion, he believes, is rooted in an instinct which has survived because it has proved useful. Those races are most vigorous which do not " breed in and in." Westermarck freely concedes that the instinct does not show itself in a distaste for sexual intercourse *between relatives;* for ignorance of relationship has not infrequently led to sexual love between near kin. He holds rather that the instinct expresses itself in indifference or aversion to cohabitation with household associates. Tylor, on the other hand, finds the origin of exogamy in the desire of savage groups to cement friendly relations with each other through intermarriage.[1]

Effects on the Family. — Whatever may be the true explanation of exogamy, however, its effects upon family life have, on the whole, been beneficent. Not only has it operated quite generally to prevent sexual intercourse between kindred living under the same roof, but it has brought new blood into the clan, thus maintaining its vigor. The whole question of the evil effects of inbreeding is under discussion by biologists and anthropologists at the present time, and cannot be regarded as fully settled. Yet it is well to remember that the most " in and in bred " people of whom we have any knowledge, the Veddahs of Ceylon, are described as short of stature, vacant in expression, and so infertile that the race is rapidly becoming extinct.

AFFECTION AND FREEDOM OF CHOICE IN PRIMITIVE MARRIAGE

Reference has been made to wife capture and wife purchase as modes of obtaining mates which were widely prevalent among savages. But what can be said of mutual choice and affection in primitive marriage? It seems clear enough that wife purchase could not have been the original custom of

[1] See *The Matriarchal Family System,* in the *Nineteenth Century,* July, 1896.

securing wives; for this implies a higher degree of social and economic development than was reached by primitive peoples among whom the property sense is rudimentary. On the contrary there is some evidence to show that in the lowest groups a considerable degree of freedom of choice is allowed to the woman. Westermarck has collected some valuable material which indicates that, at the beginning of human history, marriage was grounded in the mutual attraction and consent of the parties.[1] With rare exceptions the male among the rudest peoples appears as the wooer. The female, less dominated by sexual passion, must be courted; and thus she plays a prominent rôle in sexual selection. Nor is this fact surprising. Darwin,[2] Groos[3] and others have shown that courtship, in one form or another, very generally prevails in the animal kingdom. Male birds and animals alike not only fight fiercely with rivals of their own sex for their mates, but follow these conflicts up with attempts to charm the female onlookers in various ways. Why should not primitive man have employed the same tactics? In a state of nature, where each individual man or woman was his own food provider, the female, as previously stated, was very nearly the equal of the male in strength and self-reliance, and was by no means so dependent upon his prowess in war and skill in the hunt as she later became. Hence she could, and probably did, choose among her suitors. It may be objected that the sale of girls as wives is a common practice among primitive groups; but it should be remembered that, although purchase marriage is and has been a general custom among savages, most of these peoples are far from living under primordial conditions. The Australians, Bushmen, Hottentots and Gold Coast Negroes, who frequently arrange for the sale of infants in marriage shortly after their birth, are by no means in an absolutely primitive social condition.

[1] *Human Marriage*, chs. VII–XIII.
[2] *Descent of Man*, ch. VIII.   [3] *The Play of Animals*, pp. 257–71.

Even among savages who contract for the marriage of their children with complete indifference to their wishes, the engaged couple sometimes break the contract, when they reach maturity, and the girl elopes with another suitor. Elopements used to be common among the Dacotah Indians and are stated to be the rule among the Kurnai of Australia. A few North American Indian tribes were surprisingly generous in permitting freedom of choice in marriage to their girls. Among the Creeks the consent of the woman was regularly obtained by courtship; and no Pueblo girl was forced to marry a suitor against her will. The rude Maoris of New Zealand have a proverb which runs: " As a kahawai (a fish) selects the hook which pleases it best out of a great number, so also a woman chooses one man out of many."[1] Another instance is furnished by the Dyaks of Borneo, among whom the women are apparently given entire liberty in the choice of a husband.

Thus, marriages grounded upon mutual liking are not quite so rare in savage groups as certain anthropologists would have us think. Indeed, there is some reason to believe, as Howard[2] has suggested, that marriage began in free choice, passed through the stage of contract and purchase arranged by family or clan, and with the decay of the kinship group and paternal power, became, very slowly, once more an individual matter as in modern times.

FORMS OF MARRIAGE

Monogamy. — The different forms of marriage and family organization which have prevailed among savage peoples are three in number, *monogamy*,[3] *polygamy* and *polyandry*. Of these three monogamy, or the union of one man and one woman for a varying period of time, has been the persistent type. The

[1] Quoted by Westermarck, *op. cit.*, p. 217.
[2] *A History of Matrimonial Institutions*, Vol. I, p. 202.
[3] More correctly *monandry*, a transitory form of monogamic union.

controlling reason for the prevalence of monogamy is a biological rather than a social or psychological one. It lies in the fact already mentioned that among most peoples the sexes are nearly equal in numbers. It cannot be expected that primitive man would be aware of the physical, moral and social advantages of monogamic marriages, much less be governed by such considerations.

Polygamy, — or that form of marriage in which one man has two or more wives at the same time, has been a widespread type and is still held in honor among Oriental peoples. Unquestionably the causes leading to polygynous marriage are economic and social as well as personal. Obviously enough a plurality of wives satisfies the ill-regulated sex impulses of the savage more completely than monogamy. But such marriage also adds to his wealth and social standing and thus gives him a distinct advantage over the monogamist. The outward and visible signs of his power and wealth are evident to all. Hence polygamy is largely confined, of necessity, to the powerful and the prosperous, — to the chiefs and well-to-do men of the tribe. Other less successful members must be content with one wife or none at all.

The effects of polygamy upon the position of women and children in the home must be briefly considered. There can be little doubt that the status of the woman, where polygynous marriage prevails, is relatively degraded. She must compete with other wives for the favor of the head of the household; and when her attractions fade, as they quickly do because of grinding physical toil and prematurely advancing age, she is likely to be thrown aside for younger and more pleasing wives. Such conditions are not favorable to the growth of affection between husbands and wife; and where such affection has developed in the woman, as sometimes happens, her finer feelings are outraged by the presence of rival wives in the home. It is true that instances are recorded where overworked women in savage communities have urged their husbands to obtain other wives in order that their heavy toil might be lightened. But the weight of the evidence goes to show that polygamy is generally unpopular among savage women. Such a form of marriage divides the family into jealous and clashing groups occupying different huts and nourishing petty and bitter grudges. The effect of the custom upon young children is no less harmful. The extreme sexual indulgence of the father tends to react unfavorably upon the physique of his offspring. Moreover, the numerous children are deprived very largely of the father's personal care and of the affection which closer association with him might develop. Too often they are regarded by the fathers as more or less valuable property and are very early required to labor in the fields. At puberty the daughters are frequently sold as wives to the highest bidder and thus the hard lot of the mother becomes their own.

Polyandry. — A third form of marriage existent among primitive peoples is *polyandry*, or the union of one woman with several husbands. This practice is confined at the present time to a very few groups, notably to the Todas of India and the inhabitants of portions of Ceylon and Thibet. Among the leading causes of polyandry is the numerical disproportion between the sexes. In certain rugged and relatively barren countries male births largely outnumber the female for reasons not yet well understood, but quite possibly connected with the food supply. There is some evidence to the effect that scanty nourishment tends to an excess of male births. Nature may thus protect groups living in barren areas by limiting their reproductive capacity. Again, as Westermarck has pointed out, there seems to be a close connection between endogamy, or marriage within the group, and the practice of polyandry. Polyandrous peoples are almost without exception also endogamous. Marriage within the clan apparently tends to increase the proportion of male births, and thus it may well be a factor in the development of polyandrous marriages. Female infant-

icide has often been pointed out as a powerful cause of polyandry, but the evidence does not support this theory.   Neither
the Todas nor the Thibetans, who are the leading polyandrous
peoples, practise female infanticide if we are to believe the reports of travellers who have lived among them.   We are almost
forced, then, to the conclusion that polyandry is closely bound
up with a marked excess of male births in any community.

Despite the attempts of certain social writers to show that
at the beginning of human society polyandry was a widely
prevalent form of marriage, the theory has little to support it.
On the contrary, as we have seen, there is good reason to
believe that monogamy was the original form of marriage.
Furthermore, among peoples practising polygyny at the present time the majority of the men are monogamous for lack
of sufficient females to serve as wives.   Thus in Turkey,
where polygyny flourishes, about ninety per cent of the men
are monogamous by force of circumstances.

DIVORCE AMONG PRIMITIVE PEOPLES

Freedom of Divorce. — Nothing appears more striking to
the student of the primitive family than the instability of
marriage.   In many instances the most flimsy pretexts are
sufficient to bring about a divorce which is usually accomplished without any formalities whatever.   Marriage is commonly regarded as a private contract and as such may be
dissolved at the will of both parties or of only one.   Such facility of divorce of course implies that the affections are not very
deeply involved in marriage.   In many savage groups incompatibility of temper, the aging of the wife and hence her
depreciation in value as a worker, petty quarrels and other
causes equally slight are regarded as constituting grounds for
divorce.

The greatest variety with respect to freedom of divorce
may be discovered among savage tribes.   Some rude peoples
permit the utmost liberty to both husband and wife. · Thus

among the Point Barrow Eskimo, the negroes of the Gold
Coast of Africa and certain tribes of Asia and America, the
marriage bond is easily broken at the whim of either party.
But this is not always the case. There are tribes as, *e.g.*,
the Karo-Karo of Sumatra, who permit divorce *only by
mutual consent*. In West Victoria (Australia) a man can
divorce his wife only after the consent of the chiefs of her
family and of his own has been obtained. The wife herself
has little or no liberty of divorce although she may complain
of mistreatment to the chief who, if he sees fit, may send the
husband away for a brief period as a punishment.[1] On the
Slave coast of Africa a wife who is grossly abused may leave
her husband without repaying the " head money " if she can
prove her case before the headmen of the village.[2] In such
instances, where the tribal chiefs or a family council control
all divorces, it seems clear that marriage is regarded as a
public concern, affecting the clan or gens, rather than as a
purely private affair.

Wife purchase, as might be inferred, has operated to curtail
the liberty of divorce accorded to the woman. In a majority
of savage tribes, where the custom of purchase marriage prevails, the sole right of divorce lies with the male. Such is
the case among the Aleutian Islanders, the Dacotahs and
Abipones in America and among many African tribes. Even
here, however, custom has tended to mitigate the unjust
treatment of the wife. In some groups the husband who
casts off his wife without cause must forfeit the purchase
money paid down for her. Even in cases where the dissatisfied husband may claim a return of the purchase price after
unjustly divorcing his wife he has to fear the vengeance of
the woman's relatives who may promptly declare a blood
feud. It should further be noted that in a number of tribes
which restrict the right of divorce to the male the causes for

---

[1] Howard, *History of Matrimonial Institutions*, Vol. I, p. 229.
[2] Ellis, *The Ewe Speaking Peoples of the Slave Coast*, ch. X.

divorce are clearly laid down. Adultery on the wife's part, or the loss of virginity on the part of a betrothed girl, are very generally recognized as just occasions for repudiation of the guilty partner. Childlessness is another cause which has obtained wide recognition, not only among primitive peoples, but among the ancient Hebrews and Romans. Laziness, desertion and incompatibility of temper serve as grounds for divorce in the custom of some tribes.

Curiously enough a few of the rudest people of whom we have any knowledge do not permit divorce under any circumstances. Such are the Veddahs of Ceylon and the Papuans of the Island of New Guinea among whom death alone may serve to unloose the bond of marriage.

Disposal of Wife and Children after Divorce. — But, although marriage is easily dissolved and frequently of short duration among primitive peoples, their customs in regard to the disposal of the repudiated wife and her children show a considerable degree of sound sense and regard for justice. No woman, except in case of gross misconduct, is turned adrift in the world after her divorce. Usually she returns to her own people who provide for her until she marries again, as she frequently does. The children are divided between the parents according to various customary rules. Sometimes the mother takes the female children and the father the male. Again, where the maternal kinship system prevails, the children quite often follow the mother, just as in cases where the group is patronymic they remain with the father, since they belong to his kindred. Again, if the children of a divorced wife are very young, it is usual to leave them under the care of the mother. In certain tribes custom requires that, if the divorced woman is the guilty party, she pay a fixed sum to her husband for every child she takes away with her.

Property Arrangements. — No less reasonable are primitive customs regarding the disposal of property after divorce. Very generally the guilty party is discriminated against.

The wife discarded because of adultery or barrenness, must repay the purchase price or obtain it from her kindred. In addition she must sacrifice all gifts bestowed on her at her marriage and all property accumulated afterwards. Likewise the husband who divorces his wife without due cause usually forfeits the price paid for her and in some cases, though by no means in all, he must hand over the children to the mother. In a few instances the man and woman receive the property owned by each at the time of marriage and divide any property accumulated afterwards. Westermarck cites the case of the Manipuris among whom custom requires that the wife divorced without just cause shall take " all the personal property of her husband, except one drinking-cup and the cloth round his loins." [1]

Tendency toward Group Regulation of Divorce. — From the above discussion it appears that divorce is not restricted to civilized nations but is a custom as old as marriage. Indifference, personal dislike or incompatibility play their part in determining divorce among primitive races as among modern. Very early, also, customary law serves more or less to regulate these separations and to determine the disposal of wife, children and property. Even among some of the least civilized peoples may be observed the rudimentary tendency to bring divorce under the control of the group as in modern times.

SERVICES RENDERED BY THE PRIMITIVE FAMILY TO CIVILIZATION

Social Services. — In the rude ages that mark the beginning of human history the family, as we have seen, appears to be the earliest, because the most natural organization of society. Before the recognition of kinship bonds had developed the clan, and long before clans had become amalgamated into tribes, the natural family of two generations was probably

[1] Westermarck, *op. cit.*, p. 531.

in existence. The dependent offspring of sexual unions, which otherwise might well have been merely temporary, served as a bond uniting the male and female in a common service of protection and nurture. In the family, then, as the matrix of organized society, were nourished those altruistic virtues which, when carried beyond the boundaries of the family and the kinship group, were to prove the greatest unifying force in society. When savage man extended the instincts of sympathy, fellow-feeling and coöperation to all those united to him by the blood bond and later to all members of the tribe, the foundations of justice, law and progress were securely laid.

But the primitive family doubtless performed another social service of no small importance. Long before the medicine-man, the shaman or the tribal elders had taken the group customs into their peculiar charge, the family must have been the custodian of such crude human experience as seemed most worth preserving. From father to son, from mother to daughter, were passed on the small but precious hoards of knowledge painfully wrested from nature. Thus the family in its simple or its group form, as the only social organization, exercised a variety of functions now widely distributed. The home was the centre of such crude industry as then existed. It was in addition the sole training school of the young in the virtues most prized by the savage, as well as in the arts of warfare, the hunt and agriculture.

The Primitive Family as an Industrial Unit. — The earliest human groups doubtless had no economy, *i.e.*, no practical adjustment of means to ends. The lowest peoples of whom anthropologists have knowledge, the Veddahs of Ceylon, the Bushmen of South Africa, the Negritos of the Philippines and certain Australian tribes, are even now engaged in a daily, almost hand-to-hand struggle with nature to obtain a bare livelihood. Such a struggle for existence reveals no attempt to adapt present means, in respect to food supply and clothing, to future needs. The first genuine economy was practised not by primitive groups, but by savage peoples a little higher in civilization, and is closely bound up with the life of the household. Indeed it is well to remember that our word " economy " is derived from a Greek term signifying the practical administration of *household* affairs. In the family was developed the original division of labor upon the basis of sex differences. To the restless male with his greater physical strength and relative freedom from the care of off-spring fell the task of supplying the family with animal food in the intervals of warfare. His were the more stimulating duties of hunting and fighting. Upon the female, forced to be more stationary by the demands of motherhood, devolved less exciting and more irksome burdens. She must provide a constant supply of vegetable food at the same time that she bore and reared her offspring. From the beginning of human history mankind have been more dependent upon plant food than has been generally recognized. Game was often scarce and uncertain and primitive groups thus found their most reliable source of subsistence in roots, seeds and fruits. To the woman, the home-maker, fell the task of collecting nature's products in the region around the home, while the man roamed far, alone or with others, in search of game. It is probable, then, that woman was the most reliable food provider among primitive peoples.[1]

The old saw that " necessity is the mother of invention " is well illustrated in the crude industries of primitive women. A long forward stride was made by civilization when woman, no longer content to gather the meagre products of an un-cultivated soil, conceived the idea of planting seeds to secure a richer harvest. First with her hands she scraped the soil and dropped her seeds. The need for a more satisfactory implement led her to invent a rude digging stick. From this bent stick, in response to a daily challenge upon her inventive-

[1] See Karl Bücher, *Industrial Evolution*, ch. II.

D

ness, woman evolved the hoe and later a crude plough which she herself dragged over the soil in default of domesticated animals. To woman's constructive instinct may be traced the first primitive mill for grinding seeds, where one stone is made to move over another. The metate and muller, likewise used for grinding grain, was her invention. It was the primitive housewife who discovered that from steatite (soapstone) could be made a cooking pot which would stand the heat of the fire without cracking. In the pursuit of her multifarious tasks she was forced to be inventive; and the crude spindle, the weaving frame with its heddle, the scraper, the stone knife, the adz and other rude implements, witness to her success. Such achievements constitute an honorable record for primitive womankind. There are writers, however, who maintain that woman's inventiveness never advanced very far. They point out that the domestication of cattle and their use in drawing the plough, important improvements in the plough itself and above all the progress from crude stone implements to more serviceable metal tools were all the work of man when his attention could profitably be diverted from war to industry. These facts should not, however, blind us to the truth that in the invention of the first agricultural and household implements woman was the pioneer. And it is perhaps the earliest human inventions that require the highest degree of constructive imagination.[1]

With respect to variety of pursuits the primitive housewife was clearly in the lead. The man fought, hunted, fished, made nets and weapons and sat around the camp-fire for hours or even days at a time. In contrast to this simple industrial programme the occupations of the wife and mother seem varied indeed and the demands upon her versatility persistent and exacting. In addition to her labors as an agriculturist, she must prepare granaries to store seeds against a period of scarcity and want. She must go out and find the game her

[1] See Oliver T. Mason, *Woman's Share in Primitive Culture, passim.*

husband had carelessly thrown down and cut it up into food portions, after stripping off the hide to be converted into leather by simple processes she had herself discovered. She was more often than not the tailor, the shoemaker, the food preparer, the potter and the basket maker of the family. At times she was even the builder of the hut or tepee. And these labors were hers in addition to her cares as a mother. Truly the home, among more advanced savage tribes, was a hive of industry centering about the wife and mother. Her life stands out in striking contrast to that of the idle " lady " of modern times — a type developed among civilized nations. Primitive woman was a producer of the utmost economic importance — not merely a consumer like the luxurious " lady " of Europe and America.

One further point should be noticed in connection with primitive industry. It can hardly be questioned that the pursuits of the male — war and group fishing and hunting — demanded powers of coöperation and organization not exacted in nearly the same degree of the female by her more individualistic tasks. These demands developed in man a stronger sense of social solidarity and social obligation than was possible to the woman, confined as she was largely to the home with its personal interests. Through the long course of social history, this division of labor on the basis of sex has operated to develop in man a larger social and political interest and a greater capacity for organized effort than the home-staying woman has ever possessed. The feminine virtues and accomplishments most emphasized in all ages have been precisely those relatively individualistic ones developed by the domestic wife and mother. Therefore it is not strange that women as a whole have a more restricted social interest and vision than men. But despite this fact one of the most striking and hopeful features of our modern age is the ability shown by women to organize and coöperate in behalf of important social ends, now that the sphere of their activities and interests is no longer bounded entirely by the home.

The Family as the Earliest Educational Institution. *Status of Children in the Primitive Household: Parental Affection.* — The status of children in primitive tribes is generally determined less by fixed custom than by the caprice of the parent. In the lowest groups the power of the father over his children is absolutely unlimited, extending to the taking of life or sale into slavery. Among the Ewe-speaking people of the Slave Coast the terms for father mean " he who maintains," " he who owns." Falkner in his *Description of Patagonia* states of the savage inhabitants of that land that, although parental love seems highly developed among them, the men not infrequently sell wives or children for Spanish brandy. And this is by no means an isolated case. In the words of Herbert Spencer : " The status of a primitive man's child is like that of a bear's cub. There is neither moral obligation nor moral restraint; but there exists the unchecked power to foster, to desert, to destroy, as love or anger moves." [1]

There is reason to believe that in many savage tribes the new-born child was not held to be a *person* until it had sucked in its mother's milk or later until it was given a name. Even after their claims to personality had been established children among savages were very generally regarded as chattels at the disposal of one or both parents. In this connection a recent writer states that " the child was *property*, valuable property, and usable property. Whether he was a *person* first and only through pressure of untoward circumstances came to be regarded as a *thing*, perhaps we cannot say, since the savage's sense of personality is so obscure. But there is no doubt that he was a *thing*, an asset, a resource, a marketable good." [2] The author cites a mass of testimony to bear

[1] *Principles of Sociology*, Vol. I, p. 747.
[2] Todd, *The Primitive Family as an Educational Agency*, New York, 1913, pp. 101–2.

out this statement. Panlitschke writes of the children of the Northeast Africans : " They are the property of the father for whom they must work, from whom they must buy themselves off, who can kill them, and from whom they must be purchased. . . . Thus their labor power belongs to the father until the moment they leave the family and become themselves the heads of families." And the Yakuts of the frozen north frankly declare : " Children are our capital if they are good. It is hard to get good labourers, even for large wages, but a son, when he grows up, is a labourer who costs nothing." [1]

Such being the status of children in primitive households, we are not surprised to learn that infanticide was freely practised whenever circumstances seemed to warrant it. The motives actuating parents who destroyed their new-born children were doubtless chiefly economic. Would the food supply of the family suffice for a new member? Or, if the group were migratory, always on the search for fresh hunting or fishing grounds, could the infant be easily transported? If there were already a child in arms and one or two toddlers besides, the death sentence of the newcomer would probably be pronounced and promptly executed. Then, too, other motives were no doubt at work, such as the unwillingness of an overworked mother to assume the added burden of rearing an infant, or the deformity or weakness of the child.

Such statements as the foregoing will perhaps provoke the question : " Is not the parental instinct present and sometimes even very strong among savages? " Apparently it exists quite generally, but in a rather crude form. Like other instincts it is a product of biological and social development by means of natural selection. It manifests itself among many savage parents in the form of animal-like emotion and thoughtless indulgence, rather than in self-sacrificing affection and intelligent care. There is much evidence to show that parents in

[1] *Ibid.*, pp. 102-3.

primitive groups are fond of their children and grant them almost unlimited indulgence. But very frequently, especially in the lowest groups, their affection lacks reason and foresight and it will often weaken under the strain of famine, severe inconvenience or actual danger. Sad tales are told by travellers and anthropological writers of the obliteration of parental feeling under stress of hunger, fear or even anger. Of the Bushmans it is related: " When their supply of provisions begins to fail, or when they are pursued by enemies, or when a wife has been abandoned by her husband, their children are considered to be a burden too heavy to be borne, and to get rid of them they will strangle them, smother them, cast them away in the desert, or even bury them alive." [1] Similar evidence of the weakness of parental love is afforded by tribes in Central Africa, the Fijians, the Fuegians and many other peoples.[2] On the other hand the Pueblos of North America seem to have developed a rational affection for their offspring and a family discipline quite unusual among savages. The same is true of certain Indian tribes, the Eskimos and the peoples of the Sahara. On the whole, however, the statement of a modern writer seems fairly correct when he says that the affection of savages for their offspring " is an instinct of race preservation analogous to that of the lower animals, and gratifying itself without restraint. The savage knows little of that higher affection subsequently developed, which has a worthier purpose than merely to disport itself in the mirth of childhood, and at all hazards to avoid the annoyance of seeing its tears." [3] Furthermore it must be remembered that in many tribes parental love seems barely to outlast the period of early childhood. The period of helplessness among savage children is surprisingly short, and they are very early expected to shift for themselves. As soon as they can collect berries, seeds, shell-fish, whatever

[1] Featherman, *Social History of Mankind*, Vol. I, 532–3.
[2] See Todd, *op. cit.*, pp. 110–17.   [3] Quoted in Todd, *op. cit.*, p. 96.

food Nature freely provides, the affection of the parents, like that of animals, seems to cool and in some instances to change to positive indifference. Such is the case, for example, among the rude peoples of Guiana, Tierra del Fuego, Australia, Brazil and the Fiji Islands. Too often, when such indifference has developed, children are ruthlessly exploited for their labor. The boys especially, as among the Kafirs, are very early set at long and wearisome tasks in the fields or among the cattle. Only when they have undergone the tribal initiations that accompany the period of puberty, and have married and set up a home for themselves, are they free from the authority of the father. But in fairness it should be remembered that the exploitation of children, as well as the cruelty sometimes shown toward them in times of famine or danger, is due in large measure to the hard conditions of savage life and gradually gives way to more considerate treatment when those conditions become less harsh and exacting.

The Nurture of Infants. — When the parents in primitive society are agreed that their offspring shall live, what care do they bestow upon the new-born child? The accounts of travellers reveal a wide variety of customs in respect to the nurture of children. Some tribes show a commendable desire to start the infant aright on that path of custom which is regarded as safe and honorable. Occasionally an expectant mother modifies her food for the sake of her unborn child. Thus, among the Kafirs, she refrains from eating the flesh of the buck lest her child be ugly, and the under lip of the pig lest the lower lip of her baby be too large.[1] In the Banks Islands of the Pacific both parents eat only such food as would not cause the illness of a new-born child. Such food taboos seem fairly general among savages and are not always relaxed until a considerable time after the birth of offspring. For example, the Eskimo mother must refrain from eating raw meat a whole year and during this period is expected to put a

[1] Kidd, *Savage Childhood: A Study of Kafir Children*, p. 8.

little of her food into a skin bag after each meal. Although none of this stored-up nourishment is given to the child, the custom is called "laying up food for the infant." and is probably designed to ward off a possible future famine from its life. Quite often parental concern for offspring does not stop with food taboos. Charms are plentifully used to drive off the ever present evil spirits who might work terrible injury on the helpless child. The peoples of the African Slave Coast employ priests or priestesses to offer purifying sacrifices shortly after the birth of a child in order that malicious spirits may be kept from inflicting harm. These purification rites are very general among savages and have the further purpose of cleansing the mother and child from uncleanness; for everywhere birth is regarded as in some sense involving impurity. The superstitious Kafirs make generous use of charms. A Kafir woman smokes her infant over a fire of scented wood to ward off lurking demons; while the father causes his boy child to inhale the smoke of a vulture feather to make him brave.[1] It is interesting to note that the custom of hanging charms about the necks of infants is as ancient as primitive society. The savage Kafir, the Gold Coast negro, the ancient Roman and some modern peoples are all alike in maintaining this superstitious custom.

Unfortunately charms and food taboos do not prevent an enormous infant mortality among savages. A priest laboring among the primitive groups in Lower California relates that he baptized in succession seven children of one mother and buried them all " before one of them had reached its third year. . . ." Another writer cites the cases of four women among the Yakuts; one bore nine children and raised one; another also had nine and lost them all; another bore eight, all of whom died; another brought up two of the ten infants born to her. Commenting on these facts, Todd writes : " Probably these figures could be matched almost at random among

[1] Kidd, *op. cit.*, pp. 18–19.

savage and barbarous peoples, but it has always proved extremely difficult to collect child-mortality statistics among
them, largely on account of their feeble memorial powers in
this particular." [1] The inability of savages to remember
events that have occurred a year or two in the past is noto-
rious. Apparently their memories are strong and active
only in relation to the persistent demands of daily life such as
getting food and propitiating spirits. These oft recurring
needs serve as constant stimuli to their feeble powers of
recall. Hence the names and even the existence of deceased
children are quite frequently soon forgotten.

It is not difficult to account for the appalling mortality-
rate among savages. Ignorant as they are of the merest
essentials of proper child nurture, primitive parents cheerfully violate every principle of infant hygiene. The advantages of cleanliness, fresh air and suitable food are ignored at
every turn. Yakut babies are permitted to lie in damp,
unventilated rooms neglected for hours at a time; Thlinkeet
infants are kept in a condition of filth which produces sores
that scar their bodies for life; and Igorot children fare little
better. Many tribes look askance at bathing; and the young
suffer accordingly. Then, too, the food given to children is
often quite beyond their powers of digestion. We are told
that Bushwomen from the birth of their children " feed them
with roots and meat which they chew for them. They are
taught to chew tobacco when very young, and have scarcely
any human protection or attention whatever." Unfortunately primitive peoples have little knowledge of the virtues of
cow's milk as an infant diet; for even in tribes where cattle are
domesticated and milk can be easily procured it is quite often
not given to babies. Savage mothers, to be sure, suckle
their children much longer than do mothers in civilized
societies, the suckling in many instances not ceasing until
the child is four years old. But this custom makes it very

[1] *Op. cit.*, p. 123.

difficult for the child when weaned to digest the coarse food eaten by adults.[1]

Home Training and Education. — If the infant is vigorous enough to withstand the effects of his oft-mistaken nurture and grows to self-reliant childhood, his training and education may begin. This falls naturally into two divisions, (1) the social and moral, and (2) the practical. Of course the amount of moral training given in the primitive home depends largely upon the degree in which group customs have become fixed and authoritative. Where a tribe has well-defined notions concerning sex relations, treatment of women, attitude toward parents, food taboos, methods of warding off evil spirits, etc., the family has the important task of starting the education of the unformed child in the group way of thinking and acting in these respects. But it must not be supposed that any conscious ethical aim is present in the minds of the parents. So far as they pay any attention to the moral education of their children, this takes the form of training them in certain habits by an appeal to unthinking imitation. Discipline in savage households is generally lenient. The child is usually neither scolded nor whipped unless the parent falls into one of those sudden fits of uncontrollable passion to which primitive peoples are subject. In such cases punishment may be swift and cruel. Among more advanced groups, as the Pueblos of North America, a high value is consciously set upon obedience of elders and observance of moral customs. This obedience, however, is not secured by corporal punishment, but by the use of weird tales told by the older men over the evening fire, — tales carefully designed to arouse superstitious fear in the shuddering boys and girls.

The part played by the mother in the moral training of her children varies with her status in the household and the group. Among tribes such as the Kafirs and the Fiji Islanders, where women are little more than beasts of burden

[1] Todd, *op. cit.*, p. 120.

held in scorn and contempt, the influence of the mother must be slight indeed, at least upon her male children after the stage of infancy. Sex antagonism and sex taboos are highly developed among some primitive peoples and have worked havoc with the mother's control of her children. Webster [1] tells us that, during their initiation into full tribal membership, Hottentot youths are encouraged by their fathers and the older men publicly to flout and deride their own mothers; and in New Guinea boys are deliberately taught to beat them as a mark of manliness. Then, too, in those tribes where the sexes remain rigidly separated, little boys are taken at two or three years of age from the mother and brought up in the " Men's House." Such club-houses are common in the Pacific Islands and even among the Southwestern tribes of the United States. On the other hand, among the more civilized Iroquois and Wyandottes, where women were the heads of households and had no little economic and political power, the influence of the mother in shaping the character of her children must have been important and lasting.

At puberty the moral education of the boys among most primitive peoples is taken out of the hands of the parents and given over to the older men of the tribe. Indeed there is good reason to believe that the initiation rites, so common in savage groups, constitute by far the most important part of the moral training of the youth. By means of fasting, ordeals, dramatic representations, songs and dances, together with some explanation by way of interpretation, the tribal elders seek to impress indelibly upon the boy's excited mind the moral ideas and customs of his people. The chief interest of these puberty rites for the student of the family lies in the fact that some of the ceremonies are definitely designed to prepare the boy for marriage. Also the boy learns at this time the totem groups or classes into which he may marry and those which he must

[1] *Primitive Secret Societies*, p. 24.

carefully avoid when taking a wife. He is made by the elders
to understand that he must consider the interests of the tribe
in choosing a mate, and select a woman likely to bear children.
After the long ordeals are over the youths are regarded as men
and are permitted considerable sexual license before they
marry.[1]

In some tribes, as puberty approaches, the girls are kept in
close seclusion and required to fast rigidly. During or after
this period they may receive instruction from adult female
relations in such sexual customs as it is essential for them to
know.[2]

The *practical education* of boys and girls in primitive families, like their moral training, is gained quite often by blind
imitation of their elders accompanied by little or no instruction. In this respect, however, marked differences exist
among savage peoples. For example the Lower Californians,
the Seminoles, and the tribes of New Guinea and the Caroline
Islands pay little attention to the training of the young, while
the Apache Indians, the Blackfeet, the Pueblos and the
islanders in Torres Straits take much pains to train their children in practical duties. When the children grow old enough
to share in the tasks of the household, they assist the mother
in bringing wood and water, hunting for shell-fish, lizards,
edible weeds, roots, etc. Very early in their lives sex division
of labor becomes marked. The boys learn by imitation of
their fathers to make the weapons, traps and nets used in
warfare, hunting and fishing; while the girls imitate the work
of their mothers in cooking, weaving, skin-dressing, pottery-
making and the grinding tasks of crude agriculture. In some
tribes, as the Eskimos, the Sioux and the Dacotah Indians,
the value of directing the early play activities of children seems

[1] See Webster, *op. cit.*, p. 43, who cites Toplin's *The Native Tribes of South
Australia*, and Helms, *New South Wales*.
[2] Frazer, *The Golden Bough*, III, 204–33; Crawley, *The Mystic Rose*, pp. 215–
21, 294–314.

to have been more or less consciously felt by the parents. Thus the Eskimo boy is given a tiny bow and arrows and is encouraged to shoot at a reindeer fœtus set up for him. The Dacotah girl has a little work-bag containing an awl and some sinew; and while her mother makes moccasins she watches and imitates her.[1] Describing his boyhood among the Sioux Indians Dr. Eastman says: " Our sports were moulded by the life and customs of our people; indeed we practised only what we expected to do when grown. Our games were feats with the bow and arrow, foot and pony races, wrestling, swimming, and imitation of the customs and habits of our fathers. We had sham fights with mud balls and willow wands; we played lacrosse, made war upon bees, shot winter arrows (which were only used in that season) and coasted upon the ribs of animals and buffalo robes."[2] So far as the parents directed this training, as they certainly did in the more advanced tribes, the home may rightly be called a school of apprenticeship.

SELECTED BIBLIOGRAPHY

SOURCES.

Boas, Franz. *The Central Eskimo*, in *Report of the American Bureau of Ethnology*, VI, 516–526.

Codrington, R. H. *The Melanesians* (1891), chs. II, IV.

Danks, Rev. B. *Marriage Customs of the New Britain Group*, in *Journal of the Anthropological Institute*, XVIII, 1889.

Eastman, C. A. *Indian Boyhood*, 1902.

Ellis, A. B. 1. *The Tshi-speaking Peoples of the Gold Coast*, chs. XVII, XX.

　　　　　2. *The Ewe-speaking Peoples of the Slave Coast*, chs. X, XVI.

　　　　　3. *The Yoruba-speaking Peoples of the Slave Coast.*

Hiller, H. M., and Furness, Dr. W. H. *Notes of a Trip to the Veddahs of Ceylon*, London, 1902.

Howitt, A. W., and Fison, L. *Australian Class Systems*, in *Journal of Anthropological Institute*, Vol. XVIII.

[1] Todd, *op. cit.*, p. 164.　　　[2] *Indian Boyhood*, p. 64.

Kidd, Dudley. *Savage Childhood: A Study of Kafir Children,* London, 1906.

McGee, W. J. *The Seri Indians,* in *Report of American Bureau of Ethnology,* XVII, Part I, pp. 269–87.

Murdock. *The Point Barrow Eskimo,* in *Report of the American Bureau of Ethnology,* IX, pp. 410–23.

Powell. *Wyandotte Government,* in *Smithsonian Miscellaneous Collections,* 1879–80, Vol. XXV, pp. 76 ff.

Rivers, W. R. H. *The Todas* (1906), chs. XIV, XXII.

Spencer and Gillen. 1. *The Native Tribes of Central Australia,* chs. II, VII, XVII, and pp. 406–7, 469–71.

2. *The Native Tribes of Northern Australia,* pp. 27–49, 70–74, 133–142, 606–18.

Stevenson, Matilda Coxe. *The Zuñi Indians* in *Report of the American Bureau of Ethnology,* XXIII, 1901–2, pp. 94–107, 290–305, 349–54.

Thomas, W. I. *Source Book for Social Origins.*

SECONDARY REFERENCES.

Bachofen, J. J. *Mutterrecht* (1861).

Bosanquet, Helen. *The Family,* ch. I.

Bücher, Karl. *Industrial Evolution* (1904), pp. 25–43.

Chamberlain, A. F. *The Child and Childhood in Folk-Thought,* chs. VII, XIII, XIV.

Frazer, J. G. *The Golden Bough,* III, 204–233.

Giddings, Franklin T. *Principles of Sociology,* pp. 256–90.

Giraud-Teulou, A. *Les origines du mariage et de la famile* (1884), chs. I, II, V, VI, VIII, XIX.

Grosse, Ernst. *Die Formen der Familie und die Formen der Wirtschaft* (1896), chs. II–IX.

Hartland, E. S. *Primitive Paternity,* Vol. II, ch. I.

Hobhouse, L. T. *Morals in Evolution,* Vol. I, ch. VI.

Howard, E. G. *History of Matrimonial Institutions* (1904), Vol. I.

Létourneau, Charles. *The Evolution of Marriage and the Family,* London, 1891, chs. I–III, V–VII, IX–X.

Lubbock, Sir John. *Origin of Civilization,* chs. I–IV.

Maine, Sir Henry. 1. *Early Law and Custom,* ch. VII.

2. *Ancient Law,* pp. 124–66.

McLennan, J. F. *Studies in Ancient History* (1886), *Primitive Marriage,* pp. 87 ff., chs. V–VIII.

Mason, O. T. *Woman's Share in Primitive Culture.*

Morgan, Lewis H. 1. *Houses and House-Life of the American Aborigines*, chs. III–VI.

2. *Ancient Society*, Part II, chs. I, II–V, VIII.

Parsons, Elsie Clews. *The Family.*

Ratzel, F. *History of Mankind* (1989), Vol. I, pp. 114–452.

Spencer, F. C. *The Education of the Pueblo Child*, pp. 45–56 and ch. IV.

Spencer, Herbert. *Principles of Sociology*, Vol. I.

Starcke, C. N. *The Primitive Family in its Origin and Development* (1898), pp. 1–126.

Summer, W. G. *Folkways; A Study of the Sociological Importance of Usages, Manners, Customs, Mores and Morals*, 1907, pp. 343–476.

Todd, A. J. *The Primitive Family as an Educational Agency* (1913), pp. 96 ff.

Tylor, E. B. 1. *The Matriarchal Family System,* in the *Nineteenth Century,* July, 1896, Vol. 40, p. 81.

2. *Anthropology*, ch. XVI.

Webster, H. *Primitive Secret Societies*, chs. I–V.

Westermarck, E. *The History of Human Marriage* (1901), chs. I–VIII, XIV–XXIII.

CHAPTER III

THE PATRIARCHAL FAMILY: THE HEBREW TYPE

Sources of Knowledge of the Patriarchal Hebrew Family. —
The most fruitful sources of information concerning the
Hebrew family are found (1) in the Old Testament, especially
in the *Pentateuch* and the *Book of Ruth*, and (2) in the *Talmud*,
an ancient work consisting of the commentaries of the sages
and rabbis of Israel on the Mosaic law. These commentaries
on the oral law are said to go back to the period of Simon the
Just, who lived at the beginning of the third century B.C.
From this time to the close of the second century A.D. an
unbroken succession of Jewish rabbis and judges had interpreted and reinterpreted the law of Moses as given on Mt.
Sinai. About 200 A.D. the Mosaic law with its various commentaries and interpretations was codified by Rabbi Jehuda
the Nasi and this code formed the *Mishna*, one of the important divisions of the Talmud. The *Mishna*, in turn, served
as the basis of a later body of commentaries called the *Gemara;*
and these two treatises together constitute the Talmud. This
entire body of oral and written law was codified by Maimonides
in 1180 and again by Joseph Karo of Adrianople in 1554.
The latter code, best known as the *Shulhan Arukh*, is, with
some changes, an authoritative exposition of Jewish sacred
law at the present time. The treatises of the Talmud devoted
to marriage and divorce are (1) *Kiddushin* (on betrothal);
(2) *Kethuboth* (on dower or marriage settlements); (3) *Yeba-
moth* (on prohibited marriages and levirate); (4) *Sota* (on the
woman suspected of adultery); (5) *Gittin* (on divorce). In

addition to these treatises there are numerous references to the duties of parents and children scattered through other books of the Talmud.

Stages of Hebrew Civilization. — Like most Semitic peoples, the Hebrews have passed from the stage of nomadic, pastoral life to the agricultural stage in which land tends to supplant cattle in property value. The legends of the Old Testament patriarchs picture them as shepherds dwelling in tents and moving from place to place in search of better pasture for their flocks and herds. Such was the life of Abraham and Lot in the Bible story. But in course of time the traditions change, — the tent of the nomad gives way to the fixed abode of the dwellers in village communities; and the villages, in turn, expand into prosperous towns and cities. Flocks and herds no longer occupy the foreground, but make place for vineyards, olive gardens, orchards and cornfields. Little by little the strong tribal feeling of the Israelites becomes weaker and yields in some measure to the neighborhood tie furnished by the common interest in agricultural lands. Obviously a large tribe cannot cultivate vast arable tracts in common. Hence agriculture has commonly had the effect of breaking up the tribe into smaller groups forming village communities. These are probably the " families " or " houses " so frequently referred to in the Old Testament (see *I Sam.* XX, 29; *Judges* XVIII, 1–2). They consisted of several households united by actual kinship or by the artificial relationship furnished by adoption into the " family." In the words of Sir Henry Maine : " The community is a community of kinsmen, but though the common ancestry is probably to a great extent real, the tradition has become weak enough to admit of considerable artificiality being introduced into the association . . . through the adoption of strangers from the outside." [1] Within the village community or " great " family, the basic family, consisting of parents, children, and often grandparents

[1] *Early History of Institutions*, pp. 80, 81.

E

and grandchildren, remains intact and has its own homestead. The heads of these households constitute the village council of elders or " fathers." During this early period individual ownership is restricted to cattle and movables; pastures and cultivated land are held in common and portioned out to the homesteads. But by the time of King David (c. 1055–1015 B.C.) villages are expanding into cities; and in the age of Solomon, his successor, there is evidence that individual ownership of land as well as movable property is becoming more general. Commerce and industry have developed; a navy for trade with Ophir and Tarshish has been organized; and merchantmen are rising into prominence (cf. *I Kings*, ch. X). In the days of Ahab, King of Israel (c. 875–853 B.C.), private ownership of land is clearly established, as is shown by the attempt of Ahab to get possession of the vineyard of Naboth (*I Kings*, ch. XXI). Yet when tribal control has been almost completely superseded by that of the family the men of Judah are always careful to preserve the tradition of their particular " families " or " houses " within the tribes of the sons of Jacob.

With the advance of the Hebrews in civilization went a progressive softening of the early rigorous laws and customs. This had its effect upon the provisions of the Rabbis with respect to marriage, divorce and the rights of the man as head of the household. Little by little more consideration was shown to women and some limitations were put upon the power of the husband and father over his wives and children.

ORGANIZATION OF THE HEBREW FAMILY

The Family as Patriarchal in Type. — In the earliest times of the Old Testament narrative the Hebrew family was patriarchal in type, although it furnishes no such perfect example of this form of family organization as is afforded by ancient Rome. It is probable that the domestication of cattle and the pastoral and nomadic life which followed have had much to do with the development of the patriarchal type of family. The owner of large flocks and herds must wander in search of fresh pasture lands. He needs a numerous following to assist in tending the sheep and cattle. Thus the tendency is for a group, bound by ties of blood, to wander away from the tribe, and find its common interest in the care and protection of the herds. Such an isolated pastoral life is usually attended by two important results: (1) the owner of the flocks seeks to subordinate all the group to his control; (2) paternal relationship is made prominent and important rather than maternal kinship. Certainly, in patriarchal times, the Hebrews very generally traced kinship through males (*Numbers* I, 22; III, 15–20), although evidence is not lacking that this patronymic system had supplanted an earlier maternal kinship system.[1] Vestiges of this more primitive method of reckoning relationship are found in *Genesis* (ch. XXXVI) where the " generations of Esau " are traced through his wives, and in the *Book of Ruth* where Leah and Rachel are referred to as the women who " did build the house of Israel " (*Ruth* IV, 11).

With the development of the paternal kinship system among the ancient Hebrews went a steady increase in the power of the head of the family — the patriarch — over wives, children, slaves and the *ger* or stranger within his gates. All these, with, not infrequently, the daughters-in-law of the patriarch, were almost absolutely under his authority. It would be a mistake to regard any Israelitish woman of Biblical times as a free agent. She was all her life under male control, — that of her father, older brother, husband, or father-in-law. Only the widowed mother, who frequently dwelt under her son's roof after the death of her husband, held a free and dignified position in the household. The male head of the family had been trained in respect and obedience

---

[1] See Fenton, *Early Hebrew Life* (1880), pp. 2 ff.

to his mother, whereas his wives and concubines were regarded, at least in early times, as his property. Even in the Talmud women are frequently grouped with slaves and children.[1] Yet the affection of the husband for his wife, the influence of the wife's family and the force of public opinion must in course of time have assisted in raising the status of the married woman above that of a mere chattel. Moreover, nowhere do we read that the patriarch held the power of life and death over his wives save in the one case of adultery (*Genesis* XXXVIII, 24).

Like their mothers, Hebrew children in early times were almost completely under the authority of the father. That this control extended to life and death in the rude days of the patriarchs is made plain by Abraham's attempt to sacrifice his son Isaac as a burnt offering. Yet very early the Israelites were forbidden by Mosaic law to burn their children upon the altars of Moloch (*Leviticus* XVIII, 21). In but two other respects was the power of the patriarchal father restricted: he might not make his daughter a prostitute (*Leviticus* XIX, 29), nor might he sell her to a stranger (foreigner). Within these limits he had full authority and might marry his children as he saw fit or even sell them as slaves to a fellow-countryman (*Exodus* XXI, 7-9). The utmost respect and reverence toward parents, coupled with the most scrupulous obedience, was exacted of all Hebrew children. The Mosaic law required that the child who smote or cursed his father should be put to death (*Exodus* XXI, 15, 17); and the stubborn or gluttonous son was condemned to be stoned by his fellow-Israelites after the father and mother had testified against him before the elders (*Deut.* XXI, 18-21). Apparently the father did not himself carry out the awful punishment prescribed by the law of Moses; hence it is probable that the power of life and death was not so completely in his hands as in those of the Roman father.

[1] See Bennett, *The Hebrew Family*, in Hastings's *Dict. of the Bible*, Vol. I, pp. 846-49.

The Israelitish household likewise included slaves and sometimes strangers sojourning in Israel who placed themselves under the protection of the patriarch. So long as they remained, these individuals were substantially members of the family, *i.e.*, they were under the control of its head. As for the Hebrew slave his path seems not to have been a thorny one. Instances are not lacking where a female slave became her master's concubine (*Genesis* XXX, 1–14) and a male slave his owner's son-in-law or even his heir (*Genesis* XV, 3). By the law of Israel the *purchased* slave must be set free within seven years; hence the relation of the home-born slave to his master was more firm and intimate than that of the slave born outside the family.

The Hebrew Family as a Religious Organization. — In addition to its other functions the Israelitish family was a religious organization of great strength and unity. At the head of the family the patriarch served as priest in the various ceremonials connected with the feasts and fasts of the Jewish religion. These elaborate religious observances were intimately connected with the home [1] and served to bind its members in religious unity. The detailed regulations of the Mosaic law concerning ritual cleanness, the strict observance of the Sabbath and the Passover, must have had the effect of making family life a continuous round of ceremonial observances. It is quite possible that at the dawn of Hebrew civilization the people were ancestor-worshippers. The Teraphim, or images, referred to in *Genesis* (XXXI, 30–34) and held in high veneration, are regarded by some writers as symbols of family ancestors. Furthermore the family burial place was a sacred spot to every son of Israel as to the Greeks and Romans, among whom ancestor-worship was thoroughly established. Thus it may well have been true that, before the Hebrew tribes were welded into a strong nation with a national religion, each family practised religious rites of its own, connected with the

[1] The Passover is essentially a family rite.

worship of ancestors.   But before the dawn of Hebrew history
such family cults had yielded place to the tribal and national
worship of the one true God of Israel — Jahweh.

Inheritance of Property among the Ancient Israelites. —
In early times the stability and unity of the Hebrew family
were further secured by the preservation of landed property
within the family.   Even in patriarchal days the sons inherited cattle and movable property from the father ; and it
was specially decreed that the first-born son should have a
double portion (*Deut.* XXI, 15–18).   At first daughters
seem to have had no share in the inheritance.   Later the
Biblical narrative relates that the daughters of Zelophehad
protested to Moses against the extinction of their father's
name in Israel because he had no son.   Then " the Lord spake
unto Moses saying, The daughters of Zelophehad speak right ;
thou shalt surely give them a possession of an inheritance
among their father's brethren : . . .   And thou shalt speak unto
the children of Israel saying, If a man die and have no son, then
ye shall cause his inheritance to pass unto his daughter."
Further instructions were given to Moses that in default of
children, male or female, the estate should pass to the brothers
or uncles of the deceased man and if none were living then
the lands should be given to the next of kin (*Numbers*
XXVII, 1–11).   This " next of kin," or Goël, seems to have
been a prominent figure in the Hebrew patriarchal family.
Upon him devolved such important duties as the care of the
widow and orphaned children of his deceased relative, the
management of the property of the minor heirs, and the
avenging of his kinsman's injury or death upon his enemies.

The Levirate. — Such was the desire of the Hebrew to preserve his name and estates within the tribes of Israel that a
curious practice developed in primitive times and persisted
long after the dawn of the Christian era.   This was the
custom of *levirate* whereby the brother of a man who died
childless was expected to marry the dead man's widow and

" raise up seed " unto his brother " that his name be not put out of Israel." The first-born child of this union became the heir of the departed Israelite and was generally regarded as his son (*Deut.* XXV, 5, 6). Such a primitive custom, existing in full force among certain savage groups to-day, was bound to meet with some opposition on the part of the brother thus used as an instrument; and even in patriarchal times a way was opened up for his escape from the distasteful duty. It was provided (*Deut.* XXV, 7–10) that if a man were averse to meet this obligation of raising up " unto his brother a name in Israel " he should so declare himself in the presence of the Hebrew elders and his brother's widow. The repudiated woman was then privileged to loosen the shoe of her dead husband's brother and to spit in his face with the words : "So shall it be done unto that man that will not build up his brother's house." This crude ceremony was called *chalitza*. As civilization advanced and the aversion to levirate marriage waxed stronger among the Jews, *chalitza* was frequently resorted to as a means of escape from an irksome obligation. The custom of levirate seems in direct opposition to the Mosaic law expressed in *Leviticus* (XVIII, 16; XX, 21) which forbids marriage with a brother's wife. However, the explanation of the apparent conflict is probably that the law of levirate in *Deuteronomy* applied only to a special case, — that of the childless man whose name and family were threatened with extinction after his death. Thus it seems closely connected with the ancient agrarian law of Israel which was designed to retain all property intact within the tribe and family. The custom of levirate may also serve as a curious and interesting survival of the primitive tendency to look upon women as property who may be handed over with children and slaves to the next of kin. Be this as it may, the practice appears by no means to have died out in the time of Christ (see *Matt.* XXII, 25 ff.); but the decisions of the rabbis during the Middle Ages were, on the whole, in favor of abandoning it. The ceremony of *chalitza*, however, persisted into modern times, even though it had long since become meaningless through the decay of levirate marriage. At the Rabbinical Conference held in Philadelphia in 1869, it was considered advisable formally to declare the custom obsolete in the following words: " The precept of levirate marriage, and eventually of Chalitza, has lost to us all meaning, import and binding force." [1]

The Hebrew Family as Polygynous in Form. — Unlike the patriarchal family as it existed among the Greeks and Romans, the Hebrew family was polygynous. The marriage of one man with several wives was general among the patriarchs and kings of Israel (see *Judges* VIII, 30; *II Sam.* V, 13; *I Kings* XI, 1–3). Moreover, the practice was expressly recognized in Mosaic law (*Deut.* XXI, 15), although some attempt was made to limit the number of wives one man might possess (*Deut.* XVII, 17). Female slaves were quite frequently the concubines of their masters, and the law of Moses sought in some degree to protect their interests, especially by the provision that they be not sold to foreigners (*Ex.* XXI, 7; *Deut.* XXI, 10–14). In early times, slave girls were sometimes voluntarily handed over by Hebrew wives to their husbands to serve as concubines. Sarah, Leah and Rachel all gave their personal slaves to their husbands as concubines and claimed the offspring of the union as their own. This custom has been found among other early societies, notably among the Spartan Greeks. Apparently the lawful wives of Hebrews did not have great advantages over concubines. Probably the children of wives inherited a larger share of their father's property than did the offspring of concubines (*Gen.* XXI, 10). Probably also a wife was treated with somewhat more respect and consideration than was accorded a concubine. This would depend largely upon her husband's favor, as well as upon the power and prestige of her own family. There can be small doubt that the custom of polygamy brought dis-

[1] Mielziner, *The Jewish Law of Marriage and Divorce*, p. 58.

harmony and division into the households of Israel, especially during the centuries following the age of the patriarchs, when advancing civilization brought refinement of sentiments and ideals. Probably the practice resulted in the division of the household into small groups each consisting of the mother and her offspring. Certainly in early patriarchal times each wife had her own abode. Thus Isaac brought his bride Rebekah "unto his mother Sarah's tent" (*Gen.* XXIV, 67) ; and Jacob's several wives and concubines had separate tents (*Gen.* XXXI, 33).

But widespread as was the practice of polygamy among the Israelites it was doubtless restricted in several ways. As we have seen, the numerical proportion of male and female births among most peoples is nearly equal, although at maturity the females commonly outnumber the males because of the more dangerous pursuits, especially warfare, in which men engage. This fact alone must have made monogamy a necessity for the majority of the adult Jewish population. Then, too, the provision requiring that every man secure to his betrothed before marriage a dowry to be paid in case of his death or her divorce without just cause no doubt prevented many a plural marriage. Furthermore, enlightened public opinion gradually became increasingly hostile toward polygynous marriage. There is an implied protest against it in the later prophetical writings, notably in *Hosea* (II, 19–23), where monogamous marriage is used as a symbol of the union of Jehovah with Israel, and in *Isaiah* where idolatry and polygyny are conceived as counterparts (LVII, 3–8). Again, the prophet Malachi, writing in the fifth century B.C., extolled absolute conjugal fidelity (*Mal.* II, 14, 15). Yet beyond question polygynous marriage was permitted by the rabbis for many centuries during the Christian era. Writing in the second century after Christ, Justin Martyr states that Jewish law permitted a man to have four or five wives.[1] This statement is borne

[1] *Trypho*, p. 134. Quoted in Bennett, *The Hebrew Family*, in *Dict. of the Bible*, I, p. 848.

out by a similar declaration in Josephus.[1] It is probable, however, that the custom of polygamy gradually died out among
the Hebrews during the Middle Ages and had become practically extinct before it was formally prohibited. This prohibition was pronounced at the famous rabbinical Synod of Worms
in the beginning of the eleventh century by Rabbi Gershom
ben Jehuda; and thus Jewish law was brought into harmony
with the existing practice of monogamy.

MARRIAGE LAWS AND CUSTOMS

Respect in which Marriage was Held. — For several reasons
marriage was held in high esteem among the people of Israel.
Doubtless in rude pastoral times economic and social causes
were at the basis of this esteem.   Large families were a blessing to the patriarchs, since the boys could render valuable
assistance in tending the flocks, tilling the fields and guarding
the homestead of their father.   The girls, though less highly regarded, were yet of value for domestic service and for the price
they brought as wives or concubines.   Then, too, marriage was
looked upon as a family affair rather than a personal one; indeed
the generation of offspring was the supreme motive of every
union to the end that a man's " house " or family might not die
out in Israel.   The present conception of marriage as the completion of the personal life and happiness of the man and woman concerned would have been incomprehensible to the
Hebrews of old as to all ancient peoples.   Later, in the age of
the Messianic prophecies, marriage gained an added sanctity
from the precious possibility that the fruit of the union might
be the promised Messiah of the Jews, its long-desired saviour
from oppression.   It is probable also that the more reflective
of the Hebrews recognized the value of early marriages in
securing purity of life.   In the Babylonian Talmud Rabbi
Huna states: " Whoever is twenty years old and has not taken

[1] *Antiquities of the Jews,* XVII, I, 3.

a wife his days are all polluted with sin. . . . All his days are defiled with sinful thoughts." And Rabbi Chisda, commenting on the same theme of early marriage, further states: " If I was better able to learn than my companion, it has this explanation, for I married at my sixteenth year. And if I had married at my fourteenth I should have said to Satan: A dart in thine eyes." [1] All these reasons, together with a highly developed parental instinct, combined to secure for marriage, especially when blessed with children, an honorable place in Hebrew life.

Conditions Necessary to a Valid Marriage. — The Mosaic law and the later commentaries upon it laid down certain conditions which must be complied with if a marriage were to be valid. These conditions were concerned with (1) prohibited marriages, (2) the legal age of the parties and (3) their consent to the marriage.

Prohibited Marriages. — In the Books of *Leviticus* and *Deuteronomy* prohibitions are declared against marriages within certain degrees of relationship. A man may not marry his half-sister, his daughter-in-law, his aunt, his uncle's or his brother's widow, or his wife's sister *during the lifetime of the wife* (*Lev.* XVIII, 18; XX). The rabbis later extended these prohibitions to ascending and descending lines of whatever degree of relationship, although they permitted marriage between cousins and between step-brothers and sisters. These marriage prohibitions reflect the well-defined knowledge of relationships that had developed among the Israelites as well as their desire to safeguard the chastity of women within the family circle. It is possible, also, that the Jews, always an intelligent people, had discovered the harmful effects, in the form of physical degeneration and feeble-mindedness, which sometimes follow close intermarriage. By later Talmudic law the above prohibitions were enlarged

[1] Wünsche, *Der Babylonische Talmud* (ed. 1878), *Tractat Kidduschin*, III, pp. 87, 88.

to include the following: (1) A man might not marry his divorced wife who had remarried and become a widow, or been again divorced. It has been suggested that this regulation was designed to prevent a current practice of exchanging wives.[1] (2) A man was not permitted to remarry a wife divorced for barrenness or bad reputation. The desire of the Hebrews for offspring led them frequently to dissolve an unfruitful marriage as not having accomplished its true function. In such a case it was held that the union should not be renewed. (3) A man who had committed adultery with another man's wife or who was under suspicion of so doing was forbidden to marry the woman after she had been divorced. Such a prohibition seems designed as a penalty exacted for this supreme marital offence. The children of the foregoing prohibited unions were regarded by all Hebrews as bastards or " mamzers " and were forever sternly denied the privilege of marrying Jewish women or men of legitimate birth.

The Element of Consent. — Quite early in Hebrew history the law required that the consent of the parties to a marriage be a condition of its validity. Furthermore it was stipulated that this consent should not be forced. Probably the woman was favored in this regard, since the law declared that if her consent were compelled, the marriage was *ipso facto* null and void. If, on the contrary, the consent of the male were forced, no such consequence followed, since he could at once free himself by divorce. Neither idiots nor the insane were regarded by the Jews as capable of contracting a valid marriage since the union depended upon intelligent consent. Curiously enough, also, the consent of parents to a marriage was not a legal requirement if the parties were of age; yet respect for parents was so thoroughly ingrained in Jewish children that marriages against their will must have been very rare.

Legal Age for Marriage. — By Talmudic law the legal age for contracting marriage was fixed at puberty — the completed

[1] See Mielziner, *The Jewish Law of Marriage and Divorce*, p. 42, foot-note.

twelfth year in females and the completed thirteenth in the case of males. Marriage under that age was void. Nevertheless the father was permitted to contract for the marriage of his daughter before she had attained puberty; but if on reaching legal age, the girl refused to carry out the contract, it became null and void. In this regard Talmudic law seems distinctly in advance of the marriage laws of Greece and Rome; yet this advantage may be more apparent than real. Few young girls or boys brought up in the spirit of respectful awe and submission toward parents so thoroughly inculcated in Hebrew homes, would ever attempt defiance of parental wishes. And such defiance might easily have met with stern punishment and ultimate defeat. Moreover, girls, at least, soon learned that marriage meant security and assured social position. In the half-barbarous ages of the patriarchs, and for a long period thereafter, the condition of the unmarried woman without a male protector must have been forlorn indeed. Having no independent existence, either legally or from an economic standpoint, her lot was bound to be a cruel one if she lacked father, brother or husband to protect and support her. For in ancient society *families*, not individuals, were in a far truer sense than to-day the units of society. Outside some family the individual was virtually an outcast. This condition gave rise to the custom of contracting very young girls in marriage, — a custom that flourished during the Jewish persecutions of the Middle Ages. Yet not all rabbis approved of this practice and at least one well-known Talmudic authority protested against it as early as the third Christian century: " It is a moral wrong," he urges, " that a father should contract a marriage in behalf of his daughter before she has attained the age of consent." [1]

Legal Formalities in Contracting Marriage. — Apparently the law of Moses made little distinction between betrothal and marriage (see *Deut.* XX, 7; XXII, 23, 24). The be-

[1] Mielziner, *op. cit.*, p. 83.

trothed woman was practically a wife. And this was once the custom among many early peoples, *e.g.*, among our own Teutonic ancestors. But after the Babylonian Captivity, when the law of the rabbis developed as an extension of the primitive Mosaic law, betrothal and nuptials were established as two distinct ceremonies.

Betrothal. — As among most ancient peoples, the ceremony of betrothal was the actual beginning of marriage, although the union was not consummated until later. Consequently the girl who proved faithless to her betrothed was treated as an adulteress, and received the cruel punishment meted out to that offender among the Israelites. Betrothal was a solemn contract of marriage involving certain customary formalities. Either of two rites might be chosen since both were perfectly legal: (1) *Kaseph* (money); (2) *Sh'tar* (a written instrument). According to the first the man gave to the woman a coin of small value with the words, " Be thou wedded (or consecrated) to me." Even the Peruta, a copper piece of the lowest denomination, was frequently used. This little ceremony is of interest since it appears to have been the last vestige among the Jews of marriage by purchase — once probably a common practice. In patriarchal times Abraham's servant gave rich " gifts " to Rebekah's mother and brother that he might win the damsel for his master's son Isaac (*Gen.* XXIV, 51–53); and Jacob, who was an exile without property to exchange for a wife, was obliged to serve his uncle Laban fourteen years for Rachel (*Gen.* XXIX, 16–30). Again Hamor, prince of the Hivites, sought to win Jacob's daughter Dinah to be his son's wife by offering " never so much dowry and gift " (*Gen.* XXXIV, 12). Clearly, in these rude days, and for ages after, women were regarded, quite frankly, as having a property value. But by the time of the Roman rule, the crude act of purchase had become a mere symbol. Indeed, certain writers maintain that the custom of betrothal by *Kaseph* did not originate before the age of King Herod (reigned 40–4 B.C.) and was probably borrowed from a similar marriage form in use among the Romans (*coëmptio*). Be this as it may, the custom persisted quite through the Middle Ages, although a ring came to be used instead of the coin. In betrothal by *Sh'tar* the groom gave to his bride a written document containing the words: " Be thou consecrated unto me." In both ceremonies of betrothal the presence of two qualified witnesses was essential. After this simple rite a benediction upon the young couple was pronounced, in which references were made to Jehovah's sanctification of marriage and to the Talmudic law that the marriage must not be consummated until after nuptials. This benediction might be pronounced by a rabbi, invited to be present, or by the male relative of the bride who gave her in marriage.

Nuptials. — Quite commonly a year intervened between betrothal and the nuptial rites which concluded the marriage. Essentially, nuptials consisted in the conduct of the bride in gay procession, surrounded by her friends and greeted by songs, to her husband's home. By this act she was brought under his marital control; and with the commencement of their life together the marriage was held to be consummated. The wedding procession was followed by a banquet after which friends of the bride led her to the nuptial chamber. By Talmudic law simple religious rites, such as the recital of benedictions, accompanied the wedding festivities. The presence of a rabbi at nuptials was not a legal requirement, however, and the benedictions might be pronounced by the bridegroom himself or by any of the ten witnesses demanded by the law. Thus it will be seen that both betrothal and nuptials were regarded by the Hebrews as largely *private* matters, in which neither civil nor religious authorities were required to take part. Indeed a marriage was recognized as legally valid without any religious rites whatever, although, since these were held to add solemnity to the contract, their omission was probably rare. Apparently the custom of requiring the presence of a rabbi at nuptials was not thoroughly established until late in the Middle Ages.[1] It is noteworthy that this private character of Hebrew marriage is common to the rites of nearly all ancient peoples. Only very gradually does private contract marriage yield to the control of religion and later of the state.

The Kethuboth or Marriage Deed. — Hebrew law intervened even further in the marriage formalities to protect the interests of the wife. About a century before the Christian era, Simon ben Shatach, President of the Sanhedrin [2] in Jerusalem, promulgated the law of the marriage deed or Kethuboth. This far-seeing act required that every husband before nuptials should sign a deed conveying to the bride a sum from his estate, in case of his death or her divorce without due cause. The minimum was fixed at 200 silver *denarii* [3] (about $32) for a virgin and 100 *denarii* for a widow; but this amount could be increased at the desire of the husband. The law further required that for the due security of the wife's claim the real and personal property of the husband should be mortgaged. No doubt this marriage deed served as a restriction upon hasty divorce and was so intended by the rabbis. The requirement of a dowry remained in force until the eleventh century A.D. when the Sanhedrin of Mayence so limited the rights of the husband in respect to divorce as to lessen its importance.

The Duties and Rights of Husband and Wife. — In the Tractate *Kethuboth* of the Talmud are laid down certain regulations concerning the rights and duties of husband and wife. The basis of these regulations is found in the law of Moses where the command is given that a man shall not

[1] See Mielziner, *op. cit.*, p. 83.

[2] The supreme council of the Jewish people consisting of 71 priests, scribes and elders.

[3] A *denarius* was a Roman coin worth about sixteen cents in our money.

fail to furnish food and raiment, and " her duty of marriage "
to his first wife when he takes a second (*Ex.* XXI, 10). This
simple requirement was the germ out of which grew the
elaborate provisions of the Talmud. Evidently the rabbis
regarded marriage as a contract involving reciprocal duties
on which it was well to bestow the powerful sanctions of
law and religion.

Husband's Duties and Rights. — The husband's obligations
were clearly defined. He must furnish his wife with all
necessaries and maintain her according to his means and
station in life. The husband who neglected this duty of
support might be compelled by the court to fulfil it. The
husband was also adjudged liable for amounts borrowed by
his wife during his absence from home, if these were necessary for her support. Furthermore, the husband must provide suitable care for his wife when she was ill and proper
burial in case of her death. If she were made a captive he
must secure her ransom. Finally, he must not refuse to
cohabit with her no matter how many wives he might possess.
This was the extent of the husband's duties and they were
accompanied by certain definite rights. (1) In early times
he had an almost unlimited privilege of divorce. (2) If
his wife died before him he became her sole heir. (3) He
was entitled also to the usufruct of all property brought
by his wife at marriage and to all of her earnings if she
engaged in industry outside the home. This latter provision was regarded as a fair offset to the husband's
duty of support. In case the wife waived her right to
be supported she was permitted to retain her earnings.
Apparently, then, the Hebrews of Talmudic times were
more generous in regard to this question than were most
of the commonwealths of the United States until after the
middle of the nineteenth century. In several far Western
States at the present time, the wages of the wife are
regarded as " community property " and are entirely under

F

the control of her husband, although in law belonging equally to both.[1]

The Wife's Duties and Rights. — The duties of the Hebrew wife were numerous and well-defined; on the contrary, her rights were few and, at least in early times, rather vaguely understood. Great stress was laid upon the obligations of the married woman as a mother and housewife. All the multifarious tasks of the home devolved upon her almost as heavily as upon primitive woman. No matter how many slaves belonged to a Hebrew household the wife must not live in idleness. She must direct the work of her servants, nurse and instruct her infant children herself, and perform certain loving services designed to promote her husband's comfort and happiness. These duties are laid down in great detail in the Talmudic treatise *Kethuboth*.

The property rights of the wife were limited even in the later days of rabbinical law. Her possessions at marriage were divided into two kinds, (1) *dotal*, (2) *paraphernal* or personal. These, as we have seen, were under the absolute control of her husband, who also enjoyed all income and profits from the same. At his death, however, both kinds of property must be returned to his widow; the former in the condition it was at her marriage, no matter how much it might have increased or decreased in value. In the case of the paraphernal property, on the contrary, the husband was not responsible for loss. Apparently, also, the wife might possess certain personal property if such were given her for her exclusive use by her husband or some member of her family. This, however, she might not alienate, since her husband was entitled to inherit it on her death. Such were the laws of the Jews regarding women's property rights until late in the Middle Ages, when the rabbis of France and Northern Italy adjudged that the dotal property of a

[1] See Wilson, *Legal and Political Status of Women in the United States*, 1912, p. 88.

childless wife dying in the first year of wedded life should be returned to her father or to his heirs.[1] This last provision is interesting as evidence that the Hebrews, like all peoples, ancient and modern, looked upon the wife's dowry as provision for her support and, in part, for the support of such children as she should bear her husband. In case of her death shortly after marriage it was held that the property in justice should return to her family.

DIVORCE AMONG THE HEBREWS

Rights of the Husband. — From the days of the patriarchs until the Christian era no restrictions were placed upon the right of a Hebrew to divorce his wife. The Mosaic law (*Deut.* XXIV, 1, 2) states that if a wife find no favor in her husband's eyes because of " some uncleanness in her: then let him write her a bill of divorcement and give it in her hand, and send her out of his house." But long before the birth of Christ the later prophets had expressed their strong disapproval of divorce, and Malachi (450 B.C.) declared in no uncertain tones that Jehovah looked upon the custom with hatred (*Mal.* II, 14, 16). About the time of Christ the opposed Rabbinical schools of Shammai and Hillel disagreed concerning the meaning of the Biblical expression " some uncleanness." The School of Hillel interpreted the term to mean anything displeasing to the husband and thus countenanced the current practice which gave to the husband unlimited freedom of divorce. On the contrary the School of Shammai understood the words to mean serious moral fault or actual unchastity, and would thus have sharply curtailed the husband's privileges. However, the customary interpretation of Hillel prevailed for many centuries. As is well known, Christ disagreed with the views of his age and recognized no right of divorce save for the cause of adultery

[1] Mielziner, *op. cit.*, p. 106.

(*Matt.* V, 32), but His teachings seem to have had no effect upon Hebrew custom in this respect. In the early centuries of the Christian era the moral sense of the rabbis clearly revolted against the custom of unrestricted divorce. Rabbi Yohanan (199–279 A.D.) boldly declared that " He that putteth her [his wife] away is hated of God." By this time also enlightened public opinion tended to regard with disapproval the divorce of the wife save for certain definite moral offences such as adultery, flagrant disregard of moral decency, refusal to cohabit for a year or more, change of religion, refusal to carry out the ritual law in household management and insulting the husband or his father in his presence. Physical disability, such as leprosy and barrenness, was likewise regarded as just ground for the divorce of the wife. Early in the eleventh century, however, at the Sanhedrin of Mayence, Rabbi Gershom ben Yehudah declared : " To assimilate the right of the woman to the right of the man, it is ordained that even as the man does not put away his wife except of his own free will, so shall the woman not be put away except by her own consent." [1] Presumably this ordinance did not affect the right of the husband in cases of adultery or grave moral delinquency.

Privileges of the Wife. — In the days of the patriarchs the Hebrew wife had no rights of divorce whatever save in the one case cited in *Exodus* XXI, 7–11. Here it is provided that the bondwoman, raised by her master to the status of a wife (or concubine) shall go free if her husband fails to provide for her. She shall receive no money, but her husband is bound to give her a bill of divorcement. Some writers maintain that this provision was the germ out of which grew the wife's right to demand divorce for certain causes, a right which they claim was very early extended to free wives in Israel. No clear evidence of such a privilege exists, however, before the period of the Roman occupation of

---

[1] Amram, *The Jewish Law of Divorce*, p. 52.

Palestine (after 65 B.C.). Under the influence of Roman law and custom, the practice of the divorce of the husband by the wife gradually became general. The causes recognized by Rabbinical law were (1) physical impotence if admitted by the husband, (2) change of religion, (3) extreme dissoluteness, (4) refusal to support, (5) continued ill-treatment, (6) commission of a crime followed by escape from the country, (7) affliction with a loathsome disease or pursuit of a disgusting trade, both acquired after marriage. It is interesting to note that most of these causes are recognized by many states in America to-day as constituting just grounds for divorce. Likewise it is noteworthy that adultery on the part of the husband was not regarded in rabbinical law as a serious offence against the wife giving her the right of divorce. Until comparatively recent times Western nations likewise held this position, a position having its foundation in the double standard of morals which condones as venial in the man an act regarded as beyond forgiveness in the woman.

Status of the Divorced Woman. — The social position of a divorced wife was vastly more independent than that of her unmarried or married sisters. She was for the first time in her life entirely in " her own power " (*sui juris*). Not only was she freed from the control of husband and father, but, in a *legal* sense, she was no longer a member of her father's family, since in families of the patriarchal type, this membership fundamentally consisted in being under the power of the male head. If a divorced woman were innocent of any grave fault, she lost nothing in social standing by her divorce and she gained the priceless privilege of marrying in accordance with her own desires. Moreover, the Kethuboth, or dowry, was an inalienable right of the divorced wife if she were innocent of wrong. In cases where the wife was convicted of moral offences or breach of the law of ritual cleanness in household management, she lost all right to the dowry. And be it remembered that "immorality" in a wife was not restricted in ancient times to adultery, but included such relatively trivial offences as going abroad bareheaded with her hair loose, spinning in the streets, flirting with strange men or scolding so noisily as to disturb the neighbors. Women who refused to cohabit or who deserted their husbands also lost all claim to the Kethuboth.[1]

Control of Divorce by the Courts. — In early times divorce, like marriage, was purely a private concern with which neither law nor rabbis interfered. It consisted simply in the husband's handing the wife a " Get " or Bill of Divorce containing the words " Be thou divorced (or separated) from me." At a later period, however, the rabbis, looking to the protection of the woman, prescribed, in minute detail, the formalities to be gone through with in writing and handing over the bill of divorce. These regulations were probably designed to afford an angry husband time for reflection and reconsideration. The court further encroached upon the earlier private character of divorce by *enforcing separation upon husband or wife* in cases where the marriage was opposed to rabbinical law, *e.g.*, where the wife was found guilty of adultery, where either party was afflicted with a loathsome and incurable disease, or where the marriage was childless. In the latter case the essential purpose of marriage was held to have been unfulfilled and therefore the union was dissolved by the rabbis with or without the consent of the parties. It is evident that the control of divorce, as well as of marriage among the Hebrews, was more and more taken over by the religious authorities. And this has been the history of the marriage institution among our forefathers in Western Europe until a comparatively recent period, when divorce cases have been relegated to the secular courts.

Custody and Support of Children of Divorced Parents. — In ancient times the offspring of any Israelitish marriage

[1] Amram, *The Jewish Law of Divorce*, p. 123.

belonged to the father and remained with him as his property after the wife's divorce. But with the advance of civilization more just ideas prevailed concerning the mother's rights in her children. During the early Christian era the rabbis rather tended to favor the woman in their judgments on this question, probably because of the boundless rights of divorce possessed by the husband. The law came to demand that the divorced mother of a suckling child be provided for by the husband until the child was weaned. Toward the close of the third century A.D. certain rabbis of Palestine and Babylon took the ground that a divorced mother could keep her son with her until his sixth year and her daughter permanently. The husband was liable for his son's support during the time that he remained with the mother and was also liable for the support of his daughter until her marriage. Furthermore, if the mother for any reason declined to keep the children, the father was bound to do so. In the event of the father's death the children became " wards of the congregation." An impartial survey of these Talmudic regulations shows how far the Hebrews had travelled in the direction of equity with respect to women since those primitive ages when a woman was regarded as the property of father or husband. Although she was still a minor before the law and under the control of some male authority, she was coming to be regarded as nevertheless an individual possessed of certain positive rights.

JEWISH HOME LIFE AND TRAINING

The Economy of the Hebrew Household. — After the pastoral age among the Hebrews there ensued, as we have seen, a period when agriculture was the dominant pursuit. In these patriarchal days the land was held in common, and certain portions were given out to individual homesteads for cultivation. As the generations passed, however, communal ownership gave place to private, and great estates came into the possession of single families. Within each separate household division of labor, as in primitive times, was upon a sex basis. The man pursued agriculture or trade and fulfilled such political and religious duties as devolved upon him as a citizen and head of a family. In his home were carried on various productive industries all under the direction of the Hebrew housewife. Indeed the households of Israel were well-nigh self-sustaining in Old Testament times. That beautiful chapter in *Proverbs* (XXXI, 10–31) which extols the virtues of a good wife sketches in clear outlines the numerous activities of a Jewish woman. Apparently she sometimes purchased the fields and planted the vineyards in which she raised the raw products to be manufactured in the household. She spun and wove the wool and flax that later she fashioned into garments for her entire family. She embroidered tapestries and made clothing of silken stuffs. Also the Biblical narrative tells us that she sold " fine linen " and " girdles " of her own making to the merchant. From her stores she gave out daily to her servants the supplies of food necessary for the family and kept careful oversight of their work when she did not herself prepare the food for the table. Her children were the objects of her special care; and as they grew up they did not fail to " call her blessed." Even the poor and needy at her gates were the recipients of her thoughtful bounty.

To her other duties the Hebrew woman added the solemn obligation of preparing all food used by the family in strict accordance with the ritual law. She must never serve as food the flesh of animals which do not cleave the hoof and chew the cud, such being regarded as ritually unclean. Moreover all clean animals must be slaughtered according to the elaborate prescriptions of Talmudic law; and the flesh of these animals must be rejected if certain specified defects or taints were discovered in the organs. The vessels and utensils used in the Feast of the Passover must be carefully cleansed without water and put away for use at the return of the sacred festival. The housewife, furthermore, must separate " the first of her dough " for the priest if she would bring a blessing on her house and avoid misfortune. Then, too, she must follow exactly all the minute and detailed regulations of the Talmud concerning the right observance of the Sabbath. As we have seen, failure to comply with any of these elaborate ritual laws constituted valid ground for divorcing the wife.

The tracts of the Talmud treating of the Sabbath shed a flood of light on the employments of the Hebrew housewife. These regulations make it clear that bleaching linen thread in ovens prepared for the purpose and the making of ink and dyes for woollen cloths were domestic industries. Olives and grapes were crushed in " press-pits," and dates were put up in the home for sale in the market. The Talmudic tracts also mention a wide variety of household implements and utensils such as spindles, shuttles, mortars, skimmers, kneading-troughs, pottery and hand-mills.[1] Most Hebrew families owned hand-mills which were usually worked by slaves, or, in poorer homes, by two women of the family. From all this it is clear that the housewife in Israel was a valuable economic factor. In the words of Solomon : " . . . her price is above rubies for she looketh well to the ways of her household and eateth not the bread of idleness."

The Jewish Home as a Training School of the Young. — But the Hebrew home had other highly important functions to perform which were regarded as of the utmost value to the families and tribes of Israel. The household was the only educational institution for the masses of the people until the time of Christ, and the parents were the chief teachers. The relation of Hebrew parents and children was such as we should expect to find in a family of the patriarchal type. In the

[1] Cf. *Babylonian Talmud* (trans. by Michael Rodkinson), Vol. I, pp. 23, 24, 27–28, 41, 55; Vol. II, ch. XVIII.

hands of the father reposed great power with respect to the training of his children and the direction of their lives, even after they had married in accordance with his desires. Great respect and reverence toward parents, coupled with exact and unquestioning obedience, were demanded of all Hebrew children from their babyhood; and even at the present time the affectionate consideration of Jewish children for their aged parents is often in pleasing contrast to the attitude of the children of other races.

But the powers of the father in Israel carried with them certain serious responsibilities. Upon him rested the duty of bringing up his offspring in the fear of Jehovah and in the knowledge of His law. It was expected that he " command his children and his household after him, and they shall keep the way of the Lord, to do justice and judgment " (*Gen.* XVIII, 19). By the law of Moses every Hebrew male child must be circumcised on the eighth day of his life and thus set apart to Jehovah (*Gen.* XVII, 10). Then, too, the first-born son must be redeemed by the payment of five shekels to a *cohen* or descendant of Aaron. In the Babylonian Talmud it is written: " Our Rabbis have taught: The father is obliged to circumcise his son, to redeem him, to teach him the Books of Moses (Torah), to marry him and to have him taught a trade. According to many he must also let him learn to swim." [1] But the father did not carry this responsibility alone. He was assisted by the mother who took an active part in the child's training until he was five years of age. At his mother's knee the boy learned brief prayers and passages from the Books of Moses. As soon as he could speak he was taught to say: " The law which Moses commanded us is the heritage of the congregation of Jacob." His mother also taught him to utter the inspiring words: " Hear, O Israel, the Eternal our God is one God." After his fifth birthday the boy came more directly under the care

---

[1] Wünsche, *Die Babylonische Talmud*, p. 90.

of his father, who instructed him in the Torah (Mosaic law), and such portions of the Talmud as it was essential for every good Israelite to know. Furthermore, every father owed it to his son to teach him a trade as a means of livelihood. In the Babylonian Talmud Rabbi Jehuda is credited with the saying: " Whoever does not permit his son to learn a trade it amounts to the same as if he had taught him robbery." [1] That it was customary for the ancient Hebrews to employ " artisan masters " for the instruction of their sons seems evident from the prohibition in the Talmud forbidding such teachers to be engaged on the Sabbath.

Every son of Israel thus carefully trained was expected to fulfil certain obligations laid down in the Talmud where it is written: " In what does the fear and reverence which the son owes to his father consist? The fear (or awe) shows itself in this that the son does not stand or sit in his father's place in the congregation, does not speak in opposition to him and also does not take upon himself judgment against him (in any controversy). Reverence consists in this, that the son give his father food and drink, clothe and shelter him and lead him in and out. Some one has asked: Out of whose means (shall this be done)? According to Rabbi Jehuda, out of the son's means, according to Rabbi Nathan bar Oschaja, out of the father's means." [2]

It was Rabbi Joshua ben Gamla to whom the honor is due of having instituted schools apart from the homes in every town and village of Palestine. This great work was undertaken about the time of Christ and aroused profound interest throughout the nation. An ordinance was made providing that the inhabitants of every town must establish a school which children at the ages of six or seven should be compelled to attend. The chief subject-matter in the new schools continued to be the Mosaic law and the two portions of the Talmud called the *Mishna* and the *Gemara*. Probably

[1] *Ibid.*, p. 87.   [2] *Ibid.*, p. 97.

the Greek language was also studied, since intercourse between Greeks and Hebrews had been greatly stimulated by trade and travel. Advanced students likewise paid some attention to the sciences of geometry and astronomy.

Hitherto nothing has been said of the education of girls. Yet their intellectual training was not wholly neglected. Certain passages in the Talmud seem to point to private instruction of girls in the Jewish religion and ritual. Indeed this training would appear to be imperative if Hebrew women were to conduct their households in accordance with ritual law. Occasionally, also, a Jewish girl was taught a foreign language, usually Greek.[1] There can be little doubt, however, that the education of girls was above all things designed to fit them for their special sphere — the management of a household — and was therefore almost wholly domestic. Young women of every rank in life were taught cooking, spinning, weaving and making garments. Such religious and moral training as they received, through participation in family worship and study of the sacred writings, served to make them better mothers, capable of giving wise assistance to their husbands in the responsible task of bringing up their children in the fear of Jehovah.

The Hebrew family, then, was a school of great moral and social value. Representing as it did a strongly knit organization, with well-defined social, religious, economic and educational functions, the Jewish household affords a contrast little less than startling to our modern individualistic homes which have long relegated many of these duties to such specialized social agencies as the school, the church and various clubs and organizations for children.

SELECTED BIBLIOGRAPHY

SOURCES.

Babylonian Talmud (English translation by Michael Rodkinson), *Tracts on the Sabbath*, Vols. I, II.

[1] Spiers, *Education in the Talmud.*

Bible. Books of *Genesis, Deuteronomy, Leviticus, Numbers, Judges, Ruth.*

Wünsche, Aug. *Der Babylonische Talmud,* Vol. II, 1, 2, pp. 82–97.

SECONDARY WORKS.

Amram, D. W. *The Jewish Law of Divorce.*

Barton, Geo. A. *A Sketch of Semitic Origins.* New York, 1902, ch. II.

Bennett, W. H. *The Hebrew Family* (in Hastings's *Dictionary of the Bible,* I, 846–50).

Benninger, I. *Hebraische Archäologie,* 1907, pp. 102–29.

Edersheim, A. *Jewish Social Life,* chs. VI–VIII.

Ellis, A. B. *Marriage and Kinship among the ancient Israelites* (in *Pop. Sci. Mo.,* XLII, 325–37).

Ewald, H. *Geschichte des volkes Israel bis Christus,* Vols. 2–3, pp. 215–249.

Fenton, John. *Early Hebrew Life,* pp. 1–45, 53–65.

Gide, P. *Étude sur la condition privée de la femme,* pp. 58–66.

Jewish Encyclopedia, articles on *Marriage,* the *Family, Woman, Divorce.*

Hobhouse, L. J. *Morals in Evolution,* pp. 200–3.

Kayserling, M. *Die jüdischen Frauen in der Geschichte, Literatur und Kunst,* pp. 119–133.

Mielziner, Dr. M. *The Jewish Law of Marriage and Divorce,* 1884.

Morgan, L. H. *Ancient Society,* pp. 366 ff.

Patterson, W. P. *Hebrew Marriage* (in Hastings's *Dictionary of the Bible,* III, 262–77).

Schuster, E. J. *The Wife in Ancient and Modern Times,* ch. I.

Spiers, Rev. B. *Education in the Talmud,* London, 1898.

CHAPTER IV

THE PATRIARCHAL FAMILY: THE GREEK TYPE

Relation of the Athenian Family to the Gens and Tribe. — In the time of the lawgiver Solon (c. 600 B.C.) the Athenian Greeks were divided into four tribes. Each tribe was organized into three phratries, or religious brotherhoods, and these in turn were divided into thirty *gentes* or " great families " tracing descent to some common ancestor. This being was quite generally believed to be of divine origin or one of the renowned heroes of Greek antiquity. The gens or " great family " had important functions to perform. Upon it devolved the responsibility of investigating the legitimacy of every new-born child within its midst. In the case of male children this legitimacy, as well as the child's descent from pure Athenian ancestry on both sides, must be established before the name of the boy could be entered upon the register of the gens as a future citizen-member. In no period of Greek history do we find property held in common by the gens as was the case among the early Hebrews. The institution of private property seems established even in Homeric times, although the gens could prevent the alienation of lands from the kinship group. To this end, if the head of a family died leaving no sons, his daughter, if he had one, was forced by her kinsmen in the gens to marry the nearest male relative of her father. In some instances this custom forced the uncle of an heiress, himself already married, to divorce his wife in order to marry his niece and thus become the head of the family in the place of his deceased brother.

The Greek Family as Patriarchal in Form. — The Greek family, like that of the Hebrews, was patriarchal in type; that is, all power was centred in the father as the governing head. Indeed the word for " father " in the Hebrew, Greek and Roman tongues signified, fundamentally, not paternal relationship, but authority, dignity and power. Yet there was clearly a difference between the source of patriarchal authority in the case of the Hebrews and of the Greeks. In the former instance the father was an absolute monarch in his own right, patterning his government after that of an all-powerful Jehovah. The Greek father, on the contrary, derived his authority from the fact that he was the trustee of the family estates and power and priest of the domestic worship of ancestors. The family, then, not the patriarch, was the unit of power in Greece, and the father's authority was derivative, not inherent.

The Kinship System of the Greeks. — Although the Greeks in the historic period traced kinship exclusively through males, certain evidences may be found in their literature of an earlier custom of reckoning relationship through mothers. In the *Iliad*, when Lycaon, half-brother of the hated Hector, beseeches the mercy of Achilles, he does so on the ground that he is not the brother of the Trojan hero by the same mother. Apparently at this time uterine brothers were looked upon as more closely allied than brothers by the same father. However, the few instances in the Homeric poems which may point to an earlier practice of tracing descent through females almost exclusively refer to gods or foreigners. The Greeks as a people had beyond doubt adopted the paternal system of tracing kinship. This fact is clearly brought out in the drama of Æschylus called the *Eumenides* (Furies) where the mother's share in the generation of offspring is stoutly denied. Apollo, addressing the gods who are sitting in judgment upon Orestes for the murder of his mother, utters these remarkable words:

> " . . . The mother's power
> Produces not the offspring, ill called hers.
> No, 'tis the father, that to her commits
> The infant plant; she but the nutrient soil

> That gives the stranger growth, if fav'ring Heaven
> Denies it not to flourish : this I urge
> In proof, a father may assert that name
> Without a mother's aid ; an instance sits
> Minerva, daughter of Olympian Jove :
> Not the slow produce of nine darkling months,
> But formed at once in all her perfect bloom ;
> Such from no pregnant goddess ever sprung." [1]

The Greek Family as a Religious Organization. —The authority possessed by the Greek father as head of the family probably had one important source in economic causes. Not only was the man the protector of the family in times of warfare, but when he turned his attention to the domestication of cattle and to agriculture his economic effectiveness became relatively greater than that of the woman and his power was accordingly increased. But the authority of the Greek patriarch was further enormously enhanced by the institution of ancestor-worship which made of every Hellenic family a closely knit religious organization bound together by the worship of the family gods around the family altar. Indeed certain writers maintain that the true bond of the Greek family as of the Roman " was the religion of the sacred fire and of dead ancestors. This caused the family to form a single body both in this life and in the next." [2] In the central court of the Greek home stood the altar of *Zeus Herkeios*, protector of the family circle. Here the father, as priest of his household, offered sacrifices in behalf of his family. Opening into the court was a reception-room, the *andron*, in which was usually placed the hearth, the true centre of domestic life in Greece. Around this family hearth occurred many of the solemn religious ceremonials that were believed to secure the welfare of the home. The origin of the sacred hearth-fire, always carefully tended, dates far back into the earliest life of the Aryan races. " Agni," says the Indian

[1] *Op. cit., Morley's Univ. Library* (trans. by Robert Potter), p. 240.
[2] De Coulanges, *The Ancient City*, pp. 51, 52.

Rig Vega, " must be invoked before all other gods." In a field, not far from the Greek house, stood the tomb of the family ancestors. Here, on certain days, the household gathered to offer a funeral meal of cakes and wine or to burn the flesh of an animal as a sacrifice to the spirits of the dead. These offerings made, the living members of the family called upon the shades of the departed, now revered as gods, to bring fruitfulness to their fields and happiness to their home. The family spirits were believed to be divine and joyous only so long as funeral repasts were offered them by the living members of the family. Deprived of these offerings, the household gods were transformed into malignant demons, dangerous to the peace and prosperity of the home. Because of this ever present need of propitiation of ancestral spirits it followed that every family must seek to perpetuate itself without break; therefore it was of supreme importance that there be male descendants to offer sacrifices at the tomb of the ancestors.

Membership in the Greek family was based, not upon ties of blood relationship, but upon (1) sharing in the worship of the family gods, and (2) coming under the power of the family head. A son, once emancipated by the father from his control, no longer shared in the family worship. Therefore he became *ipso facto* an outsider. Likewise a daughter, when married, was received by solemn ceremonial into the family circle of her husband and invoked his domestic gods instead of those of her girlhood home of which she was no longer a member. On the other hand, a youth of another kin adopted by appropriate ceremonies into any Greek family became a real member of it, since he shared in the cult of its household gods. De Coulanges has pointed out that one of the meanings of the Greek word " family " is " that which is near the hearth." And Plato has referred to kinship as " the community of the same domestic gods." [1] Since men

[1] The *Laws*, V, 729 (Jowett trans.).

G

alone could carry on the ancestral worship, relationship and descent were reckoned through males only, — the kinship system known as *agnation*. Hence adopted sons might be agnates, while daughters by blood and their offspring were not.

The Powers of the Greek Father. — As among the Hebrews so among the Greeks large governing powers resided in the father as head of the family. Indeed it might truly be said that ancient law had its source in the family and was chiefly concerned with family relationships, powers and duties. True to the patriarchal type, the Greek family included parents, children and slaves unified into a society in little by the authority of the male head. Before the time of Solon the father had the right to sell both his son and daughter. Probably, however, the sale was not of the person *of the child, but only of his labor, as he still remained under the father's authority. With the gradual refining of customs and ideas that accompanied the advance of Greek civilization, the sale of offspring fell into disrepute. By a law of Solon a father was forbidden to sell his daughter and this act may have extended to his son also. However, a Greek father always possessed the right to accept a child at birth or to reject and condemn it to exposure. Like the Hebrew, he had the further right to bestow both son and daughter in marriage. But, unlike the Jewish custom, there was no law in Greece requiring the consent of the children to the marriage contract. Finally, the father's powers included the right to emancipate his son, *i.e.*, exclude him from the family and release him from paternal authority. Probably, in early times, the authority of the Greek patriarch continued to be exercised over the son as long as the father lived. But by the time of Solon the son, on reaching a certain age, was freed from paternal control.

The Status of the Greek Wife. — As head of the household, the powers of the husband over the wife were no less clearly defined than those exercised over the children. Since the family must not die out, a Greek husband might repudiate his wife for barrenness, which of course defeated the true purpose of the marriage. After Homeric times the dowry brought by an Athenian wife belonged absolutely to her husband during his lifetime. If the wife were employed in some gainful occupation, as frequently happened among the poorer class, the fruits of her work were the unquestioned property of her husband. The person of the wife was, further-more, completely under her husband's control; and, if the family were of good social standing, she could not leave her home without his permission. Indeed, the position of a Greek wife within the family circle must have been little above that of her own children. Women were regarded by all Ionian Greeks as a distinctly inferior order of beings to men and were guarded within the home with almost Oriental strictness. " The male," says Aristotle, " is by nature fitter for command than the female, just as the elder and full-grown is superior to the younger and more immature." [1] Among the Spartan Greeks, on the contrary, the position of women seems to have been much higher than in Athens. The wife was given the significant title of " mistress " by her husband; and although she was expected to be the home-keeper she was granted liberty to go abroad. Unmarried Spartan girls were permitted a large amount of freedom and were criticised by men of the other Greek states for their pert forwardness. In the period of Homeric folk-lore, all Greek women seem to have been strikingly free from the narrow restrictions of a later age. Youths and maidens met with some freedom in the house of the girl's father, and even danced together in the vintage festivals. Apparently their relations as depicted in the *Iliad* and the *Odyssey* were frank and natural. The lovely Helen freely entertained Paris, the faithless guest of her husband Menelaus. Andromache left the palace of Priam and hastened to the Secan gates to watch the progress

[1] *Politics* (Jowett trans.), Bk. I, 12; 1239 b.

of the battle raging between Greeks and Trojans. The princess Nausicaa rode with her maids to the riverside to wash the family clothing. And when Odysseus, cast up from the sea, naked and forlorn, besought her aid, the princess, deserted by her attendants, bravely stood her ground and heard his tale of manifold woes. Then to the house of her father she directed his steps. All this betokens a freer life than was ever led by a well-born Ionian Greek woman in historic times.

Doubtless the influence of the Orient was obscurely responsible for the limitations put upon the liberty of the women of Athens, Thebes and other Ionian city-states. Under tutelage all their lives as minors, having no legal status, ill-educated and treated as moral and intellectual inferiors, Ionian wives were poorly fitted to be in any sense the companions of their husbands. Although they were admitted to the family worship round the sacred fire, their presence at the sacrifices was not necessary as in Rome, and hence no offerings were made at their tombs after death. Even when widowed, the Ionian woman was not free, but came under the guardianship of some man appointed by her husband. Needless to say, being herself under perpetual tutelage, she was not at any time the custodian of her children, who, like herself, passed under the control of an appointed guardian. This custom of refusing a woman the guardianship of her own offspring has been remarkably long lived and persists in many states of America at the present time.

Property Rights and Inheritance. — In earliest antiquity, as we have seen, the Greeks had developed the institution of private property. Even in Homeric times there was no community of property, but the family estates were held by the patriarch and passed on to his eldest son. With the development of ancestor-worship, custom and law forbade that the family house and lands be alienated since they were the abiding place of the domestic gods. When a new family hearth was established, the god took up his abode near the sacred fire and remained there as long as the household endured. Thus the family, grouped around the altar, was fixed to the soil. Even the free space which the law required to be left around each house was a sacred enclosure, for the altar fire of one god must not be mingled with that of another. It was a legend of the Greeks that the sacred fire taught men to build houses. " The walls are raised around the hearth to isolate and defend it." [1] Likewise the field which contained the tomb of departed ancestors was regarded as sacred ground. Hence, until the time of Solon, no Athenian Greek might sell his burial field ; and, although Solon removed the prohibition, he punished the sale by a heavy fine and loss of the rights of citizenship. [2]

As the eldest son had the responsibility of continuing the domestic religion he alone inherited the family estates. In no case could a daughter inherit since she ceased to be a member of the family at her marriage. If an Athenian Greek died leaving a son and daughter, the son as the sole heir must provide a dowry for his sister and arrange for her marriage. As we have seen, if the deceased left only a daughter, his nearest male relative must marry the girl even if he divorced a wife to do so. By such drastic measures the Athenians prevented the alienation or dismemberment of family property. Apparently another scheme was sometimes resorted to in order that estates might remain intact. A father who had no son might contract his daughter in marriage to some man with the express stipulation that the first male child of the union be given to him as his son. This suggests the similar custom of levirate among the Hebrews. The restriction of inheritance to males did not exist in Sparta, however, and women there might freely inherit lands and personal

[1] De Coulanges, *The Ancient City*, pp. 81–2.
[2] *Ibid.*, p. 90, citing *Diogenes Laertius*, I, 55.

property. Aristotle tells us that "nearly two-fifths of the whole country are held by the women; this is owing to the number of heiresses, and to the large dowries which are customary." [1] In Athens, where the "privilege of elder" existed with respect to house and lands, the movable property only was equally divided among the sons after the father's death. The younger sons, as they married, left home to found new households and light sacred fires of their own.

MARRIAGE AMONG THE ANCIENT GREEKS

The Greek View of Marriage. — As in all societies of the patriarchal type, marriage was held in high esteem in Greece and was looked upon as a sacred ceremony. By means of such union the family was perpetuated, the inheritance of property provided for and the worship of ancestral spirits continued. Therefore celibacy was regarded as a serious offence — a crime against the household gods. So strong was this feeling in Athens that a law was enacted enjoining the first magistrate of the city to see to it that no family became extinct. And in Sparta Plutarch tells us that the man who did not marry lost certain rights and was not treated by younger men with that respect so scrupulously accorded by Spartan youths to their elders. [2] Clearly in Greece as in Palestine marriage was regarded as a contract entered into for *family ends* and as such was arranged for by parents with small attention to the preferences of their children. Doubtless some of these unions ended happily; but the very general absence of sentiment in the customary preliminaries, together with the prominence of financial considerations, must have told rather heavily against the prospects of married happiness for the man and maiden thus contracted.

[1] Aristotle, *Politics*, II, 9; 1270 a.
[2] *Life of Lycurgus*, Bohn's Classical Library, Vol. I, p. 81.

Preliminaries of Marriage. — In Homeric times marriage was a crude affair. " Gifts," usually of cattle, were made to the bride's father and the maiden was shortly after handed over to the groom with simple ceremonies and a wedding feast. Sometimes the bride-price was not paid all at once, but in instalments. Instances are not uncommon in folk-lore where a bride was given to some hero in return for valuable services rendered the maiden's father. Thus Perseus was rewarded by the gift of Andromeda as his wife after he had saved her from the dragon. Usually, however, the woman was the prize of the suitor who bore the richest " gifts." No dowry was needed by a woman in the Homeric age in order to attract a husband; but before the time of Solon the custom of setting aside a sum of money and personal effects for each daughter's dowry had become thoroughly established in the families of well-to-do and poor alike. In his life of *Solon* Plutarch tells us that the lawgiver introduced an act limiting the amount of the bride's dowry. This restriction, however, probably referred to the clothes and ornaments she might bring in marriage. In any case the obligatory provision of the dowry must have been a burden upon many fathers; and this accounts for the rather frequent exposure of female infants among the Greeks. In accordance with the practice of most ancient peoples, the ceremonies of marriage consisted of (1) betrothal, (2) nuptials.

Betrothal. — Betrothal was a contract of marriage concluded between the parents or the appointed guardians, with no attempt to secure the formal consent of the girl or the youth. This consent was taken for granted and the presence of the parties most interested was not even necessary at the betrothal. Financial arrangements played a prominent part in the formalities. The bride's dowry was agreed upon and securities given for its payment as well as for its return in case of her divorce without just cause. Sometimes special arrangements were made for community of goods between man and wife after marriage. No religious rites accompanied this business-like contract which was essentially a legal act.

Nuptials. — It was regarded by all the Greeks as highly important that the final marriage ceremonies should occur on an auspicious day. The time of the full moon was regarded as favorable, the period of the waning moon as unfavorable. In the *Politics* [1] Aristotle mentions winter as the usual and most suitable time for marriages, although he gives no reason for the preference. At the approach of the nuptial day, the bride, often a mere girl of fifteen or sixteen, performed certain acts pathetically symbolic of her farewell to girlhood and her acceptance of the duties of a married woman. Thus she dedicated her maiden girdle, her doll and other toys of childhood and sometimes a lock of her hair to the virgin goddess Artemis or to some local divinity. On the chosen wedding day rather elaborate ceremonies took place which were sanctioned alike by custom and religion. Early in the morning bride and groom each bathed in the water of a sacred stream or spring brought to their homes by members of the family. In Athens the fountain Callirrhoë was used for the bridal bath; in Thebes water was brought from the Ismenos, a sacred spring. As daylight waned the groom, dressed in festal attire and crowned with a wreath, went to the home of the bride, where were gathered the family friends invited to attend the ceremony. As each guest entered the house he was given a cake made of pounded sesame seeds mixed with honey. The eating of this ancient prototype of the modern wedding-cake was an essential part of the nuptial ceremony, and was never omitted. When the guests were all assembled, the bride's father offered sacrifices to the gods of marriage, — Zeus, Hera and Artemis. Great care was taken to remove the gall of the victim that no bitterness might enter the married life of the young pair.

[1] *Politics*, Bk. VII, 16; 1335 b.

The sacrifice performed, the father handed over his young daughter to her husband with a sacramental formula which freed her from his control and from the worship of his family gods. With the utterance of these solemn words, the bride ceased to be a member of her father's family and entered into the family of her husband under whose authority she passed. It is noteworthy that these religious ceremonies were entirely private. The father himself served as priest and no other representatives of religion were necessary. Marriage was essentially an inter-family affair in which neither state nor national religion interfered.

After the transfer of the bride to her husband a marriage banquet followed, at which women were graciously allowed to be present, although it was customary for them to sit at tables separate from the men and to remain partially veiled. As evening approached the mother performed her part in the marriage ceremonies by handing over her young daughter to the groom. Shy and shrinking in the midst of this unwonted publicity, the girl was lifted into the bridal chariot, drawn by mules, which was then quickly surrounded by the wedding guests. Led by flute players and torch-bearers, the procession made its way through the streets to the home of the groom, the marchers singing the nuptial hymn to Hymenæus. Some writers assert that the bride's mother followed the chariot bearing torches. It is possible, however, that she merely lighted the nuptial torch which was then borne by a family servant at the head of the gay procession. Arrived at her husband's home, the portals of which were decorated with garlands, the bride feigned reluctance and, after a mock struggle, was carried over the threshold in the arms of the groom. This symbolic act probably marked the fact that the wife had as yet no assured rights in her husband's home, the abode of his household gods, and therefore she must be introduced by force. However, the ceremony may have been a relic of a primitive age of wife capture.

After the entrance of bride and groom the final ceremonies took place with impressive simplicity. The bridal pair, dressed in white and crowned with garlands, drew near to the family hearth, the shrine of the domestic gods, which the young wife sprinkled with lustral water. Then she approached her hand to the sacred fire, after which certain prayers were repeated commending her to the favor of the gods of her new hearth and home. Finally the husband and wife ate together a cake of sesame seeds to symbolize their communion with each other and with the domestic divinities. By these acts the wife was received into the family worship of her husband. She was then led into the *thalamos*,[1] at the door of which a chorus of maidens sang the epithalamium or bridal hymn. By a law of Solon it was prescribed that the bride should eat a quince — the symbol of fruitfulness — before entering the wedding chamber. Sometimes a pestle for crushing grains was hung at the door of the room to remind the young wife of the household tasks which would be hers.

In Sparta the marriage ceremonies were much more crude and simple. Here, after the preliminary arrangements between parents had been made, the groom forcibly carried off the bride to his own house. In his *Life of Lycurgus* [2] Plutarch relates that, after the bride had been thus rudely brought to her new home, a bridesmaid " received her, cut her hair close to her head, dressed her in a man's cloak and shoes, and placed her upon a couch in a dark chamber alone." Here the bridegroom found her when he returned from dining as usual at the barracks. By Spartan custom, so restricted was the social intercourse between husband and wife that many a man, visiting his wife only at night and then by stealth, had not seen her face in daylight until months had passed after the marriage.

Relations of Husband and Wife. — Since the preliminaries of marriage were arranged by the parents, no doubt it often

---

[1] Bridal chamber.   [2] Bohn ed., p. 81.

happened that the bride and groom saw each other for the first time on the wedding-day. Such ignorance of each other's temperament and character must have been a serious handicap to happy marriages. The situation was rendered still more difficult by the shyness and immaturity of the bride whose early secluded life apart from men, remote from all developing social influences save those of her own family and a few friends, ill fitted her to become the companion of a husband whose personality had been developed by careful training and broad social experience. The docility of a typical girl-bride is well portrayed in the *Economics* of Xenophon where the husband Ischomachus is described as introducing his wife to her household duties. To the attempts of her husband to explain the partnership involved in marriage the girl replies: " But how can I assist you? what is my ability? Nay everything depends on you. My business, my mother told me, was to be sober-minded." [1] Apparently, however, Greek wives were not invariably sober-minded, even though we are informed by Aristophanes that a married woman commonly shrank back and blushed if she were by chance seen at a window by a man. However this may be, adultery on the part of Ionian women seems not to have been an altogether rare occurrence; and even intercourse with slaves was not unknown. These lapses from virtue appear to the student of social life as mute evidences of the truth we are just beginning to comprehend, that purity in its truest sense cannot be secured by ignorance and seclusion. In those instances where the marriage of his son was resorted to by an anxious Greek father as a means of bringing to an end the youth's flagrant debaucheries, the bride must have been looked upon by her unwilling husband as a penalty to be endured rather than as a wife to be cherished. Custom, however, exacted that, whatever his feelings, the

[1] The *Works of Xenophon* (trans. by H. G. Dakyns, 1897), Vol. III, Part I, p. 228.

husband should carefully abstain from indecent language in his wife's presence and from any act which might lower his dignity or detract from the respect in which his wife was bound to hold him.

Although the Greek wife of the higher classes was allowed somewhat more liberty than the unmarried girl, yet she was closely confined to the *gynæconitis*, or women's apartments, and was certainly not expected to leave the house without her husband's permission. When she did go upon the streets she was carefully veiled and invariably attended by a slave assigned to her by her husband for that purpose. While the man spent most of his day abroad, in the market-place discussing public questions, or in the state gymnasium outside the city, the woman remained at home directing the work of her slaves or whiling away the hours as best she might. Although husband and wife commonly took their meals together, the arrival of her lord with male friends meant the prompt withdrawal of the wife to the women's apartments. No Greek woman who had the least regard for her good name would think of attending a banquet given by her husband to his friends or even of being present when her husband brought a single guest to share his meal. Thus the life of man and wife flowed on in widely separate channels; and as he developed in mental power and increased the range of his interests and activities the woman, with her narrow outlook on life, limited wholly to personal and household concerns, must have appealed to him less and less as a companion. It followed that a marriage which began in indifference, not infrequently ended in cold estrangement, if not in positive aversion. In their conception of women and of the whole marital relation the Greeks showed a blindness, even a stupidity, which is in striking contrast to the intellectual brilliancy they brought to bear upon other phases of life. Plato saw the evil in the marriage system of his day and suggested that more kindly relations might be established between husband

and wife if the young people were given more frequent opportunities of seeing each other.[1]   But the practice of isolating women was too firmly established in the Ionian states to be modified, even at a much later period.

Although Euripides, last of the great tragedians of Greece, is generally regarded as a woman-hater, yet his evidence concerning the general attitude of his day toward women is not wholly untrustworthy.   In the drama of *Hippolytus* he puts these words into the mouth of the hero:

> " How great a pest
> Is woman this one circumstance displays:
> The very father who begot and nurtured,
> A plenteous dower advancing, sends her forth,
> That of such loathed incumbrance he may rid
> His mansions: but the helpless youth who takes
> This noxious image to his bed, exults
> While he caparisons a worthless image,
> In gorgeous ornaments and tissued vests
> Squandering his substance. . . ." [2]

In the *Medea*, however, Euripides, in a moment of rare sympathy, reverses the shield and presents to us the woman's side.   The wretched queen exclaims:

> " Of all things upon earth that bleed and grow,
> A herb most bruised is woman.   We must pay
> Our store of gold, hoarded for that one day,
> To buy us some man's love; and lo, they bring
> A master of our flesh !   There comes the sting
> Of the whole shame.   And then the jeopardy,
> For good or ill, what shall that master be;
> Reject she cannot; and if he but stays
> His suit, 'tis shame on all that woman's days.
> So thrown amid new laws, new places, why,
> 'Tis magic she must have, or prophecy —
> Home never taught her that — how best to guide
> Toward peace this thing that sleepeth at her side.

---

[1] Plato, *The Laws* (Jowett trans.), VI, 771–2.

[2] Euripides, *Hippolytus*, Morley's Universal Library, pp. 290–91.

> And she who, labouring long, shall find some way
> Whereby her lord may bear with her, nor fray
> His yoke too fiercely, blesséd is the breath
> That woman draws! Else, let her pray for death.
> Her lord, if he be wearied of the face
> Within doors, gets him forth; some merrier place
> Will ease his heart; but she waits on, her whole
> Vision enchainéd on a single soul." [1]

Concubinage and Prostitution among the Greeks. —
Although the family in the historic age of Greece was, on
the whole, monogamous, yet, from the earliest antiquity,
concubinage had existed. In the age of the Homeric epics
the distinction between wife and concubine consisted in this:
the wife was honorably purchased of her father and was
married with customary ceremonies; while the concubine
was the prize of war and was in effect the chattel of her captor.
Numerous references in both the *Iliad* and the *Odyssey* make
it clear enough that concubinage was a common practice in
times of war.   In the Trojan epic the virgin Chryseis, daughter
of the priest of Apollo, is given to Agamemnon as his concubine; and when a pestilence, sent by the god, ravages the
Greek camp and Agamemnon is forced to accept a ransom
for the maid he exclaims:

> " . . . 'Twas my choice
> To keep her with me, for I prize her more
> Than Clytemnestra, bride of my young years,
> And deem her not less nobly graced than she,
> In form and feature, mind and pleasing arts." [2]

And again he protests in bitter indignation:

> " This maiden I release not till old age
> Shall overtake her in my Argive home,
> Far from her native country, where her hand
> Shall throw the shuttle and shall dress my couch." [3]

[1] Euripides, *Medea* (trans. by Gilbert Murray), p. 15.
[2] *Iliad* (trans. by Bryant), Bk. I, ll. 146–50.   [3] *Ibid.*, ll. 38–41.

The last lines make plain the position of concubines within the Homeric family: frequently of noble birth they were employed like slaves in personal, if not menial, services for their lord and captor. It was for the sake of his concubine Breseis, unjustly taken from him, that Achilles sulked so long within his tent. Again, the murder of Agamemnon by his false wife Clytemnestra was defended by her on the ground that her lord had brought the princess Cassandra from fallen Troy to serve as his concubine within the palace.

But concubinage was apparently not confined to rude Homeric times. In the *Oration Against Neæra*, ascribed to Demosthenes, the orator makes a statement which sheds a flood of light upon the modified monogamy of the Greek family: " Mistresses we keep for pleasure, concubines for daily attendance upon our person, wives to bear us legitimate children; and be our faithful housekeepers." [1] It is probable, then, that when concubines were kept by a Greek householder these women were usually selected from among the household slaves. Certain it is that their children were never regarded as true members of the family, since they could not share in the worship of the domestic gods. Therefore such offspring had no rights of succession to any part of the family patrimony.

The Hetairæ. — The integrity of Greek family life was further threatened by another custom. In most of the cities of Greece, notably in Corinth and Athens, there existed a class of young women called hetairæ who were trained from childhood to a life of immorality. Some of these unfortunates were the exposed children of families respected in the community who had fallen into the hands of unscrupulous persons and were ruthlessly exploited. Among this class were young women of foreign birth distinguished not only for their beauty, but for their wit and intellectual attainments. Such were the renowned Aspasia, the mistress and

[1] Demosthenes, *Orations*, Bohn's Classical Library, Vol. V, p. 272.

subsequently the wife of Pericles,[1] Lamia, daughter of a citizen of Athens, Phryne, and Laïs of Corinth. A famous hetaira of Arcadian birth was at one time a pupil of Plato and another attended the discourses of the philosopher Epicurus.[2] Although these were probably exceptional cases, yet most of the hetairæ were well educated, well informed on public affairs and socially gifted.

In addition to this select group, who were accessible only to the wealthy or the socially prominent, there were the common prostitutes living in houses licensed by the state.

It is a curious fact that the Greeks so generally neglected the education of their respectable women, who thus proved, in many instances, dull and naïve in the company of their cultivated husbands, while they freely granted to dissolute women the intellectual training so conspicuously lacking in their own wives. In consequence Greek statesmen and scholars eagerly sought the more stimulating society of these attractive hetairæ. Nor was such action on the part of married men harshly condemned by public opinion.

DIVORCE IN ANCIENT GREECE

Rights of the Husband. — In the *Iliad* and the *Odyssey* there is not a single mention of divorce; therefore we are justified in believing that such separations were not an established custom in primitive times. But in the historic period of Greece divorce was far from unusual. As with the Hebrews, so with the Greeks, larger rights of divorce were conceded to the husband than to the wife. A Greek might simply dismiss his wife in the presence of witnesses if he found her unattractive or uncongenial. Although such separations were probably not uncommon, yet they were not

[1] Authorities disagree on the question of the marriage of Pericles and Aspasia; but it is certain that his son by the famous courtesan was made legitimate by a special act of the people.   [2] Becker, *Charicles*, p. 248.

wholly unrestricted, both because public opinion did not approve them, and also because in such a case the husband must return his repudiated wife's dowry to her father or guardian. In two instances the husband was very generally considered to be justified in divorcing his wife: (1) in case of barrenness, (2) in case of adultery. As respects the first cause, the Greeks held that the fundamental purpose of marriage, — the generation of offspring to perpetuate the worship of ancestors, — had not been realized and therefore the fruitless union ought to be dissolved. For this reason childless women sometimes procured exposed infants, whom they passed off as their own, in order to escape the odium attached to barrenness.[1] Adultery on the part of a wife was visited with severity by Greek law and custom. If surprised in the act, the man might be put to death by the outraged husband; and there is reason to believe that the same fate was meted out to the woman also. If the husband took time for reflection, however, he was not permitted to kill his offending wife, but might inflict corporal punishment upon her and keep her in close confinement within the house. In case the affair became public, the wife was made infamous and by law was denied all right to participate in the national religious rites and sacrifices or even to enter the temples. The adulteress who attempted to attend the public sacrifices might " suffer any maltreatment short of death with impunity." Moreover, in cases where the wife's adultery became known, the law commanded the annulment of the marriage.[2] The Spartans often boasted that adultery was far less common with them than among the Ionian Greeks; indeed they declared that the evil did not exist among them. But this is only to say that sex relations were much freer among the Spartans than the Athenians. If a Spartan had no children or had become old, he might and frequently did encourage his wife to have intercourse with some younger

[1] *Ibid.*, p. 497.   [2] *Ibid.*, p. 497.

H

and more vigorous man in order to raise up children to continue his name. Plutarch tells us that Lycurgus " permitted men to associate worthy persons with them in the task of begetting children, and taught them to ridicule those who insisted on the exclusive possession of their wives." [1] The reason for this apparent laxness is clearly stated : " Lycurgus did not view children as belonging to their parents, but above all to the state ; " and a military state was naturally concerned to obtain a goodly number of future citizens born of sound stock.

Rights of the Wife. — As may be supposed, the Greek woman had few rights in the matter of divorce. Adultery on the part of her husband, even continual and open resort to the houses of hetairæ, gave the neglected wife no ground for separation in any Greek state. Only if the husband's debaucheries resulted in the gross neglect of his family, or in genuine cruelty was his wife justified in seeking a divorce. But, even then, the undertaking was very difficult. She must submit a written complaint in person before the chief archon of the city ; and it was quite possible for a suspicious husband to prevent this by forcibly confining his wife to the house.[2] Even if the woman obtained a divorce, she must return to her old home, perhaps as an unwelcome member, and must submit once more to the authority of father or brother. Yet Greek husbands and wives not rarely resorted to separations by mutual consent, even though the wife thereby lost the small degree of freedom accorded the married woman.

Divorce, like marriage, was looked upon by the Greeks as a private and family matter not under the authority of religion or of the state, save in the single case of the wife's adultery, when the law intervened to dissolve the marriage.

[1] *Life of Lycurgus*, Bohn Library, I, p. 82.
[2] Cf. Gulick, *The Life of the Ancient Greeks*, p. 125.

THE GREEK HOUSEHOLD AS AN ECONOMIC INSTITUTION

Slavery. — It is impossible to consider the economic functions of the Greek household without recognition of the institution of slavery which was closely interwoven with all forms of home industry. The origin of slavery among the Greeks is buried in antiquity; certainly it was a well-nigh universal institution in Homeric times. In those early days of war and rapine, slaves were obtained by conquest and by open piracy; but in the historic period slaves were most frequently barbarians purchased in the market-towns of the Black Sea and Asia Minor. This class was further recruited from among exposed children, large numbers of whom were rescued to be brought up as professional dancers and flute-players. In the heroic age, when life was simple and patriarchal, the condition of the slaves was probably little inferior to that of other members of the household. Since they came under the power of the family head they were regarded as part of the family, and were treated with a kind friendliness which at times is sharply contrasted with their treatment in the historic age. Quite frequently, in these early times, slaves were intrusted with responsible posts of superintendence on the farm and in the household and lived on a familiar footing with their masters, even eating at the same table and sharing in their pleasures. Such conditions had largely disappeared in the fifth century B.C., although they tended to persist in remote pastoral sections such as Arcadia. Since slaves were not persons in the eyes of the law, they could not contract legal marriages. Yet unions were formed between slaves, with the consent of their masters, and slave-families were established. The members, however, might at any time be separated by sale or otherwise, at the will of the owner. Upon the slaves, of course, devolved all the heavier and more distasteful labors of the household, such as farm work, cattle and sheep tending, and grinding grain in the rude hand-mills of early times.

The Household as an Industrial Centre. — In the Homeric age the home was still the nucleus of most of the industries of the community. On the lands of the chiefs and their followers were produced nearly all the necessities required by the patriarchal family. Each well-to-do household had its own cattle, sheep and goats, its farm and grazing lands, its mill, its implements for converting raw materials into food and clothing. The distaff and spindle were in daily use and weaving was highly developed, although the loom was still primitive in form. So much we learn from the patient labors of Penelope in the *Odyssey*. Homer's epics show nothing of the contempt for hand labor so widespread among the Greeks in historic times. Even the gods are represented as workers: Hephæstos labors at the forge; Athena spins and weaves. The nobly born are not ashamed to work as carpenters or to make the various implements needed in household industry. Yet, although the family in the heroic age was largely self-supporting, certain industries had even then been organized into crafts which were carried on outside the home. Such were the trades of carpenters, masons, smiths and workers in precious metals.

By the fifth century, however, the household had, in many instances, ceased to be an economic unit. Only on the country estates of the rich, where large numbers of slaves were employed, do we find grain threshed and ground, grapes and olives pressed into wine and oil, bread and cakes baked in the family ovens, and all the processes concerned with making woollen and linen cloth and fashioning it into garments carried on by the members of the household. In Athens tanning of leather had become a distinct trade pursued by law outside the city because of its unpleasant smell. Shoemaking, hat manufacturing, pottery making, metal-working in iron, bronze and gold had become separate crafts doing a thriving business in special streets named for these trades. All these facts concerning extra-domestic industries may be drawn from the illustrations on Greek vases. No longer did each household grind its own grain. Instead large public mills did most of this work, at least in the cities, and sold the flour to public bakers. The bakehouses contained enormous earthen ovens for baking loaves of the standard weight and size fixed by the city's market commissioners. The Athenians prided themselves on the quality of the bread and sweetened fancy cakes prepared by these public bakers. The comedies of Aristophanes convey the impression that bread was rarely baked at home, but was quite commonly bought of women venders who set up their stalls in the market-place.[1] Then, too, certain processes connected with the making of clothing had likewise been taken over by craftsmen. Except on large country estates, the fleeces of sheep were commonly cleansed and dyed by professional fullers and dyers who had prac-tised these crafts for generations. Tailoring establishments existed in all the more important Greek cities where cloth was cut, fitted and even made up into garments for those of the wealthier classes who chose to have this labor performed outside their homes. There is reason to believe that linen goods, at least, were not even woven on household looms, but almost exclusively by the tailors in these cloth factories.[2] Division of labor in some industries seems to have been almost as minute as it is to-day. For example, certain establish-ments manufactured only women's garments, others only men's. In the manufacture of household furniture we find one group of workers making beds, another chairs, another chests for clothing, and still another bronze doors and gates, mirrors, and even hairpins of metal. The making of pottery for domestic use, once no doubt the province of Greek women as it still is of the women in primitive tribes, had become a thriving extra-household industry. Athens was especially famed among the cities of Greece for the beauty and durability

[1] Cf. Becker, *Charicles*, p. 289.
[2] See Gulick, *The Life of the Ancient Greeks*, p. 229.

of its pottery, no doubt because of the beds of clay in Attica which were peculiarly adapted to such uses.

Thus conditions were at work in Greece in the fifth century B.C. to withdraw from the household a goodly number of the industries which had for centuries been exclusively carried on within its walls. Yet it would be a serious mistake to regard the well-to-do Greek woman of the age of Pericles as a " lady " in our modern economic sense; *i.e.*, as chiefly a consumer of the goods produced by the working-classes. Most Greek women spun and wove the woollen if not the linen garments worn by the slaves as well as the free women of the household, besides doing some of the family cooking. In the homes of the wealthy, it is true, the women probably directed these labors more than they shared in them; but, with a numerous family of slaves, such direction must have consumed much time. In addition, the women of Greece were experts in the art of embroidering. This is made plain by the various vase paintings which depict them at work and reproduce the exquisite designs they embroidered on the borders of chitons and other garments. In several Greek states corporations of women wove and decorated the festive robes thrown over the statues of their patron gods and goddesses. We are told that the maidens of Athens were required every four years to weave a peplos for the statue of Pallas Athene in the Parthenon to be used at the return of the great Panathenaic festival. Into these garments were woven the portraits of the nation's great men so that they served, like the tapestries of the Middle Ages, as a chronicle of the heroes of the city-state.

Xenophon, the Greek historian and soldier of the fifth century B.C., has bequeathed to future ages a delightful picture of the household pursuits of the Greek wife and the careful economy of the average Greek home as it existed in his own day. The discourse is in the form of a dialogue between Ischomachus, a young Greek husband, and Socrates, who, according to his wont, is in search of knowledge. Ischomachus relates, with pardonable pride, that he has trained his girl-wife in her household duties entirely by himself, since she was less than fifteen years of age at her marriage and " had spent the preceding part of her life under the strictest restraint, in order that she might see as little, hear as little and ask as few questions as possible." The young husband describes to the delighted Socrates the instruction he gave to his bride in the management of what he is pleased to call, with rather unusual generosity, their " common household." He explains the primitive division of labor which assigns to males the production of the necessaries of life out of doors and to females the rearing of children, the care of supplies and the manufacture of raw materials, — pursuits which can best be carried on under shelter. Very ingeniously Ischomachus presents the time-worn argument that " the gods . . . have plainly adapted the nature of the woman for work and duties within doors, and that of the man for works and duties without doors." With much patient detail he relates how he introduced his wife to her specific tasks and responsibilities. She must take charge of and keep strict account of all supplies; take care that garments were made for all who needed them from the raw wool brought into the house; and see to it that the dried provisions were fit for eating. Upon her fell the burden of nursing the sick slaves until their recovery. She it was also who must train the unskilled slave girl to be an expert spinner. She must learn what were the best places in the house for storing wine and corn, and for putting away couch coverings, vases, household vessels, implements and utensils for spinning, cooking, kneading bread, etc. Finally she was to " consider herself the guardian of the laws established in the house, and inspect the household furniture whenever she thought proper . . .; to signify her approbation if everything was in good condition, as the senate signifies its approval of the horses and horse-soldiers; to praise and honour the deserving like a queen, according to her means, and to rebuke and disgrace any one that required such treatment." By these wise instructions the young wife of Ischomachus was clearly informed of her functions in life, — to be the director of the household slaves and guardian of the household supplies, and " to produce offspring, that the race may not become extinct." Nowhere in literature is there a more sane and temperate exposition of the age-old masculine theory of the duties of womankind; nowhere is there a more complete failure to recognize this woman as an *individual* with personal tastes and capacities worthy of consideration and development.

HOME NURTURE AND EDUCATION

Birth and Early Training. — If Plato is to be believed, the Greek home played an important rôle in the early training of children. " Education and admonition," he writes, " commence in the first years of childhood and last to the very end of life." [1] At the birth of a Greek child the joyful event was announced by symbols fastened to the door of the house. If the newcomer were a boy, an olive wreath was used to signify the public honors and preferment that might be his. But if the infant were a girl, a piece of wool was attached to the door as a symbol of the household industries to which most of her life would be devoted. On the fifth, or as some writers assert on the seventh day after birth, the ceremony of *Amphidromia* occurred. At this family festival the nurse, or some female relative, carried the new-born infant around the sacred hearth of the home. The ceremony was clearly intended to introduce the child into family membership which, as we have seen, included the spirits of departed ancestors. At this time, the father, as the supreme family head, probably made formal declaration that he accepted the responsibility of rearing the child. Otherwise the infant was ruthlessly exposed. Exposure was sanctioned by law, but was probably

[1] Plato, *Protagoras*, 325 c.

not so frequent as some writers would have us think. More commonly this fate was reserved for girls and for illegitimate children, although boys were sometimes exposed by poor parents to escape the burden of rearing them, and by well-to-do parents to avoid too minute a division of the family property. A letter has come down to us from the year B.C. 1, in which a certain Greek named Hilarion writes to his wife Alis from Alexandria as follows: " If — good luck to you — you bear offspring, if it be a male, let it live, if it is a female, expose it." [1] The laconic quality of this statement is matched by its utter failure to recognize any right of the mother in the child she had borne. On the tenth day after birth there occurred a more imposing ceremony consisting of solemn sacrifice at the family altar followed by a banquet. To this festival relatives and friends were invited, and the new-born infant was named. Usually this little ceremony was performed by the father, and at its close presents were showered upon parents and child by the guests and even by the family slaves.

After formal acceptance into family membership the Greek child of well-to-do parents was nurtured chiefly by slaves. Few mothers of the wealthier classes suckled their own children: except in Sparta, wet-nurses were very generally employed for this purpose. Apparently the first nurse was not always a slave, for Plutarch informs us that Spartan mothers, famed for their skill and good sense, were sometimes hired by Athenians to suckle and train their infants. Thus the wet-nurse of Alcibiades was a Spartan woman. Boys and girls remained under the care of nurses and mothers until the sixth or seventh year and were brought up in close association. We know that they had much the same playthings as modern children; for frequent references are made in Greek literature to rattles, go-carts, dolls of painted clay, hoops and tops. Aristophanes in his comedy of *The Clouds* refers to a cockchafer fastened by a thread as a popular toy.

[1] Milligan, *Greek Papyri*, p. 81.

In the matter of discipline, the child was by no means neglected. The Greek parents of the more favored classes sought carefully to maintain their dignity in the presence of children and insisted upon prompt obedience. Personal chastisement with sandal or slipper was the approved form of punishment, although Greek nurses and mothers, like those of later times, did not hesitate to make frequent dark references to popular bogeys as a means of frightening children into docile behavior. Slave nurses had a rich fund of myths and tales of heroes which they were fond of relating to their charges. Because of the profound influence exercised by these stories upon the child's moral nature, Plato emphasizes the care with which they should be selected. He even goes so far as to eliminate the Homeric poems from the educative material given to children on the ground that they portray the gods in immoral and undignified situations. " Then the first thing," he urges, " will be to have a censorship of the writers of fiction and let the censors receive any tale of fiction which is good and reject the bad; and we will desire mothers and nurses to tell their children the authorized ones only. Let them fashion the mind with these tales, even more fondly than they form the body with their hands; and most of those which are now in use must be discarded." [1] According to Plato the training of children in harmony with approved moral standards was vigorously carried on in the Greek home. In the *Protagoras* he describes this training: " Mother and nurse and father and tutor are quarreling about the improvement of the child as soon as ever he is able to understand them; he cannot say or do anything without their setting forth to him that this is just and that is unjust; this is honorable, that is dishonorable; this is holy, that is unholy; do this and abstain from that. And if he obeys, well and good; if not he is straightened by threats and blows, like a piece of warped wood." [2]

[1] *Republic*, Bk. II, 377.   [2] *Op. cit.*, 325 c.

At seven years of age the lives of sisters and brothers in Greek families began to diverge. Under the charge of his pedagogue, the boy was sent to palæstra and music school and later to the public gymnasium to receive that carefully planned education, terminating for the favored youth only with his legal majority, which was designed to fit him for full citizenship. All his education from this time forward was carried on outside the family; there is no mention by Greek writers of any regular home instruction after the boy had attained school age. While her brother's education was thus proceeding, the Greek girl was leading a highly restricted life, rarely leaving her home, and receiving no definite instruction save in spinning, weaving, embroidering and probably cooking if her family were not well-to-do.

It would appear, then, that in Greece, as in the modern countries of Europe and America, the educative influence of the home was chiefly confined to the early years of the boy's life; and that his musical, literary, moral and physical education was handed over to institutions such as the music school and gymnasium, followed by the organized military training of the ephebic period. That the family exercised a valuable influence in shaping the moral and religious nature of both boys and girls can hardly be doubted. Yet it appears equally certain that the inferior position of the Greek mother, her lack of knowledge of the world and of life, — a knowledge commonly gained either through direct experience or through the medium of literature, — must have served to lessen enormously the degree and the value of her influence over her children. The moral guidance of an ignorant, inexperienced, imperfectly trained mother can hardly be either sound or enlightened save in very rare instances. The egregious blunder of intelligent Greek men in almost totally neglecting the intellectual and social education of their women of good repute must have been paid for in the relative ineffectiveness of the wives and mothers.

THEORIES OF GREEK PHILOSOPHERS CONCERNING THE FAMILY

Any discussion of the Greek family would be manifestly in-complete without some reference to the views of the great philosophers of Greece on this subject. Both Plato and Aris-totle, viewing the whole question of the family and the training of offspring from the high standpoint of the needs of society, would empower the state to interfere in the making of mar-riages and in determining the fitness of the offspring of these unions to live. In the *Republic* Plato sets forth radical views with respect to the regulation of marriages by the state. Men and women of the " guardian " or ruling class are to choose their mates by lot at great nuptial festivals appointed and directed by the state. Plato advocated that the guardians of the state juggle these lots in such a way as to bring together the more vigorous and intellectual men and women and thus determine, as he thought, the character of their offspring. Thus he says : The " best of either sex should be united with the best as often, and the inferior with the inferior, as seldom as possible ; and . . . they should rear the offspring of the one sort of union, but not of the other, if the flock is to be maintained in first-rate condition." [1] Parents are to separate after the birth of children and the offspring, if permitted to live, are to be promptly sent to state nurseries, there to be reared by public nurses properly trained for their duties. The bereft parents, Plato holds (and be it noted that this idealist was unmarried), will console themselves by developing warm parental feeling for all children born at about the same period as their own child ! To the proper state officials Plato com-mits the whole matter of determining which of the new-born infants shall be reared and which shall be exposed as weak-lings, likely to grow into undesirable citizens. All children born of unions not sanctioned by the state are to be exposed.[2] It will be seen that Plato, the world's first eugenist, fearlessly

[1] *Republic*, V, 459.　　　　　[2] *Ibid.*, 457–62.

adopts the ground that marriage as well as the procreation and rearing of offspring are, above all else, matters which profoundly concern the State.

As regards the early education of children no writer of ancient times has written more suggestively than Plato. He clearly recognized the impressionability of young minds and the lasting character of early ideas and habits. Hence his careful censorship of literature and music and his belief that children from their earliest infancy should be surrounded with beautiful forms, in art and architecture, in literature and in conduct.

But beyond question Plato's most radical theory was the view that women have the same natures, the same gifts and capacities as men, only in a lesser degree. Therefore he holds that they should receive the same education and be admitted to the same spheres of work and of public service. " And so, my friend," he writes, " in the administration of a State neither a woman as a woman, nor a man as a man has any special function, but the gifts of nature are equally diffused in both sexes; all the pursuits of men are the pursuits of women also, and in all of them a woman is only a weaker man." [1] It is surprising to learn that Plato forestalled, by nearly twenty-three centuries, the views that are rapidly gaining headway in the modern world. That his voice was merely " lifted in the wilderness " to the unheeding multitude of his own age hardly needs to be stated. The Greeks were very far indeed from accepting, much less carrying out, the theories of their great idealist.

Aristotle, being less speculative and more scientific than his master, reckons with conditions as they exist and thus is more conservative. We find no recommendation in this philosopher's writings that the family be undermined or destroyed. Nevertheless he believes in State intervention in marriage, for he suggests that " the *legislator* ought to take care that the bodies of children are as perfect as possible "; there-

[1] *Ibid.*, 455–57.

fore " his first attention ought to be given to matrimony; at which time and in what situation it is proper that citizens should engage in the nuptial contract." [1] Apparently he would have the State determine the marriageable age for men and women. He deplores too early marriages as productive of " very small and ill-framed children "; and would have the " succession of children " fall within the time when their parents have attained bodily perfection. Legislators must see to it that pregnant women get sufficient exercise by commanding them " once every day to repair to the worship of the gods who are supposed to preside over matrimony." Like Plato, Aristotle does not rise above the views of his age regarding child exposure. Thus he writes: "As to the exposure and rearing of children, let there be a law that no deformed child shall live. . . ." [2] Here pagan disregard for the value of the individual human life is allied with a wholesome concern for the well-being of the city-state.

While their philosophers thus discussed and wrote, the established Greek practices with respect to marriage and family life went on practically unchanged. It is true that Greek comedians toward the close of the fifth century represent women as seeking a larger measure of freedom and influence,[3] but there is little evidence that their strivings ever resulted in a fuller and more satisfying life.

SELECTED BIBLIOGRAPHY

SOURCES.

Aristophanes.   1. *Lysistrata.*
              2. *Ecclesiazucæ.*

Aristotle.   *Nichomachean Ethics*, Bk. VIII, ch. XII.   (Jowett trans.)
           Politics (Jowett trans.), Bk. I, pp. 5, 22–6, 52–3, 238–43.

Demosthenes.   *Oration against Neæra* (Bohn Classical Library), Vol. V, 1889.

---

[1] *Politics*, VII, 16.   [2] *Op. cit.*, VII, 16; 1335 b.
[3] See the Comedies of Aristophanes, — the *Lysistrata* and the *Ecclesiazucæ*, Bohn Classical Library, London, 1853, Vol. II.

Euripides.   *Medea* (Gilbert Murray trans.).

   Hippolytus (Morley's Universal Library).

Milligan, G.   *Greek Papyri*, pp. 1–4, 8–11, 41, 81, 85, 104.

Monroe, Paul.   *Source Book in the History of Education for the Greek and Roman Period.*

   Xenophon's *Economics*, pp. 37–50.

   Plato, *The Republic*, pp. 173–79.

   Plato, *The Laws*, pp. 243–4.

Plato.   *The Republic* (Jowett trans.), Bk. V, pp. 455–67.

   The Laws (Jowett trans.), pp. 294–5, 312–13, 342–47.

Plutarch.   *Lives* (Bohn Classical Library, 1908), Vol. I, pp. 80–3, 147–8, 150.

SECONDARY WORKS.

Becker, W. A.   *Charicles*, Excursus to Scene I, pp. 217–27, 236.

   Excursus to Scene II, pp. 241–50.

   Excursus to Scene III, pp. 251–71.

   Excursus to Scene XII, pp. 462–98.

Blümner, Hugo.   *Home Life of the Ancient Greeks*, pp. 129–83, 202–08.

Botsford, G. W.   *The Athenian Constitution*, chs. I, III.

Bruns.   *Frauenemancipation in Athen*, 1900.

Bücher, Karl.   *Industrial Evolution*, pp. 95–7.

Decharme, P.   *Euripides and the Spirit of his Dramas*, pp. 93–112.

de Coulanges, Fustel.   *The Ancient City*, pp. 41–71.

Dickinson, G. Lowes.   *The Greek View of Life*, pp. 71–80, 154–67.

Donaldson, J.   *Woman, her Position and Influence in Ancient Greece and Rome . . .*, chs. I–III.

Garnier, C., et Ammann.   *L'Histoire de l'habitation humaine*, pp. 456–78.

Gide, P.   *Étude sur la condition privée de la femme* (1885), ch. III.

Guhl and Koner.   *Life of the Greeks and Romans*, pp. 75–85.

Gulick, C. B.   *The Life of the Ancient Greeks* (1907), chs. VI, IX.

Harper's *Dictionary of Classical Literature and Antiquities*, articles on *Adulterium, Amphidromia, Divortium, Matrimonium.*

Linton, E. Lynn.   *Womanhood in Old Greece* (in *Fortnightly Review*, XLII, pp. 105–23, 715–31).

Mahaffy.   *Social Life in Greece*, pp. 146–53, 224–7.

Murray, Gilbert.   *The Rise of Greek Epic*, 16–22, 124–26, 150–53.

Putnam, Emily.   *The Lady*, ch. I.

Schuster, E. J.   *The Wife in Ancient and Modern Times*, chs. II, IV.

St. John, J. A.   *Manners and Customs in Ancient Greece* (1842), Vol. I, 107–64, 369–401; II, pp. 1–28, 75–125.

Zimmern, Alfred.   *The Greek Commonwealth* (1911), pp. 65–71, 319–43.

CHAPTER V

THE PATRIARCHAL FAMILY: THE ROMAN TYPE

Periods in the History of the Roman Family. — The history of the family in ancient Rome, unlike that of Greece, is markedly progressive in character. This makes it necessary to divide Roman family history into two periods widely divergent in ideals and customs. The earlier period begins with the dawn of Roman legend and extends approximately to the close of the Punic wars (753–202 B.C.). During this period the prevalent ideals of marriage and family life are stern, simple and wholesome, although harsh and rigid. The later period covers the centuries from the end of the Punic wars (202 B.C.) to the fourth century A.D. when Christian influence begins very gradually to modify pagan marriage and family customs.

THE ROMAN FAMILY IN THE EARLY PERIOD (753–202 B.C.)

Its Patriarchal Character. — Prior to the time when the Romans began that ruthless career of conquest, which resulted in transforming all their social institutions, the family presented the most complete example known to history of the patriarchal type. The early Roman family, consisting of wife, children, sometimes grandchildren and slaves, was a religious, legal and economic unit. Its integrity was preserved through the centuries because in its oldest male head was vested all religious rights, as priest of the family ancestor-worship, all legal rights, as the only ‘person’ recognized by law, and all economic rights as the sole owner of the family property, both real and movable. Unlike the custom in Greece, the power of the family head over all adult male members was permanent, enduring throughout the lifetime of the patriarch. Gaius, in his *Institutes of Roman Law*, makes the following statement concerning the complete subordination of the members of a Roman family to its ruling head : " It should be noted that nothing can be granted in the way of justice to those under power ; *i.e.*, to slaves, children and wives. For it is reasonable to conclude that, since these persons can own no property, they are incompetent to claim anything in point of law." [1] But this vast power, reposed in the *pater*, was, after all, delegated power as was the case in Greece. Not as an absolute monarch did the Roman patriarch exercise this authority, but as the representative of the family in its cult of ancestors. He alone knew the traditional ceremonials by which ancestral spirits could be appeased and transformed from malign into beneficent forces ; and he alone as household priest could pass on this important knowledge to his eldest son.

In its strongly unified aspect the Roman family institution most vividly contrasts with the modern, which is composed of individuals with approximately equal rights before the law and with a disposition to assert those rights in ways likely to weaken the unity of family life. The prevalence of divorce and of family desertion as well as the increase in the numbers of young people breaking home ties to " start out for themselves," or throwing off parental authority as soon as they become self-supporting, are but so many indications of a spirit of individualism in the modern household quite unknown in the family of ancient times. Indeed, in those simple days, there was no place for the individual outside the family institution, — to be a free-lance, not owing obedience to a family head, was to be a social outcast. In progress of time, however, as Roman society developed, and customs changed with the

---

[1] *Op. cit.*, II, 96 ; quoted by Couch, *Woman in Early Roman Law, Harvard Law Rev.*, VIII, p. 43.

I

change of ideas, the family in Rome became more individualistic until, in late Imperial times, it resembled in more than one respect the American family of the present age.

The Patria Potestas. — The power of the father (*patria potestas*) was expressly recognized in the Laws of the Twelve Tables,[1] and extended to life and death. The *pater familias* might scourge his children, sell them into slavery, banish them from the country or put them to death. In one respect only was his authority as the legal judge and executioner of his children at all limited. In case a child had committed any grave offence, the patriarch must summon a council of the adult male members of his *gens* or " great family " and confer with them before passing sentence on his son which would condemn him to slavery or death. If he differed from the views of the majority, however, he was apparently free to carry out his own judgment. Although the Laws of the Twelve Tables expressly recognized the father's right to sell his offspring, there seems to be no instance in history of the exercise of this power. By the quaint ceremony of *emancipation*, which consisted in a fictitious sale formally carried out three times, the son was set free from the *patria potestas*, and thus ceased to be a member of the family. But, since sons were highly valued by the father as the maintainers of the family religion, this ceremony was comparatively rare. On the other hand adoption was widely practised among the Romans as among the Greeks. Where no son was born to the family head, a youth was adopted with proper ceremonial into the family membership and was taught the cult of the sacred hearth fire and of the domestic gods (Lares). Even after his marriage a son remained under the *potestas* of his father and the grandchildren likewise came under the authority of the patriarch at their birth. No male under power could control his property or his earnings nor could he make a will as long as his father lived. Thus the Roman family was

[1] Compiled about 450 B.C.

a state *in parvo*, consisting of wife, children, grandchildren and slaves, all ruled by an absolute head. Such was its character until the later centuries of the Republic.

Manus: The Status of the Roman Matron. — The power of the Roman husband over his wife was called *manus*. In the rude centuries of the kingdom and the early Roman Republic, women seem to have had few, if any, legal rights. As we have seen, a woman could not control property and hence was not regarded as a ' person ' before the law. At her marriage her husband acquired her *dos* or dowry, of which he had the entire management and profits. The wife merely passed from the *potestas* of her father to that of her husband who sat as judge over her if she were accused of serious offences. It is true that the husband must summon a tribunal of his own and his wife's male relatives to consider her case before he was permitted to pass judgment. But the matter once discussed in this family council, the husband might himself condemn his wife to death for a capital offence committed by her. If he discovered her in adultery, he might put her to death at once with no obligation to call a council of relatives. A Roman husband had also the power of personal chastisement and correction of his wife. Moreover it is probable that in cases where the wife had committed offences entailing fines upon her husband, who was legally liable for her actions, he might sell her labor, if not her person, in order to indemnify himself for the expense he had incurred.[1] Likewise he could surrender his wife to a plaintiff who brought suit for any civil offence she had committed, thus relieving himself of liability for her action.[2] Cato the Censor, that stern old Roman of the early type, in a fragment called *De dote*, writes thus of the husband's power: "The husband is the judge of his wife. If she has committed a fault, he punishes her; if she has drunk wine,

[1] Cf. Becker, *Gallus*, p. 156.

[2] Bryce, *Marriage and Divorce under Roman and English Law*, in *Studies in History and Jurisprudence*, p. 790.

he condemns her; if she has been guilty of adultery, he kills her." [1]

Yet, in spite of all these restrictions upon her freedom, it remains true that the Roman matron, in early times, was thoroughly respected and held a place of dignity and honor within the family and the State. She was unquestioned mistress of the household as the man was master. After she was lifted over the threshold of her husband's home at her marriage, she calmly faced him with the ancient formula: " Where thou art Caius I am Caia " (*Ubi tu Caius, ego Caia*) ; *i.e.*, " Where thou art lord, I am lady." And these were no idle words. The Roman matron was not confined to the women's apartments like her Greek sister. Instead she took up her abode in the *atrium*, the central room of the family life. Here she sat, spinning and weaving, and directing the labors of her household. Within the apartment in early times, stood the bridal bed (*lectum genialis* or *adversus*), the outward and visible sign of honorable married life. Marked respect was accorded the Roman wife as the guardian of the family honor, and the partner of her husband in the education of their children. In all the ceremonies of family worship she officiated at the altar as priestess beside her husband. She might even walk abroad with considerable freedom. Custom alone restricted her movements in this regard, not the command of her husband. When she did appear upon the narrow streets robed in the *stola maternalis*, men were expected to make way for her as a mark of their respect for a matron of Rome. Apparently, also, if one may judge from the early pictorial work which has come down to us, Roman wives joined their husbands at table, perhaps even at banquets. Since women had no legal status they probably could not appear in a court of law as complainant or defendant. Yet Becker holds that in very early times women might give evidence in court and might even appear to make complaint for another, until the

[1] See Cato's *Quæ Extant* (ed. by H. Jordan, Leipsic, 1860), p. 68.

abuse of the privilege led to its withdrawal by edict.[1] This right must have been very rarely used in ancient times, however, and seems in direct contradiction to legal opinion and precedent, which denied women individuality before the law.

Thus the Roman wife and mother was at once honored and subordinated; she was thoroughly respected and yet granted almost no legal rights. To quote Mr. James Bryce: " One can hardly imagine a more absolute subjection to one person of another person who was nevertheless not only free but respected and influential, as we know that the wife in old Rome was." [2]

Property Rights in the Ancient Family. — In prehistoric times, prior to the reforms of Servius Tullius, landed property was quite probably held by the *gens*. But long before the Laws of the Twelve Tables were framed property had become individual to the extent that it was held and administered by the family head for the benefit of its members. At the death of the *paterfamilias* his possessions were equally divided among the members of his family who were under his power (*in potestate*). Thus the widow and the unmarried daughters received equal shares with the sons. Primogeniture seems to have been unknown among the Romans; yet some writers [3] have assumed that it existed in order to account for the fact that estates long remained undivided within a family. A more probable explanation is that the estates were commonly held together in two ways: (1) by agreement of the heirs, (2) by provisions in the testament of the deceased father. A married daughter lost all right to inheritance and such was the law as late as the age of Justinian (6th century A.D.). If the decedent left no immediate heirs, his property was divided among his nearest agnates; *i.e.*, relations descended from a not remote ancestor through the male line. If no

---

[1] *Gallus*, p. 153.   [2] *Op. cit.*, p. 790.
[3] Cf. De Coulanges, *The Ancient City*, pp. 94 ff.

agnates were living, the inheritance passed to the members of the deceased man's *gens; i.e.,* those claiming common descent from some long dead and perhaps mythical ancestor. As in Greece the *gens* controlled the estates of a member in two ways : (1) lands could not be alienated from the *gens;* (2) daughters who had inherited property could not marry without the consent of the *gens* nor could they alienate their share of the family lands by sale or otherwise. Guardians or ' tutors ' were appointed for a woman from the *gens* of her father at his death. In early times these tutors kept a rigid oversight and control of the property of an heiress, and arranged for her marriage with great care.

Marriage in Ancient Rome. — *Matrimonium Justum and non Justum.* — Only when the parties to a marriage were of equal social rank could that form of marriage which conferred upon the man the civil rights of *patria potestas* and *manus* be entered upon. This form of marriage, entailing full rights to the husband and children, was called *matrimonium justum.* In earliest times it could not be contracted between a patrician and a plebeian; but this restriction was removed by law in 445 B.C. Another form of marriage existing in ancient Rome was called *matrimonium non justum* and was contracted with a man or woman of inferior social rank. This form did not carry with it the rights of *manus* and *patria potestas* although it was legally and morally binding. Children of such marriages could not become full Roman citizens. *Matrimonium justum* could be performed either with *manus* or without it. In the former case the wife passed under her husband's power ; in the latter she remained under the power of her own father. In earliest times by far the larger number of marriages were performed *cum mano,* thus placing the wife in the position of a daughter to her husband and making her an integral member of his family. Like all ancient peoples the Romans looked upon marriage as a sacred and important act and stamped celibacy with public disapproval, since it was disadvantageous alike to the State, which needed supporters, and to the family which needed sons to continue its domestic worship.

The Ceremonies of Espousals and Marriage. — Unlike the Greeks the early Romans did not regard the betrothal ceremony as legally binding on the parties. Espousals or betrothal consisted first in obtaining the consent of the girl's father to the marriage and in arranging the amount of the *dos* or dowry brought by the bride to her husband. Either party to the engagement could withdraw from it and such withdrawal did not constitute ground for legal action. In early days, however, unchastity on the part of an engaged girl was probably regarded as adultery, and so punished.

Let us suppose that two people of equal social condition have agreed to contract *matrimonium justum* with *manus*. What are the ceremonies connected with such marriage? First there must be the formal *consensus*, or consent of the parties, which was the essential step in any valid marriage. Then, in order that the woman might be brought under the power of her husband any one of three formalities might be followed: (1) *confarreatio*, (2) *coëmptio*, (3) *usus*. The first was a solemn religious ceremony, most commonly employed by the patrician class in Rome. The rites of confarreatio were performed at the home of the bridegroom in the evening after the bride had been carried in brilliant procession (*deductio*), lighted by torches, from her father's house and had been lifted over the threshold of her new home. At this point the bride, turning to her husband, uttered the significant words already quoted, " Where thou art Caius I am Caia," thus reminding him of her honorable position as mistress of his household. The ceremony of confarreatio followed. This essentially consisted in the eating by the bride and groom of a sacred cake, made of the ancient Roman " far." [1] The simple rite was performed in the presence of the Pontifex Maximus [2] the Flamen Dialis [3]

---

[1] *Far* was a grain like spelt.
[2] Chief of the college of priests or pontiffs.   [3] Priest of Jupiter.

and ten other witnesses. It was followed by the joining together of the hands of the young couple, probably by the chief priest. Following this ceremony the auspices were carefully taken and a sheep was sacrificed upon the family altar. The skin of the slain sheep was then stretched over two seats on which the bride and groom seated themselves, thus signifying that they were united by one bond despite their different duties within the family. After a gay banquet shared by the bridal couple and the assembled guests, the *pronubæ* [1] led the bride to the marriage-bed which had been placed in the atrium on the day of the wedding. Standing before the door of the bridal chamber they sang ancient hymns and songs in honor of marriage which would doubtless sound coarse and even indecent to modern ears. These marriage songs were likewise common in Greece and among all Aryan peoples.

Marriage with *manus* was also effected by the ceremony of " coëmptio." Here again, the formal consent of the two parties constituted the essential step in marriage. The rite called coëmptio followed this consent and included many of the ceremonies of confarreatio, — viz., the procession by torch-light, the lifting of the bride over the threshold of her husband's house, the salutation " Where thou art Caius, I am Caia," the taking of auspices and the joining of hands. But instead of the religious rite, which consisted in eating the sacred cake, a symbolical sale of the woman to the man took place. A coin of small value was generally used and the sale was purely symbolic of the fact that the woman was brought under the *manus* or hand of her husband. That this quaint ceremony was the last relic of purchase marriage is highly probable although not an established fact.

In one other way might the woman be brought under her husband's power, and that was by the ancient custom of *usus*.

---

[1] These were young Roman matrons, only once married, who served as attendants to the bride.

When a woman had given her consent and had lived in the marriage relation with her husband for one year, during which time she had not remained three days absent from his home, she automatically came under his power and became an integral part of his family, thus losing membership in her own. This marriage custom was very general during the early centuries of Roman history, although it was largely confined to the plebeian class. Since it was lacking in all religious sanction or ceremonial dignity it was never popular among the Roman patricians until a much later period.

Concubinage. — The monogamic character of marriage was far more strictly preserved by the early Romans than by the Greeks. As among most peoples of antiquity, concubinage existed as a recognized institution; but it was carefully regulated by the State. Concubinage consisted in the legalized union called *matrimonium non justum* where a citizen lived with a woman of inferior social rank with whom he could not by law contract *matrimonium justum*. There was also the sex-relationship not sanctioned by public opinion or law where a man lived with one or more mistresses. In the first case the relation was formally recognized by law and custom, although the offspring of the union were not members of their father's family and thus could not inherit his property. But the second relation was as thoroughly condemned by the wholesome public opinion of the early Roman Republic as it is in the Western world to-day. Hence prostitution was comparatively rare before the period of the Punic wars.

Divorce.— That the right of divorcing his wife belonged to the Roman husband in very early times cannot be doubted, since it is expressly recognized in the Laws of the Twelve Tables. But during the first centuries of the Republic this privilege was carefully restricted and apparently was rarely used. Indeed marriage with *confarreatio* could be dissolved with great difficulty if at all and only after a ceremony of *diffarreatio* or breaking of the marriage bonds, to which all those present at the earlier ceremony of union were invited. The causes justifying the divorce of the wife were the commission of capital offences, adultery, and wine-drinking, which last was always severely condemned and punished among the early Romans. One writer adds to this list the offence of counterfeiting the keys intrusted to the wife as *domina* or house mistress.[1] Yet, even when one of these acts had been clearly committed, the husband was compelled to call a council of his own and his wife's male relatives and lay the matter before them ere he could pronounce the customary words of separation. Only in the case of the wife's adultery could the husband dispense with the advice of the family council before taking her life. On this point Cato the Censor writes: " If you were to catch your wife in adultery, you would kill her with impunity without trial; but if she were to catch you, she would not dare to lay a finger upon you, and indeed she has no right." [2] The formula of repudiation, as given in the Twelve Tables, was: " *Tuas res tibi habeto.*" [3] This was sometimes followed by a command to leave the house (*foras exi*). Although the husband had sole rights of divorce in this early period (save in the case of separation by mutual consent, which rarely occurred), yet if he exercised this right for causes not recognized by law and custom, he brought upon himself both public disapproval and the sharp reproof of the Censor. It is probable, therefore, that divorces were rare occurrences. Indeed Plutarch refers to the case of Spurius Carvilius Ruga (230 B.C.) as the first instance of the repudiation of a wife at Rome. This can hardly, however, be in accordance with the facts. Historians are inclined to believe that Plutarch's statement should be interpreted to mean that Sp. Carvilius was the first Roman to divorce his wife for any but the three causes mentioned above. It is well known that the wife's repudiation in

---

[1] Cf. Lynton, *Fortnightly Review*, Vol. 42, p. 43.
[2] Fragment, *De Dote*, in the *Quæ Extant* (Leipsic, 1860), p. 68.
[3] Keep your own property for yourself.

this historic case was due to the fact that she had not borne a child. She had failed in her supreme duty, from the ancient point of view, of bearing a son to her husband to maintain the family name and worship. Yet, even then, public disapprobation of the act of this Roman citizen was expressed in no uncertain tones.

It will be seen from the above account that divorce was largely a private matter in ancient Rome. Even when custom was violated in respect to divorce the State intervened only by way of the rebuke of the Censor. Thus Rome is in agreement with the other nations of antiquity in regarding marriage and divorce as concerns of the family or of individuals interested.

The Early Roman Household as an Economic Unit. — Perhaps in no respect is the national spirit of the Greeks and Romans more strikingly contrasted than in their attitude toward industry. Prior to the Punic wars the Romans were a hard, stern, simple people with a high regard for manual labor; whereas the Greeks, as we have seen, held all pursuit of trade and industry which demanded actual manual work in genuine contempt. In the early days of the Republic, before Rome was launched upon her wars for conquest and expansion, the number of slaves in any household was small. As in Greece they were not only an essential part of the family,[1] but lived in somewhat friendly intimacy with its free members, despite the unlimited power of the master over their persons. In his life of Cato Major, Plutarch relates that the whole family ate in common although the slaves probably sat on benches placed at the foot of the *lecti* or couches on which the rest of the family sat.[2] These household servants relieved the well-to-do Roman matron of the more burdensome and unpleasant forms of household labor and left her free to carry on her special pursuits of spinning and weaving which were held in high esteem.

[1] The Roman word *familia* was a term first applied to household slaves.
[2] The custom of reclining at meals belongs to a much later period.

In the early days of the kingdom almost every free Roman possessed a few jugera [1] of land which he frequently cultivated by himself, or with the assistance of a servant or two. Most of the Romans of this period were farmers, who, clad in woollen tunics, drove their crude bronze-shod ploughs over the family acres. One of the highest ideals of their lives was to become good ploughmen; just as their ideal of womanhood was the chaste and industrious housewife spinning wool far into the night. Such a man was Cincinnatus, called from his plough to take command, as dictator, of the defeated Roman forces in their war against the Sabines and Æquians. The most eminent men of the early Republic were content with the simple life of the farmer. Valerius Maximus [2] tells us: " At that time there was little money; there were few slaves, seven jugera of land, poverty in families, funerals paid for by the state, and daughters without dowry; but illustrious consulates, wonderful dictatorships, and countless triumphs, — such is the picture of these old times ! "

Probably these early Roman households were largely self-supporting, — the father furnishing the food supplies of grain, green vegetables and *legumes*, and the raw wool and flax which were prepared within the house by the matron and her few family slaves. Division of labor other than that on a sex basis had hardly begun before the Punic wars. No slaves skilled in cookery were found in the households, nor were special bakers kept until after the wars in Asia.[3] All the labors concerned with cooking and baking fell upon the housewife. Even in early times, however, certain industries had been carried outside the home. Roman women rarely washed the family clothing at home, but sent all garments to professional fullers to be cleansed in great tubs filled with alkaline water. The later processes of cleansing garments are

---

[1] A *jugerum* was a little more than half an acre.
[2] A Roman writer of the age of Tiberius Cæsar (14–37 A.D.).
[3] Cf. Becker, *Gallus*, p. 452.

pictured in the wall-paintings of a fuller's establishment in Pompeii, which was unearthed years ago.   Not only did these men cleanse clothing, but apparently they cleaned and dressed cloth sent to them fresh from the loom.[1]   Very early, also, the crafts of the dyer, currier, coppersmith and gold-smith had developed into gilds called " colleges."   Plutarch, in his life of Numa, the fabled successor of Romulus in the kingship, states that popular legend ascribed the founding of these primitive " colleges " of craftsmen to that king.

The Roman Home as a School. — For several centuries after the mythical founding of Rome (753 B.C.) the home was the only institution directly concerned with the education of youth.   Within its revered precincts, — sacred to Vesta, god-dess of the hearth, to the Lares, spirits of ancestors, and to the Penates who blessed the family store, — the child was nurtured in rigorous simplicity and trained in those hardy virtues and habits of industry and self-control which were of the utmost value to the family and the state.   In spite of the narrowness of this training from our modern view-point, there was far more of true family life and spirit in the early Roman home than in the Greek.   This was due to the higher and more dignified position of the Roman mother, who not only care-fully instructed her children in their early years, but super-intended them as long as they remained at home.   In his life of the Gracchi, Plutarch has described the noble nature of the Roman matron Cornelia and the intelligent care she bestowed on the upbringing of her sons.   So honored was this Roman mother that a statue was erected to her memory by the state.[2]

The numerous references made by early writers to the practice of child exposure make it clear enough that the Roman custom of putting an unwelcome child out of the way was similar to the Greek, although there is reason to believe that

[1] *Ibid.*, p. 449.
[2] Plutarch, *Life of Tiberius and Caius Gracchus* (Bohn Library), 1, 95.

it was not as freely practised. Nine days after the birth of a boy and eight days after that of a girl the ceremony of *lustratio* took place, and was celebrated as a family festival. On this happy occasion the child was lifted from the floor and named by his father, after which it received numerous small gifts from parents and friends some of which were afterward worn suspended from its neck. The *bulla* was an amulet of gold worn at first only by children of patrician birth. It was no doubt hung about their baby necks as a protection against evil charms. After the family ceremony of *lustratio* the child's name was entered in the public registers of Rome which were carefully kept in order that the age and social station of any person might be readily established.

Unlike the Greeks, Roman parents did not commit their children to the care of slaves. Every Roman mother in ancient times nursed and reared her own offspring. In those stern and simple days education at the mother's knee was no idle expression. Great care was taken that the children should hear no evil speech and that the household attendants should be discreet in word and action. Boys were instructed first by the mother, later by the father, in those family and civic virtues of frugality, self-control, gravity, piety, courage and loyalty to the state upon which the early Romans set such high value. To inculcate the national ideals of conduct the Roman mother told her boy tales of the bravery and devotion to the state of his honored ancestors, as well as legends of the nation's heroes. In the atrium of every patrician home were placed images and waxen masks of dead ancestors, and children were very early trained to know and to honor the brave deeds of their forefathers. At a later day Cato the Elder wrote histories for his son telling of the glorious achievements of illustrious Romans and the honored customs of the country. There was little or no intellectual education in this early time. Yet every boy was taken to the forum by his father and required to learn by heart the Laws of the Twelve

Tables. By the stern regulations of this code he must guide both his public and private life. Elementary schools called *ludi* [1] were introduced into Rome before 450 B.C., but, as their name implies, they were not taken very seriously. The schools were taught chiefly by freedmen and gave instruction in reading, writing and calculation, the latter a study in which the children were encouraged to use their fingers as a means.

After his early moral education at the knee of his mother the boy, at about six or seven years of age, became the constant companion of his father, who took his son about with him from place to place as his duties on the farm and in the military field or the forum demanded. Thus the Roman boy was trained in the school of life to perform the tasks so soon to be laid upon him. He learned by actual practice to drive the oxen at the plough and to oversee the workmen on the farm. His drill in the Campus Martius made of him a hardy soldier. His visits to the forum, the law courts and later to the Senate, where he waited upon his father if he were a member, taught him legal procedure and acquainted him with public affairs. When a great Roman died the boy was taken by his parents to hear the funeral oration in which the virtues of the dead were extolled. Plutarch's *Cato* and Varro's *Monnius* paint the simple, hardy training of this early time. Cato the Elder says that from his first years he was brought up to be frugal, industrious and unquestioningly obedient. His body grew hardy and strong, due to his strenuous work on the family farm in the Sabine region, where the soil was stony and infertile. Plutarch, in describing the education of the younger Cato, states that his father "was as careful not to utter an indecent word before his son as he would have been in the presence of the Vestal Virgins." [2]

---

[1] *Ludus* means a sport, a game. Probably the serious Romans regarded intellectual education as something of a pastime, aside from the stern business of life.　　[2] *Life of Marcus Cato* (Bohn Classical Library), II, 119.

The religious education of boys and girls was as carefully looked after as their moral and practical training. When quite young they were taught to assist in all the sacrifices and rites of family worship in the capacity of *camilli* and *camillæ* (acolytes). It has been suggested that the reason why boys were permitted to wear the *toga prætexta* with the purple stripe, which was otherwise restricted to the use of magistrates and priests, was because of their active participation in the worship of the domestic gods.

When the boy had reached his sixteenth year, or thereabouts, he exchanged the *toga prætexta* for the *toga virilis*, which symbolized his growth to manhood. The change was accompanied by a solemn ceremony held on the day called *Liberalia* — the sixteenth of March. Probably the day began with sacrifices to the Lares at the family altar on which the youth laid the insignia of his boyhood. Among these were his favorite toys and the *bulla* that he had worn around his neck since his naming day. It is probable that the toga of manhood was donned at home; but this little ceremony was immediately followed by a more imposing one in the forum. Surrounded by a brilliant train of friends and retainers, the patrician youth was led to the forum and afterwards to the Capitol, where public sacrifices were offered. After these ceremonies the boy was put on probation for a year, during which his conduct was carefully observed by public officials. Meanwhile his life became more free and public. He took prescribed exercises in the Campus Martius, frequented the tribunals and the forum and sought by these means to prepare himself for public life. Thus carefully did the ancient Romans introduce their youth to the duties of manhood; and their painstaking efforts contrast very advantageously with the happy-go-lucky methods of modern states. These domestic and public ceremonies, together with their direct contact with public affairs, must have made a deep impression upon the minds of adolescent Roman boys, who were thus made to feel the responsibility and dignity of the life of a true Roman citizen.[1]

Not very much is said by Roman writers about the education of girls in this early period. It is certain, however, that they received a careful home training in their future duties as Roman housewives and mothers. They were taught especially to spin, weave and fashion garments; for upon women, in these ancient days, rested the entire responsibility of clothing the family. Also girls were at least occasionally sent to the *ludi*, or private elementary schools. The historian Livy relates that Virginia, the lovely daughter of a plebeian, was seized by order of Appius Claudius while on her way to one of these schools. Probably the *ludi* were attended almost wholly by girls of the middle class. Although it may never have been a general custom to send girls to school, it is probable that they were not left in complete ignorance as were most Greek maidens, but were given some instruction in reading and writing at home.

THE ROMAN FAMILY FROM THE CLOSE OF THE PUNIC WARS TO THE LAST CENTURIES OF THE EMPIRE

Changes in the Status of Women. — In the hotly contested campaigns of the two Punic wars,[2] Rome matched her mettle against an ancient and powerful foe. She emerged completely victorious and vastly elated at the humiliation of her dreaded enemy. But during the thirty and more years of actual warfare a large proportion of all able-bodied Romans saw service in the field. This meant that husbands were away from home for years at a time and the management of their estates and households devolved upon their wives. Many women thus received a training in self-reliance and efficiency in responsible positions. It can hardly be doubted that this educa-

---

[1] Fowler, *Social Life at Rome*, pp. 192–3.
[2] The first war extended from 264–249 B.C.; the second from 219–202 B.C.

K

tion was admirably calculated to develop in them vigorous personalities, accustomed to the exercise of power. Such women would submit with an ill grace to the restrictions upon their daily lives and interests imposed by the husband on his return from the wars. *Manus* would seem, no doubt, a tyranny. Matters were not improved when the campaigns in Spain, Greece and Asia carried the family lords and masters once more overseas to extend the boundaries of Rome's dominion. Owing to difficulties of communication, husbands and fathers holding military or political posts in the conquered provinces must have heard very rarely from their wives and children; and some of them no doubt ceased in time to care about them.

Such conditions had far-reaching effects upon family custom. First, wealth began to flow into Rome from the subject provinces, and to accumulate in influential families. Quite naturally fathers grew more and more reluctant to see not only the rich dowry given to their daughters at marriage but all gifts and bequests made to them after marriage passing into the absolute control of their husbands. In consequence there gradually grew up, after the Second Punic War, the custom of marriage without *manus*. Such a marriage left the wife nominally in the *potestas* of her father, who was usually too much engaged with personal and public affairs to interfere with her actions. In the event of her father's death, the married woman passed under the control of an appointed guardian or " tutor," who granted her a considerable degree of liberty. In time important results followed from the practice of marriage without *manus*, for women who brought large dowries and had independent means tended to claim from their husbands a freedom of opportunity and even an equality of right hitherto undreamed of. So wealthy did certain Roman women become that two laws were passed in different periods which were designed to limit both their riches and their extravagance. The Oppian Law (215 B.C.) restricted the value and kind of ornaments and apparel worn by women.

But so great was the opposition of the fair sex to this ordinance that it was repealed in the lifetime of the elder Cato, (B.C. 195) despite his bitter opposition. The *Lex Voconia* (169 B.C.) forbade any Roman owning property of 100,000 *asses*[1] or more in value, to make a woman his heir. The law, however, was evaded by the creation of trusts for the benefit of women. A second effect of the almost continuous wars of the third and second centuries B.C. was a marked decrease in the male population of Rome due to death, enslavement or absence on duty. As the men diminished in numbers, and as the authority of absent husbands passed to their wives, the social status of women was steadily elevated. Their power, to be sure, was a delegated one, and was promptly withdrawn on the return of the family head from foreign campaigns, if he did return. But this did not in the least prevent its inevitable result, — the growth within the women, thus raised to positions of responsibility and power, of a sense of their own personal worth and a sturdy desire for broader opportunity and influence. Indeed the elder Cato (d. 147 B.C.) bitterly complains that " all men rule over women, we Romans rule over all men, and our wives rule over us." [2] Thirdly, the conquest of Greece led to an influx of Greek scholars and teachers into Rome. Not only did the Roman men profit by this introduction of a higher culture into their midst, but apparently the women were gradually influenced by it. Roman matrons deliberately sought to become learned and clever. In the age of Cicero (107–43 B.C.) Clodia and Sempronia led the band of brilliant and often unscrupulous women who were not only versed in the learning of their time but were a power in politics. It was against such women that Juvenal in a later age launched his biting satire: " Let not the matron that shares your marriage bed possess a set style of eloquence, or hurl in well-rounded sen-

[1] A Roman *as* at this time was a copper coin worth about 7.9 mills in American money.   [2] Plutarch's *Lives* (Bohn Library), II, 105.

tence the enthymeme [1] curtailed of its premiss; nor be acquainted with all histories. But let there be some things in books which she does not understand. I hate her who is forever poring over and studying Paleamon's treatise; who never violates the rules and principles of grammar; and, skilled in antiquarian lore, quotes verses I never knew; and corrects the phrases of her friend as old-fashioned, which men would never heed. A husband should have the privilege of committing a solecism." [2]

Changes in Marriage and Family Customs. *Marriage and Property Rights.* — As we have seen, the practice of free marriage; *i.e.*, marriage without *manus*, grew up in Rome after the wars for conquest and became an established custom in the late years of the Republic. In Imperial times the sacred rites of confarreatio marriage, which brought the wife into the family of her husband and under his iron rule, had well-nigh disappeared, save in the marriages of priests. So likewise had the ceremony of *coëmptio* and the custom of *usus* which also resulted in bringing the wife under marital power. Marriage came to rest wholly upon the formal consent of the parties to the union; hence the Roman maxim " Marriage is by consent only " (*Nuptiæ solo consensu contrahuntur*). The formal betrothal, which included an oral agreement concerning the *dos* or bride's dowry, was still customary. Also the wedding procession by torchlight and the marriage banquet in the home of the groom were popular customs. The former was chiefly important, however, as evidence of the union already contracted by free consent. Marriage in Rome had become a purely private matter which required no religious rite, although it was customary for the auspices to be taken at weddings and for priests to be present. Since marriage no longer entailed *manus* the wife remained in her own family and was almost independent of her husband,

---

[1] An incomplete argument; a syllogism with the minor premise lacking.
[2] Juvenal, *Satires* (trans. by Evans, 1890), Satire VI, pp. 55–56.

who had little or no legal power over her conduct.   Although her *dos* was administered by her husband, who enjoyed its income, the ultimate ownership rested nominally in the father, often actually in the wife.   In case of the husband's insolvency the wife's *dos* could not be used to satisfy his creditors.   Moreover it became a common practice for fathers to endow their daughters at marriage with personal property designed for their independent use.

During the later period of the Empire another kind of matrimonial property was introduced which was called the ' gift for the sake of marriage ' (*donatio propter nuptias*).   It consisted in a portion of the husband's estate set apart for the bride, although remaining with the residue of his property under his own control.   If the husband became insolvent, however, his wife's *donatio* could not go to the payment of his creditors.   But the effects of " free marriage " were not wholly advantageous to the married woman.   As the Roman wife of Imperial times was not a member of her husband's family she had only a limited right of succession to his property should he die intestate.   Only after relatives as far as second cousins had obtained their share could the widow receive any consideration.   Indeed, in the sixth century A.D., the Emperor Justinian so far extended the list of relations who could inherit in case of intestacy as practically to exclude the wife. Only if she were in actual need was provision made for the widow from her husband's estate.   The laws of Hadrian and Marcus Aurelius, however, recognized the close relationship of mother and child by granting to them reciprocal rights of inheritance.[1]

The Roman matron was thus, to all intents and purposes, a free agent controlling her own actions and to some extent her property.   Before noting the abuses which crept into family life in the days of the Empire, it would be well to

[1] Cf. Bryce, *Marriage and Divorce under Roman and English Law* in *Studies in History and Jurisprudence*, pp. 790–8.

recognize explicitly the worthy ideal of marriage which prevailed during the late Republic. That the ideal was not realized in many instances does not impugn its high and honorable character. This conception of marriage made the wife the equal of her husband and recognized her right to the full and free development of her powers as an individual having responsibilities and privileges. A famous jurist has defined free Roman marriage as " a partnership in the whole of life, a sharing of rights both sacred and secular. . . ." [1] It is interesting to note that this pagan ideal of marriage is accepted in large measure by modern nations. It cannot be too emphatically pointed out that the evils characteristic of sex relations and family life in the Roman Empire were signs of the general social and moral degeneracy of the times, rather than the direct outcome of the increased liberty accorded to women. Moreover writers have tended to exaggerate the extent of the immorality of the Imperial period, and especially the deterioration in family ideals. The pure and devoted married life of Pliny and his noble wife Calpurnia is evidence that Roman society as a whole was not infected by the decadence so glaringly apparent among many of the wealthy and influential class. It is probable that the earlier conception of marriage, narrow and yet wholesome in some respects, was still active in the great body of the middle class as well as in individuals of higher social rank. Fortunately a lengthy inscription on the tomb of a Roman matron who died about 8 B.C., has come down to us. It was the tribute of Q. Lucretius Vespilla to his wife Turia and reads as follows : " You were a faithful wife to me and an obedient one; you were kind and gracious, sociable and friendly : you were assiduous at your spinning (*lanificia*) : you followed the religious rites of your family and your state, and admitted no foreign cults or degraded magic (*superstitio*) : you did not dress conspicuously, nor seek to make a display in your

---

[1] Quoted by Bryce, *op. cit.*, p. 798.

household arrangements. Your duty to our whole household was exemplary: you tended my mother as carefully as if she had been your own. You had innumerable other excellencies in common with all other worthy matrons, but these I have mentioned were peculiarly yours." [1] Similar eulogies of Roman wives have likewise been copied from the ancient tombstones.[2]

Decline of the Patria Potestas. — The decline of the patriarchal power of the husband over the wife was followed by a similar weakening of the *patria potestas*. Augustus Cæsar conferred upon a son under power (*filius familias*) the right to dispose by will of whatever he had acquired in the active exercise of his profession as a soldier. The Emperor Hadrian extended this privilege to sons honorably discharged from military service. Later the son *in potestate* was permitted to dispose by will of all that had come to him directly or indirectly in connection with his military service. The doctrine of a "natural law" based on justice, in accordance with which legal principles must be patterned, was gaining strong hold upon Roman conceptions of law in the first centuries of the Empire. This accounts for the marked tendency of the Emperors to restrict the rights of a father over his son. Parents were still permitted to expose their infants, but no father was allowed in the capacity of household judge and executioner, to put his son to death. In the reign of Alexander Severus (191–211 A.D.) the father's power over the person of his son was limited to moderate chastisement; for serious offences the son must be turned over to the ordinary tribunals for trial. Also the father's right of sale was restricted to young children and even then could be exercised only when he was unable because of extreme poverty to support them. Yet the *paterfamilias* was still regarded as the rightful owner of

---

[1] Paraphrased by Fowler from the mutilated original in his *Social Life at Rome*, pp. 166–67.

[2] See Friedländer, *Roman Life and Manners*, I, 264–66.

all the earnings and acquisitions of his children outside of those obtained through military service.

Growth of Celibacy. — During the later Republic as well as in Imperial times, the marked decline of the marriage rate was a cause of great concern to statesmen. It is probable that this social phenomenon was partly due to the increased wealth and prestige of women. Roman men resented the household authority assumed by wives whose possessions exceeded their own, and who showed in consequence a tendency to dominate. Of these women Plutarch writes: " Men who marry wives that are much their superiors in riches, often become, before they are aware of it, not the husbands of their wives, but the slaves of their marriage portion." [1] Then, too, some Romans did not take more kindly to learned women than did their poet Juvenal; nor were they disposed to bring into their homes as helpmeets ambitious wives who might and sometimes did use their influence over men to direct the course of politics, and thus possibly to involve their husbands in serious difficulties. Of the political activity of women in Imperial Rome, a modern historian writes: " On the walls of Pompeii female admirers posted up their election placards in support of their favorite candidates." [2] Here and there married women exercised a powerful indirect influence in governmental affairs under the first Emperors, — and that not always for good.

But the cleverness and dominating character of these newly emancipated Roman matrons can account only in part for the enormous increase of celibacy during the last centuries of the Republic and the first of the Empire. The tendency was fundamentally due to the steady deterioration of the ancient family ideals; and this, in turn, was part of the widespread decline of moral standards following upon Rome's wars for dominion. The vast influx of wealth flowing from

[1] Plutarch, *The Education of Boys* (Syracuse, 1910), p. 82.
[2] Dill, *Roman Society from Nero to Marcus Aurelius*, p. 81.

pillage and tribute, and the spread of slavery through conquest, combined to produce, on the one hand, a leisure class bred in luxury and idleness, and on the other, a steadily increasing group of landless men whose small farms had been bought up or seized by wealthy Romans to enlarge their country estates. Small landowners tended to disappear and to give place to a troublesome proletariat, incapable to a large degree of self-support, since at this time most labor was in the hands of slaves. Such conditions do not furnish favorable soil for the growth of healthy ideals of civic or of family life. Men and women alike were infected with the dry rot of selfishness and a frenzied pleasure-seeking; in consequence they looked upon the earlier almost religious conceptions of family duties and responsibilities as troublesome and outgrown. When marriages were contracted, the motives were too often mercenary or concerned with mere personal gratification. Rarely, in the senatorial class, was marriage any longer regarded as a solemn obligation to the State and to the domestic gods. Concubinage and prostitution grew by leaps and bounds as men sought to satisfy their passions without assuming the cares of married life. In time the vices of the men, darkly painted by Juvenal in his second *Satire*, infected the women and produced the Messalinas, the Julias, and the Poppæas of the early Empire. These women, reared in an atmosphere of extreme moral laxness and political intrigue, are described as " the cruellest and most wanton women of antiquity."

So serious did the evils of celibacy become that as early as 131 B.C. Metellus Macedonicus, the Censor, publicly urged Roman men to marry for the sake of maintaining the vigor of the State. In his oft-quoted speech he caustically remarks: " If we could do without wives we should be rid of that nuisance; but since nature has decreed that we can neither live comfortably with them nor live at all without them, we must e'en look rather to our permanent interests than to a passing pleasure." [1] But the speeches of public men had little effect in increasing the marriage rate. Julius Cæsar, in his brief period of power, sought to encourage marriage by rewards. Likewise in the year 9 A.D. Augustus Cæsar, in the famous *lex Julia et Papia Poppæa*, issued stern decrees against celibacy and offered substantial benefits to those married couples who had three or more children. Such parents could inherit legacies without the limitations attached to inheritance by celibates or by childless husbands and wives. Persons remaining unmarried after a fixed age were rendered thereby incapable of inheriting any property left them by will; while childless couples could take only half their inheritance. Such property reverted to the State. [2] These laws, however, seem to have had little effect, since Tacitus in his *Annals* writes: " It was next proposed to relax the *Papia Poppæa* law which Augustus in his old age had passed — for yet further enforcing the penalties on celibacy and for enriching the exchequer. And yet marriages and rearing of children did not become more frequent, so powerful were the attractions of a childless state." [3]

Childlessness. — As suggested above, the spread of celibacy was not the only social evil of the age. Even where marriages were contracted in the higher social ranks there was often little disposition on the part of either husband or wife to rear a family. When a child was conceived by an unwilling mother, abortion was freely practised or infanticide was promptly resorted to after its birth. These practices constituted part of those flagrant social abuses in Imperial Rome against which Christianity sternly set its face. They illustrate the general pagan tendency to regard human life as not valuable in itself, and therefore to be taken if circumstances seem to require it. In that bitter indictment of Roman women in the sixth

[1] Quoted by Fowler, *Social Life at Rome*, p. 150, from Livy, *Epistle* 59.

[2] Cf. Muirhead, *Historical Introduction to the Private Law of Rome*, pp. 285–6.

[3] *Op. cit.* (trans. by Church & Brodribb), III, 25.

Satire of Juvenal, the author rails against the wives of his day for their refusal to assume the cares of motherhood and for the wide prevalence of abortion and exposure of new-born infants.

In time the evils of childlessness were so apparent in the wealthier classes that adoption of an heir to the family estates became a widespread custom. This adoption was secured by a ceremony similar to that of *lustratio* by which the new-born child was received into family membership.[1] Such a custom was fruitful in evil results. Poor men became shameless hangers-on and sycophants of the rich in the hope of receiving fat bequests at their death, if not of inheriting the entire estates (*familia*). Of this hateful custom, Ammianus Marcellinus[2] writes in the fourth century A.D.: "Some persons look on everything as worthless which is born outside the walls of the capital save only the childless and the unmarried. Nor can it be conceived with what a variety of obsequious observance men without children are courted at Rome."[3] Legacy hunting seems to have been a favorite pursuit of worthless scoundrels. Pliny the Younger describes such an individual in one of his letters to Calvisius. "The fellow gets estates," he writes, "he gets legacies conferred upon him as if he really deserved them." In another letter Pliny relates how this same Regulus freed his son from his power in order to entitle the youth to an estate left him by his mother; for even in this period sons *in potestate* could not inherit during the father's lifetime. After his son was set free Regulus "fawned upon the lad with a disgusting show of fond affection." Finally the son died and Pliny satirically describes the ostentatious grief of the legacy-hunting father who thus fell heir to the young man's fortune.

Divorce under the Empire. — Although divorce was uncommon in the early period of Roman history, it had ceased

---

[1] See above, p. 126. [2] A Roman historian who died about 390 A.D.
[3] Quoted by Davis, *The Influence of Wealth in Imperial Rome*, p. 298.

to be a rare occurrence in the second century B.C. Since marriage rested solely on the consent of the parties, it followed that each party agreed tacitly or otherwise to continue the union only so long as the other desired it. This meant, of course, that marriage could be dissolved at pleasure. Such freedom requires a highly developed sense of moral responsibility in those exercising it; and, as we have seen, the ethical standards of the age were steadily deteriorating. In such a period of moral decadence every institution of society was affected; and perhaps marriage and family life suffered most of all. Plutarch's *Lives* are full of instances of the carelessness with which marriage was contracted and the ease with which the loosely knit bonds were broken. In his *Life of Æmilius*[1] the writer gives us an admirable statement of the attitude of many men of the time toward the question of divorce. Æmilius was asked why he had divorced his wife Papiria and he replied, stretching out his shoe: " Is it not beautiful? Is it not new? But none of you can tell where it pinches me. In fact some men divorce their wives for great and manifest faults, yet the little but constant irritation which proceeds from incompatible tempers and habits, though unnoticed by the world at large, does gradually produce between married people breaches which cannot be healed." Such a statement is illuminating; for it shows that the spirit of individualism was even then in conflict with the earlier civic and religious ideals that had led men to contract marriage for social and religious ends. And this new spirit, asserting as it did the right of the individual man to complete his own happiness through marriage and to dissolve the association when it no longer served his personal ends, was speedily communicated to the women. These Roman wives of the late Republic and the Empire were dominant types, as determined as their husbands to secure power and pleasure and " the fullness of life " as they conceived it. Such independent matrons were

[1] Lived in the second century B.C.

no whit more willing to bear the yoke of an irksome or unhappy marriage than were their husbands.

And so the practice of divorce spread rapidly, until in the Augustan age it had become a public scandal. This Emperor tried to restrict the practice by requiring the active party in the divorce to declare his or her purpose in the presence of seven witnesses, all full Roman citizens.[1] But the law seems to have had little or no effect in stemming the flood of divorces, although it was on the statute books for more than five centuries. Men in public life were no more serious in their attitude toward marriage than were private citizens. Cæsar divorced Pompeia, his wife, on the merest suspicion of laxity of conduct; Cicero repudiated his wife, Terentia, in middle age to marry a young and wealthy girl of whose property he had been made guardian. This unsuitable marriage was unhappy from the outset and was soon dissolved. But the matrimonial affairs of Pompey best reveal the disregard of marital rights and responsibilities into which many influential Romans had sunk. Sulla, the famous Roman general and consul, was desirous to reward Pompey for his services in war, and at the same time to win his support in the furtherance of his own (Sulla's) interests. Therefore he persuaded Pompey to divorce his wife Antistia, who was mourning the recent death of her father, and to marry Sulla's step-daughter Æmilia. Æmilia herself was not only married, but was an expectant mother. The shameful bargain was nevertheless accomplished, and it promptly brought tragedy in its wake; for the mother of Antistia committed suicide and Æmilia died in child-birth shortly after her marriage to Pompey.[2]

As we have seen marriages were frequently made at this time for purely political or economic reasons and were followed by divorce within a few days, when the specific end had been

---

[1] In the famous *Lex Julia de adulteriis*, passed in 18 B.C.

[2] Plutarch's *Lives* (Bohn Library), Vol. II, pp. 203-4.

attained. Thus a Roman Quæstor [1] was deposed by the Emperor Tiberius for marrying a woman two days before the lots for office were drawn and divorcing her the day after in order that he might appear as a married man and thus fulfil the state requirement for public officials. Seneca says of the women of his day that they counted their years not by consuls, but by their husbands; and Juvenal, always harsh in his judgment of women, charges some of them with divorcing their husbands before the marriage garlands had faded on the lintels. That such statements are exaggerations can hardly be doubted; but that they have a solid groundwork of fact seems equally true from the evidence at hand. Thus Quintus Lucretius Vespilla, Consul in 19 B.C., inscribes these words upon his wife's tombstone: " Seldom do marriages last till death undivorced; but ours continued happily for forty-one years." [2] It is well to bear in mind such cases as this, lest we fall into the error of believing that the divorce evil had penetrated all grades of society alike. Fortunately such abuses rarely make such devastating headway among the sober, industrious middle class, on which the well-being of the nation so largely depends, as among the rich and luxury-loving.

Imperial legislation after Augustus sought to restrain divorce to some extent by imposing pecuniary penalties on the culpable party. To this end it was decreed that in case of the wife's infidelity the husband might retain one-sixth of her dowry on divorce. In case of lesser offences on the wife's part he might retain one-eighth to which one-sixth was added for each child — the whole, however, not to exceed one-half of the dowry. The custody of the children belonged to the father, as the family head, and the sums deducted were held to be contributed by the offending mother toward their support. On the other hand if the husband were the guilty

[1] Two quæstors were appointed yearly to keep the treasury in the Temple of Saturn.   [2] Cf. Friedländer, *op. cit.*, I, 243.

party, he must restore the entire amount of the wife's dowry at once.

Household Economy in the Imperial Period. — The vast changes introduced into Roman society as a result of the nation's aggressive wars and conquests made themselves felt no less radically in the economic life of the family than in its social and moral life.   Even in the time of Cicero, landed property on a large scale was regarded as the only source of wealth worthy a free Roman citizen of senatorial rank.   The rude, simple farming life of the early Romans had begun to disappear even in the days of Cato the Censor (232–147 B.C.). Trade and industrial pursuits hitherto largely in the hands of free plebeians, tended more and more to be turned over to slaves, of whom vast numbers were brought to Rome as captives at the close of each campaign of conquest.   In Imperial times most of the trade and industry of Rome and the Latin cities were controlled by slaves or freedmen; the former supplying all the varied needs of the wealthy household, and the latter selling their wares in shops.   Every Roman of wealth and assured social standing attempted to maintain at least two households — a city home and a villa in the country.   Pliny the Younger describes with enthusiasm and in minute detail every feature of his charming villa at Laurentium, and in another letter sets forth the beauties of his Tuscan country home.[1]   As town and country houses grew more spacious and luxurious, the number of slaves required to manage them vastly increased.   Especially when great manorial estates took the place of the old-time country farms a large staff of out-of-door laborers was required in addition to the house servants.   The slaves attached to the country villa were called *familia rustica;* those belonging to the city house were called *familia urbana.*

Division of Labor. — The wealthy households of Imperial Rome were characterized by division of labor so minute as in

[1] *Letters* (Bosanquet, ed.), Bk. II, Letter XVII; Bk. V, Letter VI.

part to defeat its own end. In the villas, besides the agricultural slaves proper who were employed in ploughing,
sowing, reaping, and tending grape-vines and olive trees,
there were also slaves trained as gardeners, poulterers,
gamekeepers, tenders of bee-hives and fish-ponds. On the
largest estates several thousand slaves were thus employed.
Hence the villa of a wealthy Roman was not only a
haven of rest and delight in days of leisure but it was
also the source of supply of most of his daily wants — a
highly organized economic institution independent of most
of the outside sources of industry and supply. Within the
household, division of slave labor was even more minute.
Here were staffs of expert handicraftsmen in almost every kind
of work. One group of slaves was trained for dining-room
service and was under the direction of a head called the
triclinarchus.[1] Another group had charge of bedrooms and
living rooms. In the kitchen was a staff of skilled slaves, including plain cooks, pastry cooks, bakers, etc.; for most
wealthy households in Imperial times maintained large bak-
eries. Many families boasted their own tailors, spinners,
weavers and hairdressers. Frequently physicians and sur-
geons were attached to the largest households. These men
were usually slaves or freedmen, carefully trained by the master
for their work of healing. Every great house had also its private architects, its secretaries and men of literary attainments,
and its skilled musicians, jugglers and mimics to entertain the
master and mistress and their guests. Occasionally even a
philosopher was attached to the household to instruct the
mistress in the theories of Stoic and Epicurean. At the entrance to city house or villa sat the *ostiarius*, or doorkeeper,
who kept watch over the house, admitted visitors and clients
and passed them on to servants who announced them. So
great was the number of slaves retained on the largest estates
that it was necessary to divide them into groups of ten

[1] From *triclinium*, the name for dining-room.

(*decuriæ*) which were put under the authority of higher slaves called *ordinarii*, whose business it was to direct their work and to keep them from disturbing their owners by loud talking or laughing.

This lavish provision for slave labor rendered it quite unnecessary for the mistress of such a household to ply her earlier, honorable tasks of spinning and weaving or even to direct the work of her slaves, except when she so desired.   Thus there appeared in Rome the pleasure-loving " lady," so well known in modern times, with little to do except beautify her person and attend the circus, theatres and banquets.   The more intelligent and able of these women, however, ill satisfied with lives of empty enjoyment, sought to become forces in politics, writers of verse, literary critics, even students of the sciences. Plutarch says of Cornelia, wife of Crassus and later of Pompey, that she added the graces of music, geometry and literature to the charms of her beauty, and had even attended courses in philosophy.   The changes in the mode of living of these Roman ladies were reflected in the *atrium*, once the centre of the household activities, where its mistress spun and wove surrounded by her maids and children.   The slaves were now removed to apartments in the rear; the family hearth was also banished to a more private spot; the household gods were tucked away in a special *sacrarium*, or sacred place;   the family meals were no longer served near the hearth, but in various dining-rooms in different parts of the house.   In course of time the *atrium* became little more than a reception room for guests.   Yet the marriage bed, now a mere symbol, remained in its ancient place;   and the images and waxen masks of famous dead with " relics of their valour " still adorned the walls.

But, although women of wealth and social position had become mere consumers of the goods produced by slaves, the wives of the middle class and the poor still performed their household tasks as of old, feeding and clothing their families by their own efforts, assisted, perhaps, by a few slaves. Again the tombstones erected to the memory of their wives by men of simple birth bear eloquent testimony to the virtues of these industrous Roman matrons even in a decadent age. One such inscription reads: " Short, wanderer, is my message; halt and read it. The loathly stone covers a lovely woman. Claudia her parents called her: she loved her husband; bore him two sons; — She was of proper speech and noble gait, kept her house and spun. This is all. Go." [1]

The Roman Home in its Educational Aspect. *Early Home Training.* — Such profound changes in family life and ideals as have been described above were necessarily reflected in the nurture and training of children. Far from being the sole teachers of their offspring, the Roman fathers and mothers of Imperial times showed much the same disposition to turn over their responsibilities to servants and teachers as do parents to-day. The literature of the first century A.D. abounds in bitter criticism or earnest exhortation of unworthy parents. Plutarch advises fathers " who wish to beget noble children not to associate with women of doubtful reputation, . . ." and not to be " unduly fond of wine " if they do not wish to see their sons drunkards also. Turning to the women he urges them to nurse and care for their own children rather than turn them over at birth to slaves. If nurses are employed, says Plutarch, they should be " Greek by birth and training," since it is " important to train and develop harmoniously from the beginning the disposition and character of children." Then follows a satirical account of the practice of his own time in respect to choice of nurses: " What is done at present by many men is in the highest degree absurd. They select from among their slaves some to work in the fields, some for service at sea, and some to look after their merchandise. They pick out others to oversee their household affairs and still others to manage their finances. But if they happen to have a slave who

[1] Cf. Friedländer, *op. cit.*, I, 265.

is given to drink and gluttony, who is in fact good for nothing, to this fellow they assign the oversight of their boys." [1]

But the deficiencies of parents were unfortunately not confined to careless selection of nurses for their children. The lax conduct and improper language of parents in the presence of boys and girls of tender age, as well as their too luxurious nurture of their children, provoked sharp comments from the writers of the time. Thus Quintilian [2] exclaims : " Would that we ourselves did not corrupt the morals of our children ! We enervate their very infancy with luxuries. . . . What luxury will he not covet in his manhood, who crawls about on purple ! We form the palate of children before we form their pronunciation. They grow up in sedan chairs ; if they touch the ground, they hang by the hands of attendants supporting them on each side. We are delighted if they utter anything immodest. Expressions which would not be tolerated even from the effeminate youths of Alexandria we hear from them with a smile and a kiss. Nor is this wonderful ; we have taught them ; they have heard such language from ourselves. They see our mistresses, our male objects of affection ; every dining-room rings with impure songs ; things shameful to be told are objects of sight. From such practices springs habit, and afterward nature. The unfortunate children learn these vices before they know that they are vices ; and hence, rendered effeminate and luxurious, they do not imbibe immorality from schools, but carry it themselves into schools." [3] In the same spirit Plutarch tersely remarks : " Those men who live a life constantly open to criticism cannot consistently correct even their slaves, much less their sons."

Education Shifted to the School. — Yet it can hardly be doubted that the stern moral training of an earlier age with its sincere reverence for the purity of childhood, lived on in

[1] Plutarch, *The Education of Boys* (Syracuse, 1910), pp. 47-54.
[2] A famous teacher of grammar and rhetoric in Rome in the first century A.D.
[3] *Institutes of Oratory* (Bohn Library series), ch. II.

families untainted by wealth.   Horace (65–8 B.C.) pays ardent
tribute to his father's solicitude for his education : " And yet,"
he writes, " if the faults and defects of my nature are moderate
ones, . . . if (that I may praise myself) my life is pure and
innocent, and my friends love me, I owe it all to my father;
he, though not rich, for his farm was a poor one, would not
send me to the school of Flavius, to which the first youths of
the town, the sons of the centurions, the great men there,
used to go . . .; but he had the spirit to carry me, when a
boy, to Rome, there to learn the liberal arts which any knight
or senator would have his own sons taught. . . .   He himself was ever present, a guardian incorruptible, at all my
studies.   Why say more?   My modesty, that first grain of
virtue, he preserved untainted, not only by an actual stain,
but by the very rumor of it; . . ." [1]   The reference makes
plain the change that had come over Roman education owing
to Greek influence.   Ever since the Punic wars the grammar
school and the rhetorical school for training orators and statesmen, both modelled after Greek institutions, had been gaining a foothold in Rome despite the opposition of a powerful
conservative group.   In Horace's time the long struggle was
ended; Roman education was carried on largely outside the
home and had become more and more literary and intellectual
in character.   As in the present age the home had shifted to the
shoulders of the schoolmaster the burden of responsibility
for shaping the youth intellectually and morally; and the
schools were already demonstrating their insufficiency for the
task without the coöperation of the home.

The Home Training of Girls. — In conclusion brief mention
should be made of the education of girls in Imperial Rome.
After the early years of childhood under the care of a
nurse, sometimes a Greek slave, the girl's instruction began.
It is probable that only the daughters of the higher class re-

[1] Satires of Horace I, 6; in Monroe, *Source Book in the History of Education,*
p. 397.

ceived much intellectual training, and these girls were taught at home under the direction of tutors. Martial and Ovid make brief references to the nature of this education. Apparently it was literary in character like that of the boys, designed to give a thorough linguistic training as well as appreciation of the poets and prose writers of Greece and Rome. Music and dancing were held to be important parts of a girl's education. Ovid calls a well-trained voice irresistible, and enthusiastically praises the adept lyre-player and the rhythmical movements of the skilled dancer. Even in St. Jerome's day (331–423 A.D.) music was still looked upon as an essential part of a girl's training; for this Latin Father urges that " Christian maidens should have no ear for organ, flute, lyre, or cither." Only in the homes of the middle class were daughters given the old training in the use of the spindle and the loom. Yet in the early days of the Empire the daughters of Augustus Cæsar had not been ashamed to spin and weave the garments worn by the Emperor and his family; and the custom still lingered on in old-fashioned homes, even among the well-to-do. As late as the sixth century A.D. Ausonius [1] mentions the " busy spindle " of his mother; and Symmachus [2] thanks his daughter for a garment woven by her hands.[3]

When the girl had reached her thirteenth year, her parents began to seek out a husband for her. An unmarried girl at nineteen was distinctly an " old maid "; indeed at twenty a woman who had not become the mother of legitimate children was liable to incur the penalties laid down in the *lex Julia* of Augustus.[4] Although the law required that the girl's consent to the union be secured, it was always assumed as given unless she openly refused it. In reality the parents' will was absolute in most instances; and their choice was governed by considerations of wealth and family convenience. Often girls

---

[1] Ausonius was a famous teacher of rhetoric.
[2] Symmachus was also a well-known rhetorician.
[3] Friedländer, *op. cit.* p. 230.   [4] See above, p. 138.

were betrothed in their childhood, the arrangements being made in a businesslike way by professional intermediaries or " marriage-brokers." It is a significant fact in this connection that the Latin language contains no words corresponding to " court " or " woo " in our English tongue.

After the wedding festivities were over, the girl-wife of the senatorial class tasted a freedom of life which must have been in pleasant contrast to the seclusion and constant surveillance of her girlhood days at home, where she was still under the *patria postestas*. As a married woman she was to all intents and purposes as free as her husband. To quote Friedländer; " In the microcosm of a great house, with its scattered properties, legions of slaves and retinues of clients and subjects, her will granted or withheld fortune or even life. . . . Whatever claims to admiration she might have, wit, talent or education, her position ensured her success." [1] She attended banquets, theatres, the circus, and mingled freely with her peers in the social world of her time. Instances are on record of women who were promoted to consular rank by will of the Emperor. The privileges of such women were very great, and it is questionable whether men even of the grade of præfect [2] could take social precedence over them. Roman married women of senatorial rank were organized into a gild, the *conventus matronarum*, which was a sort of feminine senate. At times this body was consulted by certain of the emperors on minor questions of state.[3]

Comparison of the Roman Woman of the Empire with the Modern American Woman. — A review of family history in Rome brings into glaring relief the divergence between the customs of the early and the later period. The simple restricted home life of the Roman wife and mother of primitive times is separated by a wide gulf from the almost unlimited social and economic freedom of her sister

[1] *Op. cit.*, I, 240.   [2] A præfect was ruler of a Latin city.
[3] Friedländer, p. 240.

of a later age. This matron of the Imperial period has far more in common with the emancipated American woman of the twentieth century than with her country woman of the early Roman Republic. Just as the legal, economic, educational and personal rights of the Roman woman were restricted by the early law of the Republic, so were those of the American woman under the English common law. As the rights of Roman women were gradually extended after the Punic wars, in an age when the wealth and culture of Rome were steadily increasing and the stern patriarchal ideas were dying out, so have the rights of American women been extended and their disabilities lessened, due to much the same causes. With wealth usually come leisure and opportunity for reflection; and these bring in their train an amelioration of ideas and of manners. But the parallel can be carried further. As in Rome women eagerly sought outlets for their trained capacities in social, intellectual and political activities, so likewise do American women in the present day. As the nobly-born wives and mothers of Imperial Rome chafed against the physical burdens and the exacting demands upon time and strength of child-bearing and rearing, so likewise does a group of American women to-day, who strive for complete freedom to live their lives and develop their talents outside the limits of the home. The decline of marriage among the intellectual class in America parallels the more general decline in Imperial Rome; the increase of divorce in one country bears striking likeness to that of the other. But in one respect the parallel ceases. American women of to-day, educated to a realization of practical, social issues, show a far more dynamic interest in the lot of the working classes and in the betterment of their living conditions than was ever revealed by the hard and brilliant women of the first centuries of the Roman Empire. Moreover social consciousness has attained a higher development in the modern world than in the ancient. This is revealed in social groups at present by a spirit of self-criticism and a desire for better things that promises well for the future, and especially for the family as the basic social institution. The unrest and apparent disintegration of the modern family may be the precursor of a better state of things — of a type of family life more nearly adapted to the conditions of the twentieth century.

SELECTED BIBLIOGRAPHY

SOURCES.

Arnaud, Germain. *La vie privée des Romains decrite par les auteurs latins* (1899), chs. I, V, VI.

Catullus, *Carmina*, LVI, LXI, LXII.

Juvenal, *Satires* (trans. by Rev. Lewis Evans, London, 1890). *Satires* II, VI, XIV.

Monroe, Paul. *Source Book in the History of Education for the Greek and Roman Period.*

Tacitus, *Dialogues concerning Oratory*, pp. 361–3.
Suetonius, *Life of Cæsar Augustus*, pp. 375–6.
Musonius on the Education of Women, pp. 401–6.
Juvenal, *Satire XIV*, pp. 419–20.
Laws of the Twelve Tables, pp. 337–8.
Institutes of Quintilian, pp. 451–9.

Pliny the Younger. *The Letters of Caius Plinius Cæcilius Secundus* (Bosanquet ed. 1900).

Book I, Letters IX, XIV; Book II, Letters IV, XVII, XX; Book III, Letters I, XIV, XVI, XX; Book IV, Letters II, X, XIX; Book V, Letters VI, XVI; Book VI, Letter IV; Book VII, Letter V.

Plutarch. *The Education of Boys* (ed. by W. H. Super).

Lives (Bohn Library, 1908), Vol. I, pp. 47–84, 56–7, 95, 196–7; Vol. II, pp. 105, 384–7, 430; Vol. III, pp. 203–4, 390–9.

SECONDARY WORKS.

Becker, W. A. *Gallus*, pp. 151–187, 199–225, 231 ff.

Bosanquet, Helen. *The Family*, ch. I.

Bryce, James. *Marriage and Divorce under Roman and English Law* (in *Studies in History and Jurisprudence*, 1901, pp. 782–833).

Couch. *Woman in early Roman Law* (in *Harvard Law Review*, VIII, pp. 39–50).

Dill. *Roman Society in the Last Century of the Western Empire*, pp. 130, 134, 163–4, 208.

Donaldson, J. *Woman; her Position and Influence in Ancient Greece and Rome.*

Encyclopedia of Religion and Ethics, Vol. V, pp. 746–9.

Ferrero, G. *Woman and Marriage in Ancient Rome* (in *Century,* 82, pp. 3–14, May, 1911).

        The Women of the Cæsars.

Fowler, W. W. *Social Education in Rome,* chs. V, VII, VIII.

Friedländer, L. *Roman Life and Manners under the Early Empire,* Vol. I, ch. V.

Gide, Paul. *Étude sur la condition privée de la femme* (1885), chs. IV, V.

Guhl and **Koner.** *Life of the Greeks and Romans,* pp. 355–65, 371–5, 511–523.

Harper's *Dictionary of Classical Literature and Antiquities,* articles on *Adulterium, Connubium, Divortium, Dos, Emancipatio, Familia, Liberalia, Lustratio, Matrimonium, Manus, Voconia Lex,* etc.

Inge, W. R. *Society in Rome under the Cæsars,* pp. 61–70, 159–62, 172–83, 245–62.

Johnstone, H. W. *Private Life of the Romans,* chs. I, III–VIII.

Lacombe, P. *La famille dans la société romaine; étude de moralite comparée* (1889), Part II, chs. II–V.

Morey, Wm. C. *Outlines of Roman Law,* pp. 5–7, 29–37, 239–49, 313–34.

Muirhead, James. *Historical Introduction to the Private Law of Rome* (1886), pp. 24–36, 43–9, 64–9, 115–26, 345–8, 415–26.

Pellison. *Roman Life in Pliny's Time,* chs. II–IV, pp. 131–5.

Preston and **Dodge.** *Private Life of the Romans,* chs. I–III.

Putnam, Emily. *The Lady,* pp. 39–68.

Schuster, E. J. *The Wife in Ancient and Modern Times,* chs. V, VI.

Tucker, T. G. *Life in the Roman World of Nero and St. Paul,* chs. IX, X, XVI, XVII.

CHAPTER VI

THE INFLUENCE OF EARLY CHRISTIANITY UPON MARRIAGE AND FAMILY CUSTOM IN THE ROMAN EMPIRE

Views of the Church Fathers concerning Marriage. The Respective Merits of Virginity and Marriage. — There can be no reasonable doubt that the views of the early Christian Fathers concerning the marriage bond were profoundly influenced by the opinions of St. Paul. The doctrines of this great leader are so familiar that only brief reference need be made to a few of the more influential of them. He writes: " Nevertheless, *to avoid fornication*, let every man have his own wife, and every woman have her own husband." [1] But he promptly follows this doubtful sanction by the words: " But I speak this by permission and not of commandment. . . . For I would that all men were even as I myself. . . . I say therefore to the unmarried and widows, It is good for them if they abide even as I. But if they cannot contain, let them marry; *for it is better to marry than to burn.*" [2]

From these passages and many others similar in spirit it seems evident that St. Paul looked upon marriage as a substitute for a worse state — that of illicit sexual intercourse. Better is marriage than fornication; but, after all, the choice lies between two evils of greater and less degree. There is no hint in Paul's writings, nor does it clearly appear in the treatises of the later Church Fathers that marriage is a spiritual as well as a physical union, and that the latter should be impossible without the former. It is true that the earlier Fathers have a worthier ideal of marriage than their succes-

[1] *I Cor.* VII, 2. Italics mine.   [2] *Ibid.*, 7–9.

sors.   Thus Clement of Alexandria declares that marriage " as
a sacred image must be kept pure from those things which
defile it." [1]   Likewise Ignatius in his *Epistle to Polycarp* and
Athenagoras in his *Plea for Christians* maintain the purity of
the marriage state.[2]   But the dominant note in the later
patristic writings is a frank recognition of the physical basis of
marriage, with a rather grudging acceptance of its necessity —
an acceptance that becomes more and more reluctant as the
spirit of asceticism gains headway within the Christian body.
At the opening of the third century Tertullian in his *Letter to
his Wife* writes: " We do not indeed forbid the union of man
and woman, blest by God as the seminary of the human race,
and devised for the replenishment of the earth and the furnishing of the world, and therefore permitted, yet singly."   Later,
however, in referring to Christ's saying that the man who looks
upon a woman to lust after her hath committed fornication
already in his heart, Tertullian comments: " But has he who
has seen her with a view to marriage done so less or more? "
In reply to the question of a critic whether he is not destroying
even single marriage he boldly answers: " And not without
reason (if I am) ; inasmuch as it, too, consists of that which is
the essence of fornication."   In the same treatise he asserts
of a married woman: " . . . nor yet is the means through
which she becomes a married woman any other than that
through which withal (she becomes) an adulteress." [3]   Obviously these pronouncements show scant appreciation of the
uplifting and strengthening influence of a true marriage — of
its power to quicken and deepen all worthy emotions.   Thus
it is that the reading of the marital views of the later Church
Fathers is a distasteful task, from which the student willingly
turns.

Yet it would be manifestly unfair to judge these writings,
covering the period from the days of Tertullian to those of St.

---

[1] Cf. *Ante-Nicene Fathers*, Vol. II, 377–9.   [2] *Ibid.*, I, 95; II, 147.
[3] *Ibid.*, Vol. XVIII, p. 14, *An Exhortation to Chastity.*

Jerome and St. Augustine, solely from the standpoint of the twentieth century. It should be remembered that the struggling company of early Christians, striving as they were to realize on earth the pure ethical teachings of their Master, found themselves in the midst of a corrupt and degenerate society the leaders of which were in many instances shamelessly licentious. In the preceding chapter the great laxity with respect to sex relations and divorce that prevailed in Imperial Rome has been indicated. Although the gross immorality of Roman social life has doubtless been exaggerated by well-meaning moralists, a sufficiently solid basis of fact remains to explain, if not to justify, the attitude of the leaders of the Christian Church toward all sexual relationships. To their minds, bent upon purification of conduct, as of inner motive and ideal, most of the shameful misdeeds of their age might be traced to the attraction of one sex for the other. Gourmandizing, drinking, brutalizing games and exhibitions of all sorts, bad as they were in their immediate results, served the further vicious end of arousing animal passions which, in court circles, at least, not infrequently sought outlet in unrestrained sexual intercourse. Thus, in the final analysis, the love of the sexes appeared to the Church Fathers to be the root of many evils — if not of all.

But this does not wholly account for the scant approval of marriage accorded by the later Church Fathers. Very early in the history of the Church the idea of virginity, as a state of special purity pleasing to Christ, took root among Christians and received the sanction and encouragement of the Fathers. If sexual love is responsible, not only for gross immorality, but also for a worldly absorption in the joys and cares of family life instead of in the unseen world of the spirit, should it be placed on the same plane of holiness as the virgin state which demanded no such fealty to earthly things? One and all, the later Church Fathers answered this query in the negative. Yet they did not and could not openly condemn marriage, since it had received the sanction of Christ himself as well as the more reluctant recognition of St. Paul. Moreover, the Fathers themselves could hardly overlook the necessity for marriage from the standpoint of the renewal of the race. Also, if virgins were to be dedicated to the service of Christ they must be the fruit of unions sanctified by the Church. Hence marriage is never explicitly condemned or forbidden by Christian teachers; but it is placed third and lowest in the scale of Christian purity. Highest and best is absolute virginity, and next lower is placed that incomplete and belated, yet acceptable celibacy that is voluntarily adopted after marriage or after the death of husband or wife.[1]

St. Jerome, writing toward the close of the fourth century, leaves the reader in no doubt as to his position concerning the moral beauty of celibacy. In his famous Letter *To Eustochium*, a young Roman girl who had dedicated her life to Christ in perpetual virginity, he admonishes her: " Do not court the company of married ladies or visit the houses of the high-born. . . . Learn in this respect a holy pride; know that you are better than they." And again: " To show that virginity is natural while wedlock only follows guilt, what is born of wedlock is virgin flesh, and it gives back in fruit what in root it has lost." In reply to his critics who had attacked his views of marriage St. Jerome declares: " I praise wedlock, I praise marriage, but it is because they give me virgins." [2] But it is in his well-known treatise *Against Jovinian* that Jerome allows his growing antipathy to the married state to find full expression. Referring to the oft-quoted words of St. Paul, " It is better to marry than to burn," Jerome comments: " It is good to marry simply because it is bad to burn." And commenting further on the statement of the apostle that

[1] Tertullian, *Exhortation to Chastity*, in *Ante-Nicene Fathers*, Vol. XVIII, p. 2.

[2] *Letters* of Jerome, in *A Select Library of Nicene and Post Nicene Fathers* . . , ed. by Schaff and Wace, Vol. VI, pp. 28–30.

" Such [*i.e.*, married persons] shall have trouble in the flesh," he sarcastically exclaims : " We in our ignorance had supposed that in the flesh at least wedlock would have rejoicing. But if married persons are to have trouble in the flesh, *the only thing in which they seemed likely to have pleasure, what motive will be left to make women marry?* for, besides having trouble in spirit and in soul they will also have it even in the flesh." [1]

But St. Jerome was by no means alone in sounding the praise of virginity and in declaring the married state to be morally inferior to it. In his treatise *On Widows* St. Ambrose writes : " The apostle has not expressed his preference for marriage so unreservedly as to quench in men the aspiration after virginity ; he commences with a recommendation of continence, and it is only subsequently that he stoops to mention the remedies for its opposite." Likewise St. Augustine's enthusiasm for the virgin life is repeatedly expressed in his *Letters*. Writing to the Lady Juliana, whose daughter had taken the vow of chastity, he says : " For she did not contract an earthly marriage that she might be, not for herself only, but also for you, spiritually enriched, in a higher degree than yourself, since you, even with this addition, are inferior to her, because you contracted the marriage of which she is the offspring." In another letter in praise of this same maiden Demetrius he exclaims : " May many handmaidens follow the example of their mistress ; may those who are of humble rank imitate this high-born lady. . . ." [2]

Influence of Asceticism. — Teachings such as these, from Christian leaders in high places, bore their inevitable fruit. A blow was struck at the purity and honorable nature of the married state from which it had not recovered at the close of the Middle Ages. This is true despite the fact that early in its history the Church declared marriage to be a sacrament and had thoroughly established this doctrine by the middle of the

---

[1] *Library of Nicene and Post Nicene Fathers*, Vol. VI, p. 77 ; *Against Jovinian*, I, 13. Italics mine. [2] *Nicene and Post Nicene Fathers*, Vol. I, pp. 504, 549-50.

twelfth century.[1] As asceticism spread over the Western world, the praise of celibacy became more insistent and the depreciation of marriage more positive. The efforts of the Church to deny matrimony to the secular and regular clergy, who were held to be dedicated to a life of especial purity, steadily gained headway, even though they were not crowned with success until centuries later. The attitude of monks and other Christian ascetics toward all women, even those of their own immediate family, was unwholesome and even prurient. Woman was viewed wholly from the physical standpoint of sex and was condemned because of the carnal pleasures and temptations she suggested. Commenting on the harmful effect of asceticism upon mediæval ideas of marriage, a modern historian writes: " History all too plainly shows that the benefits conferred by monasticism and the enforced celibacy of the secular clergy come far short of balancing the evils flowing from the conception of wedlock as a ' remedy for concupiscence.' The influence of the church did, indeed, tend to condemn the breach of conjugal fidelity by the husband as equally sinful with that of the wife; although this righteous principle has by no means always been observed in Christian legislation. On the other hand celibacy bred a contempt for womanhood and assailed the integrity of the family." [2]

Second Marriages: Continence in Marriage. — Very early the Christian Church took a firm stand against second marriages. In the well-known *Letter to his Wife* above referred to, Tertullian sets forth the doctrine of the Church in this regard. " How detrimental to faith, how obstructive to holiness, second marriages are, the discipline of the church and the prescription of the apostle declare, when he suffers not men twice married to preside [over a church], when he would not grant a widow admittance into the order unless she had been

[1] The first *explicit* recognition of marriage as one of the seven sacraments of the Church is made in the *Sentences* of Peter the Lombard in 1164.

[2] Howard, *History of Matrimonial Institutions*, Vol. I, 331.

' the wife of one man '; for it behooves God's altar to be set forth pure." St. Jerome, while granting a reluctant permission to any widow to re-marry, lest she fall into the sin of fornication, justifies his consent on the ground that " It is preferable that she should prostitute herself to one man rather than to many." [1] Second marriages were strongly discountenanced by the Christian Emperor Theodosius and his successors, and finally such unions entailed forfeiture of the dower or *donatio*, as the case might be, in favor of the children of the first marriage.[2]

Many of the patristic writings comment favorably upon continence within the marriage bond and the lives of Christian ascetics abound in tales of such renunciation. In his *History of European Morals* Lecky mentions half a dozen or more of such cases taken from the legends of the saints.[3] So much bitterness of spirit and alienation were naturally produced within families by these one-sided resolves to remain virgin after marriage that the more prudent of the Church leaders became alarmed; and it was later ordained that the abstinence of married pairs from sexual intercourse in accordance with the prevalent ascetic ideal should be only by mutual consent.

The Influence of Early Christianity upon the Status of Women. — In the Gospel story women occupy a prominent and honorable position. Mary and Martha, the sisters of Lazarus of Bethany, are counted among the closest friends of Christ. To the woman at the well of Samaria Jesus discoursed of profound truths. To Mary of Magdala, we are told He first appeared after His resurrection. Yet Christ advanced no new theories with respect to the nature, position and influence of womankind. He accepted the marriage state as it existed among the Jews with the proviso that this union could not be dissolved save for adultery only. Man and wife " are no more

---

[1] Letter *To Pammachius, op. cit.*, p. 70.
[2] Muirhead, *Historical Introduction to the Private Law of Rome*, p. 388.
[3] *Op. cit.*, Vol. II, pp. 324–5.

twain but one flesh." It remained for the apostle Paul to express the earliest authoritative opinions of Christian leaders in regard to the status of women. In *I Corinthians* he urges that a woman should cover her head or be shorn. " For a man indeed ought not to cover his head, forasmuch as he is the image and glory of God : but the woman is the glory of the man. For the man is not of the woman; but the woman of the man. Neither was the man created for the woman, but the woman for the man." [1] In such plain language St. Paul declares his belief in the essential inferiority of women. Again he writes : " Let your women keep silence in the churches : for it is not permitted them to speak; but they are commanded to be under obedience, as also saith the law" (*I Corinthians* XIV, 34). Obviously the Apostle speaks here as a firm believer in the patriarchal family idea so long upheld by his Hebrew countrymen. Women shall " adorn themselves in modest apparel, with shamefacedness and sobriety "; for not Adam but the woman was deceived by the serpent and therefore in transgression (*I Timothy* II, 14). In this original sin of Eve all women have a share — all are tainted with the same offence, by which man fell and sin was brought into the world. Woman, then, shall be in subjection to her husband who yet shall give " honour to the wife as unto the weaker vessel." These, and other similar statements, faithfully set forth the attitude of St. Paul toward womankind. Furthermore they furnished the standards that determined the status of women under Christianity for many centuries.

Yet, at the time the Apostle wrote these oft-quoted sayings women in the imperial city of Rome, as we have seen in the preceding chapter, had advanced to a position of great social, economic and intellectual freedom. Unquestionably the influence of St. Paul had much to do with the spread of a reactionary tendency among Christians toward restricting the life of women very narrowly to the home and the Church.

[1] *I Cor.* XI, 7–9.

To be sure, during the first years of the Christian era, women played an important rôle as teachers and prophetesses. But this activity was soon curtailed, until women could publicly work within the Church only as widows and deaconesses, if we except their splendid service as martyrs to the faith. From the first the Christian Church supported its own poor, including dependent widows and orphans. To assist in this work widows of at least sixty years of age were appointed by Church officers to visit the sick, to aid poor women and to care for friendless orphans. Such women were carefully selected with respect to character and skill and their duties were clearly defined and restricted. Following out the exhortation of St. Paul, they were strictly forbidden to teach religious doctrine. In course of time the class of widows tended to give place to the order of deaconesses. It has been suggested that this change was due in part to the fact that " widowhood had fallen in the spiritual market and virginity had risen." [1] Be this as it may, by the middle of the third century the order of deaconesses had become well established. But let it not be supposed that these women held a position of freedom and responsibility within the Church; on the contrary, their work was almost as narrowly restricted as that of the widows. The writings of the Fathers show that the deaconess prepared the women candidates for baptism by immersion; and after the deacon had anointed the head of the baptized woman with oil the deaconess was permitted to anoint the whole body. The deaconess also took up the work of ministering to the sick and caring for the needy. As in the case of widows she was expressly prohibited from teaching the doctrines of the Church; and although she was ordained for her office, yet it was not endowed with any spiritual function. Tertullian in his treatise *On Baptism* states positively that no woman should ever administer that sacrament. He justifies his position by refer-

[1] Donaldson, *Woman; her Position and Influence in Ancient Greece and Rome and in early Christianity*, p. 139.

ence to St. Paul's well-known views: " For how credible
would it seem that he who has not permitted a woman even
to learn with overboldness, should give a female the power of
teaching and baptizing." " Let them be silent," he says,
" and at home consult their own husbands."

So much for the position of single women as active workers
within the Church. What of the status of women in general —
as daughters and wives and mothers? From the beginning of
its history the early Church clearly recognized the *spiritual*
equality of women and men. Both had been redeemed by
the Saviour of the world and their souls were alike precious
in the sight of God. Thus Clement of Alexandria in his work
on the daily conduct of the devout Christian declares: " The
virtue of man and woman is the same. And those whose life
is common have common graces and a common training." [1]
Yet in the same treatise he sounds the warning of St. Paul:
" But above all, it seems right that we turn away from the sight
of women. For it is sin not only to touch, but to look; and he
who is rightly trained must especially avoid them." [2] Tertullian is frequently harsh in his denunciations of women and
in his exhortations to them as the daughters of Eve to walk
shamefacedly before men. In his Letter *On Female Dress* he
breaks forth in bitter invective: " And do you not know that
you are (each) an Eve? The sentence of God on this sex of
yours lives in this age: the guilt must of necessity live too.
You are the devil's gateway: *you* are the unsealer of that
(forbidden) tree: *you* are the first deserter of that divine law:
you are she who persuaded him whom the devil was not valiant
enough to attack. *You* destroyed so easily God's image,
man. On account of *your* desert — that is, death — even the
Son of God had to die. And do you think about adorning
yourself over and above your tunics of skins? " [3] These two
passages sound the dominant chord of most of the later patris-

[1] *The Instructor*, in *Ante-Nicene Fathers*, Vol. II, p. 211.
[2] *Ibid.*, p. 291.   [3] *Ibid.*, Vol. XI, p. 305.

tic writings on women. As a dangerous seducer of man, as the prime cause of his fall from Eden, let woman seclude herself, dress in sober garments, veil her face and walk humbly in the world. By the age of Tertullian, if not earlier, married women were exhorted to remain in the seclusion of their homes, engaged in housewifely duties and in prayer.

The foregoing passages show that the status of the married woman within the family probably became less free after the establishment of Christianity. The words of St. Paul concerning the subjection of the woman to her husband fell on fertile soil and bore fruit for many centuries. The wife tended once more to become in theory and practice, if not in Roman law, the obedient handmaiden of her husband who was lord of her person and her services. In his work, *The Instructor*, Clement of Alexandria admits the need of all for physical exercise and permits men to attend gymnasiums as conducive to health. Women also need bodily exercise: " But they are not to be encouraged to engage in wrestling or running, but are to exercise themselves in spinning and weaving, and superintending the cooking if necessary. And they are with their own hand to fetch from the store what we require. And it is no disgrace for them to apply themselves to the mill.[1] Nor is it a reproach to a wife — housekeeper and helpmeet — to occupy herself in cooking, so that it may be palatable to her husband."

THE REGULATION OF MARRIAGE BY THE EARLY CHRISTIAN CHURCH

Betrothal and Nuptials. — During the first three centuries the Church did not interfere with the betrothal and marriage customs then in vogue in the Empire. Rather did it take up the task of working out an elaborate scheme of degrees of kinship within which marriage was prohibited. At the same time

[1] The ancient hand-mill in which one heavy stone is made to turn upon another. Usually worked by slaves.

it attempted to enforce single marriages upon Christian clergy and laymen alike. In his scholarly work on *The History of Matrimonial Institutions*, Professor Howard writes: " It is a noteworthy fact that the early church accepted and sanctioned the existing temporal forms of marriage. Her energy was directed mainly to the task of enforcing her own rules relating to marriage disabilities, such as those arising in affinity or nearness of kin; to devising restraints upon the freedom of divorce and second marriage; and to administering matrimonial judicature." [1] The Church, then, sanctioned in the first place the Roman forms of betrothal and nuptials, just as, after the barbarian invasions, it recognized the customs that prevailed among the various tribes of the North. This means that for many centuries Christian marriage, like pagan, rested upon the free consent of the contracting parties and was not essentially a religious ceremony. Betrothal was not the actual initiation of marriage, as was the case among the Teutonic peoples, but was simply an " engagement," giving neither party the right of legal redress in case of breach of contract by the other.

Yet, although the Christian Church accepted current marriage customs, it reserved the right to hallow the union by bestowing upon it the blessing of God. Not that the early Christian leaders required that marriage be performed within the church, for apparently they did not. Indeed, Christianity had no formal marriage ritual for centuries; nor did pagan usage prescribe any religious ceremony. But the Church did urge upon its members the duty of seeking the blessing of the priest upon their betrothal and nuptials; and this was probably a fairly well established custom in the first century A.D. In the fourth century Ambrose declares that " marriage should be sanctified by the priestly veil and by benediction . . ."; but this does not remotely imply that the marriage was not legal without this ceremony, or that it was not quite frequently contracted without it. By the time of St. Augus-

[1] *Op. cit.*, I, p. 291.

tine, however, and thereafter, it was probably customary for the newly married pair, after the nuptials had been privately celebrated, to attend the ordinary religious services within the church, partake together of the sacrament and receive the benediction of the priest upon their married life. Professor Howard quotes an interesting letter written about 860 A.D. by Pope Nicholas to the Bulgarians who asked for counsel regarding Christian marriage rites: " First of all they [*i.e.*, the bridal pair] are placed in the church with oblations, which they have to make to God by the hands of the priest and so at last they receive the benediction and heavenly veil." [1] From this it is safe to conclude that by the ninth century the custom of marriage within the church had been very generally established in Rome, although not even then universally adhered to. The reference in the quotation to the " heavenly veil " needs a word of explanation. Originally the veil was used by Christians in the betrothal ceremony and was worn by the betrothed maiden as well as by the newly married woman. Later, however, the ceremony of veiling seems to have been restricted to nuptials. In the Eastern Church crowning the bride with flowers or olive wreaths took the place of the veiling ceremony of the West.

Prohibited Degrees. — In the pagan Empire the earlier restrictions upon the marriage of second cousins had disappeared and even first cousins married freely.[2] But under the Christian emperors this freedom was very largely curtailed. Theodosius I forbade the marriage of first cousins under pain of death by burning. The penalty was reduced at a later period; but the prohibition remained in force in the Western Church. The sons of Constantine went further and expressly forbade marriage with a deceased wife's sister or a deceased husband's brother, and this prohibition was adopted by the Emperor Justinian. These early regulations mark the be-

[1] *History of Matrimonial Institutions*, Vol. I, 295, note 6.
[2] Tacitus, *Annals*, XII, 6.

ginning of a long series of similar decrees, issued by church councils during the Middle Ages, which culminated in the prohibition of marriage within the seventh degree of consanguinity from the common ancestor.   At the Lateran Council of 1214 Pope Innocent III relaxed the prohibition so as to include only those within the fourth degree of consanguinity.   Marriages within these degrees were not only forbidden but were declared null and void.   Such restrictions produced endless confusion and numberless difficult cases to be settled by the ecclesiastical courts.   A modern historian comments on the effect of these canonical prohibitions as follows: " Reckless of mundane consequences, the church while she treated marriage as a formless contract [*i.e.*, resting on the mere verbal consent of the parties] multiplied impediments which made the formation of a valid marriage a matter of chance." [1]

ATTITUDE OF THE EARLY CHRISTIAN CHURCH TOWARD THE EVILS OF PAGAN FAMILY LIFE

Adultery. — From its earliest history the Christian Church proclaimed purity as the chief of all virtues and set its face like flint against the pollution of marriage which was so common in the pagan world.   Over and over again the Church Fathers declared the lifelong union of one man and one woman to be the only form of sexual relation sanctioned by the Church. Adultery was condemned in unmeasured terms and the duty of faithfulness in marriage was enjoined upon the man as upon the woman.   St. Jerome expressly states that among Christians what is not permitted to the woman is equally prohibited to the man; [2] and St. Chrysostom writes in similar vein. St. Augustine even goes so far as to maintain that adultery is more criminal in man than in woman.   Thus the teaching of the Christian Church on this point was unequivocal and

[1] Pollock and Maitland, *The History of English Law*, Vol. II, 383 *et. seq.*
[2] *Letter LXXVII; op. cit.*

just; it maintained from the first the single standard in morals. It is much to be regretted, however, that the doctrine of the Church did not become the common sentiment of the great body of the Christians. Probably the double standard of morality was no more consistently followed in the pagan world than it has been among Christian nations almost to the present time. Thus the ideal of the Church has failed in large measure to be realized in the practice of its members. It is interesting to note that the more noble minds in the pagan world had recognized the injustice involved in exacting faithfulness of the wife while permitting constant infidelity to the husband. The Emperor Antoninus Pius, on granting a Roman husband a condemnation for adultery against his guilty wife, added this condition: " Provided always it is established that by your life you gave her an example of fidelity. It would be unjust that a husband should exact a fidelity he does not himself keep."[1] Aristotle, among the Greeks, and Plutarch and Seneca, among the Romans, had also urged the justice of reciprocal fidelity. But the principle remained in the realm of pure theory, apparently held only by a noble few among the pagans and rarely, if ever, legally enforced. The Christian Church, however, in the first three centuries of its unsullied purity and sincerity, *did* enforce the single moral standard upon its members, punishing guilty husband, as guilty wife, with exclusion from the Church and its sacraments.

Abortion, Infanticide and Child Exposure. — One of the greatest services rendered by Christianity to the advancement of morality consisted in the importance it attached to every human life and in the emphasis it laid on the gentler and more altruistic sentiments. Maintaining at all times the sanctity of human life, bought as it was with the blood of Christ, the leaders within the Christian Church harshly condemned the practices of abortion, infanticide and child exposure, then so

[1] Cf. Lecky, *History of European Morals*, Vol. II, 313, who quotes St. Augustine.

general throughout the Roman Empire. Utility and personal comfort, rather than compassion, had determined the attitude of the pagan nations toward these practices. The motives leading mothers to destroy their unborn children or to kill them shortly after birth were various. Extreme poverty, or the malformation of the child, were the least unworthy; while vanity, the shrinking from pain and care, and even gross licentiousness served as motives with those of low moral standards. From the first, Christian teachers made no distinction in the degree of guilt between abortion and infanticide. Both were crimes, excluding the guilty parent from the saving grace of the sacraments until the final hour of life. In the teaching of the Church the unborn fœtus, no less than the infant just brought into the world, was the temple of an immortal soul which would be condemned to everlasting punishment if ruthlessly cut off from life without the purifying rite of baptism. It can hardly be questioned that the doctrine of the Church concerning the damnation of the unbaptized constituted an important motive for its condemnation of child murder in all its forms.

While the best pagan thought had condemned infanticide, and pagan legislators had passed laws against it, neither public opinion nor law had done much to restrain the evil. Moreover, both popular sentiment and legal opinion in the pagan world were decidedly lenient in the matter of child exposure. Hence this evil assumed enormous proportions under the Empire. Every year new-born children were brought by scores and hundreds to a column in Rome, where they were left to perish or to meet the fate of adoption by professional panders who brought them up as prostitutes or sold them into slavery. Against this evil the Church launched the thunders of its wrath and punishment no less vigorously than against infanticide. Severe penitential sentences were passed upon parents found guilty of child exposure. Furthermore, the Church earnestly sought to arouse in its members by exhortation an effective sense of the criminal nature of the act.

Legislation of Christian Emperors. — Not content with ecclesiastical measures, the Church used its powerful influence to secure legislation against infanticide, child exposure and the sale of infant children. As we have seen, pagan law condemned infanticide but was not in any degree successful in stamping out the practice. It remained for the Christian Emperor Valentinian, in 374 A.D., to declare infanticide a crime punishable by death, and to enforce the statute against it. The exposure of new born infants proved a custom very difficult to uproot. In 331 A.D. Constantine had enacted a law designed to increase an exposed child's chances of adoption. The law provided that (1) a saviour of a foundling might hold it as his property, whether he adopted it as his child or made of it a slave; and (2) the parent of the abandoned child could never reclaim it. Lecky has pointed out that this enactment, however well-intentioned, marks a backward step in legal procedure, since an earlier decision of the Emperor Trajan had declared that an exposed child could under no circumstances be made a slave. The law of Constantine, while enhancing an exposed infant's chances of life, " doomed it to an irrevocable servitude." [1] Nevertheless, the law was in force until the time of Justinian, when it was enacted that (1) a father lost all authority over the child he had exposed; (2) the child could not be deprived of its natural liberty by the person who had rescued it. Unfortunately, this humane law applied only to the Eastern section of the Roman Empire, thus making it possible for exposed children to be enslaved throughout the West for many centuries thereafter.

Another unfortunate enactment of Constantine, passed during the disastrous civil wars that marked his reign, authorized parents in great destitution to sell their offspring. This sale of free children had been openly disapproved by

[1] *History of European Morals*, Vol. II, 30.

previous pagan Emperors and had been expressly condemned by Diocletian, although it is probable that the custom had never been stamped out before the age of Constantine. Theodosius the Great attempted to mitigate the effects of Constantine's law by providing that children sold by their parents might become free after a limited period of service without repayment of the purchase price. Apparently, however, the law did not meet with popular approval, since it was repealed by Valentinian III, after whose reign no Christian Emperor seems to have made any attempt to restrict the inhuman sale of children. This is but one instance out of many where legislation in Christian Rome lagged far behind the teaching of the Church Fathers.

The Influence of Christianity on Roman Custom and Law with Respect to Divorce. *Legal Enactments of Christian Emperors.* — Just as the early Christians accepted the current pagan ideas concerning the private and secular character of marriage, so they did not go counter to the prevailing conceptions of the private and non-religious character of divorce. So far as the law was concerned, Christian Rome fully recognized the right of married persons to dissolve their marriage without invoking the aid of either Church or State. No suit for divorce was required nor was public registration of divorces demanded. Yet, with the spread of the Christian doctrine that marriage was a sanctified union there developed the idea that it should be a permanent one. Although the Church Fathers were a little doubtful about the case of a divorce following an act of adultery, especially on the wife's part, they " had no hesitation whatever in pronouncing all other divorces to be criminal. . . ." [1] But so deeply rooted was the practice of divorce among the Roman people that Christian Emperors in the early centuries made no attempt to prohibit it. They confined their efforts rather to making divorce less desirable by increasing the pecuniary loss that fell upon

[1] Lecky, *History of European Morals*, Vol. II, 352.

the culpable party. So careful an authority as Muirhead has stated that the divorce legislation of Christian Emperors " forms a miserable chapter in the history of law." He adds that not one Emperor " who busied himself with the matter, undoing the work of his predecessors and substituting legislation of his own quite as complicated and futile, thought of interfering with the old principle that divorce ought to be as free as marriage and independent of the sanction or decree of a judicial tribunal." [1] The Emperors from Constantine to Justinian contented themselves with (1) increasing the penalties previously imposed on the guilty party to a divorce; (2) imposing pecuniary penalties on the active agent in a divorce secured on frivolous grounds. With reference to the first point, Christian legislation provided that the guilty husband should forfeit the entire dowry of his wife, instead of a fraction of it, and the guilty wife should lose the entire *donatio*, or marriage settlement of her husband. If there were offspring of the marriage the ultimate ownership of this property reverted to them, the innocent party to the divorce enjoying only the usufruct. In case no dowry or *donatio* had been provided the culpable party forfeited one fourth of his or her property. With respect to the second point, the law declared that the person who obtained a divorce on frivolous grounds was guilty of misconduct and became liable to the pecuniary penalties described above.

As late as the age of Justinian,[2] Christian Emperors permitted one-sided divorces in the following cases: (1) where one partner desired to dissolve the union in order to enter a monastic order; (2) where the husband had been five years in foreign captivity; (3) where there had never been prospect of offspring owing to physiological impediment. The last cause is interesting as evidence that Christian lawmakers were in accord with early Hebrew and pagan thought in re-

[1] *Historical Introduction to the Private Law of Rome*, p. 356.
[2] Roman Emperor, with his capital at Constantinople; reigned 527–65.

garding the essential purpose of marriage as the procreation of offspring.   Divorce for any of these three reasons was not penalized and was known as *divortium bona gratia* — divorce by good grace.   But legislation in early Christian times went even further and recognized the right of the partners to a marriage to dissolve it by mutual consent.   Such divorce was called *divortium communi consensu*.   It will be seen that considerable freedom of divorce without penalty was accorded in Rome long after Christianity had become the dominant religion of the Empire.   In consequence the writings of St. Jerome and other leaders within the Church abound in lamentations over the frequency of divorce.   St. Jerome states that he himself had seen a man in Rome living with his twenty-first wife who had had twenty-two husbands.   The Bishop of Amasia, writing about forty years before Justinian, declares that men changed their wives as easily as their garments and that marriage beds were removed from the atrium as readily and frequently as market stalls.   Such extreme cases may have been exceptional; yet they indicate the laxity of custom and law alike in the matter of divorce.

In the reign of Justinian that austere Christian Emperor made some attempt to curb the existing freedom of divorce. In one of his *Novellæ* [1] he enacted that in cases where the parties agreed to a divorce on insufficient grounds both should be compelled to enter a monastery or convent and should forfeit two-thirds of their property to their children.   Otherwise the marriage should be null and void.   This edict, however, caused profound popular dissatisfaction, since it was opposed to both the theory and the custom of the Roman people.   Furthermore, experience proved that the requirement concerning the adoption of monastic life did not tend to elevate the tone of morals within convent or monas-

---

[1] The *Novellæ* or Novels of Justinian were imperial statutes issued subsequent to the great *Code* of laws prepared under his direction and were designed to correct errors or repair omissions in this code.

tery.[1] In consequence the obnoxious act was repealed by Justin the Second, nephew and successor of Justinian. In the Eastern Empire, therefore, freedom of divorce lasted until late in the ninth century when divorce by mutual consent was pronounced invalid by the Emperor Leo the Philosopher.[2]

The Views of the Christian Church concerning Divorce. — Hitherto we have considered chiefly the legislation of Christian Emperors with respect to divorce. But it cannot be doubted that the freedom in this regard conceded by Roman law was directly opposed to the teachings of Church Fathers and Councils alike. Although, as we have seen, the early Fathers were a little hesitant to declare themselves hostile to divorces on the ground of adultery, they pronounced all other divorces to be grave offences expiable only by long and severe penance. Thus the laxity of civil law in Christian Rome is in strong contrast to the inflexibility of the Church's doctrine. This dualism in ecclesiastical and civil legislation persisted far into the Middle Ages. While the Church had from early times threatened divorced persons with the awful penalty of excommunication, it was not until the twelfth century that the civil law was brought into entire conformity with canon law by prohibiting divorce for any cause whatever. Commenting on the stringency of the Church doctrine with respect to divorce Lecky observes that its sweeping prohibition " was not originally imposed in Christian nations upon utilitarian grounds, but was based upon the sacramental character of marriage, upon the belief that marriage is the special symbol of the perpetual union of Christ with His Church, and upon a well-known passage in the Gospels." [3] It may be added that no utilitarian motive could have had the tremendous effect in restricting divorce that was accomplished by this mystical dogma of the Church, inculcated as it was with profound

---

[1] Muirhead, *op. cit.*, p. 356.
[2] Cf. James Bryce, *Studies in History and Jurisprudence*, p. 805.
[3] *Op. cit.*, Vol. II, 353.

earnestness and enforced with threats of exclusion from the Christian body and in consequence from the membership of the saved.

Remarriage after Divorce. — Opposed as they were to second marriages, the Church Fathers denounced with special bitterness the marriage of a divorced person during the lifetime of the other partner. In their eyes such marriages were little better than adultery. In one of his *Letters* St. Jerome, referring to a passage in *Romans* where a woman who had married during the lifetime of her husband is called an adulteress, declares: " A husband may be an adulterer, or a sodomite, he may be stained with every crime and may have been left by his wife because of his sins; yet he is still her husband, and, so long as he lives, she may not marry another." [1] This was the theory of the Church throughout the Middle Ages, although conditions sometimes forced Churchmen to modify the doctrine. Marriages might be and not infrequently were pronounced null and void because of some impediment recognized by canon law, such as relationship within the forbidden degrees of kinship, or force used in bringing about the marriage. In such cases, since there had never been a valid marriage in the eyes of the Church, the parties might contract a new union. But this was regarded as in no sense a sanction of divorce.

The Influence of Christianity in Modifying Family Legislation in Rome. — The influence of Christianity on Roman laws concerning marriage and family relations was comparatively insignificant until after it had been recognized as a State religion by Constantine. From the fourth century on, however, the Christian Church exercised a powerful influence on domestic legislation. (1) Numerous laws were passed imposing disabilities with respect to marriage with heretics and apostates. Very early the Church discouraged and opposed " mixed marriages," *i.e.*, unions between Christians and unbelievers; and this opposition was reflected in Roman law

[1] *Letter LV, op cit.*

under Theodosius. (2) Christianity was also directly responsible for the repeal of those provisions of the *Lex Papia
Poppæa* [1] which imposed penalties on celibacy and childlessness and encouraged fruitful marriages. With the rapid spread
of asceticism, celibacy became in the eyes of Churchmen a
virtue rather than a social evil; hence these penalties were abolished by Constantine in 320 A.D. (3) To Christian influence
may be traced the divorce legislation discussed in the previous
section. (4) Second marriages, as we have seen, came to be
discountenanced by Christian Emperors; and in the Theodosian
Code such unions entailed forfeiture of the dower and *donatio*
to the offspring of the first marriage if such existed. (5) The
custom of granting a *donatio* or marriage settlement to the
bride had grown up in the later centuries of the Empire and
had been made the subject of legislation by Theodosius and
Valentinian. But it remained for the Emperor Justinian in
his famous Code carefully to define the procedure in regard
to both *dos* and *donatio*. Whenever a dowry was furnished by
the wife a *donatio* must be provided by the husband; and if
one were increased during marriage a corresponding increase
must be made in the other. More important was the legal
provision authorizing the wife to demand the transfer to herself of both the dowry and the *donatio* in case of her husband's
insolvency. She was, however, under legal obligation to use
these funds for the support of the family. In another respect
also the legislation of Justinian was favorable to the wife, for
it provided that after the death of her husband or her own divorce without just cause she might recover both her dowry and
the *donatio*. Moreover, under certain conditions the mother
was given the right, so long denied to her, of legal guardianship
over her children. The influence of the Christian Church in
these last enactments is doubtful; they seem to be rather the
direct outgrowth of the earlier pagan tendency to free women
from all economic and legal disabilities.

[1] Passed in the reign of Augustus Cæsar.

Decline of the *Patria Potestas*. — Long before the establishment of Christianity the decline in the power of the Roman
husband and father over the members of his family had been
marked and progressive. This decline went steadily forward
in the later centuries when Christianity became supreme. In
the words of Muirhead: "With the Christian Emperors
the last traces disappeared of the old conception of the *familia*
as an aggregate of persons and estate subject absolutely to the
power and dominion of its head." [1] Husband and wife were
made equal before the law, although Muirhead is inclined to
believe that the wife was the more privileged as regards protection and indulgence. By the time of Justinian the *patria
potestas* had been so stripped of its earlier rights that it was
little more than a name. The exposure of new-born children
was prohibited in the Code of Justinian under severe penalties.
The killing of a grown-up child (except in the case of a daughter
taken in adultery and slain with her partner) was definitely
branded as murder and was punished as such. No father could
sell his child as a slave except in case of extreme destitution
and then only when the child was an infant. The ancient
custom whereby a father was set up as judge of his wife and
children and was endowed with powers of life and death over
them had long since fallen into disuse. Under Justinian a
father could no longer surrender his son to an injured party
bringing suit and thus wash his hands of legal responsibility
for his son's fines. To quote again from Muirhead: "All
that remained of the *patria potestas* in Justinian's legislation
is what is sanctioned in modern systems: the right of moderate
chastisement for offences, testamentary nomination of guardians, giving of the son in adoption, and withholding consent
to the marriage of a child. The latter was subject to magisterial intervention if unreasonable." [2] The right of a father
over the earnings of a son had been limited by Augustus and

[1] *Historical Introduction to the Private Law of Rome*, p. 387.
[2] *Op. cit.*, p. 390.

N

this limitation was extended by Hadrian and later pagan rulers. The Christian Emperors had simply carried further a tendency already under full headway when they denied the father any right of ownership over his son's property except in case of (1) acquisitions made by the son with funds advanced by the father for his separate use, (2) of bequests to the son. In one of the chapters of his *Novels* Justinian insured to a child, as his own in death as in life, all his property except the *peculium profecticium* or funds advanced by the father for his son's use. So far did legislation go in limiting a father's rights in the property of his son that in cases where the son died intestate his possessions passed to his father only by title of inheritance and in the absence of direct descendants.

From this brief study it would appear, then, that the amelioration of family laws in Christian Rome and the extension of the rights and privileges of the wife and mother were only a continuation of tendencies clearly present in the enactments of pagan emperors. But in matters of divorce, mixed marriages and second marriages, prohibited degrees and the removal of the penalties attached to celibacy, Christianity unquestionably introduced novel features into Roman legislation.

SELECTED BIBLIOGRAPHY

SOURCES.
   Ante-Nicene Christian Library.
      Ignatius, *Epistle to Polycarp*, Vol. I, p. 85.
      Clement of Alexandria, *Pedagogus or The Instructor*, Vol. II, pp. 211–93, 377–9.
      Athenagoras, *Plea for Christians*, Vol. II, p. 147.
      Tertullian, *Letter to his Wife*, Vol. XI (Vol. I of series of Tertullian's writings), Letter XI.
        On Female Dress, Vol. XI, Letter XII.
        On Exhortation to Chastity, Vol. XVIII, pp. 1–14.
        On Baptism.
        On Monogamy, Vol. XVIII, p. 21.

A Select Library of the Nicene and Post Nicene Fathers (ed. by Philip Schaff).

St. Augustine, *Letters*, Vol. I, Letter to Juliana, pp. 549–50, Letter CL to Proba and Juliana.

Confessions, Vol. I, p. 206.

St. Jerome, *Letters*, Vol. VI.

To Laeta, CVII, pp. 189–95.

To Eustochium, XXII.

To Pammachius, XLVIII.

To Amandus, LV.

SECONDARY WORKS.

Dealey. *The Family in its Sociological Aspects* (1912), pp. 52–62.

Dictionary of Christian Antiquities.

Meyrick, Article on *Marriage*, Vol. II, pp. 1902 ff.

Ludlow, Articles on *Betrothal*, Vol. I, p. 203; *Benediction*, Vol. I, p. 193.

Donaldson, James. *Woman: Her Position in Ancient Greece and Rome and among the Early Christians*, Bk. III, chs. I, II.

Howard, George. *History of Matrimonial Institutions*, Vol. I, pp. 291–9, 324–32.

Jeaffreson. *Brides and Bridals*, Vol. I.

Lecky, W. E. H. *History of European Morals*, Vol. II, pp. 20–34, 316–27, 336–47, 350–8.

Schmidt, Karl. *Social Results of Early Christianity*, Bk. II, ch. III.

Thwing, C. F. *The Family*, ch. III.

CHAPTER VII

THE FAMILY IN THE MIDDLE AGES

The Barbarian Invasions. — From the closing years of the fourth century until well into the sixth, the barbarian hordes of the North overran the empire of the Cæsars, disrupting its unity and establishing themselves in the territories won by conquest. The Vandals seized the northern coasts of Africa; the Visigoths made their home in Spain; the Franks occupied the fertile lands of Gaul and annexed in course of time the domains of the fierce Burgundians and Alemanni on their eastern frontiers. Into Italy poured the East-Goths, only to be completely routed and driven out by the armies of Justinian in the sixth century. But Italy was not permanently freed from barbarian inroads. After the death of Justinian in 565, the savage Lombards invaded the country and established themselves in the region north of the Po River, a territory which has been called Lombardy from that time to the present. To the north and east of the Frankish dominions lay the territories of the Frisians, the Saxons, the Jutes and the Angles, peoples who were not far removed in civilization from the Iroquois Indians of America at the landing of the white men. Some time after the withdrawal of the Roman troops from Britain, at the opening of the fifth century, those islands were overrun by the Angles, Jutes and Saxons, who, after repeated incursions, succeeded in thoroughly routing the native Britons. When Augustine made his missionary visit to Britain in 597, he found the invaders firmly established in the conquered islands. Such, in brief, was the geographical arrangement of the barbarian tribes in Western Europe in the sixth century.

Sources of our Knowledge of Family Customs among the Barbarians. — The most valuable source of our knowledge of the family life of the Germanic peoples in the first century of the Christian era is the *Germania* of the Roman historian Tacitus. In this account of the customs of the barbaric Teutons there is a brief description of their family life and their mode of contracting marriage. " The matrimonial bond," says Tacitus, " is . . . strict and severe among them; nor is there anything in their manners more commendable than this. Almost singly among the barbarians they content themselves with one wife; a very few of them excepted, who, not through incontinence, but because their alliance is solicited on account of their rank, practice polygamy." [1] A subsequent statement of Tacitus reveals some misunderstanding of Teutonic marriage customs. Thus he writes: " The wife does not bring a dower to her husband, but receives one from him. The parents and relations assemble, and pass their approbation on the presents — presents not adapted to please the female taste, or decorate the bride; but oxen, a caparisoned steed, a shield, spear and sword." There can be no doubt that these articles, which Tacitus mistook for presents, were really the purchase price of the bride, paid down by the rude suitor to the girl's father for the right to marry her and thus control her person.

In addition to the *Germania*, Cæsar's *Gallic War* furnishes the student with a few references to family conditions in Britain about 55 B.C. At this time the natives must have been in the lowest stages of barbarism, for Cæsar describes their family relations as follows: " Ten and twelve have wives common among them, especially brothers with brothers and parents with children; if any children are born they are considered as belonging to those men to whom the maid was first married." [2]

---

[1] *The Works of Tacitus*, Oxford trans., N.Y., 1884, p. 308.
[2] See Cheyney's *Readings in English History*, pp. 15, 16.

After the first four centuries of the Christian era, our most important sources of knowledge of Germanic marriage customs are the folk laws of the various Teutonic tribes. The earliest laws are those of the Ripuarian Franks of the fifth century. To the sixth century belong the Burgundian folk-laws; to the seventh the Visigothic, to the eighth the Salic and Saxon laws, and to the ninth the Frisian. All these collections of customary law abound in references to family relations and marriage forms. Thus they constitute a valuable source of knowledge of Teutonic family customs from the fifth to the tenth century.

The Kinship Group and the Household among the Anglo-Saxon and Germanic Races. — It is necessary at the outset to distinguish between the great family or " kin " and the separate household as these existed among the Germanic tribes. Just as we find the " house " and the gens among the Hebrews, the Greeks and the Romans, so we find the " kin " among Teutonic peoples. The Saxons and Frisians of the continent called their kinship group the *sippe*, while the Anglo-Saxons in Britain called it the *mægth*. In both cases it consisted of a group of kindred descended from the *grandchildren* of two common ancestors, the " kin " thus taking its rise not from the original pair, but from the third generation, — the children of their offspring. Although each *mægth* or *sippe* included only those united by blood or by formal adoption, any particular individual's " kin " was a union of both the paternal and maternal kinship groups. In this respect the *sippe* of the Germanic peoples is in striking contrast to the gens of the Romans. The Teutons traced kinship through both the father and the mother; hence the offspring of any marriage was a member of two kinship groups. The Romans, on the contrary, reckoned relationship from the common ancestor through males only (the system of agnation); therefore the gens included only those descended in the male line from the reputed founder of the family. It follows that the kinship groups of the Germans were intertwined in a network, while the Romans held each gens distinct and separate by ignoring kinship through women.

The great family or *sippe* among Germanic races was the fundamental institution of private law. The tribe and later the state depended upon the " kin " to keep the peace and punish crimes within its membership. In consequence the *sippe* had large powers over each household as well as over the individuals composing it. The " family " as a whole could protect a child even from his father. Likewise the members acted as guardians of widows and children, taking charge of the estates of orphans until they were of age. Even remote kinsmen, as possible heirs, could prevent the sale or alienation of family estates. It followed that the relations of husband to wife and parents to children were strongly influenced by the fact that each member of the household was bound by the general law of the *mægth* or *sippe* as well as by the more particular laws of the household. Both the kin of the father and that of the mother had rights and obligations in the new household formed by marriage, although the paternal kin assumed the larger share of both in the case of any individual. The wife remained in her own *sippe* after marriage. This meant that her kin made compensation in fines for offences committed by her and bore the " feud," *i.e.*, sought redress, in case of her gross mistreatment or murder.

The Law of the Mægth or Sippe. *Membership in the Family or Kin.* — By the law of the *mægth* and the *sippe* no child born out of wedlock had any rights of inheritance, since he was not an acknowledged member of his father's kin. He did, however, have some rights of protection since, if he were slain, his " price " or *wergild*, as the Anglo-Saxons called it, must be paid, in part to the king and in part to the paternal kindred. Even a legitimate child did not become a true member of the kin until his father had formally acknowledged him. Infanticide and child exposure were far from uncommon in the Middle Ages up to the eleventh century, largely owing, no doubt, to the harsh conditions of existence and the frequent famines that visited a rude people who had little understanding of natural laws. But the father's power of life and death over his offspring was limited by the law of the *sippe* to children who had not tasted food. If milk or honey had passed or even touched the child's lips the father must admit him into membership in the kin of both father and mother. Such membership secured to an individual the protection so urgently needed in the warlike period of the Middle Ages. If he were slain, the kin avenged his death or exacted of the slayers his *wergild*.[1] If, on the contrary, he killed a member of another family, the paternal kin, among the Anglo-Saxons, paid two-thirds of the murdered man's *wergild* and the maternal kin one-third. On the death of a father before the children had attained their majority, the father's kin assumed all rights of guardianship so far as property was concerned. Among the Anglo-Saxons, however, the actual control of the children was left with the mother. This is made clear by a law of Ine in the eighth century. " If a ceorl [2] and his wife have a child between them and the ceorl die, let the mother have her child and feed it; and let VI shillings be given her for its fostering, a cow in summer and an ox in winter; and let the kindred take care of the homestead until it be of age." [3] On coming of age, wards could sue their guardians within the kin for misuse or alienation of any portion of their property.

In addition to the rights and duties just mentioned, the *mægth* or *sippe* assumed responsibility for the conduct of each individual member, especially of landless men. These men had less incentive to an industrious and law-abiding life than their more fortunate kindred, and in consequence were in-

---

[1] A sum of money fixed by customary law as just compensation for the human life taken.   [2] A ceorl was a freeman.

[3] Young, *Anglo-Saxon Family Law*, in Adams, *Essays in Anglo-Saxon Law*, p. 180.

clined to rove about and get into brawls with neighboring groups. Thus the first police authority among our Anglo-Saxon ancestors was vested in the family. Before the Norman Conquest, however, this responsibility had been handed over to the organized courts.

With such powers of protection and control in the hands of the kin, membership in some family group was of the utmost importance to every individual during the early Middle Ages. His security from robbery, attack or injury of any kind, as well as his social position and influence, depended almost wholly on the power, numbers and wealth of his kindred. Although withdrawal from the kindred was permitted in specified instances there was little temptation for any one to forego the tremendous advantages which sprang from such membership.

The Law of the Household. — In addition to the law of the family group was the household law, regulating the relations of husband and wife, parents and children. This private law, like that of the *sippe* or *mægth*, was almost wholly the product of custom, and, as the centuries advanced, it was more and more limited and curtailed by the growing power of public law. It may be noted that this has been the history of all family law from the days of the ancient Greeks and Romans to our own times, when important family relations are wholly regulated by public law. At present the ancient rights of the father over the persons and property of wife and children have shrunk to a mere shadow.

Powers of the Father. — The power of the father over his offspring among most of the barbarian tribes was in the nature of a protectorship, and was called in Anglo-Saxon *mund*. That the father's authority was not absolute has been suggested in the discussion of the law of the *mægth*. The kindred could intervene to protect the rights of any child who had once been acknowledged by his father. An Anglo-Saxon parent could not sell his child into slavery after it was seven years of age, and before that age only under pressure of necessity.

On the continent, however, the Germanic tribes apparently did not so curtail the father's power to dispose of his offspring. One writer tells us that as late as the thirteenth century a German could sell both wife and child in time of famine.[1]

Despite the limitations set by the kin upon the father's power to kill or sell his offspring, his authority was more than ample from our modern point of view. A father had the right to chastise his children freely, and this privilege must not infrequently have been abused. The laws of the Jutes permitted a man to beat his children with a heavy staff provided he broke no bones.

Until the eleventh century the Anglo-Saxon father might bestow his young daughter in marriage with no regard to her wishes. In the *Pœnitentiale* of the English Archbishop Theodore, written in the seventh century, it is stated that a girl up to sixteen or seventeen years of age is in the power of her parents; after that age parents may not marry her to any suitor against her will.[2] Probably the absolute right of a father to dispose of daughters in marriage was lost in England by the time of the Danish King Cnut, whose oft-quoted law runs as follows: " And let no one compel either woman or maiden to him whom she herself mislikes, nor for money sell her. . . ." Yet the father's power to send his daughter and probably his son to a monastery to be dedicated to the life of nun or monk was unquestioned. Such a step must often have brought great bitterness into the lives of helpless children, quite unfitted by nature for the monastic life. In England from the sixth until late in the twelfth century the church held a girl thus dedicated to be bound by her father's action even when, after reaching years of discretion, she sought release from the convent.[3] For many centuries the father was the

---

[1] Gummere, *Germanic Origins*, p. 154.

[2] Young, *Anglo-Saxon Family Law*, p. 153. The *Pœnitentiale* may be found in Haddan and Stubbs, *Councils*, Vol. III, pp. 173–213.

[3] Thrupp, *The Anglo-Saxon Home*, pp. 113, 114.

legal representative of his children before the courts, making such restitution in fines as the law demanded for offences committed by them and securing compensation for injuries done them. Finally the father had the right to administer the property received by his children from their maternal kindred; and with the right of administration went the right to use the fruits of that property, *i.e.*, the usufruct. Among the Anglo-Saxons, however, the father never was permitted to control his son's earnings.

The Partial Emancipation of Children at Majority. — Unlike the Roman custom, the folk laws of the Middle Ages all recognize the right of the son to greater freedom on his coming of age. The age at which a son attained his majority varied among the different Teutonic peoples, and likewise changed from time to time. In the period of Tacitus (first century A.D.) a son was freed from the father's authority when he was capable of bearing arms. Certainly the age at which the German youths were admitted to the body of freemen seems very early to the modern man. It was probably twelve or fifteen years. Among the Anglo-Saxons, who had no ceremony of "emancipation," the age of majority was at first ten years; but a law of Cnut, in the eleventh century, reads: "And we will that every freeman above twelve years make oath that he will neither be a thief nor cognizant of a theft." At the completion of his twelfth year, then, the Anglo-Saxon boy was made a freeman, responsible to the law in his own person.

At the majority of his son a father's power over him was limited by household law and custom. Probably he could no longer freely chastise him nor prevent his marriage by forcible means, although his disapproval might and probably did prove sufficient in many instances. Also in the opinion of some historians the son, on coming of age, had the right of veto in all alienations of land by the father. This was an important privilege, since among many Germanic tribes the marriage of the son (usually at an early age) was accompanied by a division of the family property to enable the youth to set up a new home of his own. However, the father's control over the actions of his son did not wholly cease at the latter's majority, but continued, in a milder form, until the youth had married and established an independent household. Among the Anglo-Saxons, moreover, there is no evidence that the father had any legal rights over property bequeathed to his son when the latter had come of age.

Like the son the daughter attained majority at the completion of the twelfth year; but the freedom accorded to her was far less than that bestowed on the boy. The father still enjoyed the usufruct of his daughter's property, and the right to represent her in court. He likewise had full right to chastise and correct her by whatever means he saw fit to use. By the eleventh century, however, he had, theoretically at least, lost the right to dispose of her in marriage against her will. Even before this time Roman betrothal customs had begun to influence Saxon England. In consequence the free consent of the contracting parties came to be held as essential. It is true that parents still had the right to betroth their children as early as seven years of age. But if parent or offspring wished to terminate the contract when the child was ten years old this might be done without penalty. When the child was between ten and twelve the breaking of the agreement entailed fines for the parent, and after the age of twelve years both parent and child were liable to fines for refusal to keep the marriage contract.

MARRIAGE CUSTOMS AND LAWS IN THE EARLY MIDDLE AGES

Wife Capture and Wife Purchase. — Before the Christian era the capture of wives was probably a common custom among Germanic tribes, traces of which may be found in certain old-time marriage practices in Wales. Howard relates that the Welsh bridegroom a century ago went on horse-back accompanied by his friends to demand his bride. The bridal party, which was also mounted, refused to give up the girl, whereupon a mock fight ensued. Finally the bride was carried off by her nearest kinsman, while the bridegroom and his friends followed in hot pursuit. When horses and men were thoroughly fatigued the suitor was allowed to overtake his lady and lead her away in triumph. Then followed the usual wedding festivities.[1] In the first Christian century, however, wife capture had generally been superseded by wife purchase, as the account of Tacitus makes clear. There is ample evidence in the early folk laws to show that women were openly bought in marriage up to the tenth century. Thus an Anglo-Saxon law of Æthelbert, dating about 600 A.D., runs as follows: " If one buys a maiden, let her be bought with the price, if it is a fair bargain; but if there is deceit, let him take her home again and get back the price he paid." [2] The complete absence of affection or romantic interest from most of these old-time marriages is revealed in another law of Æthelbert, which states: " If a man carry off a freeman's wife, let him procure another with his own money, and deliver her to him." [3] Clearly any woman would do if she were strong and reasonably well favored. To avoid misunderstandings the Saxon laws of the early ninth century conveniently fixed the price of the woman sought in marriage at 300 shillings. In his work on German women Weinhold quotes a peasant saying of the present day to the effect that " It's not man that marries maid, but field marries field, — vineyard marries vineyard, — cattle marry cattle." [4] Here is indicated clearly enough a survival, among the German peasantry, of the custom of gross bargaining in connection

[1] *History of Matrimonial Institutions*, Vol. I, p. 173.
[2] Gummere, *Germanic Origins*, p. 152.
[3] Thorpe, *Ancient Laws*, Vol. I, pp. 24, 25.
[4] *Deutsche Frauen*, Vol. I, p. 319.

with the taking of a wife. Indeed the expression " to buy a wife " was in common use in Germany throughout the Middle Ages, although the actual sale of the bride had probably ceased by the tenth century.

Forms of Contracting Marriage : Beweddung and Gifta. — Among all the Teutonic peoples there were two stages in contracting marriage : (1) *Beweddung,* (2) *Gifta.* At first *beweddung* was a contract between the father and the suitor to give the girl to the man for certain stipulated valuables in cattle, arms or money. *Gifta* consisted in the " tradition " or handing over of the woman to her husband by the father. In the earliest times no doubt the bargain was concluded and the maid handed over at one and the same time. But as the centuries passed the interval between *beweddung* and *gifta* lengthened until, in the late Middle Ages, when *beweddung* had become betrothal and when this betrothal often took place in infancy, the interval was one of years. Certain other changes had likewise taken place in the *beweddung* or contract ceremony before the tenth century. (1) The bride price was no longer paid outright but had given place to *arrha,* a small sum of money given the father by the suitor as a guarantee of payment of the full bride price at nuptials. In the course of time the *arrha* was paid to the bride herself and, probably owing to Roman influence, came much later to take the form of a ring — the betrothal ring of modern times. (2) Not only was *arrha,* in one form or another, paid to the bride, but in the period from the sixth to the ninth century the purchase money itself was gradually being transformed into provision for the wife from the husband's property in case he died before her. Certainly from the tenth century onward *beweddung* was nothing but a formal contract or *wed* to pay the bride price to the wife in case of the husband's death. The contract was concluded by certain quaint ceremonies such as the exchange of straws between suitor and maid, or the breaking of a coin between them. Later in the Middle Ages these forms had largely given place to "hand-fasting" or solemn clasping of hands before witnesses. Whatever the binding ceremony, *beweddung* among all the Germanic races was the first step in marriage. Hence the infidelity of the girl was counted as adultery and was punished as such.[1]

As stated above, the second act in marriage was *gifta* or giving of the bride to the groom by the father or guardian. In early times the father handed over his daughter to her husband together with certain objects, such as a sword, hat and mantle, which served as symbols of the power over the person of the woman thus transferred from the father to the husband. Among certain Teutonic tribes the husband then very ungallantly trod upon his bride's foot as a mark of his newly acquired authority; but later this mode of asserting the dominance of the male was changed to the harmless delivery of a slipper or shoe to the bride. These marriage practices show clearly enough that *gifta* or nuptials *was a purely private matter* until late in the Middle Ages. Up to the tenth century the father gave the bride in marriage; after that time it became customary for the bride to select a guardian, her father, some near relative, or even a friend, who gave her away. Such was a common custom in the thirteenth century despite the opposition of the Church. Quite frequently, also, the simple marriage ritual was recited by the chosen guardian, or independently by the bride and groom, who thus, to all intents and purposes, married themselves. Out of this " self-gifta " has grown the common-law marriage of England and America.[2]

The Morning-gift. — In the centuries between the seventh and the tenth there had grown up the custom of bestowing upon the bride who had found favor in her husband's eyes a

[1] See Howard, *History of Matrimonial Institutions*, Vol. I, pp. 258–72, for a full discussion of "beweddung."

[2] For a full discussion of "gifta" see Howard, *op. cit.*, Vol. I, pp. 272–86.

bridal gift on the morning after the marriage. After receiving this mark of her husband's approval the Anglo-Saxon bride at once rose from her couch and bound her flowing hair about her head to signify that she was now an accepted wife and that her husband no longer had the right to return her to her family as unsatisfactory. At first the morning-gift seems to have been of little value; but as time went on its value so increased that it overshadowed the bride price in importance. Before the tenth century the man was bound by law to provide for the morning-gift as well as the bride price in the marriage contract. Noblemen and princes included slaves, horses, church revenues and even large estates in the morning-gift to their brides. History tells us that the Princess Eadgyth, sister of the Anglo-Saxon King Athelstan, received from her husband, the Emperor Otto of Germany, the entire city of Magdeburg as her morning-gift.[1] Several interesting examples of these marriage contracts, dating from the tenth century, have come down to us.[2] In course of time the morning-gift merged completely into the bride price and became provision for the wife to be handed over to her on the death of her husband.

Intervention of the Church in Marriage. — It must not be supposed that the Church was a silent and inactive party to such private and lay marriages as have been described above. After the conversion of the Germanic races to Christianity, during the period from the fifth to the eighth century, the Christian clergy exerted all their energy to enforce upon these barbaric peoples the canonical rules concerning the marriage of near and remote kin. Very wisely the Church did not at first combat the Germanic marriage forms, not even the sale of the bride. As it had previously accepted the forms in use in the Roman Empire, so it accepted the customs of the bar-

---

[1] Thrupp, *The Anglo-Saxon Home*, p. 61.
[2] See Young, *Anglo-Saxon Family Law*, pp. 171–2; Howard, *op. cit.*, Vol. I, p. 270.

barians. From the fifth to the eleventh century, however, the Christian clergy strove to impress upon the minds of the rude Teutons the sacred character of marriage. To this end the Church exercised its influence to induce the contracting parties to seek the blessing of the priest upon their nuptials. In course of time it became customary for bride and groom to attend mass on the day following the marriage, although the practice was never universal during this early period. Moreover, the bride mass was in no sense an essential part of the marriage ceremony, which still consisted in the handing over of the bride to her husband by her father or chosen guardian, after her consent had been signified. Yet the solemn service of the mass, followed by the priestly benediction upon the newly wedded pair, came to be regarded by many as a fitting ceremony to sanctify a union already consummated. It is interesting to note, however, that until *after the tenth century* the bride mass contained no special marriage ritual other than the priestly blessing. In a Kentish betrothal contract of the tenth century it is expressly provided that " At the nuptials there shall be a mass priest by law, who shall, with God's blessing, bind their union to all prosperity." [1] In England the nuptial benediction was pronounced while bride and groom stood under a veil or " care-cloth," held at each corner by the groom's friends. This seems to have been an adaptation of a similar Roman custom and is doubtless due to Roman influence, which, as we have seen, was strongly felt in southern England by the tenth century. To the same source is due the custom of crowning the bride with a wreath of myrtle or olive, as Christian brides were crowned in the Eastern Empire.

As the barbaric tribes advanced in civilization, the Church further extended its influence over the marriage rite. During the tenth century it became customary for *gifta* to take place *at the church door*, in the presence of the priest. It should be carefully noted that the essential act in marriage, —

[1] Young, *op. cit.*, p. 172.

o

the formal consent of the parties to live as man and wife, — was still regarded as a lay and private matter, since it was not performed within the church, and since the chosen guardian, not the priest, gave the bride in marriage. Howard furnishes us with an interesting copy of the marriage service in use in York about the end of the twelfth century.[1] This shows conclusively that even at this late period the ceremony of marriage in England was commonly performed before the door of the church. Here the bride's dower was assigned; here the priest asked : " Who giveth this woman to this man ? " And after the formal " tradition " of the bride by her father or guardian, the priest pronounced the benediction upon the married pair. Only then did the bridal party enter the church and participate in the bride mass, which was followed by a second blessing.

Very early the Christian Church sought to discourage second marriages among the barbarian tribes as it had done among the Romans in the first centuries of the Christian era. Doubtless disapproval of such marriages was genuine among the clergy; yet it is quite possible that a further impelling motive sprang from the desire of the Church to obtain possession of the lands and money of wealthy widows. Hence it was not unusual for the clergy to encourage a disconsolate mourner to take " vows of widowhood " shortly after the death of her husband when she was in deepest grief. Thereupon the widow entered some neighoring convent, where she wore a sober russet gown and a ring as marks of her dedication to celibacy. The monastery, of course, received all the property of the new devotee, but permitted her greater freedom than was allowed to those pledged to asceticism. As might be expected, these vows of widowhood were not infrequently repented of when the mourner's sorrow had begun to abate. The prevalence of such conditions among the Anglo-Saxons led King Cnut to pass a decree forbidding widows to take vows of celibacy " with unbecoming haste." In the end the clergy were

[1] *Op. cit.*, Vol. I, pp. 303-4.

successful in prohibiting second marriages till the close of the first year of widowhood, under penalty of forfeiture of the widow's dower. Up to the period of the Norman Conquest of England the property thus forfeited passed to the nearest kin of the deceased husband. But after that time the Church stamped the offence as ecclesiastical; hence the bishop seized the lands of erring widows for the benefit of the Church.[1]

SOCIAL POSITION AND PROPERTY RIGHTS OF MARRIED WOMEN

Woman's Status in the Family. — Since a woman among the Germanic tribes did not enter her husband's family, but remained a member of her own kin the bride's *mægth* or *sippe* was responsible for her offences after she became a wife. Therefore it was customary for the woman's relatives to give security at her marriage to answer for her conduct during her married life. Also injuries against the woman were payable in fines to her family or kin, under whose protection she remained. In a Kentish betrothal of the tenth century one article reads: " If then, he desire to lead her [*i.e.*, the bride], out of the land into another thane's land, then it is right that her friends have there an agreement that no wrong shall be done her: and if she commit a fault, that they may be nearest in the *bot*, if she have not wherewith she may make *bot*." [2] As a matter of fact, however, the woman at marriage came pretty completely under the control of her husband, who had full authority to enforce her obedience by personal chastisement. Only in case of extreme cruelty resulting in bodily injury, or in case of unjust divorce, would the kindred feel bound to interfere. Although the ancient folk laws did not deprive women of legal protection, even making the *wergild* of women in some instances higher than that of men, yet women

[1] Thrupp, *Anglo-Saxon Home*, pp. 36, 37.
[2] Young, *op. cit.*, p. 172. *Bot* was a money payment in compensation for an injury inflicted on another.

at this time were not "persons" in a legal sense. Father or brother or guardian answered for them in the courts and paid their fines. Such had long been the custom among the ancient Romans, and in all families of the patriarchal type. In the early centuries of the Middle Ages refractory wives might be sold by their husbands when bodily chastisement failed to accomplish its end. An idle, gadding woman was the especial aversion of the Anglo-Saxons, and she met with swift punishment from the male head of the family. In the quaint Gnomic verses found in the Exeter Book we read:

> " A damsel it beseems to be at her table;
> a rambling woman scatters words,
> she is oft charged with faults,
> a man thinks of her with contempt,
> oft smites her cheek."

And woe betide the woman who attempted to return upon her husband a few of the blows showered upon her. Among certain of the Teutonic peoples the woman who had struck her husband was compelled to ride on an ass through the streets, seated backwards, and holding the astonished animal's tail! So firmly ingrained among the German tribes was the idea of the supremacy of the husband that the man who meekly accepted blows from his wife would probably some day see his neighbors gather and take the roof off his house, on the ground that he who could not protect himself from his wife did not deserve to be sheltered from wind and rain.[1]

Yet the position of the married woman, even in the rude period of the folk laws, was not as abject as it may seem. Although she was expected to obey her husband, it must sometimes have happened that the wife possessed the stronger personality of the two; and in such instances it is idle to look to the laws to enforce the supremacy of the husband. By

[1] Buckstaff, *Married Women's Property in Anglo-Saxon and Anglo-Norman Law*, in *Annals of the American Academy*, Vol. IV, p. 238.

superior shrewdness, as well as by moral power, the woman no doubt enforced her will, then as now, in a score of matters affecting the daily life of the household. Nor did her position in the family rest entirely upon her strength of mind and character. Most of the barbarous races of the continent granted to women a certain degree of independence in their own sphere. Among the Danes, the wife had the custody of the household keys; and when Cnut the Dane became King of England he extended that privilege to Anglo-Saxon wives, together with the right to have a store-room, chest and cupboard of their own. This was a privilege not to be despised; for at this time if stolen goods were found in a man's house, his wife must suffer the penalty with him. The new law provided, however, that if the goods were not found in places which the wife controlled, and if she swore that she was ignorant of the theft, she escaped the cruel punishment or the heavy fines meted out to thieves. The lot of many a married woman must, also, have been made easier by the fact that her husband felt a certain respect for the capable wife who administered the complex affairs of homekeeping with efficiency and skill. Many a man doubtless learned that by giving his wife freedom in the household he received from her better work and thus the whole family profited by the concession.

It is probable that the primitive religions of the Teutonic tribes played some part in improving the position of women. In the dim centuries before the Christian era, and even in the time of Tacitus, the barbarous Germans worshipped household gods, as did all the Aryan race at one time or another. Now ancestor worship tended on the whole to cement the ties of marriage and give sanctity to the home. Tacitus tells us that the German barbarian believed that " there dwells in his women something holy and prophetic." Such reverence as attached to these women, through whom the gods were believed to speak, may have been extended in a measure to all women as possible possessors of the divine gift.

Influence of the Church on the Status of Women. — On the whole the Christian clergy exercised their influence to improve the condition of married women and girls, and to mitigate the too harsh exercise of authority by the husband and father. Yet so careful a historian as Wright does not hesitate to declare that in their efforts to undermine the powerful authority of the patriarch the clergy were looking to their own interests by seeking to substitute the influence of the Church for that of the family. Many women were doubtless drawn from their homes by priestly influence to be joined to Christ in spiritual marriage. During the last centuries of the Anglo-Saxon régime we are told that religious houses were filled with women who had left their husbands and with girls who refused to marry the men selected by their fathers.[1] However this may be, the Church rendered a service to civilization in stamping out the last vestiges of polygamy among the Anglo-Saxon peoples. Furthermore, it accomplished by its influence a gradual softening of manners and elevation of the woman's position in the home. In the tenth and eleventh centuries the status, at least of Anglo-Saxon women, had vastly improved. This is shown by quaint prints of the period which represent the wife as no longer serving her lord at table, but as sitting in dignity at his side. It is significant, also, of an improvement in the social position of women of the highest class that in 856 King Ethelwulf crowned his wife Judith at their marriage. From that period queens were crowned in England and sat beside their husbands on occasions of state. By this time, also, a woman had gained the priceless right to veto a marriage arranged by her father if it was thoroughly distasteful to her. To be sure she ran the risk not only of being beaten but of being sent to a convent for her obstinacy, especially if she

[1] Wright, *Womankind in all Ages of Western Europe*, p. 72.

were under age. But we may well believe that such penalties were not always inflicted by indignant fathers. For these mitigations of their lot women were largely indebted to the Christian clergy. Likewise the education bestowed upon the more intelligent girls of noble birth was owing to the influence of the Church. The literary tastes of King Alfred were awakened by his mother; and Alfred's own daughter Ethelfleda was highly educated for that time. In the eleventh century the queen of Edward the Confessor, last of the Saxon kings, was renowned for her learning and accomplishments. Referring to these facts Thrupp declares: " The high education bestowed on women during the last era of Anglo-Saxon civilization, and the independent position they attained, tended to place them on an equality with the male sex; and combined with the chastity and sobriety which generally distinguished them, offered a sound foundation for the chivalrous respect and devotion of later times." [1] It should be remembered, however, that the historian refers here only to women of royal or noble birth. The position of women of the lower social classes was distinctly inferior to that of their more favored sisters.

Married Women's Property Rights. — Before the days of feudalism, married women, both on the continent and in England, enjoyed larger property rights than were granted them later under the feudal régime. The early folk laws make this clear enough. Among the continental tribes the wife's property consisted of (1) the bride price (after it became customary to give it to the bride instead of the father), (2) the morning-gift, (3) the *gerade*. As we have seen, the bride price and the morning-gift later became fused into one provision for the bride which was agreed upon at the time of the marriage contract, or *beweddung*, and was confirmed at nuptials. The laws of the Ripuarians, the Frisians and the Westphalian Saxons stipulated that, if a wife bore a son,

[1] *Op. cit.*, p. 74.

she should lose her morning-gift and instead be entitled to one-half the joint acquisitions of the family. Among the Germanic tribes a bride commonly received a gift of personal property [1] from her own family, no doubt to assist her in establishing a new household. This was reserved for her own use. In it was included the *gerade*, which consisted of house linen, furniture, ornaments, money, sometimes even the poultry tended by the bride before her marriage and the sheep her hands had shorn. This personal property of the wife descended strictly to her female heirs.

How far did married women among the Teutons control the property to which they were entitled? On this point there seems some difference of opinion among historical writers. Apparently, however, the *gerade* belonged to the wife without qualification; and if this were of generous proportions, a German wife might be economically independent, especially as her separate earnings were her own. To offset these advantages, however, it is probably true that in some tribes all the possessions of the wife except the *gerade*, viz., the morning-gift, and all property by bequest, was under the management of the husband during his lifetime. Law and custom differed among the various tribes with respect to the control granted a married woman over her property. But upon one point the Germanic peoples were practically a unit. With the exception of the Visigoths, who had come under Roman influence, all the Teutons excluded women from ownership of land.

Yet, although some restrictions with respect to the control of her property were put upon the German wife, very few were placed on a widow. At her husband's death a woman entered into possession of her morning-gift *for life* and also received any other personal property bequeathed or given to her. Among the Westphalian Saxons, as has been stated, the widow who had borne sons received, instead of the morn-

[1] Called *Aussteuer.*

ing-gift, a full half of the family possessions. These she enjoyed for life, after which they passed to her husband's
nearest heirs. In early times a widow among the Germans
passed into the guardianship of her husband's kin and could
return to the control of her own *sippe* only if a price were
paid for her guardianship. But later this custom died out
and the German widow before the days of feudalism seems to
have enjoyed a considerable degree of independence.

Hitherto we have considered the property rights of married
women and widows solely among the tribes of the Continent.
What were the corresponding privileges among the Anglo-
Saxons in England? The Anglo-Saxon wife had the *full
ownership* of her morning-gift and could bequeath it as she
saw fit, unless her husband in the contract had expressly
limited her to a life use. Moreover, if the wife bore children,
she was entitled by a law of Ethelbert (584–616 A.D.) to
half the family property. If the husband had provided
no morning-gift for his wife, Anglo-Saxon law gave her a
right to " an undivided portion of her husband's property."
This meant that the husband could not alienate his land
without his wife's consent. Furthermore, there is evidence,
in the form of wills and deeds, to show that from early in the
ninth century until after the Norman Conquest, the Anglo-
Saxon wife was co-possessor of the family property with her
husband. A deed of gift of certain lands to the Church by
Thurkill and Aethgift, his wife, states that the ownership is
to be " as full and free as we two possess it, after the day of
us." [1] No restriction seems to have been placed upon the
right of an Anglo-Saxon woman to inherit land, as was the case
on the continent. In this respect there was sex equality
among the Anglo-Saxons. A father might divide his real
estate equally among sons and daughters if he chose to do so.

Anglo-Saxon widows were at first under the guardianship
of their nearest male kin. Such was the law in the sixth

[1] Buckstaff, *op. cit.*, p. 247.

century. But by the reign of Æthelred in the tenth century, widows were for all practical purposes independent agents. Not only did they own their morning-gift and property by inheritance, but they had the full management of these, and at times appear in the records as alienating or bequeathing their possessions without the consent of their sons. After the death of the husband and father the wife and children frequently remained in the family homestead and held the estates together. In such cases the consent of the sons was necessary to the sale of landed property by the widow.

DIVORCE IN THE MIDDLE AGES

Folk Laws and Customs. — In the prehistoric period the right of repudiating the wife was probably the privilege of every husband in the various barbarian tribes. But it may well have been sparingly used for fear of the blood feud or of the fines which would infallibly have been exacted by the relatives of a woman unjustly repudiated. In the folk laws of the Burgundians, divorce by mutual consent is sanctioned, doubtless owing to Roman influence. Gradually the folk laws of other tribes conceded this right to every married pair. These codes of customary law made a sharp distinction between the sin of adultery as committed by husband and wife. To be sure, a married man guilty of adultery might be slain if taken in the act; but his crime did not consist in unfaithfulness to his own wife, but in " violating the rights of another husband." [1] On the other hand, Tacitus relates that among the early Germans an adulterous woman was beaten through the village until she died because she had proved unfaithful to her own husband. On the whole the early folk laws show the influence of Christian teachings in a tendency to restrict the grounds on which a man may divorce his wife. Likewise in the monk Bede's *Ecclesiastical History* (731 A.D.), it is

[1] Howard, *History of Matrimonial Institutions*, Vol. II, p. 35.

expressly stated that barrenness, gluttony, drunkenness, quarrelsomeness and gadding about were not sufficient reasons for divorcing a wife. The law of the Visigoths is surprisingly advanced, going so far as to restrict a man's right of divorce to the cause of adultery, while granting the woman a similar right if the husband has committed " two scandalous wrongs." It is significant, however, that unfaithfulness on the part of the husband was not held by the Visigoths to be one of these " scandalous wrongs." This fact shows that the Christian principle of the equal heinousness of adultery in man or wife had made little headway in changing either sentiment or customary law among the barbarians.

Influence of the Mediæval Church upon Divorce. — The influence exercised by the Church of the Middle Ages in the matter of divorce makes interesting history. At the outset it is necessary to distinguish clearly between the Church's advocacy of the principle that marriage is indissoluble and its actual practice when brought face to face with the conditions of a barbarous society. As early as the fifth century the Council of Carthage had declared the indissolubility of the marriage bond and the Roman Popes had repeatedly forbidden divorce with remarriage. Yet the doctrine proved difficult to uphold without compromise. In consequence we find the Council of Agde (505) threatening with excommunication, not the men who divorce their wives, but those who fail to establish the causes of their divorce before the provincial bishops prior to their remarriage. Likewise the *Pœnitentiales*,[1] both on the Continent and in England, permit divorce for several causes and even permit remarriage. Thus the *Pœnitentiale* of Archbishop Theodore[2] grants a husband the right to divorce a wife guilty of adultery and to marry again. Even the guilty wife may remarry after a penance of five

---

[1] These were private manuals written by bishops for the instruction of parish priests in their relations to the members of their churches.

[2] Archbishop of Canterbury about the middle of the seventh century.

years. Likewise a man deserted by his wife is permitted to take another wife if he obtain the bishop's consent; and a woman whose husband is imprisoned for crime may also remarry. Other grounds for divorce and remarriage recognized in Theodore's *Pœnitentiale* are the conversion of one spouse to Christianity while the other remains heathen, and the capture of husband or wife in time of war. Nowhere is the spirit of compromise, forced upon the Church by barbarous social conditions, more clearly shown than in its early sanction of divorce by mutual consent. Not only is this privilege granted in the English penitential, but in the subsequent Frankish manuals modelled after it.[1]

Such was the state of affairs up to the ninth century when Church Councils took an uncompromising attitude toward divorce, and the penitentials in current use were carefully revised so as to harmonize with the Christian principle of the indissolubility of marriage. Not until three hundred years later did the great masters of canon law, Gratian and Peter the Lombard, seek to reconcile the conflicting views of the Church Fathers, the Popes and the Councils, by codifying all the canons concerning marriage and divorce. These codes became authoritative for all Christian nations and thus are marks of the growing power of the Church in all matters of marriage and divorce. This authority, however, was of slow growth. As we have seen, the Church had met great practical difficulties in enforcing its views concerning divorce upon an unwilling public accustomed to regard such separation as a private matter. The Christian clergy found the only solution of this problem in the complete control of divorce by their own body. Very early they initiated the struggle to secure supreme authority in this field and to wrest jurisdiction from the civil powers, but their efforts did not meet with success until the tenth century when the Bishop's court had become the ordinary tribunal for divorce cases among the

[1] See Haddan and Stubbs, *Councils*, III, 199.

German peoples. Before long such was the case throughout Christendom.

But although the Church triumphed in upholding the doctrine of the indissolubility of marriage, as a matter of fact divorces of two sorts were granted by the Bishop's court under certain conditions. First, the Church employed the expression *divortium a vinculo matrimonii* (divorce from the bonds of matrimony) to designate a marriage as null and void because of certain impediments such as (1) a previous *verbal* contract of marriage in words of the present tense, (2) kinship within the seventh degree or (3) the spiritual relationship in which, for example, the principals in the sacrament of baptism were supposed to stand. For example, the man and woman who had stood sponsors to a child were held by the Church to become spiritually kin by that act and therefore they could not marry. Secondly, canon law permitted *divortium a mensa et thoro* (divorce from board and bed) on three grounds: (1) adultery, (2) heresy or apostasy, (3) cruelty. In such instances the Church granted a separation order, permitting husband and wife to live apart. With respect to *divortium a vinculo* there can be little doubt that the powerful and the well-to-do frequently resorted to it as a means of terminating an unsatisfactory marriage and that the doors to fraud were thrown wide open. In this connection Howard writes: " Before the Reformation the voidance of alleged false wedlock on the ground of pre-contract or forbidden degrees of affinity, spiritual relationship, consanguinity, or on some other canonical pretext, had become an intolerable scandal." [1] " Spouses who had quarrelled," says a historian of English law, " began to investigate their pedigrees and were unlucky if they could discover no ' *impedimentum dirimens* ' or cause which would have prevented the contraction of a valid marriage." [2] Apparently money would accomplish

[1] *Op. cit.*, Vol. II, p. 59.
[2] Pollock and Maitland, *History of English Law*, Vol. II, p. 391, foot-note 1.

much in the ecclesiastical courts of the later Middle Ages. In his work on *The Family* Thwing characterizes the annulment of marriages as " a flourishing business of the mediæval Church," and adds : " No exercise of its power yielded more money, or caused more scandal."

HOME LIFE IN THE EARLY MIDDLE AGES

The Homes of Early Days. — Tacitus's famous account of the life of the Germans of the first century, so often quoted above, briefly describes their homes and mode of living. Every one, he says, " surrounds his house with a vacant space, either by way of security against fire, or through ignorance of the art of building. For indeed, they are unacquainted with the use of mortar and tiles; and for every purpose employ rude, unshapen timber fashioned with no regard to pleasing the eye. . . . They also dig subterraneous caves, and cover them over with a great quantity of dung. These they use as winter retreats and granaries, for they preserve a moderate temperature : and upon an invasion, when the open country is plundered, these recesses remain unviolated, either because the enemy is ignorant of them, or because he will not trouble himself with the search." In these rude homes dwelt our Teutonic ancestors, wearing but one garment called by Tacitus the *sagum*. This seems to have been a short square mantle made of some rough shaggy material or of the skins of animals. The dress of the women was very similar to that of the men, except, according to Tacitus, " that they more frequently wear linen which they stain with purple; and do not lengthen their upper garment into sleeves, but leave exposed the whole arm, and part of the breast." [1]

In the Anglo-Saxon era in England, every freeholder, on obtaining an allotment of land, surrounded his possessions with a mound of earth and dug a ditch around the whole.

[1] Tacitus, *Germania*, Oxford translation, pp. 306–8.

Inside the earthen wall was an open space called the yard (*geard*) within which stood the rude buildings that made up the *ham* or home of the Anglo-Saxon. The main building was called the *heal* (hall). Here the householder dispensed hospitality to all honest men who came to his doors, and here his friends and retainers slept at night, on the straw-strewn floor. In the hall the well-to-do thane entertained his friends at his generous board, and his lady served wine to her lord's guests. Even an Anglo-Saxon queen frequently left her raised seat beside the king to pass the wine-cup among his trusty followers. In the hall or courtyard, the lord and his lady dispensed clothing and loaves to the poor, hence the name *hlaf-ord* (loaf-owner) and *hlaf-dig* (loaf-giver) from which terms come our names "lord" and "lady." Thus the word "lady" in its origin was bound up with the gracious charity, which, in those early days, was regarded as the special duty of the well-born woman and her noblest grace. Separate chambers were built outside the hall to accommodate the women of the family. Each small building was connected with the hall and was called a *bur*, whence comes our expression of the "ladies' bower." Among the poorer classes the homes were rough and the bed-chambers were few or none until, in the words of Wright, "we arrive at the simple room in which the inmates had board and lodging together, with a mere hedge for its enclosure, the prototype of our ordinary cottage and garden." [1] Anglo-Saxon houses remained much the same in structure and arrangement until the end of the Saxon period. None had an upper story, but consisted only of the ground floor. Country houses were built on high ground, offering a wide prospect in all directions; and thus they afforded the protection so much needed in those warlike days.

The Home as a Centre of Industry. — Quite as truly as in primitive Palestine, Greece and Rome, the home of the early Middle Ages was the heart of the industrial life of the com-

[1] Wright, *History of Domestic Manners in England during the Middle Ages*, p. 11.

munity. The rude Teuton tilled his fields, hunted wild animals, made weapons and crude implements and went to war. When peace prevailed he lay about the house or caroused with his chosen companions. His wife, on the other hand, was engaged in a wide variety of productive occupations. In the words of Tacitus: " All the bravest of the warriors, committing the care of the house, the family affairs, *and the lands*, to the women, old men, and weaker part of the domestics, stupefy themselves in inaction. . . ." The quotation is of peculiar interest as showing that even agriculture in the first Christian centuries, was carried on by the Teutonic women. This fact is in accord with the practice of many savage and barbarous groups to-day, where the men merely clear the land and leave all the laborious processes of tilling the fields and raising the crops to their wives. Furthermore, the whole clothing industry, with its numerous skilled processes, was likewise entirely in the hands of the women. Archbishop Theodore of Canterbury, in his *Pœnitentiale* so often referred to, forbids Anglo-Saxon women to employ themselves on Sunday in such occupations as shearing sheep, carding wool, beating flax, washing garments, weaving, spinning or sewing. Although this indicates only a portion of the activities of the busy housewife of the period, it shows that in the seventh century the textile industry, woollen as well as linen, was wholly carried on by the wives and daughters of the family. Such was the case prior to the twelfth century when weaving became a skilled craft in the hands of men. But even then the preparatory work, the wool-combing, spinning, drawing out of the yarn and winding remained in the hands of women.[1] In the same way all the activities connected with the preparation of food and drink were home industries directed by the housewives. Women were the cooks, the brewers, the bakers in these early days. Later in the Middle Ages, as craft gilds grew up, men tried to

[1] See Karl Bücher, *Die Frauenfrage im Mittelalter*, p. 15.

take over in part the brewing and baking that had so long been domestic tasks. But even then women were not wholly excluded from these incorporated industries, as the town records in the Rhine cities and in Frankfort-on-Main abundantly prove.[1] Nor did the work of women end here. When candles succeeded rush-lights, chandlery developed as a domestic industry, — another occupation for the busy *Hausfrau*. Soap-making was likewise in the hands of house-wives, and it is highly probable that before tanning of skins became a male industry the processes were carried on in the home in part, at least, by women.

A favorite occupation of women of rank throughout the Middle Ages was embroidery. So skilled in this art did Anglo-Saxon women become that the finest embroidery and needlework in Europe was known in the eleventh century as "English Work." In certain early records women are mentioned as exercising the art of embroidery as a profession. Thus the Domesday Book makes mention of a damsel named Alwid, who held lands given her by the Saxon Earl Godwin as a recompense for teaching his daughter "orfrey" or embroidery in gold. Algiva, the queen of King Cnut, embroidered with her own hands a rich piece of stuff set with precious stones which were skilfully arranged to form pictures. We are told that its like could not be found in all England.[2] Bishop Aldhelm, in a quaint eighth-century work in praise of virginity, complains of the vanity of Anglo-Saxon women who "sought to arrange delicately their waving locks, curled artificially by the curling-iron, with their cheeks dyed red with stibium." Apparently these arts of allurement, so common in our own day, have an ancient history. But the worthy bishop is on less solid ground when he reproves women for changing the natural color of fleeces to red and purple, — a transformation which appears wholly

[1] Bücher, *op. cit.*, p. 19.
[2] Wright, *Womankind in all Ages of Western Europe*, pp. 60, 61.

P

for the better. The complaint is of interest, however, as showing that women understood the art of dyeing wool at a very early period. Tacitus mentions the practice as common in the first century among the German women.

Women and the Gilds. — As certain skilled trades, such as those of the tailor, the cobbler, the saddler, the weaver, were taken out of the control of women and became organized crafts for men — an evolution accomplished between the eleventh and the fourteenth century — these industries were still domestic in character.[1] Each one was pursued under the roof of a master-workman who was permitted to employ a fixed number of apprentices and journeymen. The finishing touches in many of these industries were added by the wife and daughters of the family. Women as independent wage-earners outside their homes were very rare in the Middle Ages. Yet there were always women left alone in the world and forced to shift for themselves. In the country districts, where gild organizations had developed little, the problem of the homeless woman was easily solved, since her labor was always desirable in households where so many industries were carried on. Hence orphaned girls and widows in the country found a refuge with their near or even distant relations. But in the cities of the later Middle Ages homeless women were badly off, since they were excluded from working in a large number of the craft gilds, not only because men sought to keep out women from these organizations, but also because they were founded essentially on the idea of family industry. That is, skilled crafts were looked upon as home work, to be carried on in the household of some master-workman who could direct the labor of his wives and children, together with that of the limited number of apprentices the gild permitted him to employ. Furthermore, mediæval gilds were not only industrial societies, but organizations exercising legal, political, military and administrative functions. Now

[1] See Bücher, *op. cit.*, p. 19.

the right to become a full member of a craft gild was dependent upon ability to render military service and to take part in political life. Women of course were excluded from both these spheres of activity and hence in many instances from gild membership. The universally accepted idea was that women were destined for marriage and their sphere of work was wholly the care of the household. Yet there were exceptions to the general exclusion of women from incorporated trades. In some gilds, after the death of a Master, his widow was expected to carry on his work, although the privilege of gild membership was limited in time or carried with it the condition of remarriage with a Master of the same craft. Here and there, especially on the Continent, women became independent members of certain craft gilds. The records of Bremen, Cologne, Dantzig, Speier, Strassburg and Ulm, give ample evidence of such independent membership. A Munich municipal ordinance of the fourteenth century runs as follows : " Whoever is a master weaver or a *female master weaver* shall have, if he desires, one boy apprentice and one girl apprentice and no more." [1] Likewise the Cologne statutes contain interesting references to the crafts of gold-beating and gold-spinning. At the head of each gild was not only a Master but a " female Master," whose duty it was to oversee the work of the members. One ordinance reads : " No gold-beater whose wife is a gold spinner may have more than three daughters engaged in gold spinning ; the gold spinner, on the other hand, whose husband is not a gold-beater may have four daughters and no more to spin her gold." [2] The statute is interesting as showing how largely, after all, gild industry was domestic in character. Very frequently sons and daughters served as apprentices to their own parents under the general regulation of the gild.

Home Nurture and Training in the Middle Ages. — When a child was born in the early Middle Ages, it was for the

[1] *Ibid.*, p. 16.   Italics mine.   [2] *Ibid.*, pp. 13, 14.

father, as head of the household, to decide whether the tiny infant should be reared. As we have seen, infanticide and child exposure were not uncommon at this time, owing to the hard conditions of existence. In spite of the steady opposition of the Church, which decreed severe and long-continued penances for such offences, destitute parents killed or exposed their infants in times of warfare or of scarcity of food. Even so late as the eleventh century the inhabitants of Schleswig occasionally cast unwelcome children into the sea, although these were probably isolated cases.[1] This cruel custom bore more severely on girl babies than on boys, since the latter were relied upon to continue the family name and to be the hope of the parents in their old age. In the countries of North Germany and Scandinavia, if a child were sprinkled with water and given a name, or if its lips were smeared with honey, it could no longer be killed or exposed. Little by little the custom of child exposure yielded to civilization, and as the position of women improved, their instincts of love and pity had increasing weight in determining the fate of the child they had borne. In the quaint old city of Nuremberg during the Middle Ages, provision was made for poor women about to become mothers, perhaps with a view to preventing infanticide or abortion. Midwives, who had almost wholly in their own hands the bringing of children into the world, were enjoined to make ready a bed and all necessary things for the confinement of poor women and to attend them as long as was necessary. Every year they were to present their account to the city exchequer and receive compensation for their outlay.[2]

In North Germany, Iceland and Scandinavia the new-born child was laid on the floor at the feet of its father, who then decided whether or not it should be allowed to live. If the decision were favorable, the little one was handed over to the

---

[1] Boesch, *Kinderleben in der Deutschen Vergangenheit*, p. 12.
[2] *Ibid.*, p. 11.

midwives to be bathed and probably swaddled, *i.e.*, wrapped tightly with cloths from head to feet. It was then sprinkled and given a name by the father. The nurses and midwives of these early days were saturated with superstitions and practised all manner of strange traditional rites which were believed to help the little stranger on the strenuous path of life that lay ahead of it. Sometimes a fresh egg, the symbol of fruitfulness, was laid in the baby's bath; or a coin was placed there to insure to the little one ample means in its later life. Again, after its bath, the new-born child was laid close against the left side of its mother in the belief that she would draw from it all sickness and protect it thus from child-pains, leprosy and the falling-sickness. Against these and many other superstitious practices, kept alive by ignorant midwives, municipal laws were occasionally directed. For example, an ordinance of Gotha, as late as the seventeenth century, after enjoining midwives to be God-fearing and lead Christly lives, continues: " On the contrary all superstition and misuse of God's name and word . . . such as use of written characters, drawings, gestures, and making the cross, amputation of the navel-string with certain questions and answers, . . . sprinkling before or after the bath, and such-like are forbidden, not alone to themselves, but also if they observe such unchristly and blamable practices in other people they shall dissuade them earnestly from the same and also report every case to the priest or magistrate." [1]

Very early in its life the infant was admitted to the sacrament of baptism, which apparently grew to be a costly affair in the later Middle Ages, so much so that it became necessary to regulate the expense by municipal ordinance. A Nuremberg law of the fourteenth century forbade the decoration of baptismal robes with gold, silver or pearls under penalty of a fine of two florins. Not more than twelve guests were permitted to attend the baptism and not more than three of

[1] *Ibid.*, pp. 18, 19.

these should later be entertained at the home of the parents. Even the entertainment was limited by the ordinance to spice-cake and wine. Not content with lessening the expense of baptism for the parents, the law cut down the christening gifts of dower money, made by god-parents and friends, to 32 Pfennigs.[1]

In the early centuries of the Christian era, the boys of the Teutonic and Anglo-Saxon peoples grew up naked and dirty in the rude homes of their parents. Their training consisted largely in running, jumping, learning the use of spear and javelin, training in the sword-dance and later in hunting and fighting. A *wergild* was set upon the boys of some Teutonic tribes at eight years of age. At twelve, as we have seen, the Anglo-Saxon boy was freed from the control of father or guardian so far as his estate was concerned. Likewise when the German youth was fifteen years of age he was commonly regarded as old enough to bear arms. After these had been conferred upon him, in the midst of the assembly of his people, either by the chief, his father or some member of the " kin," the boy was then admitted to the rights and duties of a freeman. From this time he was responsible for his acts before the law in his own person.

Not much can be said concerning the intellectual training of children during the early Middle Ages. Such education was distinctly the exception and not the rule, save for those children who were dedicated by their parents to the monastic life. In the time of the good king Alfred (9th century), began the custom of placing children in the houses of prominent nobles and princes to be educated. Yet the brothers of Alfred could neither read nor write, and this was true of most other nobly born children of the time. Such weak and unmanly arts were left to monks and a few women. Later, the Anglo-Saxon youths were sent to Normandy to be taught riding, hunting, fighting, grooming horses and serving at

[1] Boesch, *op. cit.*, p. 28.

table in the Norman castles. This was in the eleventh century, when feudalism was reshaping social customs and was beginning to hold up ideals of obedience and service as the qualities of a true knight.

In the homes of the early Middle Ages, then, such training as the boys received was largely physical and moral, although simple religious instruction was doubtless given in coöperation with the Church. The age was rude and half barbarous, and education reflected the low stage of civilization then attained by the peoples of Western Europe.

THE LATER MIDDLE AGES; CHANGES IN FAMILY LAW AND CUSTOM

Growing Power of the Church over Marriage and Divorce. — It will be remembered that, in the tenth and eleventh centuries, the Christian Church sought to add sanctity to marriage by insisting that a priest take part in the nuptial ceremony before the door of the church, and that subsequently a bride mass be performed within the church, followed by the benediction of the priest upon the newly married pair. After the twelfth century " self-gifta," or the giving of the woman to the man by herself alone or by some guardian chosen by herself, became a common custom. At this point the Church intervened and brought marriage more completely under its own control. So long as the father or a near relative, acting as guardian, handed over the bride to the groom the clergy did not interfere with their natural right. But when any third person, chosen by the bride herself, could perform this important act in marriage, the Christian priesthood took this function into their own hands. They went further and threatened with the awful penalty of excommunication the layman who would give a woman in marriage. Thus from the thirteenth century on the marriage rituals of continental Europe show that the clergy are the important factors in the ceremony. It is the priest and not the parent or chosen guardian who gives the woman to the man with the solemn words in the Latin tongue: " I join you in the name of the Father, the Son and the Holy Ghost, Amen." [1] Such, however, was not the custom in England. The individualistic Anglo-Saxon has maintained his right to give his own daughter in marriage down to the present day, as is shown by the Anglican marriage service in which the clergyman says: " Who giveth this woman to this man? "

Clandestine Marriages. — Doubtless the motive of the Church in taking such action was to impress upon the contracting parties the seriousness and solemnity of marriage as one of the seven sacraments of the Church. This doctrine, taught long before, was first formally promulgated in 1164 in the famous theological work of Peter the Lombard called the *Sentences.* But the Church was probably moved to take marriage into her own hands for another reason. As early as the ninth century Christianity had come into conflict with the rooted idea of the Germanic peoples that marriage is a *civil contract* — not a religious rite. As we have seen, this idea was particularly strong in England, although it was influential on the Continent as well. While the Church steadily sought to extend its control over marriage, some persons resented its action and insisted on a private lay ceremony, which was often clandestine in character. The custom of the time permitted a man and woman to take each other for husband and wife in words of the present tense, *e.g.*, " I *take* thee to be my wedded wife. . . ." In this lay and private contract may be found the source of the " common law " marriage of England and America. Sometimes this simple ceremony took place before witnesses, sometimes in the absence of any other parties. Clandestine marriages of the latter kind became so frequent from the

[1] Howard, Vol. I, pp. 309–12.

thirteenth to the sixteenth century as to constitute well-nigh a public scandal, since they not infrequently led to grave social wrongs. A man thus married could and did easily throw off the responsibilities he had assumed at marriage, and in consequence his wife and children might become public charges. Yet the Church was loath to pronounce such unions invalid, since such action would stamp the unfortunate offspring as illegitimate. Hence the canonical laws on marriage, as formulated by Peter the Lombard, tended to make a clear distinction between *legal* and *valid* marriages. A marriage contracted without the knowledge of the Church was pronounced *illegal* although not *invalid*. Such marriages were visited with ecclesiastical penalties in the form of severe penance; but they were not declared null and void, nor were the parties compelled to separate. After the Norman Conquest numerous canons forbade private marriages and prescribed penalties for the priest who performed them. In 1215, at the Fourth Lateran Council, Pope Innocent III attempted to stem the flood of clandestine marriages by requiring the publication of banns in all Christian countries. Yet, if a man and woman were contracted in words of the present tense (*per verba præsenti*) the Church continued to hold them as man and wife. This meant that a mere private verbal contract to marry, if in the form " I *take* thee to be my wedded wife," etc., was sustained by canon law against a subsequent marriage performed with due publicity by an officiating priest. In taking this ground the Church paved the way for serious abuses which were not remedied until the sixteenth century.

Effects of Feudalism upon Marriage and the Family. — When the feudal system was thoroughly established, Western Europe was divided into fiefs or landed estates, large and small, which were held on condition of military service rendered some overlord in return for his protection of the lands and persons of the holders. The lesser lords held their lands of some more powerful noble to whom they owed allegiance and well-defined services. Finally the most powerful of the nobility held their own lands as fiefs of the King, whose vassals they were. Thus was developed a landed aristocracy which assumed almost sovereign powers over their immediate vassals.

The effects of this social system upon marriage laws and family customs were profound and far-reaching.

Status and Property Rights of Women. — It will be recalled that, before the feudal system became established, women had been conceded considerable property rights. On the Continent the Teutonic woman had entire control of her *gerade* or personal property given her by her family at marriage. She could even alienate it without her husband's consent, and if it took the form of a considerable sum of money she might be economically independent. The wife also owned her morning-gift and separate earnings. Whether she *controlled* these during her husband's lifetime is a disputed point. Probably not, although mandates have come down to us wherein a wife gives her husband authority to transact business for her.[1] This seems to point to the wife's personal control of her own property. The German widow, at any rate, had the independent management of her morning-gift for life. Among the Anglo-Saxons the wife, as we have seen, became co-possessor of the family property with her husband. The latter could not alienate her property; and, since she was by law the absolute owner of her morning-gift, or, if none were granted at the marriage, of an undivided portion of her husband's property, she appears as a consenting party in sales of land or personal property made by him. On the death of her husband the Anglo-Saxon widow was entitled both to the ownership and control of her property by gift or inheritance, and to her morning-gift.

[1] Buckstaff, *Woman's Property Rights in Anglo-Saxon and Anglo-Norman Law*, p. 236.

Also toward the close of the Anglo-Saxon period, a widow was freed from guardianship save in the conduct of a legal case and apparently sometimes pleaded her own cause before the courts. A century before the Norman Conquest in England a widow named Wynflaed appeared before the court in person and pleaded her own case, producing as witnesses not only loyal thanes, but women whose testimony was accepted as valid before the law.[1]

All this was changed, however, under the feudal system which gradually curtailed the property rights of women and lowered their status. Fortunately there has come down to us a description of the laws and customs of England in the reign of Henry II (1154–89) which has been ascribed to the great Anglo-Norman lawyer Richard Glanvill. This interesting *Tractate* is of enormous value since it outlines in important features the legal practice in England almost to modern times. The document shows that the morning-gift of Anglo-Saxon days had by this time given place to the Norman " dower " or the life use of one-third of the husband's real estate *at marriage*, without regard to his later accumulations or losses. The law of Glanvill prescribed that this proportion might not be increased *even by agreement between husband and wife*. Nor might the husband give his dwelling-house to his wife as dower, since that belonged to his heir. Here we may plainly trace the influence of the ideas of primogeniture and entail which have governed the disposal of landed property in England down to our own time. In addition to her privilege of dower the wife was permitted a *life use* of one-third of her husband's personal property. But the Anglo-Norman wife had no control over her dower during the lifetime of her husband, nor could she in any way interfere with his management of it. So complete was her subordination that, even if her husband should sell the lands composing her dower, she could claim nothing after

[1] Young, *Anglo-Saxon Family Law*, in *Essays in Anglo-Saxon Law*, p. 182.

his death if it could be proved against her that she opposed him at the time of the sale. Nor did her disabilities end here. After her husband's death the widow must go through a complicated process at law to obtain her dower, and if her husband's heirs were disposed to dispute her claim, she must find a champion who would uphold her rights in open combat. Woe betide the unfortunate lady who was not charming enough to find a champion! Her property rights must have suffered sorely in a world so completely "man-made." In two respects, however, the laws of Glanvill concerning dower were softened at a later period. (1) Under Henry III, in 1217, a widow was permitted to receive as dower one-third of all the real estate of which her husband was possessed *at his death*. (2) In the reign of Edward IV a husband might, if he chose, endow his wife with the whole of his real estate for life. Apparently this privilege was very rarely used.[1]

With respect to the inheritance of estates the English woman in feudal times was placed at a further disadvantage. Under the Anglo-Saxon régime daughters might inherit equally with sons, there being no law to prevent this. But with the Norman kings came new customs. Glanvill writes concerning inheritance by women: "If anyone has a son and heir, and besides him a daughter or daughters, *the son succeeds to the whole;* . . . because in general it is true that a woman never takes part in an inheritance with a male, unless a special exception to this exist in some particular city by the custom of that city."[2] In the feudal period, also, there grew up the Roman custom whereby the parents of a girl gave her a dowry at her marriage. This property belonged to the husband so long as the marriage lasted, and he had a life interest in it if his wife died before him. At the death of her husband, however, a widow was entitled to the life use of both her dowry (*maritagium*) and her dower.

[1] Buckstaff, *op. cit.*, p. 260.   [2] *Ibid.*, p. 254.

The legal status of the woman under feudalism seems also to have been somewhat lowered. To quote from Glanvill: " Husband and wife were one person and that person was the husband." This meant, of course, that the woman was bound wholly by her husband's will and management and was represented by him in the courts. " While she was in the power of her husband," writes Glanvill, " she was not able to contradict his will in anything and so was not able against his will to look out for her own rights."[1] This grim injustice of feudal family law in England has been characterized by an eminent French writer as having " the harshness of the primitive barbaric codes."[2]

With feudalism came a further limitation of the power of English women. A widow was no longer permitted to be the guardian of the persons of her own children — a right that had been guaranteed to her under early Saxon law. The orphaned child of large inheritance usually came under the guardianship of his overlord who sometimes profited richly by " farming out " the care of the child to scheming persons who desired to marry the young heir to a daughter or son of their family. If the orphan were an only daughter, and hence an heiress, the overlord was very careful to assert his right to marry her to a man of his own selection or to one of whose loyalty he was thoroughly assured. So with the widow. She must obtain the consent of her liege lord to a second marriage under penalty of forfeiting her dower; and more often than not the overlord of a rich widow made a profitable bargain with the knight or squire who sought her hand and the management of her estates. By the opening of the twelfth century the extortions of the overlord with respect to the wards and widows under his control called forth a species of charter from Henry I. In this interesting document the King declared: " And if anyone of my barons

[1] *Ibid.*, pp. 252–3.
[2] Laboulaye, *Récherches sur la condition des femmes*, p. 276.

and men wish to give in marriage his daughter, or sister, or granddaughter, or kinswoman, let him talk to me about it! But I will neither take anything from him for this licence nor will I forbid him to give her, unless he should intend to unite her with my enemy. And if, my baron or other man being dead, his daughter remain his heir, I will give her with her land by the advice of my barons. And if, the husband being dead, his wife survive and be without children, she shall have her dower and marriage, and I will not give her to a husband, except according to her will." In closing, the King exhorts his barons to " forbear similarly towards the sons or daughters or wives of their men." [1]

The causes of the feudal disabilities just described are not far to seek. As the military tenure of land became common, the rights of women correspondingly decreased because feudalism valued the services of a man in fighting strength far more highly than the services of a woman within the home. Then, too, a suitor for the hand of some noble damsel often performed feudal services for his bride's father in order to obtain her dowry, and quite naturally such a suitor felt that he had earned certain rights in her property. Finally, it should be remembered that if a woman were permitted to hold large estates the overlord would feel by no means certain of receiving his feudal dues in military service. To quote from Mrs. Putnam's interesting study of *The Lady*, the lands of a mediæval knight were held " from his overlord on condition of the payment of rental in the form of military service. Every acre of ground was valued in terms of fighting men and only the knight in person could be sure of rallying the quota and producing them when required. If the knight died, in harness or in his bed, and left a widow with young children or a daughter as his sole heir, there was a good chance that the rent would not be paid. The overlord had a right, in view of his interests in the matter, to see that

[1] Wright, *Womankind in all Ages of Western Europe*, pp. 100, 101.

a fief should not be without a master; in other words, to marry as soon as might be the widow or the daughter of the deceased to some stout knight who was willing to take the woman for the sake of the fief. . . . In fact, it could be said of the lady as truly as of the serf that she ' went with the land.' She knew this full well herself. In the romance of *Girars de Viane* the Duchess of Bourgoyne came to the king, saying: ' My husband is dead, but of what avail is mourning? Give me a strong man to my husband, for I am sore pressed to defend my land! ' " [1]

Home Life in the Feudal Castle. — It must not be supposed that women under feudalism were always miserable and oppressed. Such was doubtless far from being the case. Nothing is more common in history than the cheerful acceptance by men and women alike of economic and social disabilities if these have long been customary and unchallenged. Then, too, it must be remembered that in the later centuries of feudalism the rude races of Western Europe were gradually taking on the customs and ideas of civilized people. With the decline in frequency of robber raids and devastating warfare, the knights and barons of feudal times had more opportunity to improve their manners in the presence of women, and to gain some appreciation for the gentler human qualities that tend to flourish in times of peace. This development in civilization was wholly favorable to the position of women in the family and was furthered by life in the feudal castle. The rude home of Anglo-Saxon days gave way, after the Norman invasion, to the fortress-castle of feudal times. Within this almost impregnable retreat the knight and his lady passed their days in an isolation so complete that it must often have driven the baron to take part in some robber foray or questionable adventure from sheer inactivity and boredom. But this very isolation of the family members tended to draw them together in a closer

[1] *Op. cit.*, pp. 116-17.

sympathy. "Never, in any other form of society," writes Guizot, "has a family, reduced to its most simple expression, husband, wife and children, been found so closely drawn together, pressed one against the other, separated from all other powerful and rival relations. . . . Now whenever man is placed in a certain position, the part of his moral nature which corresponds to that position is favorably developed in him. Is he obliged to live habitually in the bosom of his family, with his wife and children, the ideas and sentiments in harmony with this fact cannot fail to obtain a great empire over him. So it happened in feudal society."[1] But this is not the whole story. When the lord of the castle went forth with his retainers in quest of booty or in defence of his rights, his lady was left in sole charge of his fief. She was its manager in time of peace and its defender against attack. Such a situation of power and dignity must have had a potent influence in the development of the minds and characters of the high-born women of the Middle Ages. Just as in the period of the Roman conquests the responsible positions into which Roman matrons were thrust in the absence of their husbands tended to develop in them a sense of personal dignity and worth, so did similar conditions call forth like sentiments in the feudal lady. This enhanced self-esteem, when combined with real efficiency, must have contributed much toward elevating the position of women in the eyes of men. Then, too, women became heirs to vast estates in default of male issue. Indeed female owners of rich fiefs were not uncommon; and their position was one of relative freedom and power.

In the thirteenth and fourteenth centuries the status of women had greatly improved. Noble ladies who had been richly dowered at their marriage with lands and vassals became, at the death of their husbands, fairly independent agents. Such women, if allowed to remain unmarried,

[1] *Histoire de la Civilization en France*, tome III, pp. 343–6.

might be owners of castles and manors and as such might assume the rights and obligations of knights toward their overlords. As we have seen, the wife's position in the feudal castle had steadily become more honorable as sentiments and manners had improved. The very word " courtesy " refers to the manners prevailing in the court or family of the lord and lady. Outside the manor house and castle a very different code of conduct toward women was common for many centuries. Wright, in his study of *Womankind*, quotes a stanza from an ancient poem of the thirteenth century in which some troubadour ascribes the origin of courtesy to the influence of women.

> " There is reason enough why
> We ought to hold women dear;
> For we see happen very little
> Courtesy, except through women.
> Well know I that for the love of ladies
> The very clowns become courteous." [1]

Education of Pages and Daimoiselles. — Out of feudalism arose the curious custom by which the sons and daughters of lesser knights were sent to the castles of famous lords and churchmen to be educated. The lord of the castle took charge of the boys, who received a thorough training. First as pages, they were taught obedience and loyal service by the performance of certain humble tasks such as waiting on table, serving the ladies and caring for the horses and armor of the overlord. With this went education in gentle manners, such as would be pleasing to ladies, and in skilful riding. At the age of fourteen the page became a squire and for seven years more was trained in the arts of war and in personal attendance on his lord both at home and on the field of battle. When the youthful squire had been thoroughly imbued with the ideals of chivalry — loyalty to his church, his lord and his lady — he might, by acts of

[1] Wright, *Womankind in all Ages of Western Europe*, p. 161.

o

prowess, attain the coveted distinction of knighthood. For the knight of the Middle Ages was not born to this honor, but achieved it.

While the boys of the castle were thus being trained in manly pursuits and ideals, the girls were receiving the education deemed suitable for them at the hands of the lady of the castle. All the long day they sat in certain rooms of the castle, under the eye of the lady, learning how to spin and weave, to make clothing, to embroider girdles and garments, sometimes with marvellous pictorial scenes, and above all to weave the wonderful tapestries of the feudal period. In the late afternoon or early evening they repaired to the quaint conventional gardens surrounding the castle, where they were joined by the pages and squires. Very demure were these damsels of the thirteenth century, if we may judge by the illustrated manuscripts which have come down to us. Rather rigid manuals of etiquette for ladies began to be written about this time. One of the earliest French codes was entitled *Le Chastoiement des Dames*.[1] It exhorted young maidens to be modest in the presence of men, not to talk too much, to walk erect and not too fast lest they outstrip their companions, and above all not to turn to right or left when they walked abroad, or to let men kiss them. Such exhortations lead us to suspect that the very proper " daimoiselles " of the mediæval castle were, after all, much like the girls of the present day.

It is highly probable that most of these young women received some education in reading, writing and in the French language. But even if they were not so taught, the troubadours kept them well informed concerning the literature of their day, — the love-songs, romances and epics which extolled the charm of ladies and the prowess of knights. More-

---

[1] Written by Robert de Blois in the second third of the thirteenth century. See Hentsch, *De la Litterature didactique du moyen age s'addressant spécialement aux femmes*, pp. 75–80.

over, well-born women were trained as nurses and leeches throughout the Middle Ages. The young "daimoiselle" was very early schooled not to shrink from blood. She learned to bandage wounds, to prepare medicinal draughts from herbs and "to succour the men on whose lives her life depended." The romances of the period teem with references to women's skill in nursing and healing, to their knowledge of soothing ointments and herbs. Medical recipes have been handed down from the Middle Ages and testify to the importance of women as the physicians of the household.

Influence of Chivalry upon Family Life. — In the twelfth century, as we have seen, grew up that form of social discipline known as chivalry, which furnishes so rich a fund of material to the romancers of a later and more prosaic age. At its best chivalry gave to the rude nobles of the Middle Ages much-needed ideals of loyalty to Church and liege-lord, prowess in behalf of the weak and idealistic love and service of their chosen lady. To show courage and endurance of an almost superhuman order in the eyes of the maiden of his heart became the supreme ideal of many a lusty knight, and, it may truly be added, the "open sesame" to the affections of many a fair "daimoiselle." Indeed, one nobly born English maid boldly declared that she would wed no man who was not "handsome, courteous and accomplished, and the most valiant of his body in all Christendom." Her guardian thereupon proclaimed a tournament, with the damsel and her estates as the rich reward of the victor.

Much time was spent by the ladies of the castle in weaving girdles and ribbons to adorn the helmets of their chosen knights. Sometimes a maid of high degree condescended to lead her champion's horse by the bridle into the lists, where he proclaimed himself the true servant of love and beauty. Thus there grew up in those centuries of bloodshed and plunder, of oppression of the weak by the strong, the sentiment of romantic love. Rare indeed in pagan civilizations, almost unknown at the dawn of the Middle Ages, it was destined to spread over the whole of Christendom and to prove a great civilizing influence. For, when the lady comes to set a spiritual price upon her love and favor, when the knight willingly pays that price in brave devotion and courteous service, then love has risen from a purely sensual plane and has become an affair of the heart and the mind. In Provence, the home of poetry and romance, the ideal of romantic love was born; but it was rapidly carried over France and the rest of feudal Europe by the troubadours and minnesingers of the age. Indeed, love-making bade fair to become the most important business of knights and ladies; and the ability to write verses in praise of one's lady was the most highly prized accomplishment of the time. Jongleurs and troubadours were welcome guests in every castle and manor house, and often addressed their ardent yet conventional songs to the lady of the castle herself. In the twelfth and thirteenth centuries scholasticism was at its height and the organization of knowledge in accordance with the logic of Aristotle was the prevailing intellectual ideal. It is not surprising, then, to learn that formal codes of love were speedily drawn up for the use of all sighing lovers. Mrs. Putnam quotes from one of these works:

" Every lover is wont to grow pale at sight of the beloved.
" Virtue alone makes one worthy of love.
" Every action of the lover ends in thoughts of the beloved.
" The true lover cares for nothing save what he deems pleasant to the beloved." [1]

There are many pages of such declarations, followed by minute precepts concerning the manner and address of the lover. Absurd as all this may seem to the twentieth century mind, let us not ignore the tremendous significance of the chivalric movement in planting in the souls of men a

[1] *The Lady,* p. 142.

respect and consideration for womanhood, a willingness to serve women and some appreciation of the profound gulf between ideal love and brute lust.

So much for the brighter side of chivalry. That it has a darker aspect cannot be gainsaid. Married women, unhappy and lonely, finding little congeniality or companionship in the society of their husbands, claimed the right to love. Marriage, arranged by their parents, was a duty; love was a free gift and a joy. The former secured to the man a housekeeper; to the woman an assured social position; and to both the promise of offspring to maintain the family name and inherit the estates. But love implied a spiritual union, and its favors were the reward of service, the crown of true devotion. Often, however, this idealistic philosophy of affection must have given place to mere passing fancy or uncontrolled passion. Husbands were supposed to close their eyes to the amours of their wives and seek their true love in some lady to whom they owed no irksome marriage duty. A curious account of the devotion of a mediæval knight of the thirteenth century to a flint-hearted lady is found in the verses of one Ulrich von Lichtenstein. This Austrian noble, in his quaint poem *Frauendienst*,[1] describes his years of service of a noble lady, already married. For reasons not given this service carries him to Rome as a pilgrim and to Venice in the guise of a queen. Apparently the knight is really engaged in a series of aimless adventures which end in his visiting his lady in the garb of a leper. He sits at the castle gate by day and receives food from the hands of the lady's maidservants. At last his prayer is heeded and he is lifted by means of a bed coverlet to the oriel window of his lady's chamber. This he gladly enters and finds his beloved seated upon a bed and surrounded by her maids. But his hopes are dashed to earth when the lady meets his prayer for her love with the words: " Nay,

[1] *Service of Women.*

your courage may not aspire so far that I should lay you
here by my side. . . . My lord and master shall live ever
free from fear lest I should love another man than he; for
(even though I feared it not for God's honour and mine
own), yet my lord would keep close watch over me; . . ."
That Ulrich's love was not free from self-seeking appears
in his reply. Turning to his aunt, who had served as go-
between in the affair, he complains: " How shall this be?
If I get no profit of my coming, then shall I be crestfallen: . . ." Crestfallen he is, indeed, before his adventure is done, for his lady plays a sorry trick upon her amor-
ous knight. Having persuaded him to consent to be lowered
from the window on the condition that she hold his hand, she
then offers to kiss him. In the words of Ulrich, " I was so
overjoyed that I let go her hand: swift then was my downward journey; and had God not been with me, I had lightly
broken my neck." Some time later Ulrich casts off this
heartless lady and consoles himself with a more complaisant
love.[1]

Doubtless the fair " daimoiselles" of the castle as well as
the mistress were the inspirers of many romantic poems and
ardent love verses. Life in the mediæval castle admitted of
little privacy and encouraged extreme intimacy between the
sexes. The couch of my lord and lady was placed in the
main hall, separated only by curtains from this public assembling place. Pages and squires slept in one upper room
and "daimoiselles" in another; and visiting in bedrooms was a
common custom. In an atmosphere supercharged with sex-
feeling, with the loose song of the troubadour or the example
of friends to weaken her defences, many a girl must have
succumbed to the seduction of the youth with whom she
was daily brought into close contact. " Feudal society,"
says Wright, " was polished and brilliant but impure." He
might have added " insincere " ! For when love-making was

[1] Coulton, *A Mediæval Garner*, pp. 303-402.

reduced to codes and when the romantic verses of troubadours and minnesingers became conventionalized, then artificiality more and more vitiated the love affairs of knight and lady. The movement had become self-conscious, subject to detailed precepts and hence lacking in sincerity and genuineness. Yet, before it gave way to a new order, chivalry had accomplished much in giving men and women a vision of the meaning and worth of ideal love. As the centuries passed this love came to be more often joined with marriage, not opposed to it.

Home Life of the Common People under Feudalism. — Hitherto we have spoken only of the family life of lords and ladies — a life much more favorable to the growth of refinement of feelings and manners than that of their humbler vassals. Yet it is the working masses of the people that are the chief prop of any nation and form the most numerous part of its population. These plain folk were divided in the later Middle Ages into three classes: (1) the trading class, which lived in the rapidly growing towns; (2) the yeomen, or free farmers; (3) the serfs who were bound to the soil, and who owed clearly defined services in labor to their overlord. The last two classes lived in the country districts; and, whereas the serfs were often badly off, the yeomen owned their small farms and sometimes became so prosperous that poor knights sought their daughters in marriage as a means of repairing their fallen fortunes. The traders constituted the burgher or free citizen class of the towns and cities. By their own efforts they had passed through the training stages of apprentice and journeyman, had made a " masterpiece " in their craft and, if they had sufficient means, had paid the high fee which admitted them to full membership in their particular trade or industrial gild. Then they received the proud title of " Master " and their wives that of " mistress," from which terms have sprung our modern democratic titles " Mr." and " Mrs."

A wide chasm intervened between the burgher class and the society of the castle or manor. Although traders and skilled craftsmen represented an intelligent third estate and were rapidly becoming well-to-do, if not wealthy; although many had been educated in the burgher schools which sprang up during the thirteenth and fourteenth centuries in towns on the great trade routes; yet the speech of the men and women of this class was extremely coarse and their manners were almost wholly lacking in refinement. So much is made plain by the popular literature of the time. These folk tales and verses are invaluable for the light they throw on the life of the common people out of which they sprang. Sorry is the showing made by the burghers' wives of the fourteenth century, who are depicted as poorly educated, ill-tempered and gross in speech and manners. The men are likewise coarse and tyrannical in their treatment of their wives. Apparently the women were left much to themselves and were expected to remain at home immersed in household duties and in the endless task of spinning. By the fourteenth century the spinning-wheel had been invented, as is made plain by the illustrations of the period; but its use was confined to the well-to-do. Hence most thread and yarn were spun with the ancient hand spindle. Now this work could be carried on in groups as well as singly; so it is not surprising to learn that women took to " gadding about " and meeting with their neighbors for gossip, not infrequently in the taverns of the town. To this social dissipation their husbands often objected and enforced their prohibitions with smart blows. For the laws of the age permitted any husband to beat his wife into submission so long as he broke no bones nor destroyed an eye! Wright describes a scene in a French farce of the fourteenth century in which a group of husbands suddenly appear in a tavern where their wives have assembled. They try to drive the women home with angry words, and when these fail they resort to blows.

In a rage the wives resist and the scene ends in a general scuffle.[1]

But although popular literature reveals the gulf that exists between the coarse-mannered burgher or yeoman family, and the more refined society of the lord's court, yet there are evidences that already this gap was being bridged at not a few points. As the burghers gained in wealth they grew in power and influence and were able to wrest valuable rights and privileges from king and noble. They began to build substantial houses in the important trading towns; they travelled and became intelligent observers of men and affairs in other lands. Also they showed a disposition to send their daughters to convents to be educated and to dress both wives and daughters with a richness rivalling that of the ladies of the castle. These evidences of increasing wealth and refinement did not escape the notice of some of the impoverished knights of the period who had " squandered their substance in riotous living." Not a few of these wasteful gentlemen were driven to seek alliances with the daughters of wealthy burghers, trading their title and social position for the rich dowry of their brides. Needless to say such unions, entered into with contempt by the man and with discomfort and humiliation by the woman, were rarely happy. Yet they served in some measure to break down the rigid barriers between classes in mediæval times and gradually to acquaint the middle class with those more refined sentiments and manners which had come to flower in the feudal castles.

SELECTED BIBLIOGRAPHY

SOURCES.

    Coulton, G. *The Mediæval Garner*, pp. 383–402.

    Furnivall. *Child Marriages, Divorces and Ratifications* (*Early English Text Society*, 1897, pp. 56–85).

    The Babees Book (*Early English Text Society*, Vol. 32, pp. vii–xxii, lxiv–lxvi, 4–15).

[1] *Op. cit.*, pp. 269–70.

Haddan and **Stubbs.** *Councils and Ecclesiastical Documents* (Oxford, 1869–78), *Pœnitentiale of Theodore*, Vol. III, 173–213.

Paston Letters (Westminster, 1900).

Stubbs. *Select Charters*, p. 101.

Surtees Society Publications, Vol. LXIII.

Tacitus. *Germania* (Bohn Library, Vol. II).

Thatcher and **McNeal.** *Source Book for Mediæval History*, pp. 549–62, 592–602.

Thorpe, B. *Ancient Laws and Institutes of England* (Folio, London, 1840), Vol. I, pp. 11, 22–3, 123, 254–7.

SECONDARY WORKS.

Abbot Gasquet (Rev. Francis Aidan). *Christian Family Life in pre-Reformation Days* (Educational Briefs, No. 17, Phila. 1907).

Boesch, Hans. *Kinderleben in der deutschen Vergangenheit* (in *Monographien zur deutschen Kulturgeschichte*, Leipsic, 1900, pp. 6–40).

Bücher, Karl. *Industrial Evolution*, pp. 102–33.
    Die Frauenfrage im Mittelalter (1882), pp. 13 ff.

Buckstaff, Florence G. *Married Women's Property in Anglo-Saxon and Anglo-Norman Law* (in *Annals of Amer. Acad. of Polit. & Soc. Science* IV, 1893).

Encyclopedia of Religion and Ethics, article on the *Teutonic Family*, Vol. V, pp. 749–54.

Esmein, A. *Le mariage en droit canonique*, 2 vols., Paris, 1891, Vol. I, pp. 63–92 ; Vol. II, pp. 159 ff.

Gide. *Étude sur la condition privée de la femme*, pp. 388 ff.

Green, Mrs. J. R. *Town Life in the Fifteenth Century*, Vol. I, ch. I ; Vol. II, chs. I–IV.

Grimm. *Deutsche Rechtsalterthümer*, pp. 447 ff.

Gummere, F. B. *Germanic Origins* (1892), chs. III–VI.

Howard, E. G. *History of Matrimonial Institutions*, Vol. I, chs. VI–VIII.

Jeaffreson, J. C. *Brides and Bridals* (1872), Vol. II, pp. 299–325.

Lacroix, P. *Histoire de la vie privée*, Vol. II, pp. 1–60.

Lecky, W. E. H. *History of European Morals from Augustus to Charlemagne* (1881), Vol. II, pp. 340 ff.

McAnnally, D. R. *About the Wedding Ring* (in *Pop. Sci. Mo.*, Vol. XXXII, 1887, pp. 71–6).

Meray, A. *La vie au temps des cours d'amour*, 1876.

Pollock, Sir F., and **Maitland, F. W.** *The History of English Law* (1895), Vol. II.

Putnam, Emily. *The Lady*, pp. 106–45.

Reich, Emil. *Woman through the Ages*, Vol. I, pp. 170–99.

Schuster, E. J. *The Wife in Ancient and Modern Times* (1911), ch. VIII.

Smith and Cheetham, A. *Dictionary of Christian Antiquities*, 2 vols. (1875–80), article by Ludlow on *Arrhae*, Vol. I, pp. 142–4.

Sohm, Rudolph. *Das Recht der Eheschliessung* (Weimar, 1875), pp. 107–57.

Thrupp, John. *The Anglo Saxon Home* (1862), pp. 25–116.

Weinhold, Karl. *Die deutschen Frauen in dem Mittelalter*, 2 vols., Vienna, 1882.

Wright, Thomas. *The Homes of Other Days*, pp. 22–113.

History of domestic Manners and Sentiments in England during the Middle Ages, chs. 2, 3, 7, 8, 11, 12, 20.

Womankind in Western Europe from the earliest Times to the Seventeenth Century (1869).

Young, Ernest. *Anglo-Saxon Family Law* (in *Essays in Anglo-Saxon Law*, ed. by H. Adams, Essay IV).

CHAPTER VIII

THE FAMILY DURING THE RENAISSANCE

General Nature of the Renaissance. — The term " Renaissance " has been frequently criticised by contemporary historians, since it suggests a sudden outburst of creative energy, a rapid change in the interests, social, political, economic and intellectual of the European nations. Such a view is manifestly incorrect. Throughout the entire course of the Middle Ages the barbaric peoples of Western Europe were slowly learning the principles which govern civilized societies, — respect for property and law, consideration for the weak, and some regard for the finer, spiritual values of life. Very gradually the virile Lombards, Franks and Teutons, as well as the inhabitants of central and southern Italy, who were the pioneers of the new order, were educated by Church and State and the daily demands of economic and social life to the point where they may be said to have " caught up " with the civilizations of Greece and Rome. First in Italy, then in the northern countries, came an expansion of industry and trade, an influx of wealth, and with these the opportunities for leisure and the cultivation of mind and taste which commonly follow upon the solution of the more urgent economic problems of life. Hand in hand with industrial development went the establishment of stronger central governments — national, and in Italy, municipal. These governments sought in some measure to curb the lawlessness of the nobility, entrenched in castle and manor, to develop the resources of the country, to strengthen the respect for law and order and to protect the burgher or citizen class in its remarkable development of the trade and manufactures of the country. All these influences had been silently at work for centuries, and the Renaissance merely marks the beginning of the harvest which we are still gathering. Thus the intellectual and æsthetic awakening of the fifteenth and sixteenth centuries was the outcome of many coöperating forces, all tending to open the eyes of men to the wonder and complexity and interest of human nature and human life. "Humanism," or the study of the pursuits and activities proper to mankind, as the literatures of Greece and Rome revealed them, was the absorbing interest of the times. With such study there went a heightening of the sense of personal power and worth, a flowering of the spirit of individualism which revealed itself in a freedom of thinking and of living unheard of in an earlier and cruder age.

EFFECT OF THE MOVEMENT UPON THE STATUS OF WOMEN

Social Effects: Freer Social Life of the Courts. — Such a movement of intellectual and social emancipation could not leave the homes and the women untouched. So we are not surprised to learn that in some respects the condition of the women of the Renaissance was materially improved, while in others it remained practically unchanged until later influences had completed the work of emancipation. Certain it is that in France and Italy and to a less extent in Germany and England, married women of the ruling class were permitted a far greater degree of freedom in social intercourse than was countenanced in the Middle Ages. The delightful accounts of Castiglione, the famous author of *The Courtier*, written in the sixteenth century, reveal an ease, refinement and freedom in the social life of the Italian courts. Society in the castles and palaces of the princes of Italy and France was becoming cultured and brilliant, and was distinguished by the important rôle assigned to the women. They participated fully in witty or learned conversation; they set the standards in manners and morals; they were frequently as well educated in the classics and as familiar with the highly spiced romances of the period as the men. Nobles and princes pledged their devoted service to the fair ladies of the court and sought to meet their ideals of what is suitable and pleasing in conduct and speech. The tales of Boccaccio [1] vividly portray the free social relations of men and women of noble birth and reveal a licence in speech not sanctioned by cultivated society to-day. Indeed the period is noteworthy for its curious blending of the gross with the refined in conversation and manners. Castiglione and Boccaccio in Italy and Margaret of France [2] paint in glowing outlines these Renaissance " salons " in the courts of the ruling dukes and princes. Conversation was characterized by the quick stroke and parry of repartee and wit, and at times was overloaded with literary allusion.

Something of the liberty accorded to married women was extended to the marriageable girls of southern countries. In most of the cities of Italy they were not immured so closely in convent or home as had been the case during the century preceding. At thirteen or fourteen years of age, when their education was thought to have been completed, French girls of noble family were brought out into the world as in modern times. This was accomplished in two ways: either the damsel was sent to be lady-in-waiting to some woman of princely rank who kept a " school of manners " at her court, or she was launched into society at her mother's side. Old-fashioned folk and the more serious minded men, such as Vives, tutor to the Princess Mary of England, were horrified

---

[1] *The Decameron.*

[2] Sister of Francis I, King of France, a brilliant light among the intellectual women of France and author of a series of tales called the *Heptameron* which are modelled after the *Decameron* of Boccaccio.

at such laxness and insisted that girls be shut away from all social influences until their marriage. Such had been the custom in the " good old times " of their youth. But the tide in France and Italy was strongly setting against such strictness; and only Venice shut up its girls within convent walls, safely hidden from the eyes of men, until duly qualified suitors should carry away these nunlike maidens to adorn their homes.

In the northern countries of Germany and England the brilliant court circles of Italy and France were largely wanting. These nations were far slower in appropriating the elegancies and refinements of social life. The courts of Henry VIII and Edward VI showed few of the graces, intellectual and social, of the ducal courts of Mantua, Ferrara, Milan and Florence. Even in the golden days of great Elizabeth grossness of speech and manners was very general. And among the burgher or citizen class, not alone of England but of all countries, the refining influences of courtly speech and courtesy toward women very slowly filtered down. Yet we are told that as early as the fifteenth century English traders and artisans felt a growing sense of self-respect and dignity which tended to stir within them some aspiration for polite manners. From 1430 onward one *Book of Courtesy* after another appeared in England, for the use of gentlefolk and commoners alike. Clearly " manners " was becoming " a subject of serious anxiety," for might not the prosperous burgher enter the ranks of the gentleman by the judicious marriage of his son or daughter? [1] Some of these early manuals of etiquette have been collected and edited. A study of one of them, *The Young Children's Book*, [2] published about 1500, reveals clearly the need of such timely admonitions concerning manners at table and elsewhere. Children serving as pages at the tables of the nobility, or in their own fathers' castle, are warned not to spit

[1] See Green, *Town Life of the Fifteenth Century*, Vol. II, ch. 1.
[2] Furnivall, *The Babees Book*, p. 17.

over or on the table, nor to throw bones on the floor. Another work of slightly earlier date called *The Babees Book* (1475) urges boys not to scratch themselves at table, not to stuff their food into a full mouth or pick their teeth with their knives. They are earnestly enjoined also not to dip their meat in the common salt-cellar, or put their knives in their mouths or leave the table without washing their hands.[1] All these manuals reveal a growing regard for the decencies of life, a consideration for other people, which promises much for the gradual refining of life in the home as in the court.

Platonism and Platonic Love. — A study of the social changes wrought by the Renaissance would be incomplete without some mention of the profound influence of the study of Plato upon the prevailing conceptions of love between man and woman. The platonic doctrine that love aspires toward the beautiful, and by the stepping-stones of earthly loveliness is led toward that eternal and perfect beauty and goodness which is God Himself, found eager followers among the more refined spirits of the age. Even Cardinal Bembo espoused the doctrine and gave to it a marvellous impetus by his dignified plea for a more spiritual love between the sexes untainted by carnal desire. By the end of the fifteenth century we are told that " every man of polish and refinement had selected a lady and become her servant." [2] Women, especially, were profoundly attracted by the new doctrine. Married at an early age, as all of them were, to men commonly quite unknown to them, many young women who had become mothers at sixteen remained ignorant of love. Neither their hearts nor their minds had been won by the husbands and masters whom they respectfully addressed as " Sir," while they signed their wifely letters your " wife and subject " or " your humble, obedient handmaid and friend." To such

---

[1] *Babees Book*, pp. 4 ff.; see also *Stans Puer ad Mensam, ibid.*, pp. 27–33.

[2] Boulting, *Women in Italy*, p. 27.

women, disillusioned and hungry of heart, the theory of celestial love, free from all fleshly dross, made a powerfully moving appeal. Margaret of France, and Elizabetta, Duchess of Urbino, with many other noble ladies, became leaders in the cult of spiritual love. De Maulde calls these women " unhappy dilettanti of love " [1] who strove with sincere earnestness to pass from earthly passion to a union of mind and soul with the beloved.

Yet, although some women, like the noble Vittoria Colonna, friend of Michelangelo, passed through the ordeal of platonic love with unscorched garments, there were others who paid the price of playing with fire. The literature of the period reveals great laxness in morals no less than worthy ideals of purity and love. Doubtless platonism appealed less to men than to women, and its doctrines in many instances were utilized by the ambitious and the empty-headed as a means of pushing themselves forward in the world by gaining the good will of court ladies. Then, too, there must have been a goodly number of avowed platonists among men who found the doctrine of celestial love too ethereal for their complete acceptance. Such half-hearted devotees would warmly subscribe to the words of a young noble at the court of Margaret of France :

" Madam, when our mistresses stand on their dignity in halls and assemblies, seated at their ease as our judges, we are on our knees before them ; we lead them out to dance with fear and trembling ; we serve them so sedulously as to anticipate their requests ; we seem to be so fearful of offending them and so desirous of doing them service that those who see us have pity on us, and very often esteem us more simple than foolish. . . . But when we are by ourselves, and love alone doth mark our looks, we know right well that they are women and we are men, and then the name of liege lady is converted into sweetheart, and the name of servitor into

[1] *The Women of the Renaissance*, p. 186.

R

lover." [1] So the courtly service of love was soon degraded from a worthy cult into a fashionable pastime. In the sixteenth century there arose Platonic Academies which were in many respects nothing but courts of love. " Vanity strutted there and the devotees of love, in suitable Court-dress exchanged Petrarchistic wailings before admiring princesses and their maids of honour at the palace." [2]

The resemblance that platonism bears to the earlier movement of the twelfth and thirteenth centuries, in which chivalrous love was exalted into a philosophy of life and codified into a legal system, is clearly apparent. Both movements originated in idealistic feeling that prompted its subjects to cultivate the more spiritual phases of love. Both degenerated into an artificiality in many cases insincere and fantastic. But it should not be overlooked that platonism, like its forerunner, did create within the souls of the more noble-minded men and women a realization of the true nature of ideal affection. Little by little men and women, here and there, came to see that there was really no necessary antagonism between love and marriage; that, although marriage might be, for the majority, a contract of a social and economic nature, into which love did not enter, yet for a few more fortunate spirits it might be the consummation of a pure, romantic passion and thus the crown of life. Castiglione voices this feeling when he makes one of his courtiers say : " If my Court Lady be unmarried and must love, I wish her to love some one whom she can marry ; nor shall I account it an errour if she shows him some sign of love. . . ." [3] This was an advanced position for a fifteenth century writer to take, one not at all in accord with the prevailing idea that love and marriage were incompatible. The actual situation is bluntly described by Boccaccio. " Everyone will concede," says this rare teller of tales, " that he has not a

[1] *Heptameron*, Tale 40, and *Prologue* of first day; quoted in De Maulde, *op. cit.*, p. 351.

[2] Boulting, *op. cit.*, p. 33.   [3] *The Courtier* (Scribner's, 1901), p. 225.

wife to his mind, but one that fortune has bestowed." For many generations the popular proverbs about women reflected the low esteem in which they were held by all but the most enlightened. It was an old saying in Bologna that "Woman is paradise for the body, purgatory for the soul, hell for the purse;" and this proverb fairly reflected the feeling of the mass of men concerning the wives and mothers of the race. Yet the Court poets who sang the beauty and purity of women, who praised their gifts of mind and soul, not only stimulated many noble ladies to make themselves worthy of this high praise, but actually did accomplish something to elevate the conception of womanhood. So the seeds were sown in Italy which slowly ripened to the harvest of the nineteenth century.

Effects of the Renaissance upon the Legal Status of Women. Dowry, Dower and Property Rights. — If the social position of the more favored women was raised during the Renaissance, if they were educated and held in higher esteem, it yet remains true that little advancement was made in freeing them from the financial and legal disabilities of the Middle Ages. Very generally girls were regarded as eligible mates in proportion to the size of the dowry they could bring their husbands. Haggling by the parents over the essential matter of dowry was as open and unashamed as in any business transaction of the day. In Italy, at least, the wife's dowry was conveyed to the home of the husband immediately after the marriage ceremony had been performed, and a receipt was thereupon given for it. The management and profits of the dowry belonged exclusively to the husband, who quite often employed it as capital in increasing his business. He was required by law, however, to provide for the restoration of the dowry to his wife in case of divorce or his own death. In the latter event the dowry was held by the wife *in trust only* for her children. In Italy the wife's dowry seems to have been fairly well protected. The husband who squandered this property might be legally sued and required to restore not only the orginal amount but some-times a threefold sum.   On the other hand the custom of set-ting aside a definite portion of the husband's property for the life use of his widow, gained no foothold in Italy.   In France and England, however, the law required that one-third of the husband's real and personal property should descend to the wife after his death.   This represents the " dower " of common law.   At the beginning of the sixteenth century in England, however, the earlier custom of granting the wife one-third of the husband's *personal* property had fallen into disuse in many parts of the country.   This meant that in the larger portion of England a testator was no longer bound to leave his widow and children any share of his movable goods and chattels, but might bequeath all his personal property to whomever he wished.[1]

In England a married woman possessed absolutely no prop-erty at her own disposal.   In one respect only was the rigor of this law at all relaxed.   If property were left to a *trustee* in trust for a married woman and designed for " her sole and separate use, equity [2] would recognize this trust, and prevent the husband from dealing with the property in a manner detri-mental to the wife's interest."   When the property was held by a trustee for the wife's benefit, although not given to her for her sole and separate use, equity " *was bound to follow the law and allow the husband to claim it for his own;* yet it would not assist him in his claim, unless he agreed to make an ade-quate provision for her out of the fund." [3]   Even the personal effects, clothing, jewels, money, furniture, etc., which the wife owned before marriage or which were bequeathed to her afterwards, became the absolute property of her husband. However, the bed, apparel and ornaments of a widow, known

[1] Cleveland, *Woman under the English Law*, p. 173.

[2] Equity is a system of law designed to supplement and correct common law, especially where the latter seems rigorous and unjust.

[3] Cleveland, *op. cit.*, p. 108.   Italics mine.

as her " paraphernalia," were restored to her *if her husband had not sold them during his lifetime*.

From these provisions and others, which denied the wife the right of contract and suit and the right to bequeath property by will without the consent of her husband, it is evident that the legal personality of the English wife was almost wholly merged in that of her husband. Nor was this condition peculiar to England. In Italy, although girls were declared of age at fourteen they could transact no legal business without the assent of both father and husband, or of their trustees. Women in many Italian states were also deprived of the right to enter a lawsuit in their own names or to appear in person at the trial. The justification for this widespread attitude must be sought in history. During the lawless centuries of the Middle Ages, when brute fighting strength was a valuable asset in the defence of property and personal rights, women were in real need of the protection which fathers, brothers and husbands could afford them. In such periods the qualities of women as peace-lovers, home-makers and dispensers of charity always tend to be rated far below their real social value when weighed in the balance with physical force. So women came to be regarded as weak dependents upon father or husband; and the laws and customs respecting women naturally reflected popular sentiment. Then, too, it was generally believed that no association of human beings engaged in a common enterprise and life could possibly be happy and successful unless one firm hand were at the helm. In such a case there could be no division of authority. Even when civilization had advanced to a stage of comparative peace and order, as during the Renaissance, the ancient laws and customs were maintained for centuries thereafter, chiefly because they were the customary ways of meeting certain situations, and thus received the sanction of long usage.

THE CHURCH IN ITS RELATION TO MARRIAGE

The various streams of the Renaissance movement in the North rather speedily combined in one vigorous current of religious revolt called the Protestant Reformation. Luther in Germany, Calvin in France and Switzerland and John Knox in Scotland sounded the trumpet of revolt and led the masses of the people in their attack upon the abuses that had grown up within the Church. The result was apparently inevitable, — a complete breaking away from the Mother Church and the establishment of several Protestant sects instead of the former unified body of Christians. From the sixteenth century onward " the Church " is a term which may apply to the Roman Catholic communion, or to the growing body of Lutherans in Germany, of Calvinists in Switzerland, Holland and Scotland or of Anglicans in England, where the break with the Roman Church was more gradual than in Germany and was accomplished without an open revolt on the part of the English people.

The Roman Church and the Family. — In the previous chapter[1] reference was made to the fact that the Church, in taking the stand that betrothals in words of the present tense (*per verba præsenti*) constituted valid although not legal marriage, had prepared some very perplexing problems for itself. In the twelfth century Peter the Lombard had declared[2] that spousals (*sponsalia*) *per verba præsenti* (*i.e.*, in words of the present tense, as " I *take* thee," etc.) constituted a valid and binding marriage, whereas *sponsalia per verba de futuro* (*i.e.*, in words of the future tense, as " I *will take* thee," etc.) had no such binding power. This famous Schoolman is, then, largely responsible for the fact that the Church was caught in a mesh of verbal distinctions which had deplorable results. Men and women (or boys and girls) who contracted unions in words of the present tense were held to be as indissolubly bound to-

---

[1] See pp. 216–17.　　　　[2] In his *Sentences*, Book IV.

gether as if the marriage had occurred within the church before witnesses, had been duly recorded and had been consummated by physical union. Of course a marriage thus loosely
contracted, with witnesses few or none, could be easily dis-
avowed. Dishonorable men had no difficulty in finding persons to declare in the proper ecclesiastical court that they had
never really espoused the woman, but had only formed an
illicit relationship with her. Moreover, clandestine marriage
increased in frequency from the twelfth century onward. Such
unions were common in Holland, Portugal and Italy, as well as
in Germany and England. " So severe," writes Howard, " were
the provisions of Swiss legislation to check this evil, toward the
close of the Middle Ages, that even the innocent were deterred
from appealing to the courts to enforce their matrimonial
rights." [1] Endless difficulties arose with respect to abandoned
wives and children, and the Bishops' courts of the fifteenth and
the first half of the sixteenth century were kept busy adjudi-
cating such matrimonial cases. A further difficulty was
created by the fact that the difference between the present
and the future tense is not sharply defined in everyday speech
either in German or English. Martin Luther, with his wonted
bluntness and energy, has pointed out this fact: " They [2] have
played a regular fool's game," he writes, " with their *verbis
de præsenti vel futuro*. With it they have torn apart many
marriages which were valid according to their own law, and
those which were not valid they have bound up. . . . Indeed
I should not myself know how a churl [3] would or could betroth
himself *de futuro* in the German tongue, for the way one be-
troths himself means *per verba præsenti*, and surely a clown
knows nothing of such nimble grammar as the difference between *accipio* and *accipiam;* [4] therefore he proceeds according
to our way of speech and says: ' I will have thee,' ' I will

[1] Howard, *History of Matrimonial Institutions*, Vol. I, p. 346.
[2] The authorities of the Roman Church.　　　　[3] A countryman.
[4] *Accipio*, — I take; *accipiam*, — I will take.

take thee,' ' thou shalt be mine.' Thereupon ' yes ' is said at once without more ado." [1]

At the Council of Trent in the middle of the sixteenth century the Roman Church cut the Gordian knot of this perplexing problem in one clean stroke. This famous Council decreed that, whereas all marriages previously contracted by mere verbal consent of the parties and without parental sanction should be held valid, thenceforward all marriages not celebrated in the presence of a priest and two or three witnesses should be null and void. By this decree the Roman Church freed itself from the evils of clandestine and irregular marriages and took a decisive forward stride toward making marriage a public concern. Indeed a step toward publicity had been taken as early as 1215, when Pope Innocent III required that the banns of marriage be three times published in the Church before the ceremony was performed. But this decree was not rigidly enforced, although the marriage rituals of the Renaissance period all contain careful directions for asking and publishing banns. The Council of Trent, while decreeing that publication of banns be everywhere enforced, did not take the further step of making such publication essential to a valid marriage. Hence the nobility had little difficulty in obtaining a license from the bishop, dispensing with the obligation of publishing their marriage banns.[2]

With respect to divorce, the Church maintained the position which it had held during the greater part of the Middle Ages. Since marriage was a mystical sacrament ordained of God, it was an indissoluble union. Only in cases where the contracted parties were within the numerous forbidden degrees of kinship or were " spiritually related " could a *divortium a vinculo* be granted. This was in reality not a divorce but an *annulment* of a union held by the Church never to have really existed. Furthermore, in cases where adultery, deser-

[1] Luther, *Von Ehesachen* in his *Werke XIII*, 102; quoted in Howard, *op. cit.*, Vol. I, p. 341.   [2] See Howard, *op. cit.*, p. 361.

tion, impotency or extreme cruelty could be proven, the ecclesiastical courts granted the plaintiff a *divortium a mensa et thoro* which was only a legal separation. It has been pointed out in a previous chapter that during the Middle Ages annulments of disappointing marriages could be obtained by persons of wealth and influence without great difficulty. It is true that Henry VIII was unable to secure such a dissolution of his marriage with Katherine of Aragon; yet his sister Margaret Tudor was markedly successful in her "matrimonial adventures." Not only did she obtain papal sanction for her marriage with James IV, to whom she was related within the forbidden degrees, but she secured a divorce from her second husband on the trumped-up plea that James IV had lived for three years after the battle of Flodden Field and so was alive at the time of her second marriage.[1] But from the time of the Renaissance to the present the Roman Church has enforced its view of the indissoluble character of a true marriage with great consistency.

Attitude of the Anglican Church toward Clandestine Marriages. — The Established Church of England unfortunately took no such sensible stand against irregular marriages *per verba præsenti* as had the Roman Catholic Church. Hence England suffered from all the evils attendant on such marriages until the middle of the eighteenth century. Interesting evidence of the binding character of mere verbal contracts in words of the present tense is furnished in a rare old English book, *Of Spousals*, published in 1686. In this quaint work the author declares that in his own day spousals *de præsenti* were everywhere valid:

" But that woman, and that man, which have contracted Spousals *de præsenti:* as, (I do take thee to my Wife) and (I do take thee to my Husband) cannot by any agreement dissolve these Spousals but are reputed for very Husband and Wife . . .; and therefore if either of them should in fact

[1] *Ibid.*, Vol. II, p. 58.

proceed to solemnize matrimony with any other person, con-
summating the same by Carnal Copulation, and Procreation
of Children, This Matrimony is to be dissolved as unlawful,
the Parties marrying to be punished as Adulterers, and their
Issue in danger of Bastardy." [1]

Further evidence of the evils resulting from these loose
verbal contracts is furnished by Furnivall in a valuable work
on *Child Marriages, Divorces* and *Ratifications.* The evidence
consists of depositions made in trials before the Bishop's court
and the Mayor's court in Chester 1561–66. This collection
abounds in illustrations of the frequency of marriages *per
verba præsenti,* especially among the common people. It
also shows how numerous were the cases that were brought
before the Bishop's court, either for the dissolution of such
unions or for their enforcement when husband or wife refused to acknowledge the marriage.[2]

As early as 1540 Henry VIII had attempted to right this
evil by a statute which was unfortunately repealed in the reign
of Edward VI. Of this statute Swinburne writes as follows:
" Worthily, therefore, was that Branch of the Statute of noble
King Henry the Eighth, establishing (That marriages contracted and solemnized in the Face of the Church, and consummate with bodily knowledge, or fruit of Child or Children,
should be judged and taken for lawful and indissoluble, notwithstanding any Precontract of Matrimony, not yet consummate with bodily knowledge, etc.) worthily, I say, and upon
good ground was this Branch of that Statute (established by
the Father) repealed and made void by his gracious Son King
Edward the Sixth, for Spousals *de præsenti* though not consummate, be in truth and substance very Matrimony and
therefore perpetually indissoluble except for Adultery. . . ."
Yet, in spite of the binding character of such contracts, the
writer goes on to say that Spousals " *de præsenti* be destitute

---

[1] Swinburne, *Of Spousals* (ed. 1686), p. 13.
[2] *Early English Text Society,* 1897, Vol. 118, pp. 56–85.

of many legal effects wherewith Marriage solemnized doth abound. . . ." [1] These effects were, briefly, that such a contract not followed by the ceremony of marriage, cost a woman her right of dower in her husband's lands and rendered her children illegitimate. With respect to the latter point, however, the law of the English Church was not in harmony with that of the State, as Swinburne makes clear:

" Concerning their issue, true it is, that by the Canon Law, the same is lawful; But by the Laws of this Realm their Issue is not lawful, though the Father and the Mother should afterwards celebrate Marriage in the Face of the Church. Likewise concerning Lands by the Canon Law, the foresaid Issue may inherit the same, . . . But it is otherwise by the Laws of this Realm, for as the Issue is not legitimated by subsequent Marriage, no more can he inherit his Father's Land; . . ." [2]

Now, since Church law in England rested upon the sanction of the State, it was the statutes of the realm that were followed in all cases where disagreement arose. Hence many English children were rendered bastards, whose parents were held to be bound together by a verbal contract well-nigh as firmly as if their marriage had been duly solemnized by a clergyman. Nor could these children be made legitimate by the marriage of their parents after their birth. Clearly the canon law was more just in this regard than the civil statutes. In Scotland the ruling of the Church in respect to this matter was followed as it is at the present time. Hence the subsequent marriage of parents in Scotland legitimatized their children born out of wedlock.

Not only did the Anglican Church hold two persons contracted in words of the present tense to be married, but the ecclesiastical laws could force the parties thus contracted to solemnize the marriage. Should one of the parties refuse so to do, " he or she so refusing may for his Contumacy or disobedience therein, be Excommunicated: . . ." If after

[1] *Op. cit.*, pp. 14, 15.   [2] *Ibid.*, p. 223.

forty days, the party still remained obdurate, the Ordinary [1]
might crave " the aid of the Secular Power, Whereupon a Writ
de Excommunicatio Capiendo, is to be directed to the Sheriff,
for the apprehension of the Body of the same Party Excommunicated; who being apprehended by virtue thereof, is to be kept
in Prison, without Bail or Maniprise, until he or she have
humbled themselves and obeyed the Monition of the Ordinary, . . . " This being done, and the Church being satisfied, the Ordinary is to absolve the party and secure his release.[2]

**Views of Luther and the Protestant Reformers concerning
Marriage.** — It is clear enough that the English Church did
not greatly change the *form* of marriage as a result of the
Reformation, and such was the case in Germany. But a profound change of view was accomplished throughout the
Protestant world with respect to the *nature* of marriage. No
longer was it regarded as a mystical sacrament, but rather
as a civil contract necessary to society and blessed of God.
Luther is not always clear on this point, for he goes so far as
to speak of marriage as a " most spiritual " status, " ordained
and founded " by God himself. In the view of the great
German reformer, marriage and the family constitute the very
foundation stones of human society which would " fall to
pieces " without them. Yet this profound reverence for the
married state did not preclude Luther from viewing it as a
" temporal business " with which the Church should not interfere, but rather should " leave to each City and state its
own usages and customs in this regard." [3] On the whole
Luther is distinctly favorable to the view that marriage is a
civil matter to be regulated and perhaps celebrated by state
authorities; hence, as Howard has pointed out, he must be

---

[1] A bishop or his deputy acting as an ecclesiastical judge.
[2] Swinburne, *op. cit.*, pp. 231–2.
[3] Luther, *Preface to the Short Catechism* (1529); quoted in Howard, *History
of Matrimonial Institutions*, Vol. I, p. 387.

regarded as the most influential agency in bringing about civil marriage.[1] Doubtless Luther was moved to take this ground by his belief that great evils grew out of Church jurisdiction in marriage, the most flagrant being the abuses connected with the enforced celibacy of priests. Also he held, like many others in his day, that ecclesiastical jurisdiction had produced the whole intolerable burden and perplexity of clandestine marriages, since it was the ruling of a Churchman that had elevated contracts *per verba præsenti* into valid matrimony. Because he clearly saw that the clergy were not true to their vows of celibacy and that many " lived in concubinage in return for a yearly tax paid to the bishop," [2] Luther took the radical step of declaring the right of the clergy to marry, — a right that he claimed to be based alike upon nature and the Scriptures. Not only did he preach this doctrine, but in 1525 he boldly acted upon it by marrying Katherine von Bora, a nun escaped from the Cistercian convent of Nimbschen. Little by little, as his followers recovered from the first shock produced by his action, they tended to accept the theory of the right of priests to marry. Somewhat later this came to be the view in England, where, in 1548, the obstacles to the marriage of the clergy were removed by statute law, even though the act declared that " it were most to be wished that they would willingly endeavour themselves to a perpetual chastity." [3] The statute was repealed, however, in the reign of Catholic Mary (1553-8), and was not reënacted under Elizabeth, who had great distaste for the theory of a married clergy. A letter written by a married clergyman to the Archbishop of Canterbury in 1559 throws light on the unhappy position in which many married priests found themselves at this time. " The Queen's Majesty will wink at it [*i.e.* the statute above referred to] but not stablish

---

[1] *Ibid.*, p. 388.
[2] For this whole discussion see Howard, *op. cit.*, Vol. I, pp. 386-9.
[3] *Statutes at Large*, Vol. II, p. 283.

it by law, which is nothing else but to bastard our children." [1]
It was not until 1603 that the statute of Edward VI was
reënacted by James I in response to a petition addressed to
him by numerous Puritans.

An important reform accomplished by the Protestant Revolt, not only in Germany but in all Protestant lands, was the
sweeping away of many of the impediments to marriage established by the Roman Church of the Middle Ages. Quite
generally it was agreed that all barriers due to so-called " spiritual kinship " should be broken down and that persons should
be permitted to marry within the third degree of consanguinity. Unfortunately, both Germany and England tended to
find impediments to marriage in the ancient Levitical law ; [2]
and this led, in England, to those acrimonious controversies
over the right to marry a deceased wife's sister which have
been unhappily handed down to the present time. Moreover, despite the more liberal views of Luther on this matter,
Protestants in all lands at first followed the ruling of the
Mother Church, which positively forbade marriages between
Christians and non-Christians. Such unions were called
" mixed marriages " ; and German literature concerning marriage abounds in bitter discussions of the disadvantages attending such unions.

BETROTHAL AND MARRIAGE

Prevailing Customs. — As in the Middle Ages, marriage was
preceded during the Renaissance by the solemn contract of
betrothal. The student of the period is particularly impressed
by four current ideas and customs with respect to betrothal
and marriage : (1) The popular sentiment concerning the nature of marriage ; (2) the predominant part played by the
parents in arranging the marriage ; (3) the early age at which
betrothal and marriage ceremonies were performed ; (4) the

[1] Howard, Vol. I, p. 396.   [2] See *Leviticus* XVIII, 6-19.

view of betrothal as a binding contract second only to marriage in its indissolubility. Concerning the first it may be said that there was little advance over the later Middle Ages in the esteem in which marriage was held. It was still looked upon as a convenient social arrangement for securing the perpetuation of the race and advancing the social or financial status of the contracting parties. Not only was romantic love usually unassociated with marriage, since the bride and groom quite commonly had never seen each other previous to their betrothal, but it was a general belief that the two had nothing in common. " Marriage," wrote Margaret of France in the sixteenth century, " is not a perfect state; let us be satisfied with wisely accepting it for what it is, a makeshift, but reputable." [1] A social writer has further described the marriage of the Renaissance age as " a business partnership, a grave material union of interests, rank and social responsibilities, sanctified by the close personal association of the partners. . . . To mingle with it love, the absolute, great enthusiasm of heart or intellect, was to lay up for oneself disasters, or at least certain disappointment. No passion can survive the humdrum, the monotony, the deadweight of matrimonial experience, and what marriage can hold out against passion? A certain equality is the rule of passion; what it demands is a perfect union between two persons who are mutually attracted and whom there is nothing to keep apart. What would become of married life under these conditions without one to give law to the other? In regard to marriage, the time-honored principle, rigorous though protective, was this: the husband ought always to take the helm, imbecile, madman or rake though he be; woman is born to obey, man to command." [2] Such was the prevalent view of the marriage relation in all the countries of Western Europe during and long after the Renaissance period. It is not surprising, then, to read the following contemporary

[1] *Heptameron*, Tale 40, quoted in De Maulde, *op. cit.*, p. 49.
[2] De Maulde, *op. cit.*, pp. 22, 23.

account of a court marriage in England so late as the seventeenth century.

" On Thursday was a marriage at Court betwixt Lord Mandeville's eldest son and Susan Hill, a kinswoman of the Lord Marquis.[1] They were married by the Lord Keeper in the King's Bed-chamber, who took great joy in it, and blessed the Bride with one of his shoes. The principal motive of this Match, besides fair words and promises, was the paying back of £10,000 or security for it, of that sum the Lord President [Lord Mandeville, the groom's father] lent when he was made Lord Treasurer; and some say the Lord Marquis ties his own land for £5000 more; and withal he, [*i.e.*, the groom] is to have a table of ten dishes and bouche [2] at Court (as they call it), which began the day of the Marriage, till some better place fall to his lot. Indeed he had need of some amends, having forsaken a Match of £25,000 certain with the Lady Craven's daughter, that was designed and reserved for him." [3]

So these two pawns, the young Mandeville and the girl relative of the Duke of Buckingham, are married to make good a debt owed the groom's father; and the young man receives the condolences of his friends for giving up a better marriage bargain. Only among the poorer classes, who dance on the village greens and frolic together in holiday seasons, is there any free choice in marriage. And even here it is in some degree restricted by financial considerations.

The second noteworthy fact concerning Renaissance marriages is the controlling part taken by the parents in all the arrangements. There was general agreement that young girls, and, perhaps to a somewhat less degree, young men, must be prudent and not insist on marrying to please themselves if they would escape the penalties of such outrageous

---

[1] Later Duke of Buckingham, favorite of James I.

[2] *Bouche* means victuals, eating, living.

[3] Nichols, *The Progresses . . . of King James I* (collected from MSS. and rare papers), Vol. IV, p. 805.

folly. Marriage was a serious affair to be discreetly, not to say shrewdly, arranged by the parents and relatives of those concerned. Not only did all men hold this view, but it seems to have been the expressed opinion of some of the most able women of the time, such as Margaret of Valois and Anne of France, eldest daughter of Louis XI. The future husband of Lady Jane Grey, a girl of sixteen, was presented to her by her parents with not a word of warning, and she was informed that their commands concerning him would be duly communicated to her. Very rarely did a girl rebel against the matrimonial plans of her parents. Yet in 1579 Margherita Gonzaga, who had been married at sixteen to Ercole II of Ferrara, an elderly man, twice widowed, wrote to her father concerning her sister's contemplated marriage: " Having heard that a marriage is being arranged between La Polisena and Gian Francesco Mainoldo, I am anxious to write four words to your highness, and I earnestly implore you not to allow her to be married against her will. Your highness will recollect very well that when I was at Mantua and was asked if I believed she would be content, I replied that the Gonzaga knew how to endure what might be insupportable to others." [1]

The docility shown by most girls in respect to their marriage arrangements is doubtless due in some measure to the severity of home discipline. But it must not be forgotten that with the decline of monastic fervor and the closing of many convents in England and Germany, the only career open to women was marriage. Not to marry meant complete social failure, and a galling dependence upon one's family for the whole of one's days. No wonder most young women shuddered at the thought of such a life and gladly chose the lesser evil.

The third custom which strikes the student of this period with peculiar force is that of child betrothals and marriages. Among powerful families, desirous of enhancing their social and political prestige, or of increasing their wealth, such contracts

[1] Quoted in Bculting, *Women in Italy*, p. 58.

S

were very common. Children of high rank were sometimes betrothed by their relatives before they had left the cradle. Occasionally go-betweens were employed by noble Italian families to inform the relatives of a girl child of the most eligible young men in the marriage market and to negotiate the betrothal. Such betrothals often occurred when the girl was only three or four years old. The talented poetess Vittoria Colonna was betrothed to the Marquis of Pescara at this age, although the marriage did not take place until she was seventeen. This was rather unusual, as many betrothals were followed by marriage when the girl was twelve years old, this being the legal, marriageable age in most countries of Europe. In vain did physicians of the period point out that for the sake of the health of the wife and the vigor of the offspring, the consummation of marriage should be deferred until girls had reached their sixteenth year. But most parents were anxious to get their girls off their hands early in life, for it was regarded as mildly disgraceful to have a daughter unmarried or unbetrothed at sixteen or seventeen. Furthermore, since the girl's whole function in life was held to be wifehood and motherhood, and since most of her days would be spent in the home of her husband, parents rather sensibly held the opinion that a girl should go to her future home while she was in the plastic and impressionable age, before habits of thought and conduct had become definitely formed, so that she could not so easily be shaped to her husband's will. And be it remembered that quite often the husband was not of the same age as his girl-bride. Young men demanded a period of freedom before thrusting their heads into the noose of matrimony. Thus it came about that men of thirty-five were betrothed to girls of fourteen, after their wild oats had been gayly sown. At times, however, boys as well as girls were betrothed in their early childhood. In a work already cited on *Child-Marriages* . . . *in the Diocese of Chester*, A.D. 1561–6,[1] Furnivall has col-

[1] *Early English Text Society*, Vol. 118 (1897).

lected testimony, in trials conducted in the Bishop's court and entries from the Mayor's books, concerning betrothals and marriages in the English town of Chester. These all go to show that in England, as in Italy and France, children were betrothed and married by their parents when mere infants. Thus we find the case of one Elizabeth Hulse, married at four years of age to George Hulse, aged eleven, and seeking a divorce in the Bishop's court on the ground that " she could never fansie or cast favour to hym, nor never will do ; . . ." The children were married in the chapel of Knotisford and on the girl being asked how she, a mere infant, knew of this fact, " she sais she knowis not, but bie the sayenge of her father & mother, forther, she sais, she was married to hym biecause her frendes thought she shuld have had a lyvinge bie hym ; . . ."[1] This unfortunate marriage was never consummated, since both parties proved obstinately reluctant to carry out the contract ; and it was probably annulled by the ecclesiastical court. A similar case was that of Roland Dutton, married to Margaret Stanley when he was nine years of age and she but five. As was customary the two children lived apart after the marriage until the age of puberty. When the time approached for the consummation of the union, the boy declared " that he would refuse to take the said Margaret to his wief ; and that he would not consent to the said marriage which was solempnized in his minoritie. . . ." Apparently in England, in the sixteenth century, children dared to assert their will against that of their parents when it came to marriage with an unpromising mate. But these cases were doubtless exceptions to the general custom of meek compliance. Quite often the court was appealed to for ratification of a child marriage when the parties had attained a " ripe " age and desired to live together as husband and wife. Such a case is that of John Starkie and Alice Dutton, married four years previous to the action for ratification, at

[1] *Op. cit.*, p. 42.

ten years of age, and now prepared to assume the duties of man and wife![1]

The fourth custom that impresses the student of the Renaissance period is the binding character of the betrothal contract. This, of course, was a heritage from the Middle Ages when betrothal was regarded as a form of marriage and the unchastity of the engaged girl was punished as severely as adultery. Espousal or betrothal was a ceremonious contract, broken only with difficulty and with some loss of prestige. In Italy, among the nobility, the bride-elect was quite often not seen by the young man until the day of the signing of the contract. Venetian girls, clad in white or peacock blue, with their hair hanging loose, were led into the room where were gathered their family and friends, the unknown suitor and the notary public. Dutifully the girl knelt before her parents to receive their blessing. Then followed the signing of the contract with due solemnity, after which it was taken by the notary to be published in the Palace of the Doges. Yet, in the sixteenth century, betrothals were more frequently annulled in Italy than in the Middle Ages — an index of the growing spirit of individualism. In Germany, however, Luther exercised all his powerful influence in favor of the customary view that betrothal is a contract hardly less solemn and indissoluble than that of marriage.

The Marriage Ceremony. — Among the patrician classes, especially in Italy, where ceremonial was dearly loved, the rite of matrimony was performed with elaborate splendor. In the words of De Maulde: " The opening scene was as imposing and brilliant as the subsequent years of married life were to prove sombre and colourless."[2] In gorgeous procession the bride and groom walked from their homes to the door of the church where the brilliant party was met by the priest. Standing in the porch the priest put to the parties the momentous question: " Wilt thou have this woman to be thy wedded wife

[1] *Op. cit.*, pp. 49–51.   [2] *The Women of the Renaissance*, p. 37.

. . . ? " and " Wilt thou have this man . . . ? " When the
" I will " had been duly uttered, the couple were sprinkled with
lustral water, after which the wedding procession wound
through the nave to the altar rail, where the bridal mass was
sung and the benediction pronounced. Then followed feasts
and pageants, concerts, dramatic performances and dances,
lasting for days together. Brilliant pictures of the wedding
festivities in Italian cities are painted by contemporary
writers. We read of triumphal arches, decorated façades of
palaces, lavish banquets, with gold plate and ruinously costly
decorations, the performance of dramas and musical fêtes,
and the reading of poems written for the happy occasion by
renowned literary lights. Yet the marriage day of some noble
ladies was not always either happy or very brilliant. The
custom of marrying young men and women of high rank by
proxy was rather general at this time. Thus the young Duke of
Urbino, who had been married by proxy to Leonora Gonzaga,
daughter of the Duke of Mantua, had so little interest in his
bride that he had to be urged to visit her by glowing descriptions of her beauty and virtue. Even more humiliating was
the experience of Bianca Sforza, married by proxy to the
Emperor Maximilian. The ambassador who was selected to
hand over the princess to her husband at Innsbrück found
only an archduchess awaiting the bridal party instead of the
brilliant escort he had expected. Putting the best face he
could upon the matter, the ambassador gave a few balls himself in honor of the bride; then he hurried off to Vienna to
find the royal groom. But two months dragged along before
Maximilian could be persuaded to claim his bride, who still
remained in a most humiliating position at Innsbrück awaiting
her dilatory spouse.

As we have seen, not all marriages during the Renaissance
were ecclesiastical and ceremonious. Until the Council of
Trent (1545–63) pronounced such unions null and void, it was
not uncommon for a man and woman to marry themselves, in

the presence of a notary and one or two witnesses, by simply holding hands and pronouncing the words " I take thee to be my wedded wife " and " I take thee to be my wedded husband." In Italy one witness to such a marriage was deemed sufficient if he were a priest, a magistrate or a notary since these men had the necessary skill to attest the validity of the marriage in writing. Indeed a promise and an exchange of rings constituted a marriage in Italy prior to the Council of Trent, although the absence of witnesses made it easy for the man thus married to abandon his wife if he chose.[1]

Many curious and uncouth wedding customs prevailed among the humbler folk during this period. In the more remote parts of Italy the bride kept up a plaintive wailing before her marriage, which is thought by some writers to be a survival of marriage by capture. Another quaint Italian survival, perhaps of purchase marriage, was the *serraglio*. When the bride was on her way to the church she was stopped by a band of young men, one of whom presented her with a bouquet, and received from her a ring in return, after which the bridal party proceeded to the church. At the wedding feast which followed, the recipient of the ring returned it in another floral offering to the bride; whereupon the bridegroom was forced to ransom it with a sum of money which the young man and his companions spent in feasting and revels. De Maulde gives a realistic picture of French wedding festivities among the country people. " In the rural parts of France the company only rose from the table to sit down again, or to dance under the elms. Deep drinking, love, quarrels, broad jests, strange customs, such for instance as the *jus primæ noctis*,[2] or the drinking match, traditional with the country lads, — all this developed a boisterous gaiety. The bridegroom alone groaned under it,

[1] Boulting, *op. cit.*, pp. 68–72.

[2] A mediæval custom which gave to the overlord the right to lie with the bride of any of his vassals on the wedding night. Sociologists are not agreed concerning the frequency or the prevalence of this practice.

for among the middle and lower classes it was the correct thing to invite to one's wedding as big a crowd as possible. . . . When night came he had not even the right of taking his rest; ordeals of every kind lay in wait for him; and in the morning he was bound to go on laughing, to receive more visits, and profess himself the happiest fellow in the world." [1] One is perhaps permitted to wonder whether his lot was worse than that of his bride, shrinking from the rude songs and coarse pranks so popular at the time.   For in those days, when primitive impulses and customs were not held in check by refined feeling, the bride and groom were put to bed by their friends to an accompaniment of practical jokes and full-flavored jests which must have caused many a sensitive soul to recoil in disgust.   The wedding customs of the present day, too often not over-refined, are the lineal descendants of these coarser practices of Renaissance times.

HUSBAND AND WIFE

Authority of the Husband. — After the wedding festivities were fairly over, and husband and wife settled down to the daily routine of married life, the young bride had ample opportunity to discover that her path was by no means strewn with roses.   A French writer of the sixteenth century thus describes what should be the attitude of a woman to her husband: " To pay honour, reverence and respect to her husband, as to her master and sovereign lord . . . obedience in all things just and lawful, adapting herself and bending to the habits and disposition of her husband, like the useful mirror which faithfully reflects the face, having no private purpose, love or thought; . . . she must be in all and through all with the husband . . . wash his feet, keep his house." [2] Nowhere can be found a more satisfactory statement of the relations

---

[1] *Op. cit.*, pp. 38–9.
[2] Charron, *la Sagesse.*

of husband and wife during the centuries when the patriarchal family idea was paramount in Europe. The power of the husband to enforce obedience to his will by threats, blows and confinement to the house, was rarely questioned at this time. " Woman, good or bad, needs the stick " was an ancient and honorable saying in Tuscany; and its observance was general throughout western Europe. Only when the wife sustained severe bodily injuries did the law rather reluctantly intervene. Even Petrarch favored the occasional chastisement of wives; nor did he perceive any more clearly than his contemporaries the startling incongruity between the courtly service of women and the practice of wife beating.

When they reflected upon the matter at all, men asserted themselves to be the superiors of women in all respects and therefore entitled to hold them in dutiful subjection. In *The Courtier* Castiglione makes the Lord Gaspar say that " every woman universally desires to be a man " since man is " far more perfect than woman." Whereupon the Magnifico Giuliano replies : " The poor creatures do not desire to be men in order to be perfect, but in order to have liberty and to escape that dominion over them which man has arrogated to himself by his own authority." [1] As the discussion of women's weaknesses and virtues gayly proceeds among the courtiers, the lord Gaspar suggests that there are probably many husbands who " hourly wish for death " because of the " torment of their wives."

" ' And what pain,' replied the Magnifico, ' can wives give their husbands that is as incurable as are those that husbands give their wives? — who if not for love, at least for fear are submissive to their husbands? '

" ' Certain it is,' retorted my lord Gaspar, ' that the little good they sometimes do proceeds from fear, since there are few in the world who in their secret hearts do not hate their husbands.' "

[1] *Op. cit.*, p. 185.

Again the gallant Magnifico took issue with this hostile critic of women, and asserted that " wives nearly always love their husbands more than husbands love their wives . . ." and this in spite of the fact that many women known to him " suffer in this world the pains that are said to be in hell." [1]

Sometimes these unhappy women fled from their homes to escape unbearable ill usage at the hands of their husbands, only to be returned by their own fathers or brothers, " as a result of the appalling free-masonry between men."

Affection between Husband and Wife. — Yet it must not be supposed that hatred or indifference were the only feelings that animated husband and wife in the fifteenth and sixteenth centuries. The affection existing between some married pairs has come down to us in history. Who questions the love of Sir Thomas More, of Luther and of a score of lesser men for their wives, who generously returned this affection? The family relatives who selected the partners of their sons and daughters sometimes chose more wisely than could the young people themselves. An Italian husband, Giovanni Rucellai by name, wrote of his deceased wife that " she was a very dear lady to me and a good housewife and mother, preserved to me long, for she lived fifty-five years and departed this life Ap. 24, 1418, and this I account the greatest loss I ever suffered or ever could have." A century later Isabella Guicciardini wrote to her absent husband: " Realize what my condition is, always remembering that I cannot see you. . . . Do you think I am so happy, with two little maids, sometimes seeing folk and chattering, but mostly writing and praying and chaffering and keeping my accounts." [2] The love of Margaret of France for her faithless husband, Henri D'Albret, has been often related. And it may truly be said that whatever pain he may have caused her during her lifetime, he yet nourished a spark of genuine affection for his brilliant wife and sincerely mourned her death. A quaint

[1] *Ibid.*, p. 193.   [2] Quoted in Boulting, *op. cit.*, p. 100.

chronicler of the day thus describes his grief : " What shall we say of the King, bereft of his Margaret? No longer did he run a strong course. He seemed as one swaying from side to side, wretched and ill at ease, like those, who, unaccustomed to the sea, cross from one vessel to another, trying to avoid falling into the water. So this poor prince strayed hither and thither." [1]

Some husbands and wives got along happily and comfortably, even with mild affection, by seeing little of each other. In such marriages undue strain was avoided by infrequent meetings. The woman did her duty as wife and mother when called upon to perform it. At other times she tasted the joys of a free being, — free to study, to manage her household and children as she saw fit, to mingle in the social life of the court and the castle. Meanwhile her spouse likewise enjoyed his liberty, sailing the seas, going to war, engaging in affairs of state and quite often enlisting in the chivalrous service of some fair feminine platonist as he moved from court to court. The wives of Italian tradesmen, too, enjoyed some freedom, since their husbands were often absent for months at a time carrying on their business in foreign cities. Such women, however, were usually closely watched by their husbands' relatives, who in accordance with ancient custom in Italy, dwelt in the same neighborhood, as a family group, and kept a sharp lookout on the conduct of this otherwise unguarded wife. It is probable that English wives had greater liberty at this time than those on the Continent. A Dutchman writing in the sixteenth century comments thus on the liberty of Englishwomen :

" Wives are not kept so strictly as they are in Spain or elsewhere. Nor are they shut up, but they have the free management of the house or housekeeping, after the fashion of those of the Netherlands and others their neighbors. They go to market to buy what they like best to eat. They are well-dressed, fond of taking it easy, and commonly leave the care

[1] Olhagaray, *Histoire de Bearn et de Foix.*

of household matters and drudgery to their servants. . . . In all banquets and feasts they are shown the greatest honour. . . . All the rest of their time they employ in walking and riding, in playing at cards or otherwise in visiting their friends and keeping company, conversing with their equals (whom they term gossips) and their neighbours, and making merry with them at child-births, christenings, churchings and funerals; and all this with the permission of their husbands, as such is the custom. Although the husbands often recommend to them the pains, industry and care of the German or Dutch women, who do what the men ought to do both in the house and the shops, for which services in England men are employed, nevertheless the women usually persist in retaining their customs. This is why England is called the paradise of married women. The girls who are not yet married are kept much more rigorously and strictly than in the Low Countries."[1]

It should not be forgotten, in reading this rosy account of the life of English matrons, that this Dutch observer is limiting his description to the women of the upper classes. The account applies not at all to the busy housewives of the middle and lower ranks of society. Moreover, it is well to remember that the ideal of English womanhood at this time was ably expressed by Sir Thomas Overbury, a contemporary poet, in his poem " A Wife."

> " Give me next Good, an understanding Wife,
> " By nature wise, not learnéd by much Art,
>
> *   *   *   *   *   *   *
>
> " Domestick charge doth best that Sexe befit,
> " Contiguous businesse as to fix the minde,
> " That leasure space for fancies not admit,
> " Their leasure 'tis corrupteth Womankinde,
> " Else, being plac'd from many vices free,
> " They had to Heav'n a shorter cut than we.
> " Books are a part of Man's Prerogative. . . ."

[1] Quoted in Hill, *Women in English Life*, Vol. I, pp. 115–16.

Unfaithfulness in Marriage. — During the Renaissance, as at the present time, the double standard of morals prevailed. Even then, however, fair-minded men here and there questioned its justice as thousands of men and women question it to-day. On the whole, however, the unfaithfulness of the husband to the marriage bond was lightly regarded and mildly punished, while adultery on the part of the wife sometimes met with death — at least within the circle of the Italian courts. Castiglione has cleverly expressed the argument of the ages in support of a double moral standard and has met this argument with a cogent reasoning hard to refute. My lord Gaspar states the affirmative position in the following words :

" Therefore . . . it is wisely ordained that women are allowed to fail in all other things without blame, to the end that they may be able to devote all their strength to keeping themselves in this one virtue of chastity ; without which their children would be uncertain, and that tie would be dissolved which binds the whole world by blood and by the natural love of each man for what he has produced."

To which the Magnifico pertinently replies :

" But tell me why it is not ordained that loose living is as disgraceful a thing in men as in women, seeing that if men are by nature more virtuous and of greater worth,[1] they could all the more easily practise this virtue of continence also ; and their children would be neither more nor less certain, for although women were unchaste, they could of themselves . . . in no wise bear children, provided men were continent and did not take part in women's unchastity. But if you will say the truth, even you know that we men have of our own authority arrogated to ourselves a license, whereby we insist that the same sins are in us very trivial and sometimes praiseworthy, and in women cannot be sufficiently punished, unless by shameful death, or perpetual infamy at least." [2]

[1] Lord Gaspar had just contended for the greater virtue, strength and perfection of men.   [2] *The Courtier*, p. 206.

In Southern lands, in Italy and France, the immoralities of the husband were more open, although probably not more frequent, than in England and Germany. Francis I, king of France, publicly remarked that the man who lived without a mistress was a " nincompoop " ; and it is certain that term could never have been applied to him. The custom of buying slave girls, Circassians, Tartars and Russians, in the markets of Venice was quite common during the Renaissance. The dignified Cosimo de' Medici, patron of scholars and artists, was not above owning a beautiful Circassian slave girl, who served as his mistress and who became the mother of his bastard son Carlo de' Medici. Since these female slaves were very valuable, no men except their masters could debauch them without running the risk of heavy fine, imprisonment or even death if caught in the act. A modern historian mentions an Italian family in which seven children were born of slave girls in two years.[1] The wealthy burghers in Italy were as frequent offenders as the nobility in respect to keeping slave concubines or mistresses. Ostensibly these girls were employed in well-to-do middle-class families as nurses and domestic servants, but usually they were completely at the disposal of their masters. Much ill feeling was no doubt caused in families by these illicit unions; and yet few Italian women would have dreamed of making this offence a cause for separation. Such action would no doubt have held them up to public scorn and ridicule. If a woman had a comfortable home and a reasonably kind husband, why should she complain? Indeed the attitude of many good wives of the period toward their husbands' illegitimate children seems to the modern student of history surprisingly generous. Quite frequently they received these little ones into the family and brought them up with their own children. The illegitimate son of Cosimo de' Medici was reared in his own family. The noble Elizabetta, Duchess of Urbino, brought up her illegitimate niece; Bianca Maria Visconti took charge of her

[1] Boulting, *op. cit*, p. 158.

illegitimate granddaughter, Caterina Sforza, until the child's father married again, when his new wife accepted and reared her with her own little ones. This same Caterina paid her debt of generosity when she brought up her husband's illegitimate child with her own offspring.

The explanation of this liberal treatment accorded to unfortunate children born out of wedlock probably lies in the fact that in the struggle of contending factions for supremacy in the Italian cities, every child born into a family might be a source of added strength, whether legitimate or not. For the family, including all blood relations, was a far stronger and more important social unit then than it is now. Also it must be remembered that, at a time when marriages were so loosely contracted as they frequently were before the Council of Trent, concubinage was not so far removed as it is to-day from the lawful state of matrimony. For both these reasons illegitimate children, at least in Italy, were not stigmatized as in modern times. Quite often they were as well educated and almost as well placed in life as their legitimate brothers and sisters.

Yet penalties were visited upon adultery even when committed by men. In parts of Northern Italy an adulterer was condemned to lose an eye, besides paying a heavy fine, if any one chose to bring him to judgment. In other parts of Italy both the man guilty of rape and the adulterer were fined. Then, too, women of means and influence in all Christian countries could obtain legal separation from an unfaithful husband through the ecclesiastical courts; but such relief seems to have been rarely resorted to in the South, though it was fairly common in England among the well-to-do.

But were wives always faithful to their husbands, however erring these might be? Apparently not. It is not strange that, married when very young to men unknown to them, ardent women yielded to temptation and fell passionately in love. In the courts of France and Italy a degenerate platonism emphasized the importance and the joys of love;

and the whole subject of sex relations was freely and continually discussed. In an atmosphere surcharged with unwholesome sentiment not a few young wives forgot their marriage vows. Sometimes the husbands, themselves unfaithful, shut their eyes to the errors of their wives so long as they acted with some discretion. But the stern old law of Rome, repeated in the law of the Lombards, permitted a husband to put his adulterous wife to death if surprised in the act. At one time or another the wives of the proud Dukes of Ferrara, Mantua and Milan, paid with their lives for the crime of adultery.

In England a commission, which sat for twenty years during the reign of Henry VIII, made an elaborate report on the *Reformation of Ecclesiastical Laws*. In this report it was suggested that divorces *a vinculo* (giving the right of remarriage) be granted for adultery, malicious desertion and mortal enmities; and that divorces *a mensa et thoro*, which were legal separations giving no right to marry again, be abolished.[1] But England was not ready for this radical step, and legal separation granted by an ecclesiastical court remained for many years the only mode of divorce in cases of adultery.

THE HOMES OF THE RENAISSANCE

Improvements in Architecture and Furnishings. — With the growth of industry and commerce and with the resulting increase in wealth there went a marked improvement in the homes of the upper and middle classes, both in architecture and furnishings. The desire for more beautiful and comfortable homes was first felt in Italy long before the Northern countries had outgrown their taste for the uncomfortable castles and manor-houses of the late Middle Ages. One of the most splendid of the Italian palaces was that of Urbino,

[1] Cleveland, *Woman under the English Law*, p. 226.

built by Duke Federico di Montefeltro in the fifteenth century. Castiglione thus describes it:

" Among his other praiseworthy deeds, he built on the rugged site of Urbino a palace regarded by many as the most beautiful to be found in all Italy; and he so well furnished it with everything suitable that it seemed not a palace but a city in the form of a palace; and not merely with what is ordinarily used, such as silver vases, hangings of richest cloth of gold and silk, and other similar things, — but for ornament he added countless antique statues in marble and bronze, pictures most choice, and musical instruments of every sort, nor would he admit anything there that was not very rare and excellent. Then at very great cost he collected a goodly number of most excellent books in Greek, Latin and Hebrew, all of which he adorned with gold and silver, esteeming this to be the chiefest excellence of his great palace." [1]

Such a passage is valuable not only as giving the reader a peep into the luxurious homes of Renaissance princes, but also as serving to illustrate the rapid development of æsthetic and intellectual taste during the period. What noble of the Middle Ages would have spent his gold in pictures, statues and rare books in foreign tongues to beautify his castle and enrich his mind? Feudal days were past now and the homes of nobles no longer housed a company of retainers and fed them in the great bare halls. Instead there was an appalling number of trained and paid servants attached to every important household. One lady of Ferrara in the sixteenth century boasted a personal staff of four secretaries, a chief lady and seven maids of honor, six maids of the bedchamber, doctors, equerries and other servants to the number of nearly two hundred. Surrounded by this small army of attendants, the Renaissance lady of France and Italy lived amid costly and beautiful surroundings. The delicately carved furniture, stiff and uncomfortable though it doubtless was, the

[1] *The Courtier*, p. 9.

splendid plate and glass, the elaborately decorated beds with lace covers, silken hangings and gold fringe, as unhealthful as they were elegant, the tapestries and hangings of stamped leather, the walls painted in the wonderful frescoes of great artists, — all these were evidences of the luxury of princely homes.

But let it not be supposed that there is no dark side to this glowing picture. The lack of sanitary arrangements in these splendid palaces would shock to the core of his being the modern man of the middle class. The windows were still innocent of glass; and wind and rain were kept out by oiled linen, often torn and dirty. The crowd of elegant pages of the court of Ferrara were provided with but one comb and one copper wash basin among them with which to make their toilets. Indeed, the ducal family were not above using pewter dishes, when not entertaining prominent guests, and ordinarily ate simple food. Everywhere sumptuousness rubbed elbows with dirt and discomfort.

The houses of the English nobility during the reigns of Henry VIII, Edward VI, Mary and Elizabeth, were gradually made over into comfortable and even luxurious dwellings. In a *History of Leicestershire* [1] a writer of the sixteenth century describes the homes of the great nobles and the numerous staff of servants kept to manage them. As the English nobility emerged from the semi-barbarity of mediæval life in castles and manors, they found it necessary to hold in check their household staffs by a code of minute domestic regulations governing all the servants from the steward to the pot-boy. Frequently the households of dukes and earls were conducted with something of the splendor and formality of the English court. Lofty Gothic dining rooms took the place of the bare eating halls of the mediæval castle. Chapels were built in connection with every great house and choral services were held there daily until long after the Reformation.

[1] Nichols, *op. cit.*, III, 681.

T

Richly carved ceilings and armorial bearings were found everywhere, intertwined with family proverbs and devices. Privacy, almost unknown in the mediæval castle, was now dearly prized. The lord and lady no longer slept in the hall of the castle; but each had a lofty chamber, with the sleeping rooms of attendant squires, pages and gentlewomen close at hand.

The homes of the prosperous middle class in the English towns show similar improvements. As early as the fifteenth century the merchants of Bristol and other towns began building fine houses three stories in height, some of the more pretentious ones having a tower in which treasures of silver plate were securely stored. Underground were great cellars with groined roofs where wine and ale were kept. The ground-floor was commonly used as a warehouse or shop where the merchant or master craftsman plied his trade. Above were the living-rooms and bedchambers of the family, sometimes with a fine hall built out in the rear, having a lofty roof of carved timber. Wealthy burghers emulated the nobility in hanging their walls with tapestries. But few, if any, of these middle-class homes could boast a library; for English traders were practical materialists as yet, with little interest in the things of the mind.[1]

It is evident that the improvement in the architecture and furnishings of English homes did not always commend itself to conservative natures with a bent for looking back to " the good old times." In a *Description of England in Shakespere's Youth*, Harrison writes thus gloomily of the changes that had taken place:

" And yet see the change, for when our houses were builded of willow, then had we oken men; but now that our houses are come to be made of oke, our men are not onlie become willow, but a great manie through a Persian delicacie crept in among us, altogether of straw, which is a sore alteration. . . . Now have we manie chimnies, and yet our tenderlings

[1] Cf. Green, *Town Life in the Fifteenth Century*, Vol. II, p. 84.

complaine of rheumes, catarhs and poses. Then had we none but reredosses and our heads did never ake. For as the smoke in those daies was supposed to be a sufficient hardning for the timber of the house; so it was reputed a far better medicine to keepe the goodman and his familie from the quack or pose, wherewith as then verie few were oft acquainted."

One is permitted to wonder what this dissatisfied gentleman would have thought of the household improvements other than chimneys which were introduced a generation later, — such innovations as glass for windows instead of oiled paper or linen, mattresses in lieu of straw pallets and feather pillows instead of the hollowed log of earlier times. But let it not be imagined that the English homes of Henry VIII's reign or even those of Elizabeth's golden age would meet with unqualified approval in our own day. Our English forefathers tolerated much dirt in their homes and about their persons that would be highly offensive to our more delicate taste. We are told that the scullions in Henry VIII's kitchen were so filthy and tattered that an ordinance was passed in 1526 ordering that the master cooks be given twenty marks yearly to provide such scullions " as shall not goe naked or in garments of such vilenesse as they now doe, nor to lie in the nights and dayes in the kitchens. . . ." The purpose of the ordinance was said to be " for the better avoyding of corruption and all uncleannesse out of the King's house, which doth ingender danger of infection. . . ." [1]

Conveniences were scarce in those days, and even in nobles' houses the introduction of a few unexpected guests meant that the host might have to give up his own toilet accessories, since there were not enough to go around! Erasmus ascribed the frequency of the plague in England " partly to the incommodious form and bad exposition of the houses, to the filthiness of the streets and to the sluttishness within doors. The floors," says he, " are commonly of clay, strewed with rushes, under

---

[1] Furnivall, *The Babees Book*, p. lxvi.

which lies unmolested an ancient collection of beer, grease, fragments, excrements . . . and everything that is nasty." [1]

Home Industries. — Although the development of the gilds in the late Middle Ages tended to put men in control of industries previously carried on solely by women, yet there was much productive labor still remaining for the busy housewives to do. Even great ladies found their time fully occupied in directing the work of their large retinues of servants, in keeping careful accounts of household supplies and expenditures, in making conserves and brewing medicines from herbs carefully stored in the herb room of every household. All food such as butter, cheese, bread, ale and wine was carefully measured and weighed before being given to the servants; and noble ladies frequently attended to this work themselves. Caterina Sforza, wife of the Duke of Milan, was reputed to be an excellent housekeeper, and during her lifetime made a large and valuable collection of recipes. Harrison thus describes the work of the " ancient " as well as the young gentlewomen of Elizabeth's court:

" Besides these things I could in like sort set downe the waies and meanes, whereby our ancient ladies of the court doo shun and avoid idlenesse, some of them exercising their fingers with the needle, others in caulworke,[2] diverse in spinning of silke. . . . How manie of the eldest sort also are skilfull in surgerie and distillation of waters, besides sundrie other artificiall practises perteining to the ornature and commendations of their bodies. . . . Nevertheless this I will generallie saie of them all, that as ech of them are cuning in somthing whereby they keepe themselves occupied in the court, so there is in maner none of them, but when they be at home, can helpe to supplie the ordinarie want of the kitchen with a number of delicat dishes of their own divising. . . ." [3]

---

[1] Quoted in Furnivall, *op. cit.*, p. lxvi.
[2] A network made into a cap for the hair.
[3] Harrison, in *Holinshed's Chronicles*, Vol. I, p. 196.

The wives of nobles of large estates not only had household duties to perform, but, in the absence of their lords, they kept buildings in repair, supervised the labor on the land and replenished the stores. Henry Percy, Earl of Northumberland, declares that " in this state of England wifes commonly have a greater sway in all our affairs than in other nations Germany excepted." [1] In the morning hours the lady devoted much time to distilling drinks. In a quaint work on the " English Housewife," written in the seventeenth century, the writer mentions *twenty-two* distilled drinks from mint, hyssop, thistle, dill and other herbs too various to mention.

But if noble ladies were busy in directing servants and making drinks and confections, what shall be said of the wives of yeomen and tradesmen? Certain it is that they were astir with the dawn in summer, and at five on dark winter mornings. The prosperity of the whole family was felt to be in large measure in the keeping of the prudent housewife. English rhymes expressed this feeling in the jingle :

> " For husbandry weepeth
> Where huswifery sleepeth
> And hardly he creepeth
> Up ladder to thrift." [2]

So the *Hausfrau* in Germany and the " good wife " in England carried on a variety of domestic industries such as curing meats, brewing ale, dipping candles, making soap, baking bread and doing all the family cooking. A seventeenth century writer describes in detail the process of bread-making : " The bake-house with its bolting house and sieves attached, its ' troughs to lay Leven in,' its moulding tables, its brake for kneading or ' dough sheet ' for treading the dough, and its large brick oven, was the heart of the culinary department." [3]

[1] *Archæologia*, Vol. XXVII, pp. 339–40.
[2] Tusser, *A Book of Huswifery* (ed. 1812), p. 236.
[3] Markham, *The English Housewife* (ed. 1683), pp. 185–6.

If the goodwife made white bread, she ground the coarse meal upon " block stones " in good old primitive fashion, bolted it through fine bolting cloth and thus carried out all the processes from the beginning.

The author of the *English Housewife* says of the art of malt-making that the " office belongeth particularly to the Housewife; and though we have many excellent men-maulsters, yet it is properly the work and care of women, for it is a housework and done altogether within doors where generally lyeth her charge; . . ."

But these were only a part of her activities. When the food and drink was prepared, the housewife turned to her spinning-wheel, ever at hand; or she heckled hemp and flax, carded wool and scoured and bleached yarn. When the woollen or linen cloth was spun, woven, cleansed and sometimes dyed, she made it up into garments for the family. The weaving of the cloth was quite often done outside the household at this time by village weavers employing in their own homes a limited number of apprentices and journeymen. When the material, duly woven, had been returned, it was customary in some well-to-do families to send it to the village tailor to be made up, or to employ the tailor at home. Increase of wealth and luxury were causing some country people to be dissatisfied with the old home-made products and to sigh for the more elegant goods made by craftsmen in the larger cities. These skilled artisans were taking over some of the industrial processes formerly belonging to the housewife. Caps and gloves, hosiery, shoes and girdles were quite commonly manufactured by master workmen in highly specialized trades which were organized into gilds. Card-makers, combers, clothiers, weavers, fullers and dyers all plied their separate trades and had their gild organizations from which women were largely excluded, especially in England.

Home Nurture and Education. — As in the Middle Ages, midwives were very largely employed in the delicate office of bringing children into the world. Only in specially serious cases were men physicians summoned to lend their aid. A curious Renaissance custom, handed on from earlier times, decreed that the Italian mother should receive the congratulations of her friends shortly after the birth of a child. Hence there was often a stream of visitors pouring in and out of the "lying-in-chamber," felicitating the parents and admiring the infant. Frequently gifts were presented to mother and child in these days. Families were very large, and the strain upon the woman, who began her duty of child-bearing at a ruthlessly early age, must have broken her health in many instances. Quite commonly a girl-wife became a mother at sixteen, as did the young Marchioness of Este, who proudly announced to the citizens of Modena in 1499 that "this 25 Mar. at the tenth hour by the ineffable grace of God, we gave daylight to two lusty female twins." But children born of girl-wives and boy-husbands were not always "lusty." The rate of infant mortality was terribly high in this age when medicine, antisepsis and sanitation were in their infancy. Apparently girl babies received but a scant welcome, especially in powerful families, where boys were universally desired. It is related of Isabella, the beautiful and talented Marchioness of Este, that she put aside a gilded cradle, prepared for a boy, when a female child was born to her. On this melancholy occasion Lorenzo de' Medici actually wrote a letter of condolence to the disappointed father.[1]

Midwives took charge of mother and child for some days after the birth. Quite often they were ignorant and superstitious women whose skill, so far as they had any, was gained through much practice unenlightened by sound theory. A quaint book for the benefit of German midwives was published by one Rueff, about 1580. He gives the following advice to these women concerning the care of their tender charges:

[1] Boulting, *op. cit.*, p. 165.

> " Now mark with diligence what I say to you,
>   The child shall bathe every day,
>   With lukewarm water, and soon
>   After the bath thou shalt anoint it
>   With oil of roses to make it healthy.
>   Thou shalt also, at the same time,
>   Stretch its limbs up and down
>   Until it can stretch itself.
>   Thou mayst also delicately bend them for him
>   While they are still so tender
>   According to thy pleasure, as thou wilt
>   By which means they will be well-formed.
>   Likewise mayst thou also carefully shape
>   The ears of the child while they are still soft,
>   The nose in order that the outline
>   May be clear and smooth." [1]

Rueff also recommends the practice, not yet wholly forgotten, of hanging red corals around the neck and arms of
children. " This strengthens the child," says Rueff, " and
makes it happy and virtuous." The mediæval custom of
swaddling children was still prevalent in all the countries
of Europe. The wrappings were commonly retained until
the child was nearly a year old; and one wonders why such
treatment, even now quite general in the south of Europe,
did not result in the child's losing the use of his arms and legs.

Because of the Catholic doctrine that unbaptised infants
lost all share in the joys of heaven and were condemned to
the pains of hell, great care was taken that the baptism of
the child should take place at the earliest possible day. Well-
to-do families sought to make the baptismal ceremony a
sumptuous and expensive affair. In Venice the infant
of noble birth was taken to the church in pompous
procession, carried under a canopy or in a gilded chair.
Splendid baptisteries were built in many churches where
gathered the parents, god parents and friends of the child

---

[1] Boesch, *Kinderleben in der Deutschen Vergangenheit*, p. 17.

in their richest silks and brocades. Costly presents to the parents as well as the infant candidate for baptism were expected of every god parent, and the expense this custom entailed upon them was so great that sumptuary laws were passed in Italy and Germany to regulate the practice. Likewise the banquets furnished by parents to the baptismal party were lavish in the extreme. In Magdeburg in 1583 all entertainment at the baptism of a child was abolished by law, with the exception of a simple meal to the midwives.[1]

Although it was the general custom during the Renaissance for mothers to nurse their infants, yet this practice was by no means universal. Despite the protests of physicians and learned men the women of the well-to-do classes tended to shirk their duty in this respect and to turn their children over to wet-nurses. An Italian moralist of the fifteenth century declaimed hotly against the custom, declaring that mothers deserved the hate of their children who put them " to the slavish breasts of Tartars and Saracens and the women of other animal and outlandish folk." Even if the mother suckled her children, foreign-born slave nurses were employed by most prosperous Italian families to care for the little ones during childhood. Frequently the children were sent to foster-nurses in the country, where they remained until they had passed the more troublesome stages of infancy and early childhood. This custom was more general in France and Italy than in England, where the nurse, selected with some care, commonly entered the family and took charge of the children until they were fully grown. Quite commonly her position in the family was dignified and responsible, and she often won the affectionate esteem of her foster-children. An instance of this is furnished by Shakespere's talkative Nurse in *Romeo and Juliet*, who was a real foster-mother to her charge whom she dearly loved. In Act I she says:

[1] *Ibid.*, p. 28.

> " God mark thee to his grace!
> Thou wast the prettiest babe that e'er I nursed ;
> And I might live to see thee married once,
> I have my wish." [1]

Home Training. — During the Renaissance, as in all ages, the early training and education of children was confided to the mother, even where nurses were employed. She it was who formed the speech of the child with loving care, as she formed its manners and morals and gave it the earliest instruction in religion. A writer of the period pays tribute to the mothers of Ferrara who " possess a truly admirable quality ; they train their children so well in courtesy, manners and the show of breeding that all the ladies of all other lands might copy them." Numerous works appeared in the fifteenth and sixteenth centuries admonishing parents to the utmost diligence in the upbringing of their children, especially with regard to their religious and moral training. Both Catholics and Protestants vied with each other in exalting the importance of family education, and in urging parents to a fuller appreciation of the responsibilities of parenthood. In 1498 appeared in Germany the *Seelenführer*, or *Soul's Guide*, a handbook of instruction with much good advice addressed to fathers and mothers. The author declared with earnestness that all Christian instruction should begin in the family. " Let parents, therefore, be admonished to see that their children grow up in Christian fear and reverence, and that their home be their first school and their first Church. Christian mother, when thou holdest thy child, which is God's own image, on thy knee, make the sign of the holy cross on his forehead, on his lips and on his heart, and as soon as he can lisp teach him to say his prayers. Take him betimes to confession, and instruct him in all that is needful to make him confess rightly. Fathers and mothers should set their children a good example, taking them to mass,

[1] *Romeo and Juliet*, Act I, Sc. III.

vespers, and sermons on Sundays and saints' days as often as possible." [1] A catechism by Diedrich Coelde, which was published about the same time, exhorts parents to teach their children the Lord's Prayer, the Apostles' Creed and the Ave Maria. Morning and evening they should bless their little ones, then make them kneel to God in thanksgiving. Children should be taught to say "Benedicite" and "Gratias" before and after meals, to eat and drink with moderation and to behave modestly in the streets. Parents are warned that most of the sin in the world is the result of bad training in the home; and hence they are urged to be strict in discipline and not to spare the rod.

With somewhat broader outlook Luther writes on family instruction. Recognizing as he did, " three hierarchies, established of God," — the State, the Church and the family — he taught that the family was the basis of the other two. From the Fourth Commandment it is obvious that God attaches great importance to obedience to parents. " Where this is not the case, you will find neither good manners nor a good government. . . ." Family government is the basis of all other government. " For where obedience is not maintained at the fireside, no power on earth can insure . . . the blessings of a good government; . . . If now the root is corrupt, it is in vain that you look for a sound tree or for good fruit." [2] Reverencing, as he did, the married state, as well as that of parenthood, Luther writes with enthusiasm of them both. " The parental estate God has especially honored above all estates that are beneath Him, so that he not only commands us to love our parents, but also *to honor* them." Parents should appreciate profoundly the responsibility resting upon them, " to train up their offspring for society and the Church. . . ." " Let every one know, therefore, that above all things it is

[1] Quoted in Janssen, *History of the German People*, Vol. I, p. 31.
[2] *Exposition of Exodus*, 20: 12, quoted in Barnard, *German Teachers and Educators*, p. 131.

his duty (or otherwise he will lose the divine favor) to bring up his children in the fear and knowledge of God; and if they have talents, to have them instructed and trained in a liberal education that men may be able to have their aid in government and in whatever is necessary." To bad or neglected home training Luther attributes most of the social evils of his time. Hence he earnestly declares: "No one should become a father unless he is able to instruct his children in the Ten Commandments and in the Gospel, so that he may bring up true Christians. But many enter the state of holy matrimony who can not say the Lord's Prayer, and knowing nothing themselves, they are utterly incompetent to instruct their children." At least once a week the father, as head of the family, should examine his children in the Ten Commandments, the Creed and the Lord's Prayer. On rising in the morning and retiring at night children should repeat these foundation principles of Christianity, and neither food nor drink should be given them until they have fulfilled this important duty.[1]

Doubtless there was much more formal religious training given to children in the sixteenth century than now. Religion played a more prominent part in the lives of individuals and of families in those days than in this more secular-minded age. Well-nigh every noble house had its chapel, where the family assembled daily to hear priest or chaplain read the mass or the service of the reformed sects. Discipline was severe in those days, and the parent was warned by the Church itself against neglecting the rod. Although there is evidence that gentler methods were beginning to prevail in Italy, such was not the case in the Northern countries. Children knelt daily to receive their parents' blessing, addressed them in formal terms of great respect, as " Sir " and " Madam," and were rarely permitted to sit in their presence. Even when fully grown, English girls in Edward

[1] Cf. Painter, *Luther on Education*, ch. VI.

VI's time were required to stand at the side of the room during visits to their parents, unless the mother relented and gave them a cushion to kneel on. For small offences these young ladies were freely chastised with the large fans carried by their mothers, — even before company![1] Much evidence exists that severe home discipline was not only the practice but the accepted theory of the age. Vives, the Spanish Renaissance scholar, and tutor of the Princess Mary,[2] urges mothers, while loving their children, to " hide their love, lest the children take boldness thereupon to do what they list. Nor let not love stop her to punish her children for their vices, and to strengthen their bodies and wits with sad [*i.e.*, wise] bringing up."[3] Usually parents needed no urging to severity, and contemporary letters and accounts dealing with the discipline of children are painful reading to people of the present day, when regard for the individuality and self-respect of the child have perhaps gone too far. About the middle of the fifteenth century a friend of the Paston family writes thus of Agnes Paston's treatment of her young daughter:

" She was never in so great sorrow as she is now-a-days, for she may not speak with no man . . . nor with servants of her mother's, but that she beareth her on hand otherwise than she meaneth; and she hath since Easter the most part been beaten once in the week or twice, and sometimes twice a day, and her head broken in two or three places."[4]

In his quaint work, *The Scholemaster*, Roger Ascham, once tutor to the Princess Elizabeth, tells us of the upbringing of the gentle Lady Jane Grey as described by herself:

" One of the greatest benefites that God ever gave me is that he sent me so sharpe and severe Parents, and so jentle a

[1] Howard, *Lady Jane Grey and her Times*, p. 110.
[2] Eldest daughter of Henry VIII.
[3] Vives, *Instruction of a Christian Woman* (1523); edited by Foster Watson, London, 1912, pp. 128–9.   [4] *Paston Letters*, Vol. I, p. 50.

scholemaster. For when I am in presence either of father or mother, whether I speake, kepe silence, sit, stand, or go, eate, drinke, be merie or sad, be sewying, plaiyng, dauncing, or doing anie thing els, I must do it, as it were in soch weight, mesure, and number, even as perfitelie as God made the world, or els I am so sharply taunted, so cruellie threatened, yea presentlie sometyms, with pinches, nippes, and bobbes, and other waies which I will not name for the honor I beare them, so without measure misordered that I think myself in hell till tyme cum that I must go to M. Elmer, who teacheth me so jentlie, so pleasantlie, with soch faire allurements to learning, that I thinke all the tyme nothing whiles I am with him. And when I am called from him, I fall on weeping." [1]

Intellectual Education. — With the Renaissance the intellectual growth of preceding ages came to fruition. Everywhere the boys, and often the girls, of prominent families were carefully instructed in the classical learning of the time. The revival of intellectual education came first to Italy, then penetrated the countries north of the Alps. England and Germany were among the last nations to be profoundly affected by the new culture. Even so late as 1500, Richard Pace describes a conversation at an English dinner table concerning the education of children. One man had just announced his intention of finding a good teacher for his children when another "burst out furiously with these words : ' Why do you talk nonsense friend? ' he said; ' A curse on these stupid letters; all learned men are beggars: . . . I swear by God's body I'd rather that my son should hang than study letters. For it becomes the sons of gentlemen to blow the horn nicely (apte), to hunt skilfully, and elegantly carry and train a hawk. But the study of letters should be left to the sons of rustics.' " [2]

[1] *Op. cit.* (ed. by John E. B. Mayor, 1911), p. 97.
[2] Prefatory Letter to Colet in Pace's *De Fructu;* quoted in Furnivall, *op. cit.*, p. viii.

Fortunately for the future of England, however, this mediæval notion was not shared by most of the gentlemen of the day. Boys of noble families were carefully educated by tutors at home, not only in the Greek and Latin classics, but in music, " writinge, plaienge att weapons, castinge of accomptes." Quite often they were sent abroad with their tutors to travel and become acquainted with the languages and institutions of other countries, — especially France. The mediæval custom whereby boys were sent away from home to the houses of prominent nobles and statesmen to be educated had by no means died out in sixteenth-century England. In 1511 the household of the Earl of Northumberland contained several " Yong Gentlemen at their Fryndes fynding," *i.e.*, supported by their relatives in order that they might learn letters, manners and warfare in the earl's castle and later be advanced to important posts at court or elsewhere. More than half a century later the Earl of Essex sent his son to be educated, partly in the household of Lord Burleigh, and partly in that of the Earl of Sussex. In a letter to the former he states his purpose in the education of his boy to be, — " so that he might . . . reverence your Lordship for your Wisdome and Gravyty . . ." and " frame himself to the Example of my Lord of Sussex in all the Actions of his Life, tending either to the Warres, or to the Institution of a Nobleman, . . ." [1] Nor was this custom confined to the nobility, for the English practice of apprenticing children of the working-classes away from home in order that they might be educated and taught a trade in some family where their future interests would be well looked after, was very general. However, the custom was by no means as widespread as in the preceding reign of Henry VII, when it was made the basis of a harsh criticism of English parents. In *The Italian Relation of England* the author says :

" The want of affection in the English is strongly manifested

[1] *Murdin's State Papers*, pp. 301–2, quoted in *Babees Book*, p. **xv**.

toward their children; for after having kept them at home till they arrive at the age of 7 or 9 years at the utmost, they put them out, both males and females, to hard service in the houses of other people, binding them generally for another 7 or 9 years . . . and few are born who are exempted from this fate, for every one, however rich he may be, sends away his children into the houses of others, whilst he, in return, receives those of strangers into his own." [1]

The Renaissance brought not only a more liberal education to the sons of nobility and gentlemen, but it extended the benefits of culture to their daughters also. That quickened sense of the worth and possibilities of human personality, so characteristic of this age, opened the eyes of many parents to the capacities and talents of their girls and resulted in securing for them an education in the classical languages and literatures no whit inferior to that bestowed upon the boys. Many are the eulogies of learned women furnished by the literature of the time. Castiglione wrote of his ideal Court Lady, " I wish this Lady to have knowledge of letters, music, painting, and to know how to dance and make merry; . . . " [2] This view was apparently shared by many parents, not alone in Italy, but in France and England. A modern writer describing this education tells us: " Little girls sucked in Latin with their mother's milk; . . . they were given a tutor at an age when they ought to have been learning nothing but how to walk; at seven they were expected to be able to maintain a conversation, and at thirteen to have finished their studies and be ripe for matrimony." [3] The author refers here chiefly to French and Italian girls, who mature early; yet the statement needs little modification to apply to the girls of Northern lands. At the age of thirteen we are told that Mary Stuart made a public address in Latin; and at fifteen the ill-fated Lady Jane Grey was well versed in four languages and read

[1] *Camden Society Papers* (1847), pp. 24–6.   [2] *The Courtier*, p. 180.
[3] De Maulde, *The Women of the Renaissance*, pp. 91, 92.

Plato in Greek with appreciation. Quite commonly tutors were engaged to teach girls in their homes. Occasionally sisters and brothers were educated together by the same teachers. This seems to have been a common practice at the courts of Italian despots. Caterina Sforza was instructed with her brothers and so were the daughters of the Grand Duke Cosimo de' Medici and the Duke of Mantua.

But it must not be supposed that all of the reading of these girls was of a severely classical sort. The tales of Boccaccio and French romances modelled after them were eagerly read by French and Italian maidens and must have done woful harm to moral standards by implanting in the minds of these young damsels the dubious conviction that love should not be sought in marriage but rather outside its bonds.

In this brief account of the Renaissance education of boys and girls not a word has been said of the intellectual training of the common people. The reason is not far to seek, since such education hardly existed. The majority of women, at least, were very little affected by the revival of culture taking place during the fifteenth and sixteenth centuries. The wives of the respectable burghers of Germany, England, France and Italy were almost wholly uneducated in many instances, and were not at all ashamed of their ignorance, since no one looked upon it as discreditable. Their training was in household duties, and can be said to have been both varied and thorough. No girl was held to be ready for matrimony who could not spin and weave, make and mend clothing, cook and brew, and tend the sick. Even the daughters of the highest nobility received some of this training. Vives is but expressing the accepted opinion of his age when he exhorts the mother of a carefully educated girl that " she shall, beside the learning of the book, instruct [her] also with women's crafts; as to handle wool and flax, to spin, to weave, to sew, to rule and over-see an house." [1]

[1] *Of the Instruction of a Christian Woman*, p. 123.

U

Contrast between Home Education in the Renaissance, and at the Present Time. — Cursory as is this study of home training and education during the Renaissance, perhaps it will serve to make clear how vastly more important was the rôle played by the family then than now. The parents passed much more time at home than is possible for fathers and mothers in this age of factories, workshops, offices and clubs; and their personal responsibility for the religious, moral and industrial training of their children was pressed upon their attention by precept and example. The contrast presented by the home education of Renaissance girls and the almost completely *extra* home training of the modern girl, is a striking one. At present the well-educated American girl spends most of her time between seven and twenty-one in activities and interests outside the family circle; and, at the end of her formal education, she may have had no instruction whatever in the duties of wife and mother. Discipline was harsh, sometimes to the point of actual cruelty, in Renaissance days; yet the State very rarely curtailed the authority of parents over their children, as it probably would do in similar cases occurring at the present time. Clearly, this encroachment of the government upon ancient family rights had then scarcely begun. The spirit of individualism, the respect for personal rights has so developed since the eighteenth century, that not only does public opinion condemn the severe punishments of that earlier age, but the State actively intervenes to protect the child, wherever necessary, from its own parents. All these changes and many others mark the revolution that has been silently effected in the power and influence of the family since the sixteenth century.

SELECTED BIBLIOGRAPHY

Sources.

Barnard. *German Teachers and Educators*, Luther's Views of Family, pp. 131–9.

Castiglione. *The Courtier* (ed. 1901), pp. 171–94, 205–9, 218–27.

Furnivall. *Child Marriages in the Diocese of Chester (Early English Text Society, Vol. 118, 1877, pp. xxix, xxxv, xliii–liii, 56–71, 140–1, 184–202).*

The Babees Book (Early English Text Society, Vol. 32).

Harrison. *Description of England in Shakspere's Youth (in Holinshed's Chronicles, Vol. I, New Shakspere Society, 1877).*

Knox, John. *First Blast against the monstrous Regiment of Women* (English Scholar's Library, ed. by Arber, 1878), pp. 11–53.

Luther, Martin. *Vom heyligen Ehestandt und Œconomia oder Haushaltung* (in his *Tischreden*, cap. 36, folios 349b–374a).

Tusser, Thomas. *Five Hundred Points of Good Husbandry . . . together with a Book of Huswifery* (ed. by Wm. Mavor, 1812), pp. 240–79.

Vives, J. L. *Instruction of a Christian Woman* (ed. and trans. by Foster Watson, 1912), pp. 63–115.

SECONDARY WORKS.

Boulting, Wm. *Woman in Italy from the Introduction of the Chivalrous Service of Love to the Appearance of the Professional Actress* (1910), Part I, ch. I; Part II, chs. I–VIII.

Cleveland, Arthur R. *Woman under the English Law* (1896), pp. 169–236.

Hare, Christopher. *The Most Illustrious Ladies of the Italian Renaissance* (1911), pp. 6–24.

Howard, E. G. *History of Matrimonial Institutions*, Vol. I, ch. IX.

Howard, Geo. *Lady Jane Grey and her Times* (1822), pp. 86–96, 109–24, 153–63.

Lanciani, Rudolfo. *The Golden Days of the Renaissance in Rome*, pp. 195–205.

de Maulde, Réné la Clavière. *The Women of the Renaissance* (1911), Bk. I, chs. I–IV; Bk. II, chs. II–IV.

Putnam, Emily. *The Lady*, pp. 158–210.

Reich, Emil. *Woman through the Ages*, Vol. I, 227–72; Vol. II, ch. I.

Sichel, Edith. *Women and Men of the French Renaissance* (1902), ch. II, and pp. 367–77.

Wright, Thomas. *The Homes of Other Days*, chs. XXIII–XXVI.

CHAPTER IX

THE ENGLISH FAMILY IN THE SEVENTEENTH AND EIGHTEENTH CENTURIES

Social Classes and Conditions in England in the Seventeenth Century. — Although the decay of the feudal system had had the effect of weakening, in some degree, the barriers between the various social classes in England, yet these obstacles were by no means removed in the seventeenth century. On the contrary society was sharply marked off into grades, each jealously maintaining the precise degree of prestige that belonged to it and shutting its doors to most applicants for admission from other and lower social ranks. In those days it was exceedingly difficult for any man to pass from the life station in which he was born to any higher one. The ploughman, the independent farmer, the artisan seldom, by any chance, rose from their humble stations to that of the gentleman. Occasionally a man of great talent made his mark in literature or the church and was granted a half-grudging admission to the ranks of the well-born. But these climbers were the rare exceptions. Not only was it next to impossible for every man to raise his social class, but it was exceedingly difficult for the laboring man even to change his place of abode and his kind of labor. Once apprenticed to learn a trade, that trade and no other he was expected to practise. Moreover, the artisan or ploughman was forced by the English laws of settlement to ply his industry in the town or parish where he was born or trained. This economic inflexibility and its unfortunate effects upon the working-classes did not escape the more observant members of the English Government. We are told that towards the close of the seventeenth century " an attempt was made by the Commons to bring about some relaxation of the laws of settlement, in the full knowledge and avowal of the fact that such restraints created paupers, by preventing the people from seeking and from obtaining employment where the need of it existed, and by insisting upon their starving on the parochial pittance in places where it was an utter impossibility for capital to support labour." [1] But the State utterly failed to remedy the evil, which continued for generations after the seventeenth century.

At this time the English people were roughly divided into the following classes: [2] (1) the aristocracy and gentry, consisting in the year 1688 of about 16,600 families, having an aggregate income of about £6,000,000 a year derived from their landed estates. It has been calculated that of the 154,000 persons composing these families, above 80,000 were servants attached to the great households. Below the landed aristocracy were (2) the " freeholders of the better sort," numbering 40,000 and having an income of about £3,500,000 or £91 a year to each family. Every freeholder is assumed to have had two servants in his family, making 80,000 dependents in this class. Next came (3) the class of lesser freeholders or yeomen, numbering about 120,000 and maintaining (on estimate) about 60,000 dependents in their households. The total income of this class is estimated at £6,500,000 or about £55 per year to each family. These three classes, comprising nearly 176,000 families, and deriving their income almost wholly from the land, constituted about one-fifth of the entire population of England. There should further be noted (4) the professional class, consisting of nobles and gentry in the civil service, the army and the navy, together with lawyers, clergy and physicians; (5) the trading or merchant class; (6) the artisans and day-labourers. Among these last

[1] See *8 and 9 Wm. III*, cap. 3; Sydney, *Social Life in England*, p. 141.
[2] See Gregory King, *Scheme of the Income and Expense of the Several Families in England*, 1688, quoted in Sydney, *op. cit.*, pp. 136 ff.

should be included that miserable class of apprentices who were too often treated little better than slaves by the masters to whom they were bound for seven years by the Act of Apprentices of Elizabeth's reign (1562). It will be seen that, whereas the first three classes derived their income from the land, the last three were supported by their own labor in one form or another. These latter classes constituted about four-fifths of the English population in 1688.

The Household Membership: Family and Servants. — It must not be forgotten that in the seventeenth century a man's family included not only his wife and children, but all his servants and retainers, from the chaplain who conducted services daily in the chapel of the great house down to the humblest kitchen wench. In those days the master and mistress of a retinue of attendants held themselves personally responsible for the moral and physical well-being of every servant; and, although they ruled their household literally with the rod, disciplining children and servants alike, yet they admitted their dependents to a degree of familiar intercourse that it would be hard to find to-day. The servants of a noble family were most frequently drawn from the neighboring respectable tenantry and were treated, not as hirelings, but as humbler members of the household, whose interests were identified with those of their employers. Indeed the name " servant " was applied indiscriminately in the seventeenth century to any one who served another, thus including the young gentleman who waited at his lord's table, and the young lady who served in the chamber of a peeress. Of this conception of service Bishop Heber writes: " There was then no supposed humiliation in affairs which are now accounted menial, but which the peer received as a matter of course from the ' gentlemen of his household,' and which were paid to the knights or gentlemen by domestics chosen in the families of their own most trusted tenants; whilst in the humbler ranks of middle life it was the uniform and recognized duty of the wife to wait on her husband, the child on his parents, the youngest of the family on his elder brothers and sisters." [1]

It was part of the busy life of most English gentlewomen personally to superintend the work of every member of the family if not to share in it.   Only in the great households of wealthy peers did the steward take over the duties of supervision and training of servants which had always been the province of the housewife.   The Earl of Cork had so enormous a retinue of household servants that he prepared a set of rules governing such matters as their work, their behavior and the tables at which they should eat.   For be it remembered that rules of precedence, determined by fine distinctions in social station and the grade of service performed, were as important and binding in the servants' quarters as in the apartments of their employers.   With a view to the health of their souls, the Earl provided that all servants except officers " shall meet every morning before dinner and every night after supper at Prayers."   The Steward was empowered to examine and dismiss "any subordinate servant of ye whole Familie"; and he was enjoined to know all the women servants under " ye degree of Chamber-maydes " by name and not to change them often except for due cause.   Separate tables were provided for the Steward and " ye gents " and for the " Wayter " and other gentlemen; and " ye longe Table " in " ye Hall " was to accommodate all the lesser servants.[2]   In many families the servants were called to family prayers daily and were examined by their mistresses every Sunday after church with the laudable intent of discovering what spiritual nutriment they had received from the sermon and how much they knew of the catechism and the Bible.   We are told that Mrs. Walker, the pious wife of an English clergyman, taught her

[1] Quoted in *Barnard's Journal*, article on *English Home Life and Education*, Vol. 26, p. 379.

[2] See Bradley, *The English Housewife in the Seventeenth and Eighteenth Centuries*, p. 132.

servants to read a chapter from the Scriptures every day, and as soon as one of the group had learned to read intelligently, she presented him or her with a Bible. At the hour of family prayer the whole household gathered together, including the farm laborers; and if any man was paid by the piece, his loss was made up to him. On Sundays this worthy lady walked to church attended by her entire family, children and servants, and in the evening all were assembled again for religious instruction.[1] In the *Memoir* of Mary Rich, Countess of Warwick, we read: "Nov. 13, 1668. After dinner I spent the whole afternoon in examining and exhorting my servants to prepare themselves to receive the sacrament. I was enabled to speak with much seriousness and affection to them, and I did much endeavour to bring them to a seriousness in the matter of their souls."

In consequence of the personal interest in their welfare shown by master and mistress, and despite cuffings and beatings, the servants of the seventeenth century showed a devotion to the family and its interests in happy contrast to the indifference of their successors of the present day. Indeed the " domestic servant question " may be said to have been practically unknown in the country districts of England until after the Restoration of Charles II. Servants followed the heads of the family abroad in times of civil war and exile, and were frequently remembered in the wills of those they had so loyally served. Such bequests must have been especially acceptable in those days when the wages of servants varied from 30 shillings to £6 per annum !

THE POSITION OF WOMEN IN THE SEVENTEENTH AND EIGHTEENTH CENTURIES

Statutes affecting Women. — During the seventeenth and eighteenth centuries the English family remained patriarchal in type. Throughout this long period the law did

[1] *Barnard's Journal*, Vol. 26, pp. 380-2.

little or nothing to free the woman from her subordinate position in the family. Yet a few statutes were enacted which were of direct interest to women. Two of these concerned the wardship of heiresses. In those days there still existed the ancient feudal custom of " court wardships " by which minor heirs of large estates became, on the death of the father, wards of the king. Now the ruler, having no personal interest in these children, frequently granted some relation who applied for the privilege and paid well for it, the right to bring up the young heir and arrange for his or her marriage at the proper time. Otherwise the girl or boy remained a ward of the court. This meant that the child's education was quite likely to be superficial, if it were not entirely neglected. Furthermore, a royal ward might be disposed of in marriage by the king as he saw fit. A case in point is that of Mary Blacknall and her sister, who were left by the death of their father heiresses to a large property and at once became court wards. In the *Verney Papers* we learn that four of their maternal relatives " procured from the court of wards a lease of their lands, with the custody of their persons during their minorities, and the right of bestowing them in marriage, by payment of a fine of 2,000£ half of which was paid down, and a bond given for the remainder. The object of this arrangement was to secure to the young ladies a careful education and the power of choosing a husband on attaining a proper age. The 2,000£ was just so much money which it was deemed by their relatives worth while to pay out of their fortunes in order to release them from the oppressive power exercised over infant heiresses by the court of wards for the benefit of the crown." Later the older sister died and little Mary Blacknall, at eleven years of age, became sole heiress. Then it was that the temptation to marry her among themselves led three of the guardians to plan her marriage to the son of one of their number, — a Mr. Libb. However, the fourth guardian, Mr. Wiseman, defeated the scheme by appealing to the court of wards, which at once made out an order restraining the other guardians from such action. Two years later the little girl was *offered* to Sir Edward Verney for his son, the father binding himself to pay the remaining £1000 to the court. It is agreeable to learn that Mr. Wiseman gave his consent to this commercial arrangement only when it had been agreed that his ward should not be forced to the marriage against her will. In 1629 the girl was married to Ralph Verney, while still under fourteen. The young couple, however, did not live together for several years. Ralph Verney returned to Oxford to finish his studies, and only then returned home to claim his bride, who had meanwhile been living with his mother and learning the arts of housekeeping. Apparently this marriage, arranged in a purely business-like spirit, turned out to be a singularly happy one.[1]

But all court wardships did not end so fortunately. The king's need of funds led to outrageous misuse of his prerogatives with respect to royal wards and provoked sharp resentment from the English nobility. On the restoration of Charles II in 1660 action was immediately taken to abolish military tenure of lands with the rights of wardship and marriage which had belonged to such tenure since the feudal system began. The same Act of Parliament provided that a father might appoint a guardian by will to serve until his child should attain the age of twenty-one years. It will be noted that the mother is not mentioned in this Act, the reason being that she had no rights of guardianship in her children. Apparently, however, a mother might be permitted the right of co-guardianship with the nearest male relative, for, in his *Autobiography*, Lord Herbert of Cherbury relates that, after his father's death, his mother desired her brother, Sir Francis Newport, " to haste to London to obtain his (Lord Herbert's) wardship for his and her own use joyntly, which he obtained." [2]

---

[1] *Verney Papers, Camden Society Pub.*, Vol. 56, pp. 145-6.
[2] *Op. cit.* (ed. 1771), p. 35.

In 1670-71 an act was passed concerning the disposal of the property of a married man or woman who died intestate. In such cases the wife received half her husband's property for life if there were no offspring, and one-third if children were born to them. If a married woman died intestate, her whole estate was enjoyed by her husband during his lifetime.[1]

So late as 1663 the age-long right of a husband to inflict bodily chastisement upon his wife was upheld by the courts. In the case of Bradley *versus* Wife the English court " refused to bind the husband over to keep the peace, at the suit of his wife, unless it could be proved that her life was in danger, ' because by law he has power of castigation.' " [2] It is significant of a marked change of sentiment in this regard, however, that eleven years later, when Lady Leigh proved ill-treatment against her husband in the courts, Lord Chief Justice Hale gave it as his opinion that the " moderate castigation " mentioned in the legal register " was not meant of beating, but only of admonition and confinement to the house . . . and decided that a husband had no right to chastise his wife with personal correction." [3] But let it not be supposed that wife beating ceased in England after the judgment of the Chief Justice was pronounced. As is well known, the custom has persisted among the less enlightened classes down to the present time, partly because of the difficulties surrounding legal action and partly because of the wife's fear of her husband or her reluctance to bring him within the clutches of the law.

Legal Position of Women. — The status of married women in England in the last quarter of the eighteenth century is so ably discussed by a historian of that period that it seems well to quote at length from his book.[4] First he carefully de-

[1] Chapman, *The Status of Women under English Law*, p. 34; *Statutes of the Realm*, 22-3, ch. II, c. 10, sec. 6.

[2] Cleveland, *Women under the English Law*, pp. 221-2. [3] *Ibid.*, p. 222.

[4] Alexander, *The History of Women*, London, 1782 (3d ed.), Vol. II, pp. 488-511.

tails the privileges of a married woman. These consisted chiefly in her exemption from imprisonment for debt; her right to proper maintenance by the husband so long as she lives with him, or, in case of cruel treatment, her privilege of separate maintenance; her further right to demand security for the good behavior of the husband in case of gross ill-usage, and to sue for restitution of conjugal rights if she were deserted by him. A husband, although vested with power over all the goods and chattels of his wife, may not devise by will the ornaments and jewels which she is accustomed to wear, " though it has been held that he may, if he pleases, dispose of them in his lifetime." Since husband and wife are one and the husband the legal person, he " is liable to answer all such actions at law as were attached against his wife at the time of their marriage, and also to pay all the debts she had contracted previous to that period. . . . A wife may purchase an estate, and if the husband does not enter his dissent before the conveyance, he shall be considered as having given such consent, and the conveyance be good and valid. A wife who is accustomed to trade may sell goods in open market; and such goods a husband by virtue of his authority over her, shall not have any power to reclaim." [1]

The writer then goes on to describe a further privilege some-times extended to the English wife in the form of a marriage settlement. These " settlements " became very popular in the eighteenth century as a means whereby a wife might escape complete financial dependence on her husband. In the words of Alexander: " It is no uncommon thing, in the present times, for the matrimonial bargain to be made so, as that the wife shall retain the sole and absolute power of enjoying and dispos-ing of her own fortune, in the same manner as if she were not married; *by which inequitable bargain, the husband is debarred from enjoying any of the rights of matrimony, except the person of his wife.*" [2] Such generous marriage settlements, however,

---

[1] Alexander, *op. cit.*, pp. 488–95. [2] *Ibid.*, p. 496. Italics mine.

were probably the exception rather than the rule, since most men disapproved as cordially as the worthy Mr. Alexander of so "inequitable a bargain." Yet it became customary among the well-to-do for the future husband to allow his bride a fixed annual sum for her separate use. Also it was a common practice for the man to settle upon his wife a specified amount of land and money which constituted her "jointure" as it was called. This property, like the dower of common law, which it was designed to replace, was strictly reserved for the use of the wife after her husband's death, and could not be touched by his creditors. Thus, by means of jointure or dower, the wife was provided for in the event of her widowhood.

So much for the privileges of a British wife in the year of our Lord 1782. What was her position in other respects? Let us turn again to Alexander.

"In Britain, we allow a woman to sway our sceptre, but by law and custom we debar her from every other government but that of her own family, as if there were not a public employment between that of superintending the kingdom, and the affairs of her own kitchen, which could be managed by the genius and capacity of woman. We neither allow women to officiate at our altars, to debate in our councils, nor to fight for us in the field; we suffer them not to be members of our senate, to practise any of the learned professions, nor to concern themselves much with our trades and occupations. We exercise nearly a perpetual guardianship over them, both in their virgin and their married state, and she who, having laid a husband in the grave, enjoys an independent fortune, is almost the only woman among us who can be called free. Thus excluded from every thing which can give them consequence, they derive the greater part of the power which they enjoy, from their charms; and these, when joined to sensibility, often fully compensate, in this respect, for all the disadvantages they are laid under by law and custom.

" As the possession of property is one of the most valuable of all political blessings, and generally carries the possession of power and authority along with it; one of the most peculiar disadvantages in the condition of our women is, their being postponed to all males in the succession to the inheritance of landed estates, and generally allowed much smaller shares than the men, even of money and effects of their fathers and ancestors, when this money or those effects are given them in the lifetime of their parents, or devised to them by will; for otherwise, that is, if the father dies intestate, they share equally with sons in all personal property. When an estate, in default of male heirs, descends to the daughters, the common custom of England is, that the eldest shall not, in the same manner as an eldest son, inherit the whole, but all the daughters shall have an equal share in it.

*   *   *   *   *   *   *

" But besides these laws, which for the most part operate so as to hinder the fair sex from getting possession of any considerable property, the laws of marriage again divest them of such property as they really are in possession of. By marriage all the goods and chattels which belong to the woman become vested in the husband, and he has the same power over them as she had while they were her sole and absolute property. When the wife, however, is possessed of real estate in land, the power which the husband acquires over it is not so extensive, he only gains the right to the rents and profits arising out of it during the continuance of the marriage; but if a living child is born to him, though it should die in a very short time, he becomes, in that case, tenant for life, by the courtesy of the country. If there happens to be no child, then at the demise of the wife the estate goes to her heirs at law. But the property of her goods and chattels devolves upon the husband, who has the sole and absolute power of disposing of them according to his pleasure.

" Every married woman is considered as a minor, and cannot do any deed which affects her real or personal property, without the consent of her husband; if she does any such deed, it is not valid and the husband may claim the property of what she disposed of, as if no such disposal had been made. As a married woman cannot dispose of her property while living, so neither does the law give her that power at her death. In the statute of wills she is expressly prohibited from devising land, and even from bequeathing goods and chattels without the leave of her husband, because all such goods and chattels are, without any limitation, his sole and absolute property; whether they were such as the wife brought along with her at the marriage, or such as she acquired by her labour and industry afterward.

* * * * * * *

" If a husband and wife are jointly possessed of houses and lands which are settled upon the survivor, if the husband destroys himself his wife shall not have the half that belonged to him; it becomes the property of the crown, as a compensation for the loss of a subject. When a husband and wife agree to live separate, and the husband covenants to give her so much a year; if at any time he offers to be reconciled and to take her home, upon her refusal, he shall not any longer be obliged to pay her a separate maintenance. If a legacy be paid to a married woman who lives separate from her husband, the husband may file a bill in chancery to oblige the person who paid it to his wife to pay it again to him with interest.

* * * * * * *

" The power which a husband has over the person of his wife, does not seem perfectly settled by the laws of this country, it is nevertheless certain, that she is not to go abroad, nor to leave his house and family without his approbation; but what coercive methods he may make use of to restrain her from so doing, or whether he may proceed any farther than to admonition and denying her money, seems a point not altogether agreed upon.

" When a wife is injured in her person or property, so limited is her power, that she cannot bring an action for redress without the consent and approbation of her husband, nor in any way but in his name. If, however, such husband has abjured the realm, or is banished from it, he is considered as dead in law, and his wife in that case may sue for redress in her own name and authority. . . . When a widow is endowed of certain lands and tenements, and sells them, the heir at law may not only recover them of the purchaser, but also refuse to restore them back to the widow, or to pay her any dower in their stead. By the laws of England, a father only is empowered to exercise a rightful authority over his children; no power is conferred on the mother, only so far as to oblige these children to consider her as a person entitled to duty and a reverential regard." [1]

A review of this formidable array of deprivations and restrictions laid upon married women shows that the vast majority are concerned with the ownership and disposal of property. Clearly in these respects the hands of a British wife were firmly tied. Such arrangements point to the fact that monogamous marriage and patriarchal family organization were designed in large measure for the protection of private property, and for its control and inheritance by males. Other ends were doubtless served by these institutions, but the economic purpose was fundamental from the dawn of history to the latter half of the nineteenth century.

THE IDEAL OF WOMANHOOD IN ENGLAND

The Seventeenth Century Ideal. — Despite the numerous limitations with which the life of a married woman in England

[1] *Op. cit.*, pp. 505–13.

was hedged around, and the subordinate position occupied by her in family and State, yet it would be a mistake to assume that women were held in low esteem throughout the whole of this period. When the conditions of social life in the early seventeenth century are taken into consideration, the ideal of womanhood in that age seems fairly high. To be sure, that ideal might be summed up in the words " a virtuous housewife," and the feminine " vertues " most highly extolled were beyond question discreetness, modesty and humility; yet the conception was fine and worthy as far as it went. In his quaint book *The English Gentlewoman*, published in 1641, Brathwaite has happily expressed the feminine ideal of his age.

" For shee loves without any pointed pretences to be really vertuous, without any popular applause to be affably gracious, without any glorious gloss to be sincerely zealous. Her Education hath so enabled her as shee can converse with you of all places, deliver her judgment conceivingly of most persons, and discourse most delightfully of all fashions. Shee hath been so well schooled in the Discipline of this *Age*, as shee onely desires to reteine in memory that *forme* which is least affected but most comely; to consort with such as may improve her *Knowledge* and *Practise* of goodnesse by their company; . . . Diligent you shall ever find her in her imployments, serious in her advice, temperate in her Discourse, discreet in her answers. . . . Take upon her to instruct others, she will not, such is her Humility; albeit, every moving posture which comes from her may be a line of direction unto others to follow her. . . . However, she might boast of *Descent*, her desire is to raise it by *Desert*. Shee holds, no family can be truly *Generous*, unlesse it be nobly vertuous. Her *life* must express the line from which she came." [1] And again: " Shee distates none more than those busie housewives, who are ever running into discourse of others families, but forget their own. Neither

[1] *Op. cit.*, opening pages of dedication to Anne, Countess of Pembroke.

x

holds shee it sufficient to bee onely an Housekeeper; or Snayle-like to bee still under roofe; shee partakes therefore of the Pismere in providing, of the Sareptan widow in disposing; holding ever an absent providence better than an improvident presence. . . . She conceives no small delight in educating the young and unexperienced Damsels of your sexe; wherein she reteines an excellent faculty and facility." [1]

It will be noted that the author of this ideal picture does not omit all mention of the intellectual training of his perfect gentlewoman. Her education is to enable her to " converse with you of all places, deliver her judgment conceivingly of most persons, and discourse most delightfully of all fashions " (*i.e.*, customs). Yet there can be little doubt that the intellectual impulse of the Renaissance had largely spent itself in the seventeenth century. In consequence it is probable that neither men nor women were as thoroughly educated as they had been in preceding generations. It is true that gentlemen's sons very generally studied the classics at home with tutors or in the great Public Schools of England; but their training became largely conventional as the respect for learning grew less deep and less sincere. Certain it is that neither Puritan nor Cavalier set great store on the thorough education of girls. The Puritan was averse to it because he harked back to the conception of the early Church Fathers of woman as the cause of the original sin, therefore a creature to be kept under strict government. The Cavalier was more indifferent than hostile, partly because woman was tending to become for him a plaything whose sex was her most alluring charm, and partly because custom had almost wholly restricted women's education to domestic management.

After the Restoration of Charles II in 1660 a change came over the spirit of English society, at least among the wealthy

[1] *Op. cit., Address to the Reader.*

and high born. Men and women became infected with the
feverish gayety and low moral ideals of the Court and abandoned the quiet of their country estates for the excitements
of fashionable life in London. Quite often women were as
frivolous and in some instances as vicious, as the men. Of the
change that had taken place in social life and ideals Sir John
Evelyn wrote with some feeling at the close of the seventeenth
century:

" Thus you see, young sparks, how the stile and method
of wooing is quite changed . . . since the days of our forefathers (of unhappy memory, simple and plain men as they
were), who courted and chose their wives for their modesty,
frugality, keeping at home, good housewifery, and other
æconomical virtues then in reputation; and when the young
damsels were taught all these in the country and at their
parents houses, the portion they brought was more in virtue
than money, and she was a richer match than one who could
have brought a million and nothing else to commend her."
Morality and patriotism were sound and vigorous in those
days, for " men of estate studied the public good, and gave
examples of true piety, loyalty, justice, sobriety, charity,
and the good neighborhood compos'd most differences;
perjury, suborning witnesses, alimony, avowed adulteries,
and misses (publickly own'd) were prodigies in those days.
. . . The virgins and young ladies of that golden age
. . . put their hands to the spindle, nor disdain'd they
the needle; were obsequious and helpful to their parents,
instructed in the managery of the family, and gave presages of making excellent wives. Nor then did they read
so many romances, see so many plays, and smutty farces;
set up for visits, and have their days of audience, and
idle pass-time. . . . Their retirements were devout and
religious books, and their recreations in the distillatory, and
knowledge of plants and their virtues, for the comfort of
their poor neighbors and use of the family, which whole-

some plain dyet and kitchen physick preserved in perfect health." [1]

The Ideal Woman of the Eighteenth Century. — When every allowance has been made for the human tendency to look back to the " good old times " of one's youth and to disapprove of the social innovations introduced in one's old age, Sir John Evelyn's account still remains substantially correct. A profound alteration for the worse had come over the social life of his time; nor did the tone of morality improve in the eighteenth century, which is rightly known as the most artificial and perhaps heartless epoch in English history. In the *Spectator* (1712) Addison satirizes the empty life of the fashionable lady of the time in the following extract from *Clarinda's Journal :*

" Wednesday. From Eight to Ten. Drank two Dishes of Chocolate in Bed, and fell asleep after 'em.

" From Ten to Eleven. Eat a Slice of Bread and Butter, drank a dish of Bohea, read the *Spectator*.

" From Eleven to One. At my Toilet, try'd a new Head.[2] Gave orders for Veney[3] to be combed and washed. *Mem.* I look best in Blue.

" From One till Half an Hour after Two. Drove to the Change. Cheapened a couple of Fans.

" Till Four. At Dinner. *Mem.* Mr. Frost passed by in his new Liveries.

" From Four till Six. Dressed, paid a visit to old Lady Blithe and her Sister, *having heard they were gone out of Town that Day.*

" From Six to Eleven, At Basset.[4] *Mem.* Never sit again upon the Ace of Diamond." [5]

It can hardly be expected that the ideal of womanhood would be dignified and worthy at a time when social life was frivo-

---

[1] *Mundus Muliebris*, in *Literary Remains* (ed. 1834), pp. 700–2.
[2] Head-dress.   [3] Venus, her lap-dog.
[4] A gambling game of cards.   [5] *Spectator*, No. 323.

lous and unsound. On the contrary, that ideal may truthfully be said to have reached its lowest ebb. The writings of
the time abound in references to the " fair sex " and bear
eloquent testimony to the eighteenth century Englishman's
conception of woman's character and functions. The emphasis laid on "female delicacy" and "sensibility," the insistence
upon woman's dependence on man as constituting her supreme
charm, the universal tendency to place the highest value
upon qualities peculiar to sex, all conspire to make these
works almost nauseous reading. A few quotations will
bring this feminine ideal more clearly before the reader.
In his oft-quoted *Legacy to his Daughters*, Dr. Gregory
writes in 1796 :

" One of the chief beauties in a female character is that
modest reserve, that retiring delicacy which avoids the public
eye, and is disconcerted even at the gaze of admiration. . . .
When a girl ceases to blush she has lost the most powerful charm
of beauty. That extreme sensibility which it indicates, may
be a weakness and incumbrance in our sex, as I have too often
felt, but in yours it is peculiarly engaging." [1] Apparently
Dr. Gregory's ideal woman is never for one moment to be
wholly spontaneous, but must constantly hold in mind the
disturbing fact that " female delicacy " may be easily marred.
Thus he warns his daughters in dancing never to allow themselves " to be so far transported with mirth as to forget the
delicacy of [their] sex. Many a girl, dancing in the gaiety
and innocence of her heart, is thought to discover a spirit
she little dreams of." [2]

Perhaps one of the best expressions of the dominant conception of womanhood in the eighteenth century is that of
Lord Kames.

" A man says what he knows; a woman what is agreeable;
knowledge is necessary to the former; taste is sufficient to
the latter. A man who does his duty can brave censure; a

[1] *Op. cit.* (ed. 1796), pp. 35–6. [2] *Ibid.*, p. 68.

woman's conduct ought to be exemplary, in order to be esteemed by all. The least doubt of her chastity deprives her
of every comfort in the matrimonial state. *In the education
of females accordingly, no motive has greater influence than the
thought of what people will say of them.*" The mother must
take account of this, and very early teach her little daughter
submission to the will of those in authority over her. " This
is essential to the female sex, forever subjected to the authority
of a single person, or to the opinion of all." [1] When the girl
has been made duly " tractable " she should then be taught
that to " make a good husband is but one branch of a man's
duty; but it is the chief duty of a woman to make a good
wife." " Woman, destined to be obedient, ought to be disciplined early to bear wrongs, without murmuring. This is a
hard lesson; and yet it is necessary even for their own sake;
sullenness or peevishness may alienate the husband; but tend
not to sooth his roughness, nor to moderate his impetuosity.
Heaven made women insinuating, but not in order to be cross :
it made them feeble, not in order to be imperious : it gave a
sweet voice, not in order to scold : . . . it did not give
them beauty, in order to disfigure it by anger." [2]

The male writers of the age, perhaps stirred to action by a
certain restless dissatisfaction among women here and there,
leave no doubt of their belief in the essential inferiority of
the female sex. Thus in his *Strictures on Female Education*
Bennet voices the general view in the following delightful
statement :

" It may be supposed with great probability and fairness,
that their very outward frame is marked with a physical inferiority. It appears not to be calculated for such efforts
of thinking as the more abstracted sciences require. . . .
*The delicacy of the everlasting pea, which so happily unites
elegance with sweetness, would be easily oppressed.* The tender

[1] *Loose Hints upon Education* (ed. 1781), pp. 135–7. Italics mine.
[2] *Op. cit.*, pp. 228–9.

plant which is refreshed with *gentle* gales, would be entirely overwhelmed or exterminated by a *whirlwind.*" [1]

Even Erasmus Darwin, grandfather of the great evolutionist, adds his voice to the chorus. Thus in 1797 he writes:

" The female character should possess the mild and retiring virtues rather than the bold and dazzling ones; great eminence in almost everything is sometimes injurious to a young lady; whose temper and disposition should appear to be pliant rather than robust; to be ready to take impressions rather than to be decidedly mark'd; as great apparent strength of character however excellent, is liable to alarm both her own and the other sex; and to create admiration rather than affection." [2]

Foreigners visiting England in the eighteenth century comment on the low state of sexual morality. Thus Archenholz writes that it was estimated in his day that London alone harbored 50,000 prostitutes, not counting the " mistresses " kept by many men of wealth. This widely prevalent vice was hushed up as much as possible by the " taboo " long ago set upon discussion or even recognition of its existence. Women, especially, were expected to go about with eyes and ears firmly closed. Now and then fathers instructed their daughters that when married they should feign ignorance of the vicious lives of their husbands. In 1700 the Marquis of Halifax, an honorable man, embodies this counsel in his *Advice to a Daughter:* " First then, you are to consider, you live in a time which hath rendered some kind of Frailties so habitual that they lay claim to large grains of allowance." A woman should regard herself as recompensed for the strict virtue required of her by holding the honor of the family in her keeping. " This being so, remember, That next to the danger of committing the fault yourself, the greatest is that of seeing it in your Husband. Do not seem to look or hear that way. . . ."

[1] *Ibid.* (ed. 1788), p. 104. Italics partly mine.
[2] *Plan for the Conduct of Female Education in Boarding Schools* (ed. 1797), p. 10.

The foregoing panegyrics on the ideal " female " character were of course written by men and glorify those elements of passive docility, gentleness, and clinging dependence which have always appealed to the masculine sex. But it is a little discouraging to find that the literary women of the period, — such writers as Hannah More and Mrs. Barbauld, — uphold much the same ideal of womanhood. Not gifted with the far-sighted vision that would enable them to glimpse the widening opportunities in the fields of education and of employment soon to be laid open to women, they still maintain that the home is the only sphere possible to their sex. Even while urging that women should receive a more thorough and practical education than is given them in the boarding schools of the period, Hannah More appeals to " men of sense " not to oppose " the improvement of the other sex, as they themselves will be sure to be gainers by it; the enlargement of the female understanding being the most likely means to put an end to those cavils and contentions for equality which female smatterers so anxiously maintain." [1]

Yet protestants against these cramping doctrines were not lacking even among the women. Toward the close of the seventeenth century appeared a ringing *Essay* by Mrs. Bathsua Makin, urging that competent schools for girls be erected and prophesying that if women were intelligently educated, men would speedily be ashamed of their ignorance. Later were published the protests of Mary Astell, all [2] sharply criticising the current ideal of womanhood and the shallow education of her sex.

The French Revolution and Mary Wollstonecraft. — But the age was not ready for these advanced doctrines, and so the eighteenth century drew toward its close with no apparent change in the ideas and practices respecting women. Then

[1] *Strictures on the Modern System of Female Education*, p. 14.
[2] *Some Reflections upon Marriage* (Fourth ed., 1730); *An Essay in Defense of the Female Sex*, 1696; *A Serious Proposal to the Ladies* . . ., 1694.

came the revolt of the American Colonies, closely followed by the Revolution in France; and England was thereupon invaded by strange and alarming theories of liberty, equality and human brotherhood. The awful uprising of the French people against king and privileged aristocracy; the attacks directed against the Church as repressive of all freedom of thinking; the almost frenzied assertion of fundamental human rights, common to all; these were bound to make themselves felt in the most conservative English circles. The letters of Horace Walpole to Hannah More are replete with accounts of the horrors being enacted across the Channel, and are aflame with indignation against the outrages committed—an indignation which took small account of the oppressions that had provoked them. Even the women of the day read of the new social philosophy which served as the gospel of the French people in their revolt, and which was producing restless discontent among the laboring class in England. Most of them, like their husbands and fathers, were terrified by its doctrines and turned from them with strong aversion. For these educated women belonged to the aristocratic class from which the ranks of the conservative Tories were regularly recruited. In the words of a modern writer: " They had been brought up in the settled conviction that it was their duty to labour among the poor, and they could not understand the fierce cry of the poor for power to labour for themselves." [1] Nor did they understand any better the profound influence that these new theories of democracy were bound to exert upon the education and life of their own sex.

But one woman clearly saw the broader implications of this democratic upheaval, even as she saw and resented the flimsy education and superficial lives of the titled ladies of her day. Aglow with the vision and hope of a new order in which all women, — wives and mothers as well as maidens, — should play a nobler part than was possible to them under

[1] Blaese, *The Emancipation of English women*, p. 76.

the limitations of the eighteenth century, Mary Wollstonecraft wrote her *Vindication of the Rights of Women.* Ill-
organized and abounding in needless repetitions as the work
doubtless is, it yet was the most stirring and significant con-
tribution to feminist literature that had appeared among
any people. A comparison of Mary Wollstonecraft's fervid
appeal published in 1792 with the works of Mary Astell,
written a century before, reveal how far the former had progressed beyond the relatively conservative position of her
predecessor. The *Rights of Women* might be said to take
as its thesis this ringing statement: " It is time to effect a
revolution in female manners, — time to restore to them their
lost dignity, — and make them, as a part of the human species,
labor, by reforming themselves, to reform the world." [1]   Let
women fill their heads with sound knowledge and their days
with wise employments, and their " virtue " will pretty well
take care of itself, says this eighteenth-century feminist.
It has more than once been pointed out that Mary Wollstonecraft's fearless attack on the eighteenth-century custom of
emphasizing the sex qualities of women at the expense of their
intellectual gifts did much to bring about the author's condemnation by the preachers of " female delicacy." For she
sought to show in the plainest language that so long as both
men and women were agreed to concentrate their attention
on the sexual character of women, society would steadily
deteriorate in morals. " This desire of being always women,
is the very consciousness that degrades the sex." The power
women should seek is not a gross physical influence over men
but a control of their own natures by means of a trained
reason.[2]   Therefore every woman should have such education
as will " exercise the understanding and form the heart —
or, in other words, . . . enable the individual to attain such
habits of virtue as will render it independent. In fact, it

[1] *Op. cit.*, in *The Humboldt Library of Popular Science Literature*, Vol. XV,
p. 60.   [2] *Ibid.*, p. 76.

is a farce to call any being virtuous whose virtues do not result from the exercise of its own reason." [1]

One of the most radical and fervent doctrines of the writer's creed is her belief in the right of every woman to be regarded as an *individual* with peculiar capacities of her own worthy of respect and development. Therefore the end of women's exertions should be " to unfold their own faculties, and acquire the dignity of conscious virtues." [2] Even if a woman's duties are limited to managing her family, educating her children and assisting her neighbors, she cannot properly discharge these duties if she lacks, " individually, the protection of civil laws ; she must not be dependent on her husband's bounty for her subsistence during his life or support after his death ; for how can a being be generous who has nothing of its own? or virtuous, who is not free? " [3] Mary Wollstonecraft is, perhaps, the first woman of her time to perceive the dignity and independence which would accrue to women from opening to them the world of labor and permitting them to earn their own living. " How many women," she bitterly exclaims, " . . . waste life away, the prey of discontent, who might have practised as physicians, regulated a farm, managed a shop, and stood erect, supported by their own industry, instead of hanging their heads surcharged with the dew of sensibility. . . . How much more respectable is the woman who earns her own bread by fulfilling any duty, than the most accomplished beauty ! " [4] These were brave words to be uttered in the eighteenth century.

It cannot be said that the clarion tones of this new declaration of independence made a profound impression upon the English mind, for this was too busily engaged in horrified repudiation of the principles of the French Revolution and in the attempt to prevent these disturbing theories from upsetting the contented equilibrium of the masses of the

[1] *Ibid.*, p. 38.   [2] *Ibid.*, p. 42.   [3] *Ibid.*, pp. 153–4.   [4] *Ibid.*, p. 156.

English working people. In consequence, the removal of
the legal, economic and educational disabilities of women
was destined to be the work of the nineteenth century.

MARRIAGE IN THE SEVENTEENTH AND EIGHTEENTH CENTURIES

Persistence of the Idea of Marriage as an Economic Contract. — As might be expected, little change was effected
during this period in the conception of marriage as fundamentally a contract to secure social and economic benefits,
— a contract arranged in most cases by the parents. " The
girls of the seventeenth century enjoyed but a brief springtime. With dawning womanhood, while they were yet in
the schoolroom, in some cases even in the nursery, careful
parents were already considering the choice of a husband." [1]
Poor Ralph Verney, who was guardian of his five orphaned
sisters, had many anxious years of matrimonial negotiations
before the last girl was successfully married off. His difficulties were enormously increased by the fact that his deceased
father, Sir Edmund Verney, had left a marriage portion for
only one of his daughters. Very open and unashamed was
the bargaining, and many were the demands on Ralph's
slender property before he had the profound satisfaction of
giving away the last sister at the marriage altar. [2]

Early marriages were the rule throughout the seventeenth
century. Thus Lady Mary Villiers was a widow at nine;
Mary Blacknall was married to Ralph Verney at thirteen;
and Herbert of Cherbury was married at fifteen to his
cousin Mary, who was twenty-one. This latter match was
quite frankly arranged by the parents and guardians, so that
the young lady could inherit the property of her father, Sir
William Herbert of St. Gillian's, who made his daughter's

[1] Elizabeth Godfrey, *Home Life under the Stuarts*, p. 113.
[2] See *Verney Memoirs*, Vol. I, ch. XXVII.

inheritance conditional upon her marrying a man whose sur-
name was Herbert.[1] Yet here and there were parents, even
in the seventeenth century, who deliberately permitted to
their daughters freedom of choice in marriage. The fair
Lady Dorothy Sidney was sensibly left to choose her own
husband and so likewise was the Puritan maid, Lucy Apsley.
Even where the marriage was contracted for by the parents
the right of veto remained with the girl and the youth.

Occasionally a certain idealism may be found coloring the
conception of marriage in the seventeenth century, — not
that this had been wholly lacking since the Renaissance, but
that now it is becoming more apparent. Toward the middle
of the century an English gentleman, writing to felicitate
Master Hugh Penry upon the latter's marriage with his sister,
says: " . . . I heartily congratulate this marriage, and pray
that a blessing may descend upon it from that place where
all marriages are made which is from Heaven, the fountain
of all felicitie. . . ." [2] This same idealistic gentleman, reply-
ing to a friend who has urged him to marry, writes:

" 'Tis the custom of som (and 'tis a common custome)
to choose Wives by the weight, that is, by their wealth. . . .
The late Earl of Salisbury gives a caveat for this, That beuty
without a dowry . . . is as a gilded shell without a kernel;
therefore he warns his son to be sure to have something with
his Wife, and his reason is, *Because nothing can be bought
in the Market without money.* Indeed 'tis very fitting that
he or she should have wherewith to support both according
to their quality. . . . But he who hath enough of his own
to maintain a Wife, and marrieth only for money, discovereth
a poor sordid disposition." [3]

Half a century later Mary Astell denounces the prevailing
custom whereby wives are chosen for their dowries, not for

---

[1] *Autobiography of Edward, Lord Herbert of Cherbury* (ed. 1771), p. 36.
[2] James Howell, *Familiar Letters* (ed. 1645), Section 2, p. 33.
[3] *Ibid.*, Section 2, pp. 89–90.

their characters. " In a word," she declares, " when we have reckon'd up how many look no further than the making of their Fortune, as they call it; who don't so much as propose to themselves any Satisfaction in the Woman to whom they plight their Faith, seeking only to be Masters of her Estate, that so they may have Money enough to indulge all their irregular Appetites; who think they are as good as can be expected, if they are but, according to the fashionable term *Civil Husbands;* . . . when to these you have added such as marry without any thought at all, further than that it is the custom of the World, what others have done before them, that the Family must be kept up, the antient Race preserved, and therefore their kind Parents and Guardians choose as they think convenient, without ever consulting the Young one's Inclinations, who must be satisfied, or pretend so, at least, upon Pain of their Displeasure, and that heavy Consequence of it, Forfeiture of their Estate: These set aside, I fear there will be but a small Remainder to marry out of better Considerations. . . ." [1]

But such ideas and practices were deeply rooted in the past, and it is not surprising that matters had not greatly improved by the middle of the eighteenth century. Steele in the *Guardian* deplores the mistake made by parents who " make love for their children, and without any manner of regard to the season of life, and the respective interests of their progeny, judge of their future happiness by the rules of commerce." [2] Yet the occasional references in eighteenth century literature to free choice on the part of fashionable ladies, who are hard put to it to select one among their lovers [3] show that parental prerogative in the matter of arranging marriages was gradually being undermined. Writing in 1796 to his daughters Dr. Gregory says of free choice in marriage: " If I live to that age when you shall be capable to judge

---

[1] *Some Reflections upon Marriage* (ed. 1730), pp. 35–6.   [2] *Op. cit.,* No. 73.
[3] Steele, *The Tatler*, No. 258.

for yourselves, and do not strangely alter my sentiments I shall act towards you in a very different manner from what most parents do. My opinion has always been, that when that period arrives, the parential (*sic*) authority ceases. . . . If you did not chuse to follow my advice, I should not on that account cease to love you as my children." [1]

Disinclination of Men for Marriage. — Certainly the young people of the eighteenth century had larger opportunities to meet and know each other than were permitted them in previous periods. They visited in their homes, and mingled freely in the dancing academies so popular at the time. Yet a marked disinclination on the part of young men to marry became very noticeable in the reign of Queen Anne. "The whole literature of the day," says Ashton, "speaks of the tendency of young men to avoid the trammels of matrimony." [2] The author is inclined to lay this reluctance at the door of the new custom of marriage settlements whereby a generous jointure was secured to the bride on the death of her husband and "pin-money" was allowed her during his lifetime. If the pin-money were large enough, a wife might be made economically independent of her husband; hence the custom was very unpopular in Queen Anne's day, and even later. Steele in *The Tender Husband*, represents two fathers as in hot discussion over this vexed matter. One of them, Sir Harry Gubbin, exclaims:

"Look y', Mr. Tipkin, the main Article with me is that Foundation of Wives Rebellion, — that cursed Pin Money — Five Hundred Pounds *per annum* Pin Money.

"*Tipkin.* The word Pin Money, Sir Harry, is a term —

"*Sir H.* It is a Term, Brother, we never had in our Family, nor ever will. Make her Jointure in Widowhood accordingly large, but Four Hundred Pounds a Year is enough to give no account of."

---

[1] *Legacy to his Daughters*, pp. 125–6.
[2] Ashton, *Social Life in the Reign of Queen Anne*, p. 25.

Marriage Customs. *Clandestine Marriages.* — Although clandestine marriages had been common enough in the seventeenth century, their frequency had so increased in the eighteenth as to constitute a grave scandal. As early as the reign of William III (1689–1702) an Act had been passed which sought to enforce the law requiring a five-shilling duty on marriage licenses and imposing a fine of £100 on any person who married couples without a license. Yet the law seems to have been easily evaded. At this time certain chapels in London were exempted from the visitation and control of the Bishop. Of these " lawless Churches," as they were called, St. James's near Aldgate and Holy Trinity attained an unsavory notoriety as places where any unmarried couple of legal age could be united in matrimony with no preliminary formalities or embarrassing questions asked. Occasionally the rector of one of these churches fell into the clutches of the ecclesiastical authorities and was suspended from office for a few years. But as soon as he was reinstated he returned to the profitable business of marrying without license or banns.[1]

But the greatest scandal in this respect surrounded the irregular marriages performed in the prisons of the Fleet and the Queen's Bench. Early in the reign of Anne, clergymen imprisoned in the Fleet for debt began their infamous trade of marrying whatever couples presented themselves, without requiring either banns or license. These impecunious gentlemen boldly advertised their willingness to unite all comers in matrimony for a small sum. An illicit register was kept to record these marriages as early as 1674. The records show that an unprincipled clergyman named John Gaynam plied a brisk and lucrative marriage business in the Fleet between the years 1709 and 1740; and there were numerous other ordained ministers who also turned a pretty penny in the same unlawful trade. In the Queen's

[1] See Ashton, *op. cit.*, p. 29.

Bench prison matters were even worse, for there laymen officiated as well as clergymen. So great did the scandal become, that in 1712 a Marriage Act was passed (10 Anne, cap. 19) renewing the penalty of £100 attached to the performance of an illegal marriage and giving half the penalty to the informer. The Act also imposed an extra duty of five shillings on every marriage license or certificate, while it provided that " if any gaoler or keeper of any prison shall be privy to or knowingly permit, any marriage to be solemnized in his said prison, before publication of banns, or license obtained as aforesaid, he shall for every such offence forfeit the sum of one hundred pounds. . . ." [1]

Unfortunately this Act seems to have been practically inoperative from the first, and Fleet marriages continued to be performed until 1753, when the Hardwicke Act was passed.[2] By the terms of this law, which was hotly contested in the Commons, all marriages, save those of Jews, Quakers and members of the royal family, were to be celebrated only after publication of banns or securing of a license, and only during the hours from eight to twelve in the morning (the canonical hours), in an Anglican Church or chapel, and before an Anglican clergyman. " To solemnize marriage in any other manner or in any other place or without banns, except by special license of the archbishop, is punished with fourteen years' transportation, and the marriage is declared void." [3] To secure the publicity so urgently necessary, the act provided that at least two witnesses must be present at the marriage and registers must be accurately kept by the clergy. Such registers might not be falsified or destroyed under pain of death. In case of the marriage of minors by license, failure to obtain the parents' consent rendered the marriage void. Imperfect as it was, this Act marked a long

[1] Ashton, *op. cit.*, pp. 27–32.   See also Howard's exhaustive account of Fleet marriages in his *History of Matrimonial Institutions*, I, 435–460.
[2] 26 George II, c. 33.   [3] Howard, *op. cit.*, p. 458.

Y

stride forward in the regulation of marriage by the State, in contradistinction to the Church, and in the abolition of clandestine unions.

Private Marriages. — Even when couples did not seek to evade the law, private marriages seem to have been very popular in the age of Queen Anne. Doubtless this mode of tying the matrimonial knot was favored because the chief parties could thus avoid the noisy and expensive festivities that accompanied a public marriage in eighteenth century England. In his valuable study of English life at this time M. Misson describes these " incognito " marriages as follows:

" The Bridegroom . . . and the Bride . . . conducted by their Father and Mother, or by those that serve them in their room, and accompany'd by two Bride men and two Bride maids, go early in the morning with a Licence in their Pocket and call up Mr. Curate and his Clerk, tell him their Business, are marry'd with a low Voice, and the Doors shut; tip the Minister a Guinea and the Clerk a Crown; steal softly out, one one way, and t'other another, either on Foot or in Coaches; go different Ways to some Tavern at a Distance from their own Lodgings, or to the House of some trusty Friend, there have a good Dinner and return Home at Night as quietly as Lambs. If the Drums and Fiddles have had notice of it they will be sure to be with them by Day break, making a horrible Racket, till they have got the Pence, and, which is worst of all, the whole Murder will come out." [1] The writer goes on to describe in plain language the rude sports in which the bridesmaids and groomsmen indulged at the expense of the newly married pair, who doubtless were thoroughly out of patience before they were at last left in peace.

Doubtless marriage was made very easy for every one of legal age during this period. Any boy of fourteen and girl of twelve who desired to escape parental discipline and lead

[1] Misson's *Memoirs and Observations in his Travels over England* (trans. by Ozells, 1719, quoted in Ashton, *op. cit.*, pp. 32–3).

a " free " life might be indissolubly joined in the bonds of matrimony without their parents' consent and at little expense. Ashton quotes the advertisement of a Hampstead chapel which advertisement was designed to fill the coffers of the chapel at the expense of unthinking couples: " As there are many weddings at Sion Chapel, Hampstead, five Shillings only is required for all the Church fees of any Couple that are married there, provided they bring with them a license or Certificate, according to the Act of Parliament." A little later, in 1716, the chapel generously offered to marry all persons applying there without any fee whatever, provided they should " have their wedding dinner in the gardens." [1] The law requiring that banns be proclaimed three times in church before the marriage was celebrated had become thoroughly unpopular and was frequently evaded by securing a license. Misson says concerning the custom of banns that " very few are willing to have their Affairs declar'd to all the World in a publick Place, when for a Guinea they may do it *Snug*, and without Noise; and my good Friends the Clergy, who find their Accounts in it are not very zealous to prevent it."

THE HOMES OF THE SEVENTEENTH AND EIGHTEENTH CENTURIES

Architecture and Furnishings. — The homes of the nobility and gentlefolk of England in the seventeenth century must have been in many respects delightful dwelling places, full of sober beauty and charm. The revolution in domestic architecture that began during the reign of Henry VIII was carried much further in the days of Elizabeth. While the prevailing desire for privacy did not lead to the abandonment of the great hall of the mansion, it did develop private apartments such as the parlor, the withdrawing room and lofty

[1] Ashton, *op. cit.*, p. 31.

bed-chambers. The dirty rushes which strewed the floors in Henry VIII's day gave place in the seventeenth century to floor coverings of leather or to Indian and Persian carpets. The influence of the great architect, Inigo Jones, who came to England early in the seventeenth century with Anne of Denmark, was wholly to encourage the Englishman's desire for privacy in his home and for furnishings which expressed his personal taste. Under the Stuart kings the houses of the great nobles improved vastly both in comfort and elegance. Yet, with all their panelled walls, elaborate carving, hangings of silk, velvet or tapestry, glass painted in heraldic designs, and costly foreign furniture, these homes were not so essentially English as the less pretentious manor-houses, built of timbered oak, and boasting myriad windows with leaded panes. The country homes of the well-to-do in Stuart days were quite commonly self-supporting, capable of provisioning themselves with very little assistance from the outside world of industry. Each had its slaughter-house and brewery, its malt-house and sometimes its mill for grinding the grain raised on the estate. Even laundries had been added to most houses, for the family washing was now very generally done at home. Surrounding the house were spacious grounds traversed by paths which ran between stiff rows of clipped yew trees. One of these paths brought the sauntering visitor to the fish-ponds, stocked with carp ; another led to the herb garden behind its low hedge, where lavender, rosemary and thyme were carefully tended by the housewife.

To Sir John Evelyn we are indebted for a delightful description of the furnishings of a manor-house in the closing years of the Stuarts :

" They had cupboards of ancient useful plate, whole chests of fine Holland sheets, (white as the driven snow) and fragrant of rose and lavender, for the bed ; and the sturdy oaken bedstead, and furniture of the home, lasted one whole century ; the shovel-board, and other long tables, both in hall and parlour, were as fixed as the freehold; nothing was moveable save joynt-stools, the black jacks, silver tankards and bowls. . . .

" Things of use were natural, plain and wholesome; nothing was superfluous, nothing necessary wanting: . . ." [1]

Another description of a seventeenth-century home is found in Howell's *Familiar Letters*. The writer pictures it as " so virtuous and regular a House as any I believe in the Land both for æconomical government, and the choice company, for I never saw yet such a dainty race of children in all my life together, I never saw yet such an orderly and punctual attendance of servants, nor a great House so neatly kept. . . . The kitchen and gutters and other offices of noise and drudgery are at the fag end, there's a back gate for beggars and the meaner sort of swains to come in at. The stables butt upon the Park, which for a chearfull rising ground, for groves and browsings for the Deer, for rivulets of water may compare with any for its bignes in the whole land; it is opposite to the front of the great House, whence from the Gallerie one may see much of the game when they are a hunting. Now for the gardning and costly choice flowers, for ponds, for stately large walks green and gravelly, for orchards and choice fruits of all sorts, there are few the like in England: . . ." [2]

Contrast this charming picture with that presented by the homes of the poorer peasantry, described by a modern historian as almost uninhabitable. " One chimney, one unglazed window, a roof thatched with straw, and four bare walls, afforded shelter from the summer's heat and the winter's cold, but that was all. Of comforts there were none. The cottage had no flooring, save that which was furnished by nature. . . . The mud walls were rarely covered with any coat of plastering; there was no ceiling under the straw

---

[1] *Mundus Muliebris*, in *Literary Remains* (ed. 1834), pp. 700–1.
[2] *Op. cit.* (1645), Part II, p. 9.

roof, and when the hovel contained any other chamber, it was accessible only by means of a ladder or by a post indented with notches for the reception of the feet in climbing up to it. The doors and windows never closed sufficiently to exclude the rain or the snow, and in rainy weather puddles were scattered over the inequalities in the mud floor. Nor were the furniture and domestic utensils comparable in any respect with those which the households of the humblest cottagers are now found to contain." [1] Even in these days of marked inequality in the living conditions of rich and poor, it is questionable whether our tenement dwellers ever sink to such a state of abject wretchedness and discomfort as characterized the peasantry in England during and after the seventeenth century. The children born into these homes were reared in ignorance and squalor, suffered, in the fen lands, from ague and frequently died of plague or smallpox in the absence of capable medical assistance. The parish doctors of those days were apt to be quacks, whose scanty knowledge was too often the product of a dubious experience.

In the reign of Queen Anne (1702–14) the architecture of English houses underwent some changes which resulted in the red brick villas of many gables and a somewhat motley design that are commonly called " Queen Anne " houses. A recent writer is bold enough to assert that the so-called Queen Anne style " never had any existence at all except in the brains of modern æsthetics and china maniacs." [2] Be that as it may, it is certain that comfort and convenience in the interior planning of these houses were subordinated to the graceful proportion of the exterior. On the contrary the furniture of the period is marked by simplicity and elegance as well as by an admirable adaptation of each piece to the end it was designed to serve.

During the early part of the Georgian period (until 1750),

[1] Sydney, *Social Life in England*, pp. 146–7.
[2] Bradley, *The English Housewife*, pp. 267–8.

the classical designs of an Italian architect, Andreas Palladio by name, determined the style of English architecture. Although these homes were no doubt very fine and stately, it is questionable whether Italian villas were properly at home in the somewhat gray and inclement environment of England. Undoubtedly the Georgian homes built in the country were more comfortable and convenient than many of the city houses. These solid, spacious dwellings are thus happily described: " We all know the mellow brick Georgian houses with their stone facings and their spreading cedar trees about them. . . . The large square rooms could comfortably accommodate the hooped petticoat. . . . The front door is always in the center and is often surmounted by a graceful pediment. On either side are large sashed windows, the tiled roof slopes sharply up behind the parapet, and the chimneys are clustered at the four corners. We know that behind each of these houses is a large and charming garden, full of sweet-scented, old-fashioned flowers. . . ." [1]

The Economy of the English Household. — Within these country homes of the Stuart and Georgian periods the busy housewife plied her various tasks and entertained her friends with lavish hospitality. Less proficient than the elegant belles of London and Bath in the arts of the toilette and of killing time, these English wives and mothers were highly skilled in a bewildering variety of household industries. A picture of the ideal home maker of the early seventeenth century is drawn in Brathwaite's *English Gentlewoman:*

" Her household she makes her commonweale; wherein not any from the highest to the lowest of her feminine government, but knowes their peculiar office and employment; to which they addresse themselves (so highly they honour her they serve) with more love than feare. She becomes Promoter, I meane of no office to wrong her Countrey, but the tender care of a mother in behalfe of her well-educated

[1] *Ibid.,* p. 194.

progeny; . . . Markets shee seldom visits, nor any place of freer concourse; for she findes when her eyes are abroad, her thoughts are estrang'd from home." [1]

In such quaint language the author embodies the belief of the age that household duties should engross the entire interests and activities of every good wife and mother. Her home should be in very truth her world. Little marvel it is that even to-day many women are narrow individualists in tastes and employments, and are rarely moved to extend their active helpfulness beyond the walls of their home. The ideal is too deeply rooted, the custom too firmly established, to be easily modified or transformed.

The most valuable source of our knowledge of the industries carried on in an English household during the seventeenth century is probably the curious old work on *The English Housewife* written by Gervase Markham. However, this is only one of a large number of similar publications which served a valuable educational purpose. After descanting upon the moral virtues of a wife and her obligation to be temperate and modest " in her behaviour and carriage toward her Husband " even when " mishaps, or the misgovernment of his will may induce her to contrary thoughts," the writer plunges at once into his principal theme and describes in illuminating detail the duties of the housewife in the various departments of household economy. First and foremost among her " vertues " he places the " preservation and care of the family touching their health and soundness of body. . . ." To this end the housewife must know " how to administer any wholsom receipts or medicines . . . as well to prevent the first occasion of sickness as to take away the effects and evil of the same, when it hath made seizure on the body." To be sure Markham concedes that the " depth and secrets of this most excellent Art of Physick, are far beyond the capacity of the most skilful woman, as lodging only in the brest of

[1] *Op. cit.* (ed. 1683), p. 398.

learned Professors, . . ." yet this fact does not deter him from enumerating a host of minor ills which beset mankind, each with its appropriate remedy. Dandelion, poppy-seed, sorrel, lettuce, " Spinage," elder-leaves, featherfew, yarrow and " tansie " are only a few of the plants and herbs whose virtues the good housewife must know how to convert into medicinal draughts for the healing of her household.[1] No wonder the herb garden was so important a feature of the English homes of the period! Indeed some women attained great skill both in " physick " and surgery. The wife of Col. Hutchinson relates in her *Memoirs* that she attended the wounded of both sides during the siege of Nottingham.

Next in importance Markham places the art of cookery, going so far as to say that " she that is utterly ignorant therein, may not by Laws of strict Justice challenge the freedom of Marriage, because indeed she can then but perform half her vow; for she may live and obey, but she cannot cherish, serve and keep with that true duty which is ever expected." [2] Space is wanting to detail the multifarious household labors that are involved in the culinary art. It must suffice to mention that knowledge of herbs for seasoning, of the " compounding of Sallets " (salads), of fricasseeing, making of puddings, boiling, stewing and roasting meats, preparing of various sauces, making pastry, concocting marmalades, jellies, pastes and all kinds of conserves, baking " bisket bread " and plain bread, this and much more practical knowledge must be possessed by her who aspired to the proud title of skilful housewife. Some space is given by Markham to the important tasks connected with " Ordering of Banquets " both " great Feasts " and " humble " ones. Truly the quantity and variety of meats, fish, " sallets," fricassees and " Quelquechoses " figuring in a so-called " humble feast " seems overwhelming to the modern hostess. For Markham declares that the meal should include " no less than two and thirty dishes

[1] *Op. cit.*, pp. 4-48.   [2] *Ibid.*, p. 49.

which is as much as can conveniently stand on one Table, and in one mess ; . . . " [1] And the English housewife must have prepared or supervised the preparation of every dish ! [2]

An entire chapter is given up in Markham's book to " Distillations and their vertues." The housewife is advised to obtain some good stills either of tin or " sweet earth " " and in them she shall distill all sorts of waters meet for the health of her Household. . . ." There follows a formidable list of these medicinal waters, such as angelica, sage water, rosemary water, saxifrage water and water distilled from bean-flowers, strawberries, vine leaves, goats' milk, asses' milk, lilies and calves' feet, which last is best " for the smoothing of the skin, and keeping the face delicate and amiable. . . ." [3] Having distilled medicines and lotions, the busy homeworker may then turn her attention to preparing the various perfumes and sweet salves so highly valued in the seventeenth century, and to the " election, preserving, and curing of all sorts of wines, because they be usual charges under her hands, and by the least neglect must turn the Husband to much loss. . . ." [4]

" Our English Housewife, after her knowledge of preserving and feeding her Family, must learn also, how, out of her own endeavors, she ought to cloathe them outwardly and inwardly . . . the first consisting of Woollen cloth and the latter of linnen." [5] To this end " it is the office of a Husbandman at the shearing of his sheep to bestow upon the House-Wife such a competent proportion of Wooll, as shall be convenient for the cloathing of his Family. . . ." After receiving the raw wool the housewife is instructed to separate that portion she intends to " spin white " from that she intends to " put into colours." She is taught with great detail how to dye the wool, oil it, card it, and spin it " upon great wool-wheels. . . ." Then comes the careful division of the wool into parts for the warp and the " weft " respectively before it is " delivered up

---

[1] *Op. cit.* (9th ed., 1683), p. 101.   [2] *Ibid.*, pp. 49–101.   [3] *Ibid.*, p. 101.
[4] *Ibid.*, pp. 112–13.   [5] *Ibid.*, p. 122.

into the hands of the Weaver;" for, be it remembered that in the seventeenth century, most of the weaving of fabrics was done outside the household.

Having prepared her wool, the housewife may next turn her attention to the making of linen cloth. And here opens up a wide range of activities in the right performance of which she receives full instructions. She must know where best to sow the hemp and flax seed, and how to weed, " pull " and moisten the plants when they are above the ground. Much skill is required in first watering and then drying the hemp or flax. Next it must be twice " swingled " or beaten with a " Swingle-tree dagger," after which the heckling may begin. This of course consists in " combing the hemp first with a coarse wide-toothed instrument, then with a good straight Heckle made purposely for Hemp. . . ." The heckle used for flax must be " much finer and straighter " than that for hemp, but the process is the same. Then follows the spinning, reeling, scouring and " whitning " of the hempen and linen yarn, which is finally wound into balls ready for the weaver. But when the woven cloth is returned it must be again scoured and whitened before it is made up into household linen and garments.[1]

Lest the housewife find time hanging heavily on her hands she is further introduced to the mysteries of butter and cheese making, the care of the dairy and even the rearing of calves. Then, too, it is important that she know how to prepare malt from which " is made the Drink by which the Household is nourished and sustained. . . ." This is a many-sided industry in itself and leads directly to the allied art of brewing. Ale and beer were then the most popular drinks of Englishmen, and minute are the directions for the skilful preparation of these national beverages.[2]

It has seemed worth while to outline in some detail the household industries of the seventeenth century that the reader may

[1] Bk. 2, chs. V, VI.   [2] *Ibid.*, chs. VII, IX.

appreciate what an invaluable producer the English housewife assuredly was. In these days when most of the complicated processes named above have been entirely removed from the home, women of narrow education and interests, who can afford to keep a servant or two, must frequently find time hang heavily on their hands. Idleness among women is largely a phenomenon of modern times, due in part to the increase and dissemination of wealth consequent upon the Industrial Revolution, in part to the transformation of industry from the domestic to the factory system, and in part to the pride taken by successful men in maintaining their wives in an indolent luxury which is supposed to enhance their charms. Even so early as the close of the seventeenth century this parasitic type of idle, pleasure-loving woman was emerging and being shaped by a variety of circumstances. But it was during the eighteenth and nineteenth centuries that she became gradually perfected as a type.

Home Nurture and Education. — How important a part was played by English homes during this period in the nurture and training of children? A numerous offspring was the rule in these days, yet relatively few children were reared. If the literature of the time is to be believed, the child mortality was truly appalling when compared with our modern age. In her delightful *Memoirs*, Ann, Lady Fanshawe, mentions fourteen children born alive to her, between the years 1645–65, of whom only two lived to grow up![1] Seven of these little ones died in infancy, and there can be little doubt that the imperfect knowledge of child hygiene possessed by mothers and physicians at this time was chiefly responsible for this harvest of death. In the seventeenth century the swaddling of babies was no longer practised in England, so English infants, at least, were freed from those cramping bands that provoked the indignant protests of Rousseau in the *Émile*. But it is to be feared that the infant of wealthy parents received less of

[1] *Memoirs of Ann, Lady Fanshawe* (ed. 1907).

the mother's personal care than in previous periods. The nurse became an important figure in the well-to-do households of the time and exercised a control over the children, both boys and girls, which was all but supreme. Although this nursery government ceased for the boy when he was seven years of age, it frequently continued in the case of the girl until she was married. The nurse it was that taught her small charges the fascinating rhymes now gathered together in *Mother Goose*. Old King Cole, Tom the Piper's son and the Robin Hood songs were childhood favorites then as now. Also children looked to their nurse to recount those charming fairy tales that were old even in the seventeenth century — such tales as Puss in Boots, Cinderella, Sleeping Beauty and Bluebeard. The games of English children at this time are generally regarded as being more varied than ours of to-day. There can be little doubt that in the absence of our wealth of expensive toys, which are more or less exact reproductions of their complicated originals, the playthings of English children made far larger demands on their imagination and resourcefulness than do ours. The games of small boys and girls of that day were often imitations of the various industries they saw going on about them. In these they were assisted by the delightful resources of an English country house of the Stuart period. The shed of the harness maker, the blacksmith's forge and the fascinating shop of the carpenter, all could be found on the premises, and must have been unfailing sources of profitable amusement.[1]

Family discipline continued to be severe in the seventeenth century, although even then signs were not lacking that a milder order of control was creeping in. Yet the rod and strict confinement on bread and water were still freely used; and we are told that Elizabeth Tanfield, first Lady Falkland, never " addressed her harsh and autocratic mother save on her knees ! "[2] In the *Verney Memoirs* we read a pathetic letter

[1] See Godfrey, *English Children in the Olden Time*, pp. 62–3.
[2] Godfrey, *Home Life under the Stuarts*, p. 9.

in which the grandmother of Ralph Verney's little boy, who was not yet three years old, urges her son not to have the child forcibly " strudgeled " and to allow no one but his tutor to whip him. But this was perhaps an exceptional case. Gentler relations were fortunately coming to prevail between parents and children; and these were greatly furthered by the individualistic movement of the eighteenth century, especially in France. Very slowly ideas concerning the personal rights of children began to influence English society and resulted in modern legislation for the protection of children, and in an enlightened public opinion in favor of rational and kindly methods of discipline.

While still in the nursery, English children laid the foundations of their education under the guidance of nurse and mother. At two years of age, they must learn the alphabet, and for this purpose much use was made of wooden blocks with the letters printed on them, — an invention of Sir Hugh Plat in the late sixteenth century. Having mastered the rudiments of learning, the child was promoted to study of the "hornbook," the original primer of our forefathers. This quaint invention usually consisted of a piece of board on which were printed the letters of the alphabet in large and small type, the Lord's prayer, and, in Catholic countries, the " Hail Mary." Over the printed matter was fastened a piece of horn to protect it. From these humble beginnings of knowledge the child advanced to reading of the primer. Even as early as the middle of the seventeenth century this type of school-book was appearing. One of the earliest was Coote's *The English Schoole Master*, published in 1636. Very early, also, children were taught to count and to perform simple reckoning by the aid of the abacus, which was found in well-nigh every English nursery until the end of the eighteenth century.

These simple tasks, together with religious instruction and learning of the catechism — Anglican or Westminster — constituted the bulk of nursery education. But the little boys of the period had a tremendous advantage over the girls, since they were free to play out-of-doors when their tasks were done; whereas the girls must train their tiny fingers to make the samplers of fine canvas worked in delicate cross-stitch, so highly prized at the time. One is tempted to pity these small maidens thus early condemned to " keep the house " and strain eyes and nerves over intricate work too often in advance of their undeveloped powers of coördination and control. A few of these marvellous samplers have been handed down to modern times; and one wonders whether the pious and dutiful sentiments painfully worked thereon infallibly expressed the thoughts and feelings of the young needlewomen. Even when the daily " stint " on her sampler was done, the little girl could not escape into the out-of-doors. Mother or nurse was at hand to teach her to " sew a seam " with the painstaking care that evokes admiration and wonder in this more impatient and hurried generation.

After nursery days were past the education of boys and likewise of girls (so far as they received any) was frequently intrusted to a private tutor. Quite commonly tutors in French, in playing on lute and virginals, and in dancing, were engaged to instruct girls of the better classes in their homes, while their brothers were wrestling with the intricacies of Latin and Greek grammar in preparation for public school and University. We are told that Colonel Hutchinson personally supervised the education of his sons and daughters even while employing numerous carefully chosen tutors for them. But complaints were not lacking at this time of the carelessness of parents in selecting their sons' teachers. Thus Peacham, writing in 1634, says: " Is it not commonly seene, that the most gentlemen will give better wages, and deale more bountifully with a fellow who can but teach a dogge, or reclaime an hawke, than upon an honest, learned and well-qualified man to bring up their children ! " [1]

[1] The *Compleat Gentleman*, p. 31.

Nor were matters improved in the eighteenth century. DeFoe expends much biting sarcasm in attacking the English custom of entailing estates in favor of the eldest son. With his future thus provided for, the education of the heir was intrusted to inferior tutors; and the younger sons, who must shift for themselves, were carefully educated for the professions or government service. DeFoe declares that the difference between a liberal education " and the meer old woman lit-terature of a nurse and a tutor " is clearly demonstrated in English families " where the bright and the dull, . . . the man of sence and learning and the blockhead is as often to be dis-scern'd where one is untaught and good for nothing because he is to have the estate, and the other is polish'd and educated because he is to make his fortune; . . . " [1] To defects of ignorance and lack of training, DeFoe attributes the fact that many English landowners " are also in but very indifferent condicion as to family circumstances, and many even of the greatest estates are overwhelm'd in debt. . . . " [2]

But carelessness, or niggardliness, in the choice of household tutors was not the only charge brought against eighteenth century parents. The literature of the period fairly bristles with references to the neglect of their maternal duties by fashionable ladies. Thus DeFoe writes: " It is indeed too true that this wealthy age is so entirely given up to pleasure, and it prevails so much among the ladyes as well as among the men, that it grows a little unfashionable for the mothers to give themselves any trouble with their children, after they have 'em, but to order their dress and make them fine and to make a show of them upon occasion. 'Tis below a lady of quallity to trouble her selfe in the nursery, as 'tis below the gentleman of quallity to trouble himselfe with a library." [3]

Not only were the girl children of society-loving mothers confined to the nursery under the care of servants, but when

[1] *Ibid.* (ed. 1730), p. 68.   [2] *Ibid.*, pp. 104–5.
[3] *Ibid.*, p. 71.

their nursery education was ended they were quite commonly sent to fashionable boarding schools where they were taught a mere smattering of French, music, needlework and dancing, which last was a highly valued art. Even the training of the growing girl in household management and the arts of cooking was apt to be neglected in favor of elegant and often useless needlework and " accomplishments." Whereas girls in the seventeenth century were carefully instructed by their mothers in " the preparation of whatever required more art or curiosity for the closet or the parlor, as preserving, drawing spirits in an alembic or cold still, pastry, angelots, and other cream cheese . . ." and were trained in all forms of useful needlework, city girls in the eighteenth century were not uncommonly sent to the schools of professional pastry cooks to get a smattering of this homely knowledge and skill. Ashton mentions these schools and quotes from the advertisement of a famous one in Lincoln's Inn Fields which claimed to teach " all Sorts of Pastry and Cookery, Dutch hollow works, and Butter Works. . . ." [1] In his play, *The Tender Husband*, Steele represents an aunt as upbraiding her niece for her ignorance of domestic arts. The aunt informs the girl that her mother " spent her time in better Learning than ever you did. Not in reading of Fights and Battels of Dwarfs and Giants; but in writing out receipts for Broths, Possets, Caudles and Surfeit Waters as became a good Country Gentlewoman." Yet no doubt the country homes, at least, continued to give girls a careful training in household management.

But, if the education of their daughters in domestic affairs was neglected by some fashionable mothers, they never overlooked the training of their girls in social graces and in the supremely important art of getting a husband. On this point Hughes has expressed his sentiments in the *Spectator*: " The general mistake among us in the educating our children is, that in our daughters we take care of their persons, and

---

[1] *Social Life in the Reign of Queen Anne*, p. 24.

z

neglect their minds; in our sons we are so intent upon adorning their minds that we wholly neglect their bodies. . . . When a girl is safely brought from her nurse, before she is capable of forming one simple notion of any thing in life, she is delivered to the hands of her dancing-master; and with a collar round her neck, the pretty wild thing is taught a fantastical gravity of behaviour, and forced to a particular way of holding her head, heaving her breast, and moving with her whole body; and all this under pain of never having a husband, if she steps, looks or moves awry. This gives the young lady wonderful workings of imagination, what is to pass between her and this husband, that she is every moment told of and for whom she seems to be educated." [1] One is tempted to ask why, indeed, should not a girl's home education have been directed solely to one end? Since getting a husband was the goal of existence for nine-tenths of the women of England, since failure in this respect meant lamentable failure in life at a time when opportunities for single women to attain honorable financial independence were conspicuously wanting, surely few women would hesitate to exercise all their charms to capture a mate rather than sit at the fireside of reluctant relatives in the rôle of unwelcome old maids! In those days to be an " old maid " was nothing short of a tragedy; for it meant that a woman, no matter how comfortably fixed in life, would lead an empty existence, barren of purpose and large interests, and irrevocably stamped with the crushing mark of the unsuccessful. Economic and social conditions were responsible for the current ideal of woman and for her useless education; and it required an economic and social upheaval to modify both the ideal and the education. This will be discussed in a subsequent chapter.

[1] Chalmers' *British Essayists, The Spectator*, Vol. VII, pp. 25–6.

SELECTED BIBLIOGRAPHY

SOURCES.

Addison, Joseph. *The Spectator*, Nos. 92, 157.
   The Guardian, No. 155.

Alexander, Wm. *History of Woman* (1769), 2 vols. Vol. I, pp. 332, 461, 501–6; Vol. II, pp. 1, 112, 502–11.

Armytage, Geo. J. (compiler). *Allegations for Marriage Licenses . . .*, 1660–79. (*Pub. of the Harleian Society*, XXXII, XXXIV, 1892.)

Astell, Mary. *Some Reflections upon Marriage* (1730), pp. 1–55.
   An Essay in Defense of the Female Sex, pp. 5, 14, 23, 32–3, 48–9.

Bennet, J. *Strictures on Female Education* (1788), pp. 44–5, 81–124, 133–9, 144–52.

Brathwaite, Richard. *The English Gentlewoman* (1631), Introduction and pp. 397–8.

DeFoe, Daniel. *The Compleat Gentleman* (ed. 1890), pp. 68–180, 247–55.

Edgeworth, Maria. *Practical Education*, ch. XX.

Evelyn, Sir John. *Literary Remains* (1834); *Mundus Muliebris*, pp. 699–713.

Godwin, Mrs. M. W. *Thoughts on the Education of Daughters, . . .* (1787).

Gregory, Dr. *Legacy to his Daughters* (1784), pp. 18–19, 31–52, 68, 120–37.

Hayley, Wm. *Old Maids* (1792), Vol. I, pp. 7–19.

Howell, James. *Familiar Letters* (1645).

Hughes, John. *The Spectator*, Nos. 33, 53, 66.

Kames, Lord (H. Howe). *Loose Hints upon Education*, pp. 8–12, 133–6, 222–9.

Markham, G. *The English Housewife* (1683), entire.

Memoirs of Ann, Lady Fanshaw (reprinted from original Ms., London, 1907).

More, Hannah. *Essays for Young Ladies* (1789).
   Strictures on Female Education (1799), Vol. I, 64–70, 105–15, ch. VII; Vol. II, 14–31, 172–8.

Steele, Richard. *The Tatler*, Nos. 61, 141, 185, 201, 248.
   The Guardian, Nos. 73, 172.

Swinburne. *Of Spousals* (1686).

Tusser, Thomas. *A Book of Huswifery* (1812).

Verney Memoirs, 2 vols.

Verney Papers (in *Camden Soc. Pub.*, 1853, Vol. 56, pp. 145–69).

Wollstonecraft, Mary. *Vindication of the Rights of Women* (1792) (reprinted in *Humboldt Lib. of Sci.*, XV). See pp. 37–45, 75–83.

SECONDARY WORKS.

Ashton, John. *Eighteenth Century Waifs* (1887), pp. 17–30.

Social Life in the Reign of Queen Anne (1882), chs. I–III, V, VIII.

The Dawn of the Nineteenth Century in England (1886), chs. XXXIII, XXXIV.

Ballard, Geo. *Memoirs of British Ladies* (1775), pp. 204, 224, 264–6.

Bradley, Rose M. *The English Housewife in the 17th and 18th Centuries* (1913).

Chapman, A. B., and **Mary W.** *The Status of Women under the English Law.* See Acts 1492–1832.

Cleveland, Arthur R. *Women under the English Law* (1886), pp. 169–236.

Godfrey, Elizabeth. *Home Life under the Stuarts*, chs. I, II, VII–IX, XII, XIV–XVI.

English Children in the Olden Time (1907), chs. I–III, IV–VI, XI, XIII.

Hill, Georgiana. *Women in English Life* (1896), Vol. I, 145–92, 307–50.

Howard, E. G. *History of Matrimonial Institutions*, Vol. I, ch. II; Vol. II, pp. 85–109.

Reich, Emil. *Women through the Ages*, Vol. II, pp. 39–67.

Sydney. *Social Life in England*, pp. 159–63.

CHAPTER X

THE FAMILY IN THE AMERICAN COLONIES

The Early Settlements. — In the early years of the seventeenth century began the first stream of emigration from the mother country in England to the untried shores of America. Political and economic as well as religious reasons were responsible for the first colonization of the New World; although the first two motives operated more largely in the founding of Virginia and the latter in the settlement of the first New England colonies. Much has been written of the courage that burned high in the hearts of the men who left their native land to plant new homes in an inhospitable wilderness. Literature acquaints us in great detail with the cruel hardships these men endured, with their strenuous daily toil in building houses and raising crops, with their constant anxiety concerning their Indian neighbors and their brave defence of homes and families against the merciless onslaughts of the savages. But until recent years comparatively little tribute has been paid to the unflinching loyalty and courage of the wives and mothers of these pathfinders. Nor has it been clearly recognized that the crushing hardships, the enervating disappointments, which always accompany the colonization of a virgin wilderness, would have been impossible of endurance had not the women lent their invaluable aid to the work of making homes. That the English colonization of America was successfully carried out only with the help of a small band of women is stated by a modern historian to be " one of the best authenticated facts in the history of America's infancy." [1]   He cites

[1] J. A. Bruce in *Woman in the Making of America*, Boston (1912), p. 3.

as evidence the unsatisfactory conditions that prevailed in
the first Virginia colony so long as the men labored on without
wives or homes. Discontent and restlessness were rife and
were about to break forth in open rebellion when the Virginia
Company in England came under the direction of a wise and
far-sighted man, Sir Edwin Sandys, who clearly saw that the
disaffection of the colonists was chiefly caused by their loveless
lives and their homeless state. The Records of the Virginia
Company [1] contain his blunt and sensible advice to his col-
leagues: " We must find them wives, in order that they may
feel at home in Virginia." And with no unnecessary delay
wives were indeed found for these eager settlers, — young,
honest, hard-working girls, who left the mother-country for
the new land of their adoption with the wistful hope that it
might provide them with good husbands and good homes.
These courageous maids, ninety in number, were received
with the utmost enthusiasm and were eagerly besieged by
the lonely colonists who desired them in marriage. Only a
man who could demonstrate his ability to support a wife and
who could afford to pay the passage money of his chosen one,
amounting to one hundred and twenty pounds of leaf tobacco,
was granted the privilege of securing a bride from among this
bevy of English maids. Moreover, it was stipulated that he
must win the consent of the young woman, which was in no
way to be forced. In such primitive fashion was the Virginia
colony furnished with wives and mothers. The effect upon
the discontented settlers was speedy and beneficent. In the
quaint words of the chronicler, men then " sett down satys-
fied " in the homes they had founded; and they no more
sighed for the comforts of Old England.

Not only was the spirit of colonial wives undaunted by
danger and suffering, but their helpfulness was of the most
practical and energetic sort. New England women helped
their husbands in the task of building their first rude log

[1] Vol. I, p. 269.

homes and later they set to work to furnish them. This was accomplished largely through their own efforts, eked out by the household treasures brought from England. The wives of the first Pennsylvania settlers assisted in digging the caves in the high banks of the Delaware that served as their first homes. In the records of the Quaker family of Hard we may read of Elizabeth Hard's share in building such a home. The account is written by her niece :

" All that came wanted a Dwelling and hastened to provide one. As they lovingly helped each other, the Women even set themselves to work that they had not been used to before ; for few of the first settlers were of the Laborous Class, and help of that source was scarce. My good Aunt thought it expedient to help her Husband at the end of the saw, and to fetch all such Water to make such kind of Mortar, as they then had to build their chimney. At one time being overwearied there-with, her Husband desired her to forbear, saying, ' thou had better, my dear, think of dinner ' ; . . ." Unfortunately the poor lady lacked all wherewithal for a meal and walked away in discouragement, quietly weeping as she went. But soon she bravely reminded herself that she now had the priceless gift of liberty of conscience for which she long had prayed ; so, dropping on her knees, she begged God for forgiveness and help. The narrative goes on to tell us that scarcely had she risen and started to seek food when the cat appeared with " a fine large Rabbit, which she thankfully received and dressed as an English hare. When her Husband came to dinner, being informed of the particulars, they both wept with reverential Joy, and Eat their Meal, which was thus seasonably provided for them, in singleness of heart." [1] It is gratifying to learn that later, when this same Hard family, together with their relatives, the Morrises, became well-to-do and owned rich family plate, some of it was engraved with the design of the provident cat bringing the rabbit in her teeth.

[1] Quoted in A. H. Wharton, *Colonial Days and Dames*, pp. 68, 69.

Severe as were the sufferings in the Middle Colonies they could hardly compare with those endured by the settlers on the bleak coast of New England. We read in *Winthrop's Journal* [1] of the loss of precious cattle and swine through the attacks of wolves; of the bitter cold which froze feet and fingers, of the outbreak of scurvy, and of the scarcity of even the coarse Indian corn which was the staple article of food among the colonists for several years. Yet the sufferings of the colonists of Massachusetts Bay were not so cruel as those endured by the heroic company at Plymouth. In the course of a few years, however, more substantial and comfortable homes took the place of the log huts hastily built as temporary shelters from the bitter cold. About 1650 Johnson, in his *Wonderworking Providence of Zion's Saviour in New England*, quaintly describes Boston as " a City-like Towne . . . crowded on the Sea-banks and wharfed out with great industry and cost, the buildings beautifull and large, some fairely set forth with Brick, Tile, Stone, and Slate, and orderly placed with comly streets, whose continuall enlargement presages some sumptuous City. . . ." [2] No doubt this enthusiastic Puritan's account is somewhat biassed by his praiseworthy desire to glorify the " wonder-working Providence " whom he so devoutly worshipped. Apparently many of these early houses were of wood, fairly spacious and comfortable, the forerunners in architectural design of the typical colonial dwellings of a later period. Little by little, as the first hand-to-hand conflicts with an inhospitable Nature were crowned with success, life became something more than a struggle for bare existence. Gradually a few comforts crept into the homes of the settlers, scattered along the coasts from the Carolinas to Massachusetts, and these home comforts increased as the years passed by. In the plantation homes of the South, in the neat Dutch houses of Manhattan, and in the

---

[1] Edition of 1908, Vol. I, pp. 58, 68, 105.
[2] *Op. cit.*, edited by Jameson, New York, 1910, p. 71.

colonial dwellings of New England, various types of family life were developed. But in all was the true spirit of the home. These newer generations were American born and felt no such heartsick longing for the mother-country as must have frequently troubled their parents. Their traditions, their hopes, their purposes were bound up with the new land that they were so proudly and energetically developing.

THE STATUS OF WOMEN IN COLONIAL DAYS

Establishment of English Common Law. — It is not to be expected that the English colonists of America would all at once change their customary ideas and practices with respect to womankind. These men, Cavaliers and Puritans alike, had been reared amid authoritative traditions of the intellectual, social and legal inferiority of women; and these traditions they naturally brought with them to the land of their adoption. English private law became the " common law " of the colonies with a few changes that will be noted later. The details of this system of private law have been given in the preceding chapter. Therefore it is necessary only to recall that married women were controlled, both in person and in property, by their husbands, whom they were bound to serve and obey. They were in legal phrase *sub potestate viri* — under the power of the husband — and be it remembered that the husband held the purse-strings. Only in case an allowance strictly for their personal use were settled upon women at marriage were they relieved from a condition of complete financial dependence. Even the clothing and ornaments of a married woman belonged to the husband during his lifetime and might be disposed of as he saw fit; whereas her chattels, or property in money and movables of any sort, became his absolute property, as did also the wife's earnings. Likewise the husband was the sole guardian of the offspring of the marriage, and he alone could determine important questions concerning the education, religious training, preparation for life-work and marriage of his boys and girls.

The status of married women according to the English common law is thus described by Justice Blackstone, writing late in the eighteenth century:

" By marriage the husband and wife are one person in law; that is, the very being or legal existence of the woman is suspended during the marriage, or at least is incorporated and consolidated into that of her husband. . . . Upon this principle of a union of person in husband and wife depend almost all the legal rights, duties and disabilities that either of them acquire by the marriage. . . . For this reason a man cannot grant anything to his wife, or enter into covenant with her; for the grant would be to suppose her separate existence, and to covenant with her would be only to covenant with himself; and therefore it is also generally true that all compacts made between husband and wife when single are voided by the inter-marriage." [1]

Yet it should be noted that, despite her loss of legal personality, a wife might inherit property from some third person, although the husband at once assumed its control and enjoyed its profits as long as the marriage continued. Only if her husband died before her was his widow granted the management of her property. At the death of the wife the husband lost his interest in her landed estate except in case a child capable of inheriting was born of the marriage. In such an event, even if the child were not living at the time of the wife's death, the husband became vested with an estate in her lands for the remainder of his life. This is technically called his " estate by the courtesy of England " or merely his " courtesy estate." This English custom became thoroughly established among the colonies in America.

But the husband of colonial times had certain disabilities as well as advantages growing out of the marriage relation.

[1] Blackstone's *Commentaries.*

He must maintain his wife in accordance with his means, whether or not she brought him property at marriage. To be sure, the American colonists were as shrewd bargainers with respect to marriage-contracts as were their English forefathers; and they took good care to see that a dowry, big or little, went with the woman of their choice. Indeed, the higgling of the Puritan Judge Sewall over matters of dowry and settlement with the three fair widows whom he successively sought in marriage, makes interesting reading. The bargaining is quite open and unashamed on both sides.[1] Yet it must be remembered that if the advantage went against the husband he was required by law properly to support his wife and was held liable not only for her necessary debts contracted after marriage but for any unpaid debts for which she was liable before the marriage. This provision of English law led to the crude and curious custom of " smock-marriages " in some of the colonies, — a practice imported from the mother-country. It was held by certain of the more ignorant men and women of the time that if a widow were married in her smock without other clothing and without head-gear her husband would be exempt from paying her anti-nuptial debts. We are glad to learn that many of these marriages took place in the evening, thus saving some shreds of the bride's modesty. Alice Morse Earle in her delightful book, *Customs and Fashions in Old New England*, has collected some interesting instances of " smock-marriages." Certain it is that they were not confined to New England. As late as 1748 a certain Mr. Hahn, travelling in Pennsylvania, relates that a bridegroom in that colony went to meet his widow-bride on the highroad and announced in the presence of several witnesses that the clothing he considerately threw over her scantily clad person was only lent for the wedding festivity.[2]

Not only was the right of a woman to proper maintenance

[1] See Sewall's *Diary* (*Mass. Hist. Soc.*, Boston, 1882, Vol. III, pp. 269–274; also pp. 302–3).   [2] Earle, *op. cit.*, pp. 78–9.

by her husband secured to her by the common law, but her dower rights in her husband's lands were likewise carefully protected throughout the colonies. With this end in view the law required that the husband obtain the concurrence of his wife in the sale or alienation of any considerable portion of his landed estate.

So much for the wife's property rights. The colonists seem also to have taken some steps to protect the person of a married woman from assault or libel. In most of the American colonies a man was not permitted to beat his wife — a luxury which he had long enjoyed in Old England — nor could he even belabor her with his tongue too freely. Doubtless many married men in colonial times were guilty of both offences, but their wives might bring action against them at any time. In his history of *Haverhill*, Chase mentions the case of a man who, when summoned for beating his wife, boldly claimed his right so to do on the ground that she was his " servant and slave." But this was by no means the theory of his fellow citizens, as the offender no doubt discovered to his cost. Indeed, throughout the New England colonies, the charge of extreme cruelty was sufficient if established to secure for the wife a legal separation, although not often a complete divorce unless accompanied by infidelity. In the Southern Colonies, however, where the Church of England was at least nominally established, and where, in consequence, marital cases must be tried in ecclesiastical courts, no provision seems to have been made during colonial times to free a woman from the tyranny of a cruel husband.[1]

But if the wife's rights in respect to abuse, corporal and verbal, were duly protected, so also were the husband's. Everywhere in the colonies a " curst and shrewish tongue " exposed a married woman to the hateful penalty of stocks, pillory or ducking-stool. Indeed this last-named instrument

[1] See Howard, *Hist. of Mat. Inst.*, Vol. II, pp. 34–7, for Mass. Bay Colony; and for the Southern Colonies, pp. 366–76.

for the punishment of scolding wives seems not to have disappeared in a few states until early in the nineteenth century.

Right of Women to hold Lands. — In the New England colonies little encouragement was given to independent women (*i.e.*, single women and widows) to take up and develop lands. Mistress Deborah Moody, who purchased large tracts of land near Swampscott, Massachusetts, was not very cordially received by the colonial authorities and soon removed to the Dutch colony of New Netherlands. Yet the town authorities of Boston were scrupulous in including women when they made allotments of land to families according to their numbers; and the town of Salem granted " maid-lotts " to single women in the early days of settlement. The practice, however, came under the disapproval of Governor Endicott, who advised that it be abandoned, thus avoiding " all precedents and evil events of granting lotts unto single maidens not disposed of." [1]

The Southern and Middle Colonies were more hospitable to independent women settlers. Haddonfield, New Jersey, was settled by a young woman, Elizabeth Haddon by name, who came alone to the colony when she was only nineteen years old, and managed her father's extensive lands with remarkable business judgment. Another courageous woman was the widow Mary Tewee, who took up an enormous tract of land in Pennsylvania which she cleared and cultivated. But the most remarkable case of the kind is that of Mistress Margaret Brent, who, with her scarcely less capable sister Mary, emigrated from England to the Maryland colony in 1638. The two sisters took up land, built manor houses and became active in a variety of business affairs. When Leonard Calvert, Governor of the colony and brother of the Proprietary, Lord Baltimore, died in 1647 he appointed Margaret Brent as his sole executrix — a truly surprising step to take in those days! The lady seems to have distinguished herself not only in business but

[1] Earle, *Colonial Dames and Goodwives*, pp. 50–51.

in the public affairs of the colony. We read that when the small army, which had served the government in certain troubles and had remained unpaid, was on the verge of mutiny Mistress Brent took matters into her own capable hands. With no authority she sold cattle belonging to the Proprietary and paid off the angry men. Apparently Lord Baltimore wrote a tart letter of protest to this " meddling " dame, for the Assembly gallantly intervened in her behalf. In a joint letter they said:

" As for Mrs. Brent's undertaking and meddling with your Lordship's estate here . . . we do verily believe and in conscience report that it was better, for the colony's safety at that time, in her hands than in any man's else in the whole province after your brother's death." [1]

After reading this account we are not surprised to learn that this same dauntless lady in 1648 boldly entered the Assembly and, in the words of the record, " requested to have vote in the House for herself and voyce allsoe, for that on the last Court 3rd January it was ordered that the said Mrs. Brent was to be looked upon and received as his Lordship's Attorney." It is not difficult to imagine the dismay and disapproval that filled the masculine breasts of the members of the Assembly at this unheard-of request from a woman. Very promptly they put America's first advocate of woman's suffrage in her place, for the record reads: " The Governor deny'd that the s'd Mrs. Brent should have any vote in the house. And the s'd Mrs. Brent protested against all proceedings in this present Assembly unless she may be present and have vote as afores'd." [2]

Attitude toward Women in the Colonies. — In the Southern Colonies, especially in Virginia, the scarcity of women during the early days of settlement caused them to be held in high esteem and to be eagerly sought in marriage. Although the

[1] Bruce, *Women in the Making of America*, pp. 26–7.
[2] Quoted in Earle, *Colonial Dames and Goodwives*, pp. 47–8.

private law of England had been thoroughly established throughout these colonies, with all its disabilities respecting women, there sprang up and flourished in the plantation homes of the South a spirit of chivalrous courtesy and regard for women. This attitude had early characterized the finer type of English Cavalier — the type which was in part responsible for the founding of the great plantations of the South.

The spirit is exemplified in the words of Governor Spotswood of Virginia, spoken to his friend Colonel Byrd on the occasion of the latter's visit to the Governor's house " Germanna " on the edge of the wilderness. To this frontier settlement the Governor had brought his gently bred wife, who cheerfully and bravely accepted her isolated life. Of her the Governor said, when his friend rallied him on his husbandly devotion, " that whoever brings a poor gentlewoman into so solitary a place from all her friends and acquaintances, would be ungrateful not to use her with all possible tenderness." [1] And, on the whole, the well-born women of the South received a degree of tender consideration not so generously bestowed on those of the Middle and New England Colonies. Not that the women of the North were not loved and respected, for they surely were. But love in stern New England was somewhat rigidly controlled and its open manifestations were on the whole discouraged. Then, too, the Puritans, as we have seen, cordially embraced the view of the ancient Hebrews, of Paul and of the Early Christian Fathers that women were an inferior order of beings to be wisely held in control by their lawful husbands and masters. If a descendant of the Massachusetts Puritans could, in the year of our Lord 1876, write as follows of women's sphere what must have been the rooted conviction of his ancestors?

" The ordinary occupations of the female sex are necessarily of a kind which must ever prevent it from partaking of the action of life. However keenly women may think or feel,

[1] Wharton, *Colonial Days and Dames*, pp. 86-7.

there is seldom an occasion when the sphere of their exertions can with propriety be extended much beyond the domestic hearth or the social circle." [1]

Now, since the "social circle" in Puritan New England was highly restricted until after the first quarter of the eighteenth century, it is safe to assume that Puritan women's lives were almost wholly bounded by the interests of home, with the weekly visit to the meeting-house on Sunday and the "Lecture" on Thursday. But even their liberty to attend religious meetings became a subject of controversy in the Providence colony, where an order had been passed that no man should be molested for his conscience. Winthrop relates that a certain man, Verin by name, refused to permit his wife to go to the meeting held by Roger Williams " so oft as she was called for." Whereupon certain men of the colony would have summoned this husband for censure. " But," relates Winthrop, " there stood up one Arnold . . . and withstood it, telling them that, when he consented to that order, he never intended it should extend to the breach of any ordinance of God, such as the subjection of wives to their husbands, etc., and gave divers solid reasons against it." [2] No wonder married women in these days signed their letters " Your faythfull and obedient wife "; and, when they ventured to offer advice to their husbands, were pretty likely to follow it up, as did sweet Dame Winthrop, with words like these: " . . . but I shall allways submit to what you shal thinke fit."

MARRIAGE LAWS AND CUSTOMS IN THE COLONIES

Prevailing Ideas of Marriage and the Family. — Throughout the colonies marriage was held in high esteem, not only as a means of perpetuating an honored family name but also

[1] Charles Francis Adams, *Memoir of Mrs. Adams* in his *Familiar Letters of John Adams and his Wife Abigail Adams*, Cambridge, 1876, p. xxii.

[2] *Journal*, p. 155.

because large families were necessary to people the vast stretches of the new country. In New England, and to a less degree in the Middle Colonies, marriage was looked upon as a civil contract, the ceremonies of which might be conducted by a civil officer. In the Southern Colonies, however, and during the eighteenth century this was true of Maryland also, the English idea of marriage as a sacrament to be performed solely by a clergyman of the Church of England very generally prevailed.

The patriarchal idea of family organization was held by all the colonists; but the belief in the sacredness and importance of family government was even more deeply rooted among the Puritans than among their fellow colonists in the South. This was largely due to the fact that the Puritans derived most of their ideas of government — both State and family — from the Mosaic laws set forth in Deuteronomy and Leviticus. Hence we find the Puritans justifying the autocratic power of the household head by reference to the similar power held by the patriarch in ancient Israel who ruled his family as a monarch. Nor did the stern settlers of New England hesitate to carry out the grim prescriptions of the Hebraic law to the letter. Thus the early codes of Massachusetts Bay, as well as of Connecticut and New Haven, provided that the obstinate and unruly child should meet with the awful penalty of death. The law of the Connecticut colony reads:

" If a man have a stubborn and rebellious son of sufficient years and understanding, viz. : sixteen years of age, which will not obey the voice of his father or the voice of his mother, and that when they have chastened him will not hearken unto them, then may his father and mother, being his natural parents, lay hold on him and bring him to the magistrates assembled in court, and testify unto them that their son is stubborn and rebellious . . . such a son shall be put to death. *Deut.* XXI, 20, 21." The same penalty was prescribed for

2 A

the child or children who should " curse or smite their natural father and mother." [1]

It is gratifying to learn, however, that no record exists of the actual carrying out of the provisions of these laws in a single instance. But so much cannot be said of another law, likewise taken from the Hebrew code. So high was the esteem in which pure family life was held by the Puritans that they did not shrink from prescribing the death penalty for adultery with a " married or espoused wife." Only in Rhode Island and Plymouth was the law softened to severe flogging. In Plymouth was added the penalty of wearing the scarlet letter *A* upon the breast until death released the offender. Although the colonial magistrates appear to have shrunk from exacting the full penalty prescribed by law, yet the records of the Massachusetts Bay colony show that two persons were executed for adultery in 1644 and a third execution is mentioned by Cotton Mather in his *Magnalia Christi*.[2] It is a note-worthy fact that no distinction of sex was made in the Puritan laws concerning adultery. Man and woman suffered alike, in striking contrast to the Mosaic law that limited the penalty to the adulteress only.

Holding such views of the sacredness of the family and the importance of firm household government, it is not surprising to learn that the Puritan colonists looked askance upon bachelors and " antient maids " especially if these unyoked individuals sought to live independent lives. It was very generally believed that every unmarried person should be connected with some respected family which would be responsible for his morals and for his obedience of the laws of State and Church. In colonial Hartford " the selfish luxury of solitary living " was taxed twenty shillings a week; [3] in colonial Pennsylvania (1766) unmarried men sometimes paid double taxes; and in the New Haven colony it was enacted

---

[1] Trumbull, *Blue Laws True and False* (1876), pp. 69–70.
[2] Howard, *op. cit.*, Vol. II, p. 170.   [3] *Ibid.*, p. 153.

in 1656 " That no single person of either sex do henceforward board, diet, sojourn, or be permitted so to do, or to have lodging; or house room within any of the plantations of this jurisdiction, but either in some allowed relation, or in some approved family licensed thereunto, by the court, or by a magistrate . . . ; the governor of which family, so licensed, shal as he may conveniently, duly observe the course, carriage and behaviour, of every such person, whether he, or she walk diligently in a constant lawful imployment, attending both family duties, and the publick worship of God, and keeping good order day and night, or otherwise." [1]

Similar ordinances were passed by the colonies of Massachusetts Bay and Plymouth. The latter settlement enacted that " henceforth noe single person be suffered to live by himselfe or in any family but such as the selectmen of the Towne shall approve of; . . ." Offenders were to be " sumoned to the Court to be proceeded with as the matter shall require." [2] Apparently these laws were enforced for we read that in 1762 " Thomas Henshaw and Thomas Hall, singlemen, being convicted of living from under family government, . . . are ordered forthwith to submit themselves " to such government " and to appear at the next court and bring with them certificate thereof." [3] Clearly a single man in colonial New England gained his freedom with marriage, not lost it as has sometimes been ironically supposed. Indeed " ' Incurridgement ' to wedlock was given bachelors in many towns by the assignment to them upon marriage of home-lots to build upon. In Medford there was a so-called Bachelor's Row, which had been thus assigned." [4]

One is tempted to speculate concerning the feelings of these earnest Puritans, so seriously engaged in bringing single youths

[1] Trumbull, *Blue Laws*, p. 258.

[2] *Plymouth Col. Rec.*, XI, 223; quoted in Howard, Vol. II, p. 154.

[3] *MSS. Records of County Court for Middlesex*, Vol. III, p. 21; quoted in Howard, Vol. II, p. 155.

[4] Earle, *Customs and Fashions in Old New England*, p. 37.

and maids under the discipline of family government, could they come to life and behold the freedom accorded bachelors and unmarried girls at the present time. Certain it is that they would cordially disapprove not only the independence granted these 'shirkers' of family responsibilities, but also the number of single women, young and old, in modern society. In Boston all such " antient maids," we are told, were regarded as " such a curse as nothing can exceed it, and look'd on as a Dismal Spectacle. . . ." Yet the writer of this statement, an English visitor to New England, does not hesitate to pay his respects to one of these luckless virgins who, although " now about Twenty Six years (the Age which they call a *Thornback*) yet . . . never disguises her self by the Gayetys of a Youthful Dress, and talks as little as she thinks of Love: . . . The two great vertues essential to the Virgin-State, are Modesty and Obedience; and these are so remarkable in her, as if she was made of nothing else. . . . Her Looks, her Speech, her whole behaviour are so very chaste, that but once going to kiss her, I thought she'd ha' blush'd to Death." Just tribute having been paid to the modesty of this " old (or Superannuated) Maid " of twenty-six, the quaint chronicler then eulogizes her " Matchless Obedience " to her parents which " extends itself to all things that are either Good or Indifferent, and has no Clause of Exception but only where the Command is unlawfull." With admiration he relates that he has " known her Scruple to go to Roxbury [not a Mile from Boston] without her Father's Consent." Such docility furnishes the writer with opportunity to descant upon the sacred power of the parent over his offspring, a right " so undoubted, that we find God himself gives way to it and will not suffer the most Holy Pretence, no, not that of a Vow to Invade it, as we see in *Numb*. 10." [1] Apparently the views of the Englishman and the Puritan colonists in

---

[1] Dunton, *Letters from New England*, in *Publications of the Prince Society*, Boston, 1867, pp. 99–101.

respect to the autocratic power wielded by the household head were entirely harmonious.

Courtship Customs. — Throughout the colonies there prevailed the English custom that the approval of parents should be secured before courtship began. Great importance was attached to this formality in the New England colonies where numerous laws concerning courtship were passed from time to time. In the first code of Connecticut we read that " no person whatsoever, male or female, not being at his or her own dispose, or that remaineth under the government of parents, masters or guardians, or such like, shall either make, or give entertainment to, any motion or suit in way of marriage, without the knowledge and consent of those they stand in such relation to, under the severe censure of the court in case of delinquency, not attending this order; nor shall any third person or persons intermeddle in making motion to any such, without the knowledge and consent of those under whose government they are, under the same penalty." [1] The law of the New Haven colony is in similar strain prohibiting any " indeavor to inveagle, or draw the affections of any maide, or maide-servant . . . without the consent of father, master, guardian, governor . . . or (in the absence of such) of the nearest magistrate, whether it be by speech, writing, message, company-keeping, unnecessary familiarity, disorderly night meetings, sinful dalliance, gifts, or any other way . . ." under penalty of forty shillings for the first offence.[2] Truly the young men of colonial New England were compelled to walk circumspectly in love as in all else! Yet there seems to have been considerable freedom allowed young people in cases where the parents approved of their association. John Dunton, the English traveller, from whose letter regarding old maids I have already quoted, once took a long horseback journey with a fair damsel who rode a pillion behind him. And this in the seventeenth century in Puritan Massachusetts!

[1] Trumbull, *Blue Laws*, pp. 106–7.   [2] *Ibid.*, p. 242.

Yet there is evidence that such freedom was not approved by the magistrates. A statute of Massachusetts declares in unmistakable terms against this " loose and sinful custom of going or riding from town to town, — . . . ofttimes men and women together upon pretence of going to lectures, but it appears . . . much to drink and revel in ordinaries and taverns. . . ." For the prevention of such merrymakings it was ordered " that all single persons who merely for their pleasure take such journeys . . . shall be reputed and accounted riotous and unsober persons, and of ill behavior . . . and shall be committed to prison for ten days, or pay a fine of forty shillings for each offence," unless they are able to " give bonds and sufficient sureties for good behavior in twenty pounds." [1] Thenceforth, it would appear, the young man in Massachusetts who desired to take his chosen maid a-riding must first give proper guarantee of decorous conduct! Yet these strict Puritan standards had clearly broken down in the eighteenth century. Mrs. Earle cites one Captain Geolet who made a trip through New England about 1750 and had much to say of " ' Turtle Frolicks ' and country dances with young ladies of refinement and good station in life." [2] Curiously enough our modern custom of chaperonage seems to have been non-existent; for young men escorted girls to dancing parties and accompanied them home afterwards with no older person in attendance.

From the *Diary* of Judge Samuel Sewall the reader gets many a gleam of light upon colonial courtship customs in New England. The Judge's daughter Mary was sought in marriage by one Mr. Gerrish, whose father, a minister, wrote in due form to obtain Mr. Sewall's consent to his son's waiting upon the young lady. This being granted, the Judge invited the young man to his house and noted in his diary the progress of the courtship. Apparently Mr. Gerrish was anxious to proceed

[1] Whitmore, *Colonial Laws of Mass.* (1672–86), pp. 236–7; quoted in Howard, Vol. II, p. 154. [2] *Colonial Dames and Goodwives*, p. 201.

with all decorum, for the Judge records: " He asked me . . .
whether it were best to frequent my House before his father
came to Town. . . ." Having received permission, the
would-be lover made a serious misstep; for on the Friday
appointed for his call the Judge notes in his Diary: " In the
evening S. Gerrish comes not; we expected him, Mary dress'd
herself; it was a painfull disgracefull disapointment." Yet,
" painfull " as the occurrence doubtless was, it seems not to
have cost the young man his chances; for a later item reads:
" S. Gerrish comes. Tells Mary except Satterday and Lord's-
day nights intends to wait on her every night; unless some
extraordinary thing hapen." Courtships in those days were
not expected to drag along, but to be got over with decent
haste and not too much sentiment. Such was the case
with Mary Sewall's wooing, for six months later we read:
" Midweek, Augt 24. In the evening Mr. Pemberton marrys
Mr. Samuel Gerrish and my daughter Mary: He began with
Prayer, and Mr. Gerrish the Bridegroom's father concluded:
. . ."[1]

Another daughter of Judge Sewall, Betty by name, was a
shy, nervous girl who fled from the approach of lovers. In
consequence her shrewd old father, intent on his daughter's
making a good match, was disappointed in his matrimonial
schemes more than once. Thus he records under date of
January, 1698/9, that " Capt. Tuthill comes to speak with
Betty, who hid herself all alone in the coach for several hours
till he was gone, so that we sought at several houses, till at
last came in of her self, and look'd very wild." Poor, shy
Betty! At last she summoned courage to send her unwelcome
suitor away on the ground that she " was willing to know her
own mind better."[2] But her troubles were not over, for a
few months later another wooer appeared in the shape of one
Mr. Grove Hirst. The first mention of this gentleman is

---

[1] Sewall's *Diary* (Coll. of Mass. Hist. Soc., 1879, Vol. VI; *Sewall Papers*,
Vol. II, pp. 250-1, 268). [2] *Ibid.*, Vol. V, pp. 491-2.

found in a statement in the Judge's *Diary* under date of September 28, 1699. Upon returning from a short journey he records : " Find my family in health, only disturb'd at Betty's denying Mr. Hirst. . . . The Lord sanctify Mercyes and Afflictions." A month later we read : " Mr. Wm. Hirst comes and thanks my wife and me for our Kindness to his Son in giving him the Liberty of our house. Seems to do it in way of taking leave." [1] But apparently this suitor was not so easily discouraged as the Captain, for a year later the Judge inserts this brief item in his journal : " Octr 17th. 1700 . . . Mr. Grove Hirst and Elizabeth Sewall are married by Mr. Cotton Mather. . . . Sung the 128 Psal. I set York Tune not intending it. In the New Parlor." [2] So timorous Betty at last was married off and the old Judge had the satisfaction of seeing one more daughter well " set up in life." The records of this courtship are of especial interest as showing that considerable freedom was allowed Puritan girls to reject the advances of unwelcome lovers, even when they were heartily approved by the parents. Disappointed as Judge Sewall clearly was at Betty's repeated denial of her suitors, yet it seems never to have occurred to him to force his daughter's consent.

If the courtship of the Sewall girls reveals the cautious methods by which Puritan suitors secured the consent of parents to their advances as well as the independence of Puritan maids in making up their minds to marry, the wooing of numerous fair widows by Judge Sewall himself makes humorously evident the custom of bargaining over marriage settlements. Less than four months after his wife's death we find the Judge writing : " This morning wondering in my mind whether to live a Single or a Married Life ; . . ." But he does not " wonder " long ; for he soon decides to wait upon the Widow Denison whose husband has but just departed

---

[1] *Sewall Papers*, Vol. V, pp. 502–3.
[2] *Ibid.*, VI, p. 24.

this life, leaving his will to be " proven " by the Judge himself. Lest this seem indecent haste, it should be remembered that widows were not long permitted to remain in single blessedness in any of the American colonies. Life was hard in early colonial days and it was felt by men and women alike that its difficulties could best be faced in partnership. Then, too, widows were held in high regard in all the colonies. Even in Revolutionary days we are told that " the reign of widows was absolute " ; and the statement is supported by reference to the early love affairs of Washington, Jefferson and Madison, all of whom were profoundly influenced by " the characteristic glamour which hung around every widow." [1]

The courtship of the Widow Denison, however, appears not to have proceeded smoothly. It would seem that this lady was ill-disposed to give up the comfortable provision made for her in her husband's will for the less generous allowance the Judge was willing to make her. Thus we read : " Ask'd her what I should allow her; she not speaking; I told her I was willing to give her Two (Hundred?) and Fifty pounds per anum during her life, if it should please God to take me out of the world before her. She answer'd she had better keep as she was than give a Certainty for an uncertainty; She should pay dear for dwelling at Boston. I desired her to make proposals but she made none. I had Thoughts of a Publishment [2] next Thorsday the 6th. But now I seem far from it. May God, who has the pity of a Father, Direct and help me ! " [3] A few weeks later the Judge, thoroughly disheartened, decides " that it seem'd to be a direction in Providence not to proceed any further; . . ." and he so informs the fair widow. Thereupon courtship and higgling over money matters cease for a time — but not for long. Soon we find the Judge courting — and winning —

---

[1] Earle, *Colonial Dames*, pp. 30–6.
[2] The law required that the intention to marry be thrice published in town meeting or "publike lecture."   [3] *Sewall Papers*, Vol. III, p. 202.

the Widow Tilly. Unfortunately, however, his second wife died less than a year after the marriage, and the luckless widower was once more thrown upon the matrimonial market.

This time the Judge's affections speedily light upon the Widow Winthrop. But the lady meets his advances with the objection that she " could not leave her house, children, neighbours, business. I told her she might do som Good to help and suport me." [1] Mistress Winthrop, however, is not easily convinced that she will benefit herself by marrying again. Nor does she hesitate to tell her aged suitor that he is in need of " a Wigg," and, further, that his " Coach must be set on Wheels, and not by Rusting." [2] Undismayed by these plain hints the Judge patiently pursues his courtship under discouraging difficulties and finally gets down to a discussion of marriage settlements. " Told her I had an Antipathy against those that would pretend to give themselves; but nothing of their Estate. I would give a proportion of my Estate with my self. And I supos'd she would do so. As to a Perriwig, My best and greatest Friend, I could not possibly find a greater, began to find me with hair before I was born, and had continued to do so ever since; and I could not find in my heart to go to another." [3] A little later the Judge records : " Spoke of giving her a Hundred pounds per anum if I dy'd before her. Ask'd her what sum she would give me, if she should dy first? Said I would give her time to Consider of it. She said she heard as if I had given all to my children by Deeds of Gift. I told her 'twas a mistake, Point-Judith was mine &C. That in England I own'd, my Father's desire was that it should go to my eldest Son ; 'twas 20 £ per anum ; she thought 'twas forty. I think when I seem'd to excuse pressing this, she seem'd to think 'twas best to speak of it ; a long winter was coming on." [4] Clearly this New England

[1] *Sewall Papers*, Vol. III, p. 267.   [2] *Ibid.*, p. 270.
[3] *Ibid.*, p. 272.   [4] *Ibid.*, p. 274.

widow could look out for her own interests even against so shrewd a bargainer as the Judge. We may infer, also, that she did not regard her elderly wooer as a " good match "; for she finally told him very positively that " she could not Change her Condition." During his last call upon Mistress Winthrop both the widow and her parlor must have had a chilling effect upon the Judge, since he records that " The Fire was come to one short Brand besides the Block, which Brand was set up in end; at last it fell to pieces and no Recruit was made." [1] So, thoroughly discouraged, the old man takes his leave, and that, apparently, " for good."

But a few months later this persistent suitor is found writing to the Widow Gibbs proposing marriage, — under definite conditions. His financial proposition, which figures prominently in the letter, is as follows : " For your children, or some in their behalf, to give Bond to indemnify me from all debts contracted by you before the Marriage; and from all matters respecting the Administration. This, I told you [in a previous letter] I peremptorily insisted on. I was to secure you Forty pounds per anum during the term of your natural Life in case of your Survival." [2] Despite the dictatorial tone of this " love letter " and its distinctly bargaining flavor, the Widow Gibbs seems to have been reasonably satisfied with her suitor, for their banns were published a few days later. Let us hope the lady never knew how much lower she was rated by the Judge than was the Widow Denison of earlier days ! The provision for the latter, it will be remembered, was 250 pounds yearly; whereas the final object of the Judge's calculating affections was fain to be content with a beggarly income of 40 pounds in case she survived her husband.

As the eighteenth century advanced, social life became freer and more pleasure-loving throughout the colonies. The severest phases of the struggle for existence in the new land were past and even in New England the harsh Puritan spirit

[1] *Ibid.*, p. 275.   [2] *Ibid.*, p. 303.

was gradually becoming softened. In the Southern and Middle Colonies society became really gay and manners were characterized by more freedom and less delicacy than would be sanctioned in cultivated circles to-day. But it should be remembered that coarseness and lack of restraint were characteristic of eighteenth century manners in Europe, especially in England, and the colonies were merely adopting standards and practices which very generally prevailed abroad. A certain " Lucinda," known as the " Young Lady of Virginia," has left us a lively record of social customs and manners in the colony of her birth during the eighteenth century. She writes her friend Polly Brant:

" The Gentlemen dined to-day at Mr. Marionbirds. We have supped and the gentlemen are not returned yet. Lucy and myself are in a peck of trouble for fear they should return drunk. Sister has had our bed moved in her room. Just as we were undress'd and going to bed the Gentlemen arrived, and we had to scamper. Both tipsy! . . . Hannah and myself were going to take a long walk this evening but were prevented by the two Horrid Mortals, Mr. Pinkard and Mr. Washington, who seized and kissed me a dozen times in spite of all the resistance I could make. They really think, now they are married, they are prevaliged to do anything. . . ." [1]

In a society so gayly careless of conventions we may well believe that ample opportunities were afforded colonial youths and maidens to know each other and to carry on those preliminary skirmishings that sometimes lead to serious courtship. Southern girls were doubtless " sad coquettes in their youth . . . although they look so demure in their portraits, and proved such exemplary wives and mothers in later years. Duels and despairing lovers seem scarcely to have ruffled the serenity of their lovely countenances, or to have made their hearts beat faster under their stiff bodices." [2]

[1] *Journal of a Young Lady of Virginia*, 1782. (Ed. of 1871, p. 15.)
[2] Wharton, *Colonial Days and Dames*, pp. 197–8.

Even Pennsylvania damsels, if we may believe the Virginia traveller, William Black, were prone to " discourse on love " and to pull " the other Sex to pieces." And when this amusement palled these young ladies fell to " Criticising on Plays and their Authors . . . "; It is evident that " female " conversation on literary themes was not deemed fitting by this Virginia critic, for he caustically remarks that " Expressions which swim on the surface of Criticism seemed to have been caught by the Female Fishers for the Reputation of Wit." [1]

Bundling. — It is hardly possible to discuss courtship customs in colonial days without reference to the crude practice of " bundling " which seems to have been most prevalent in rural settlements along the Connecticut Valley and on Cape Cod. In his *Knickerbocker's History of New York*, however, Irving refers to this custom as having spread among the Dutch girls of New Netherland. He attributes the practice to the Yankee settlers in the colony, of whom he writes : " Among other hideous customs, they attempted to introduce among them that of *bundling*, which the Dutch lasses of the Netherlands, with that eager passion for novelty and foreign fashions natural to their sex, seemed very well inclined to follow, but that their mothers, being more experienced in the world, and better acquainted with men and things, strenuously discountenanced all such outlandish innovations." [2] It is at least questionable, however, whether this rude practice were not brought over to the new land by the Dutch settlers themselves from Holland, where a similar custom had long existed in the country districts. An account of the character and extent of the practice may be found in Howard's valuable *History of Matrimonial Institutions* [3] and a fuller treatment is given by Stiles in his book *Bundling in its Origin, Progress and Decline* (Albany, 1871).

[1] Earle, *op. cit.*, p. 191.   [2] *Op. cit.*, p. 217.   ("Geoffrey Crayon" edition.)
[3] Vol. II, pp. 181-8.

Precontract. — Very generally in the New England Colonies the ancient custom of formal, public betrothal was carefully preserved and even regulated by statute. In Plymouth the " couple — having the consent of the parents or guardians, in the case of two minors — made before two witnesses a solemn *promise of marriage in due time*, the ceremony having the formality of the magisterial wedding then in vogue." [1] In Massachusetts, New Hampshire and Connecticut, also, the customary ceremony of precontract was celebrated with much formality, although in Massachusetts it was not established by law. A Connecticut statute of 1640 reads: " It is ordered by the authority of this court, that whosoever intends to join themselves in marriage covenant shall cause their *purpose of contract* to be published in some public place and at some public meeting . . . at the least eight days before they enter into such contract whereby they engage themselves each to other, and that they shall forbear to join in marriage covenant at least eight days after the said contract." [2]

But this Puritan custom of public betrothal seems not to have been favorable to morality. In the first place the " betrothed woman was put, both by law and social custom, one step above the woman who was not betrothed, and one step below the woman who was married. This was so as respects the civil and criminal law." [3] The natural outcome was that couples thus solemnly betrothed regarded themselves as half married and not infrequently lived as husband and wife before the marriage ceremony had been performed. Indeed it has been maintained that precontract " must be held responsible for a very large share of the sexual misconduct revealed in the judicial records. Before the general court

---

[1] Goodwin, *The Pilgrim Republic*, p. 600. Italics mine.
[2] Trumbull, *Blue Laws*, p. 106. Italics mine.
[3] Shirley, *Early Jurisprudence of New Hampshire* (*Proc. of New Hampshire Hist. Soc.*, 1876–84, p. 308; quoted in Howard, Vol. II, p. 180).

of Plymouth the cases of ' uncleanness ' after contract and
before marriage are very numerous. . . . Members of some
of the most illustrious families of New England were guilty
of indiscretions in this regard." [1] Doubtless the colonial
authorities were largely to blame for this state of affairs. By
elevating the ceremony of betrothal into a public affair, announcement of which must be published eight days before-
hand, the Puritan fathers in effect placed a premium upon
illegal sex relations after precontract and before marriage.
The authorities, indeed, although they punished such social
offenses with fines or whipping, yet reduced this punishment
" in general one half, or less than one half what it would
have been had there been no betrothment." [2] Naturally,
in the eyes of young offenders, the lesser punishment indicated
a lessening of the offence, and sexual intercourse between betrothal and marriage was quite often the outcome. Nevertheless, despite the manifest evils which resulted from attaching
legal significance to the ceremony of precontract, the custom
and the law alike persisted at least up to the middle of the
eighteenth century.

Colonial Marriage Laws. — Very generally, in the American
colonies laws were passed providing that (1) due notice should
be given of the intention of marriage; (2) clear evidence of
parental consent should be furnished; (3) the marriage should
be celebrated by certain persons duly recognized by law;
(4) the records of all marriages should be kept by town or
county clerk or registrar.

Banns, Publication and License. — In all the colonies from
New Hampshire to Georgia provision was made that the banns
of the marriage should be read three times in some public place.
In Virginia banns were published on " three severall Sundays
or holydays in the time of devyne service in the parish churches
where the sayd persons dwell according to the booke of com-

---

[1] Howard, *op. cit.*, Vol. II, p. 186.
[2] Shirley, *op. cit.*, p. 308; quoted in Howard, Vol. II, p. 180.

mon prayer. . . ." [1]   And such was the custom in the Carolinas and Georgia where the Church of England had at least nominally been established.   But in these Southern colonies the parties intending marriage were also privileged to obtain a license from the Governor, or, later, from the county court, instead of publishing banns.   This privilege was welcomed by the more sensitive members of the community, who shrank with distaste from the publicity associated with the publishing of banns.

The Middle colonies varied somewhat in their laws regulating the announcement of intention to marry.   In Maryland, like her sister colonies to the South, either banns or license were demanded : whereas in Pennsylvania the parties were required to affix " their intention of marriage on the court or meeting-house door of the county wherein they dwell, one month before the solemnizing thereof " and to prove their " clearness of all other engagements " by a certificate secured from some reputable persons.[2]   Thus, owing to Quaker influences, Pennsylvania required no banns nor did it apparently adopt the custom of granting a license.   New Jersey, also, required that a notice of the proposed marriage be posted for two weeks in some public place or that banns be three times proclaimed in church.   Later, after the colony was united with New York, power was granted to the Governor to issue licenses. In New York, likewise, after England had obtained control of the colony in 1664, the English custom of banns or license was established by the so-called " Duke's laws."   This legal code clearly states that any marriage celebrated without banns or license or without minister or magistrate is void.[3]   The provision is noteworthy as one of the very few of its kind to be found in the body of colonial laws.   Most of the other colonies were apparently content to punish infringement of the mar-

---

[1] Act of 1631; quoted in Cook, *Marriage Celebration in the Colonies* (*Atlantic Monthly*, 1888, Vol. 61, p. 355).

[2] Act of 1683; quoted in Cook, *op. cit.*, p. 358.   [3] Cook, *op. cit.*, p. 360.

riage laws concerning publicity with fines or other penalties, without going to the length of declaring marriages not properly published or celebrated as null and void.

Throughout the New England colonies laws were enacted requiring banns or the posting of a notice of intention to marry in some public place. Rhode Island, in its code of 1647, provided that " No contract or agreement between a Man and a Woman to owne each other as Man and Wife shall be owned from henceforth as a lawful marriage . . . but such as are in the first place, with the parents, then orderly published in two severall meetings of the Townsmen." [1] The New Haven colony laws also provided " That no persons shal be either contracted or joyned in marriage before the intention of the parties proceeding therein, hath been three times published, at some time of public lecture, or town meeting in the town, or towns where the parties, or either of them do dwel . . .; or be set up in meeting upon some post of their meeting house door, in publick view, there to stand so as it may be easily read by the space of fourteen daies; . . ." [2] Similar laws were enacted in Plymouth, Massachusetts and New Hampshire; and each code provided that no one " under the covert of parents " should marry without their consent.

The Celebration of Marriage. — The colonies were as circumspect in their regulation of the celebration of marriage as they were in respect to its publication. In the Southern colonies, where the Episcopacy was sooner or later established, the tendency was very strong to restrict the performance of the marriage ceremony to clergymen of the Church of England. In 1661–2 a Virginia law provided that " noe marriage be solemnized nor reputed valid in law but such as is made by the ministers according to the laws of England." [3] For more than a hundred years thereafter (and indeed this had been the custom since the settlement of the colony) no lay magistrate or

---

[1] Act quoted in Cook, *op. cit.*, p. 352.   [2] Trumbull, *Blue Laws*, p. 242.
[3] Cook, *op. cit.*, pp. 353–4.

2 B

dissenting clergyman could join parties in marriage in the colony of Virginia. But in 1780 and again in 1784, after the Revolutionary War, acts were passed providing, under certain conditions, that it should be " lawful for any ordained minister of the gospel . . . to celebrate the rites of matrimony according to the forms and customs of the church to which he belongs. . . ." This concession marks the spirit of toleration that was becoming characteristic of all the colonies at this time. It was followed by another concession to the lay spirit in the Act of 1784 which granted to the courts in the remote frontier districts of Virginia the power to nominate certain " sober and discreet laymen " to celebrate marriage in those places where no clergyman could be found, according to the forms and customs of the Church of which these appointees were members. Thus Virginia, by the close of the eighteenth century, had at least partially abandoned the principle of ecclesiastical marriage and had sanctioned that of lay celebration under clearly defined conditions.

The history of the laws regulating marriage in the other Southern colonies is similar to that of Virginia. In all the Church of England was somewhat loosely established and its laws requiring marriage by a clergyman of that church were nominally enforced. But as early as 1728 the Carolinas sanctioned the performance of the marriage ceremony by " any lawful magistrate " *in the absence* of a clergyman of the Church of England, or with his expressed consent. A further step toward toleration was taken in 1766 when Presbyterian ministers were singled out from other dissenters and permitted to solemnize marriage " in their usual and accustomed manner." This paved the way for the Act of 1778, passed during the stress of the Revolution and authorizing all " regular ministers of the gospel, of every denomination . . . and all justices of the peace in this State, . . . to solemnize the rites of matrimony, according to the rites and ceremonies of their respective churches." A similar Act was passed in Georgia in 1785.

Only in Maryland was a different course pursued. Starting, under Catholic rule, with a policy of complete toleration
and recognition of either religious or civil marriage as legal,
this colony became the seat of a bitter struggle for supremacy
between the adherents of the Church of England on the one
hand and the Catholics and Quakers on the other. By the
end of the seventeenth century the advocates of Episcopacy
had won. Soon after assuming control, they passed the Act
of 1717 which provided that all members of the Church of
England desiring marriage should " apply themselves to a
minister for the contracting thereof. . . ." But unfortunately the authorities were not content to stop here. Imbued
with the idea that only a marriage celebrated by a duly ordained minister of the gospel is legal, the law-givers enacted
in 1777 that no marriage should henceforth be celebrated in
Maryland " unless by ministers of the Church of England,
ministers dissenting from that Church, or Romish priests,
appointed or ordained to the rites and ceremonies of their respective churches. . . ." The Quakers only were permitted
the privilege of lay celebration. It is an interesting fact that
this law has been made part of the present Maryland code.
Thus this state is the only one in the Union which has failed
to sanction the celebration of marriage by a civil magistrate.[1]

In the Middle colonies, where no church party gained exclusive control, religious toleration and the lay celebration of
marriage had no such hard-fought battles to wage. From its
foundation by William Penn the colony of Pennsylvania proclaimed a policy of complete religious toleration. In accordance with this principle marriages which were solemnized by
any form of religious society were recognized as both valid
and legal. It has sometimes been charged against the Quakers
that they tended to repudiate marriage or at best to celebrate

---

[1] For this whole discussion see Howard, *op. cit.*, Vol. II, 228–63, and pp.
353–7. Also see Hening's *Statutes*, Vol. I, 156–8, 181–3, 332, 433; Vol. II, 49–
51; Vol. III, 441–2.

it in a loose and irregular way. Nothing could be more un-
true to the facts. The Society of Friends indeed permitted its
members to take each other in marriage on the ground that
marriage is " God's joining not man's." But it was carefully
stipulated that this ceremony should take place in " Publick
Meeting " in the presence of at least twelve witnesses, after
due publication had been made. A later statute required that
one of the twelve witnesses demanded by the previous law
should be a justice of the peace. It is clear that the Pennsylvania Quakers held marriage in great esteem and took pains
to surround it with due safeguards of publicity and registration.[1]

In East and West New Jersey the law of 1668 permitted
the celebration of marriage by an " approved minister or justice of the peace within this province," thus sanctioning civil
marriage from the beginning. But toward the close of the
seventeenth century New Jersey was united with New York
in one royal province. Thereafter an attempt was made to
enforce the matrimonial laws of the Church of England
upon the people. But the attempt was not crowned with
success. By the Act of 1719 it was made lawful for " any
religious society in the province to join together in the holy
bonds of matrimony such persons as are of the said society.
. . ." Apparently, then, justices of the peace lost the right
to celebrate marriage at this time, although the power seems
to have been later restored; for an Act of the General Assembly of 1752 forbids ministers, *justices*, or others to join
persons in marriage without banns or license under penalty
of a fine of £200.[2] In 1795 it was clearly enacted that " every
justice of the peace of this State, and every stated and ordained minister of the gospel . . . is authorized and empowered to solemnize marriages." [3]

Under Dutch rule marriages in New Netherlands were required to be celebrated by a minister of the Dutch Reformed

[1] Howard, Vol. II, pp. 315–24.   [2] *Ibid.*, p. 313, foot-note.
[3] Cook, *op. cit.*, p. 359.

faith. But the " Duke's laws," promulgated for his colony of New York in 1664, after providing for publication of banns, public posting of intention to marry, or securing a license from the Governor, declare that " it shall be lawful for any minister or for any Justice of the Peace to join the parties in Marriage, Provided that the said partys do purge themselves by Oath before the Minister or Justice that they are not under the bonds of Matrimony to any other person." The Duke's laws were reënacted in 1684 and were changed in no important particular before the Revolution.

In the New England colonies the course of affairs was somewhat unusual. From the beginning of their history as colonizers there existed among the Puritans a strong distrust of all ecclesiastical forms sanctioned or enforced by the Church of England. This suspicion, amounting to active dislike, was extended to the ecclesiastical celebration of marriage. At the outset the Puritan colonists stoutly proclaimed the principle of Luther and Cromwell that marriage is a civil contract and should therefore be celebrated by a civil officer, duly empowered by law. Very generally the New England law and custom required that marriage be celebrated before a justice of the peace or other magistrate and did not sanction celebration by the minister of any faith. Indeed Governor Winthrop relates that on the occasion of a " great marriage . . . solemnized at Boston " the bridegroom procured the pastor of his home church in Hingham to preach. " But the magistrates," writes the Governor, " hearing of it, sent to him to forbear." One of the reasons assigned was that " we were not willing to bring in the English custom of ministers performing the solemnity of marriage, which sermons at such times might induce. . . ." [1] Yet for sixteen years no law was passed in Massachusetts enforcing the prevailing custom of civil marriage, lest such a statute be " repugnant to the laws of England." But in 1646 the colonists of Massachusetts Bay enacted that

[1] Winthrop's *Journal* (N. Y., 1908), Vol. II, p. 330.

" no person whatsoever in this jurisdiction shall join any persons together in marriage, but the magistrate, or such other as the General Court or Court of Assistants shall authorize in such place where no magistrate is near." Similar statutes were enacted in New Haven, Connecticut and Rhode Island.[1]

Toward the close of the seventeenth century, however, when the colonists' fear of ecclesiastical domination had greatly lessened, their hostility to ecclesiastical marriage rites also declined. Therefore no strong opposition was made to the order of council issued in 1686 by Dudley, as president of New England, authorizing ministers as well as justices of the peace " to consummate marriages, after three several times publication or license from the president or deputy." [2] Four days after Dudley had received his commission the " first marriage with prayer-book and ring " was celebrated in Boston and no doubt some zealous Puritans were scandalized thereby. But gradually such opposition died down in all the colonies save Rhode Island, which refused to clergymen the right to solemnize marriage until 1733. Shortly after securing their charters the other New England colonies enacted laws empowering ministers of all denominations to perform the rites of matrimony.

No prescribed ritual for marriage existed in the New England colonies in early times. The ceremony was usually performed at the home of the bride and we may be sure that prayer, exhortation and psalm-singing played a prominent part. But it was not long before a discreetly decorous merry-making followed the wedding ceremony and in the latter part of the eighteenth century marriages were made the occasion for much gay revelry in New England. Even Judge Sewall does not condemn the " Cake and Sack-Posset " which seemed invariably to follow the psalm-singing and prayers in weddings of his own day.[3]

---

[1] Cook, *op. cit.*, p. 351; also Whitmore, *Colonial Laws of Massachusetts* (1660–72), p. 172.   [2] Quoted in Howard, Vol. II, p. 135.
[3] See Sewall's *Diary*, Vol. II, pp. 403–4; Vol. III, p. 253.

Registration of Marriages. — Very generally in the colonies
provision was made for the proper registration of marriages.
In New England the town clerk or clerk of the writs was
charged with the duty of keeping a register of marriages as
well as of births and deaths. In Plymouth the clerk was allowed " thripence apece for each particular person soe registered." [1] Moreover, the parties to the marriage were required
to report it to the clerk within one month under penalty of a
fine of three shillings, half of which went to the clerk if he had
entered a complaint of neglect. By the code of 1647, failure
to publish and register a marriage in Rhode Island brought
upon the offending bridegroom a fine of five pounds paid to the
parents of the maid. All the accessories also each forfeited
five pounds, half of which was turned over to the bride's
parents. It has been pointed out by the historian that an effective system of registration was thus established in colonial
Rhode Island " such as recent legislation has attempted to
revive." [2]

Throughout the Southern colonies provision for the registration of marriages was also carefully made. In Virginia the
minister of every parish was required to keep a record of all
solemnized weddings and to make an annual return to the
quarter court on the first of June. In North Carolina in 1715
the Governor was empowered to choose from among three freeholders nominated by the inhabitants one man to be register
of deeds; and until there was a clerk of the parish church in
that district this official was to keep a record of betrothals and
marriages. In 1696 Georgia and South Carolina likewise required that every man hereafter married in those colonies
should record his marriage in the register's office within thirty
days after celebration or else forfeit " one royall " for neglect.
Furthermore, at the time of registration he must produce a
certificate under the hand of minister or magistrate, attested

[1] Howard, Vol. II, p. 144.
[2] Arnold, *History of Rhode Island*, Vol. I, p. 208; quoted in Howard, II, 148.

by six witnesses of the ceremony.[1] Similar provisions were made in the Middle colonies. By the Duke of York's laws " The Minister or Town Clerk of every parish shall well and truly and plainly " record all births, marriages and deaths in his district " in a Book to be provided by the Church-wardener for that purpose." If the master of a family or person concerned failed to report the marriage within one month, he should pay a fine of five shillings.[2] Likewise the laws agreed upon in England for the governing of Pennsylvania provided that a certificate of marriage " under the hands of parents and witnesses shall be brought to the proper register of that county and shall be registered in his office." [3]

Summary. — A review of colonial legislation with respect to marriage gives clear evidence that the first settlers made every attempt to safeguard the institution of matrimony and to prevent thoughtless persons from entering into the contract carelessly and without due formality. Parental consent, given to the town or county clerk personally or in writing, was everywhere required ; due notice of the marriage by banns or posting or, in default of banns, by license from the Governor, was demanded in all the colonies ; the solemnization of marriage was regulated by law ; and, finally, registration of the marriage in town or county clerk's office, or, in colonies where the Church of England was established, by the parish clerk, was a universal requirement. In none of the colonies was " self-marriage " (incorrectly called common-law marriage) in which the parties took each other for husband or wife without the presence of magistrate or clergyman sanctioned by law. Even in Pennsylvania the law of 1693 required that one of the twelve witnesses to the ceremony should be a justice of the peace. In all the other colonies marriage by magistrate or clergyman, or

---

[1] Howard, Vol. II, p. 260.

[2] *Colonial Laws of New York*, Vol. I, p. 19 ; quoted in Howard, Vol. II, p. 288.

[3] "Laws agreed upon in England," in Linn, *Charter and Laws*, p. 101 ; quoted in Howard, Vol. II, p. 318.

(in the frontier districts of Virginia) by a layman licensed by the courts was inflexibly demanded by law. Yet there can be little doubt that " self-marriage," contrary to legal provisions, did occur from time to time throughout the colonies. In such cases, except where the law expressly declared the marriage void,[1] the offenders were liable to punishment for contracting an *illegal* marriage, but their union was not declared *invalid*. Thus the old mediæval distinction between marriages contracted contrary to law and those which were null and void from the beginning [2] seems to have crept into colonial legislative practice. Even in the colonies where illegal marriages were also declared invalid the statute was probably itself invalid because not in accordance with the laws of England.[3]

DIVORCE IN THE COLONIES

New England Laws and Practices. — Colonial laws and practices with respect to (1) absolute divorce and (2) separation from bed and board, show marked differences. In New England, where the idea of civil marriage was so deeply rooted, it is not surprising to learn that civil divorce was likewise sanctioned and provided for. In his interesting *History of Massachusetts*, Governor Hutchinson, who was presiding officer in the divorce court for many years, makes the following statement concerning the colonial lawgivers : " In matters of divorce they left the rules of the canon law out of the question. . . . I never heard of a separation, under the first charter,[4] *a mensa et thoro*. . . . In general what would have been cause for such a separation in the spiritual courts, was sufficient, with them, for a divorce *a vinculo*. Female adultery was never doubted to have been sufficient cause ; but male adultery, after some debate and consultation with the elders,

---

[1] As in New York, until 1684, Virginia (by the Act of 1661–2) and probably Rhode Island.

[2] Because they were within prohibited degrees of consanguinity.

[3] See Howard, Vol. II, pp. 232 and 287.　　　　[4] 1630–92.

was judged not sufficient. Desertion a year or two, when there was evidence of a determined design not to return, was always good cause; so was cruel usage of the husband." [1]

During the early colonial period the authority to grant divorces in Massachusetts resided in the Court of Assistants, which held its sittings twice yearly. By the *Acts and Resolves* of November 3, 1692, entire jurisdiction over matrimony and divorce was conferred upon the Governor and Council. A later Act of 1696 empowered these authorities to assign the woman, if the innocent party, a reasonable portion of her husband's estate " not exceeding one-third part thereof " as alimony.[2] Howard has prepared some valuable tables setting forth the salient facts in cases of divorce and annulment brought before the Court of Assistants during the periods 1639–92, 1739–60 and 1760–86. A study of these tables brings some interesting facts to light. Forty cases of divorce or annulment were brought before the Court during the first period mentioned above. Of these, four were suits for annulment and the marriages were declared void. In two instances the causes assigned for annulment were bigamy and in two others " affinity," *i.e.*, marriage within the prohibited degrees. In one of these latter cases a man had married his brother's wife; in the other the man had married an uncle's widow — both unions being forbidden in the code of Leviticus and also in Puritan law. Twenty-eight of the forty divorce suits were brought by women. It is noteworthy that the Court apparently regarded the adultery of the husband as insufficient cause for granting a divorce to the wife, since in only one instance was the decree of dissolution of marriage issued on the sole ground of adultery. And even this decree was reversed on appeal. But adultery, accompanied by desertion or cruelty, or desertion, aggravated by remarriage or refusal to provide, was in every instance accounted just cause for dissolving the marriage. During the period 1739–60 only three decrees for

[1] *Op. cit.*, Vol. I.   [2] *Acts and Resolves*, I, 209.

absolute divorces were issued, together with two decrees of separation. But in the third period 1760–86 the number of divorces, separations and annulments of marriage greatly increased. Ninety-six petitions were presented to the Governor and Council, and in seventy-six cases absolute divorces were granted. In thirty-seven instances, where decrees of dissolution were issued, the husband was the plaintiff and the charge against his wife was adultery. The wife's charges were again, as in the former period, adultery accompanied by cruelty, desertion or failure to provide. In only one case, where the wife was plaintiff, that of Rosanna *v.* Wm. Scott, was the marriage dissolved on the sole ground of adultery. Decrees of separation were issued in favor of the wife in ten instances, commonly on the ground of cruelty or desertion and failure to provide.

This analysis makes clear several important facts: (1) the New England colonists did not hesitate to go counter to English law and practice in regarding the dissolution of marriage as a civil function and in endowing the legislative body with full rights in respect to such dissolutions; (2) although far more generous treatment was accorded wives, in respect to divorce or separation, than was conceded in the other colonies, yet discrimination in favor of men very generally existed. The husband could and did obtain divorce on the single ground of adultery, whereas in the vast majority of cases the wife could not. (3) The practice of granting separations on the grounds of cruelty, desertion or failure to provide became more frequent during the late colonial period than it had previously been. (4) The privilege of remarriage was granted to a woman in case the husband had been absent four or five years and his whereabouts was unknown.

Connecticut colony was unique in intrusting its divorce cases almost wholly to the courts of law. Of divorce law and practice in Connecticut Howard writes: " Perhaps in none of the other colonies was so liberal, and on the whole so wisely

conservative, a policy adopted. . . . Separation from bed
and board was rejected. . . . Reasonable and fairly liberal
causes of divorce *a vinculo* were clearly specified; husband and
wife were treated with even justice; and although legislative
divorce, always liable to abuse, was permitted, the greater
part of litigation seems always to have been intrusted to the
regular courts. In short, Connecticut, in all the more essential
respects, anticipated the present policy of civilized nations by
nearly two hundred years." [1]

Divorce in the Southern and Middle Colonies. — In the
Southern colonies, where the Church of England was established, English law and custom with respect to divorce and
separation were very generally followed. Now in seventeenth
century England, it will be remembered, the ecclesiastical
courts still had jurisdiction in such matters. Absolute divorce
was not granted by these courts, and separation from bed and
board was permitted only on the grounds of adultery, desertion
and cruelty. But the colonists of Virginia and the Carolinas
showed no desire to set up the English ecclesiastical court in
the country of their adoption. Indeed, this tribunal was
never established; nor was any other court given jurisdiction
in respect to the dissolution of marriage. The result was that
no divorces or legal separations were granted in the Southern
colonies throughout the colonial period. "Their statute
books are entirely silent on the subject of divorce jurisdiction." [2]
Of course parties might and did separate by mutual consent;
and in Virginia, at least, the county courts received and
granted petitions for alimony from parties thus separated.
Now, since no statute empowered the courts to take action
in petitions for alimony, we are forced to believe that the
authority was assumed without legal sanction because of the
exigencies of the situation.

In the Middle colonies, also, a highly conservative policy
in regard to divorce was very general. New Netherland, to

[1] *Op. cit.*, Vol. II, pp. 353–4.   [2] Howard, Vol. II, p. 367.

be sure, influenced by the doctrines of the Protestant reformers, occasionally granted a petition for absolute divorce or for separation. But when the colony passed under the rule of England the English law concerning separation was adopted. But here, again, as in the Southern colonies, no ecclesiastical court having jurisdiction in cases of adultery and cruelty was ever established. Hence neither divorces *a vinculo* or *a mensa et thoro* were granted in New York during the colonial period, except in a few isolated cases, occurring previous to 1689, when the Governor of New York seems to have arbitrarily assumed the power to grant divorces.[1] Similarly in Pennsylvania, although the code of 1682 recognized absolute divorce on the ground of adultery, yet no tribunal was empowered to grant such divorce. There are, however, two instances of absolute divorces granted by the colonial legislature in Pennsylvania. The first decree was issued by the council in 1769 and was sustained; but a later decree of 1772 was declared void by the English king in the following year.[2]

In conclusion it may be said that the strong contrasts between the procedure of New England respecting divorce and that of the Middle and Southern colonies seem largely based upon (1) religious differences and (2) the relatively non-interfering policy of England with regard to her subjects in the colonies of New England. The theory of marriage as a civil contract, which could be made binding by a civil magistrate and therefore could be dissolved by a civil court, was fundamental in the doctrine of Lutherans and Calvinists alike. The English Church had not assented to it; and therefore, wherever this Church gained even doubtful primacy in the colonies, the narrow tenets of the Anglican communion respecting marriage and divorce were made binding. It is interesting to note, however, that even in Cavalier Virginia, where the Church of England was most firmly established, the colonists were unwilling to set up the English ecclesiastical court. To that

[1] See Howard, *op. cit.*, Vol. II, pp. 383-4. [2] *Ibid.*, p. 387.

extent they refused to go; apparently sharing, in some degree, the New England distrust of the jurisdiction of the Anglican church. Doubtless, the independent and aggressive spirit of the New England colonists, their strong and prompt resentment of any encroachment upon their chartered privileges, was in part responsible for the fact that their institution of civil divorce was not declared void by the English government, as being directly contrary to the law of the mother country.

HOMES AND HOME LIFE IN COLONIAL DAYS

Houses and House Furnishings. — In New England the rude log cabins of the first settlers soon gave place to more commodious and comfortable homes, some built of brick and stone and some of wood. About the middle of the seventeenth century the houses were built of oak with great stone chimneys and sometimes had an overhanging second story to afford better defence in case of an attack by Indians. " Lean-to " houses in which the second story sloped down to the first in the rear were quite popular. Weeden thus describes their interiors: " This class of houses had four main rooms, the larger ones often twenty feet square, on one floor. On the ground was a parlor, or ' great ' room, for company; a bed-room; a kitchen, the main assembling place of the family; and a milk and cheese pantry." [1] But let it not be supposed that all classes were thus comfortably and spaciously housed. The laboring class and small farmers of this period were well content to live in one-storied houses of two rooms — a kitchen and a family bedroom. In the country districts log huts had by no means disappeared in 1650; and even the deep pits lined and roofed with boards, so often used by settlers in a new country, could occasionally be found. During the latter half of the seventeenth century, however, New England homes showed considerable improvement. Most of the better class of

[1] *Economic and Social History of New England*, p. 214.

houses boasted a second story projecting a foot or so beyond the first. Sometimes they were gabled on the front, thus allowing for bedrooms in the attic. The windows were diamond paned, with the glass cased in lead, and frequently swung outward on hinges. The house of a well-to-do Hartford merchant is described as having a parlor, hall, " spaceroom " and kitchen on the first floor, with second-floor chambers above each room and another chamber in the garret.[1] Yet, despite the increased spaciousness of colonial homes in New England the household must have been sadly crowded. An old manuscript of 1675 states that the average family comprised 9.02 persons including the servants. It was not uncommon for a New England wife to bear twenty children, although, because of the enormous child mortality, few lived to maturity. Judge Sewall had fourteen children, seven sons and seven daughters; yet, in his old age, only four were living. No wonder that " trundlebeds " were set up in every bedroom!

During the eighteenth century, especially in the latter half, were built those charming colonial houses of which too few remain in New England. One has only to visit such New England towns as Litchfield, Connecticut, and Concord and Salem, Massachusetts, to see these simple, yet pleasing homes, painted white, with green blinds, and often with beautiful colonial doorways.

In the Southern colonies the early rude shelters likewise gave place to comfortable abodes. Writing about 1705 Beverley says of Williamsburg homes : " The private dwellings are . . . very much improved, several gentlemen there having built themselves large brick houses of many rooms on a floor; but they don't covet to make them lofty, having extent of ground to build upon ; and now and then they are visited by high winds, which would incommode a towering fabric. They love to have large rooms, that they may be cool in summer. Of late

[1] Weeden, *op. cit.*, p. 284.

they have made their stories much higher than formerly, and their windows larger, and sashed with crystal glass; adorning their apartments with rich furniture.

" All their drudgery of cooking, washing, daries, &c., are performed in offices apart from the dwelling houses, which by this means are kept more cool and sweet." [1]

Thus early was the delightful plantation home of the South, in its essential features, established on Virginia soil. Of these homes Mrs. Wharton writes: " Later, there arose upon the banks of the James, the Potomac and the Chesapeake, stately mansions surrounded by plantations that rivalled the parks of old England, — Shirley, Brandon, Westover, Gunston Hall, the home of the Masons, Flower de Hundred, Wyanoke, the Hermitage, Wye House, — names synonymous with generous living, hospitality, and all the charms with which refined womanhood adorns a home." [2]

Most of the ordinary dwelling-houses, however, were small and covered with shingles of pine or cypress wood. Beverley seems inclined to complain somewhat bitterly of the " ill-husbandry " of the Virginia colonists in the matter of furnishing their homes. Thus he writes " that though their country be overrun with wood, yet they have all their wooden-ware from England; their cabinets, chairs, tables, stools, chests, boxes . . . and all other things, even so much as their bowls and birchen brooms, to the eternal reproach of their laziness." [3]

In the Middle colonies no single type of home architecture seems to have developed if we except the Dutch houses in New Netherland, which were, of course, highly typical, in some respects, of that cleanly and thrifty people. Irving humorously describes the homes in the town of New Amsterdam, later New York.

" The houses of the higher class were generally constructed of wood, excepting the gable end which was of small, black and

---

[1] *History of Virginia* (reprint in 1855 of second ed. of 1722), p. 235.
[2] *Colonial Days and Dames*, p. 81.   [3] *Op. cit.*, p. 239.

yellow Dutch bricks, and always faced on the street, as our ancestors, like their descendants, were very much given to outward show, and were noted for putting the best leg fore-most. The house was always furnished with abundance of large doors and small windows on every floor, the date of its erection was curiously designated by iron figures on the front, and on the top of the roof was perched a fierce little weather-cock, to let the family into the important secret which way the wind blew.

" In those good days of simplicity and sunshine, a passion for cleanliness was the leading principle in domestic economy, and the universal test of an able housewife, — a character which formed the utmost ambition of our unenlightened grand-mothers. . . . The whole house was constantly in a state of inundation, under the discipline of mops and brooms and scrubbing brushes. . . .

" The grand parlor was the sanctum sanctorum, where the passion for cleaning was indulged without control. In this sacred apartment no one was permitted to enter, excepting the mistress and her confidential maid, who visited it, once a week, for the purpose of giving it a thorough cleaning, and putting things to rights, — always taking the precaution of leaving their shoes at the door, and entering devoutly on their stocking-feet." [1]

Life was simple and homely in all the colonies, especially in the North where the kitchen was very generally the family living-room, not only because it was the cosiest room in the house, but also because it was the warmest. Its great fireplace and enormous brick oven served to warm at least half the kitchen, whereas in the stiff and uninviting parlor the atmos-phere in winter was frigid enough only a few feet from the fire. In the farm-houses of New England, home life centred around the hospitable kitchen fireplace until well into the nineteenth century. Whittier in *Snowbound* has painted in attractive out-

[1] *Knickerbocker's History of New York*, pp. 182–3.

2 C

lines the happy evenings passed beside the blazing logs of the hearthfire, — a picture which might easily apply to colonial New England of a century before. Another description, this time of Dutch home life around the kitchen hearth, is furnished by Irving. He says: " As to the family, they always entered in at the gate, and most generally lived in the kitchen. To have seen a numerous house-hold assembled around the fire, one would have imagined that he was transported back to those happy days of primeval simplicity, which float before our imaginations like golden visions. The fireplaces were of truly patriarchal magnitude, where the whole family, old and young, master and servant, black and white, nay, even the very cat and dog, enjoyed a community of privilege, and had each a right to a corner. Here the old burgher would sit in perfect silence, puffing his pipe . . .; the goede vrouw, on the opposite side, would employ herself diligently in spinning yarn or knitting stockings. The young folks would crowd around the hearth, listening with breathless attention to some old crone of a negro, who was the oracle of the family, and who, perched like a raven in a corner of the chimney, would croak forth for a long winter afternoon a string of incredible stories about New England witches, — grisly ghosts, horses without heads, — and hair-breadth escapes, and bloody encounters among the Indians." [1]

Furniture was plain and rather meagre in these days, save in the homes of the leading colonists. Although " Turkey Carpettes " are frequently mentioned in inventories of the seventeenth century, the term refers to table-covers. The floors were very generally uncovered although sometimes they were sanded. " Forms " or benches and stools of various heights were commonly used for seats. Chairs were less numerous; yet an inventory of the furnishings of Governor Eaton's home in New Haven, taken in 1657, shows that his living-room or " hall " boasted no less than six of these useful

[1] *Op. cit.*, p. 184.

articles of furniture.[1]   Very stiff and hard were most of these
chairs, although their wooden seats were sometimes covered
with cushions.   Not until late in the seventeenth century did
chairs with cane seats appear; and about the same time the
easy-chair came into use.   Every inventory of the period
mentions at least one chest.   These were commonly made of
oak, cedar and cypress and sometimes had drawers.   They
were designed to hold most of the family clothing as well
as table- and bed-linen.   Clocks were comparatively rare until
well into the eighteenth century, the colonial housewife being content to mark time indoors by means of an hour-glass
or a water-clock.   It is said that John Davenport of New
Haven who died in 1760 owned the first clock.[2]   Candles of the
fragrant bayberry were extensively used long before tallow
became plentiful.   Mrs. Earle describes a primitive kind of
lamp used in New England called " Betty lamps."   " They
were a shallow receptacle, usually of pewter, iron or brass,
circular or oval in shape, and occasionally triangular, . . .
with a projecting nose an inch or two long.   When in use they
were filled with tallow or grease, and a wick or piece of twisted
rag was placed so that the lighted end could hang on the nose."

As to table furnishings in the seventeenth century, the inventories make plain that most of our colonial forefathers
used napkins generously but were lacking both in the quantity
and quality of their tableware.   In an age when forks were
rare even in England it is not surprising to learn that few colonists were blessed with them until the latter half of the century
and even then they were far from common, as the inventories
of the household furnishings show.[3]   It is said that Governor
Winthrop probably had the first fork ever brought to the new
country.   In 1633 he received a letter from one E. Howes,
saying that the latter had sent him a " case containing an Irish
skeayne or knife, a bodekyn and a forke *for the useful applica-*

[1] Earle, *Customs and Fashions in Old New England*, p. 108.   [2] *Ibid.*, p. 125.
[3] Weeden, *Economic and Social History of New England*, p. 292.

tion of which I leave to your discretion." [1] But early in the eighteenth century forks apparently became common. Judge Sewall in 1718 makes careful note of a gift to the Widow Denison of two cases each containing a knife and fork.[2] Very little earthen ware, and of course no china or porcelain, was to be found in the colonies in the early days. Instead, wooden platters and trenchers were very common as well as pewter dishes which were always kept bright and shining. Of the wooden trenchers (frequently nothing but square blocks of wood whittled by hand) we are told that Harvard College purchased them by the gross for the use of students.[3]

Domestic Industry in Colonial Times. — We may be certain that the well-trained English housewives of the seventeenth century, who joined their husbands in establishing new homes in the strange land of America, did not leave their housewifely knowledge and skill behind them. After the first problem of immediate shelter had been met, the settlers turned their energies to developing a permanent food supply. Fortunately, the soil of the new country proved favorable to the production of most of the grains and fruits of England and the " lean years " which followed the landing of the colonists gave place before long to comparative plenty. In his quaint *Wonder-Working Providence of Zion's Saviour in New England*, Johnson writes in 1647 that " the Lord . . . hath blest his people's provision, and satisfied her poor with bread, in a very little space, everything in the country proved a staple commodity, wheat, rye, oats, peas, barley, beef, pork, butter, cheese . . .; and those who were formerly forced to fetch most of the bread they eat, and beer they drink, a hundred leagues by Sea, are through the blessing of the Lord so encreased, that they have not only fed their elder Sisters, Virginia, Barbados, and many of the Summer Islands that were

---

[1] Quoted in Earle, *op. cit.*, p. 136. Italics mine.
[2] Sewall's *Diary*, (*Mass. Hist. Soc. Coll.*, Vol. VII, p. 190).
[3] Earle, *op. cit.*, p. 138.

prefer'd before her for fruitfulness, but also the Grandmother
of us all, even the firtil Isle of Great Britain. . . ." [1] Of
necessity the food of the colonists was changed somewhat
from that of England to meet the new conditions. Indian corn
or " guinney wheat " soon became a staple article of diet,
which the colonial housewives from Virginia to Massachusetts
ground in stone mortars (later in hand-mills called " querns ")
and prepared in a variety of ways. Writing in 1705 Beverley
says of the Virginians : " The bread in gentlemen's houses is
generally made of wheat, but some rather choose the pone,
which is the bread made of Indian meal. Many of the poorer
sort of people so little regard the English grain, that though
they might have it with the least trouble in the world yet they
don't mind to sow the ground, because they won't be at the
trouble of making a fence particularly for it." [2]

Doubtless the colonists learned from the Indians how to
transform the " dainty Indian maize " growing in their fields
into such dishes as Indian pudding, hasty-pudding, corn-pone,
hominy and samp. They learned, too, how to prepare de-
lectable " sukguttahhash " (succotash) from beans and corn.
Kitchen-gardens soon were attached to most homes and furnished a varied supply of vegetables and fruits. Cattle at
first were scarce, so that fresh meat was a great luxury for many
years. But fish, clams and oysters were abundant and wild
turkeys and game proved plentiful and delicious until the
hunters' guns drove them away from the settlements. Apparently little malt was made at home in the early days, so
the housewife was relieved of one elaborate and tedious task —
at least for a time. Beverley tells us that most Virginia housewives brewed their beer with malt " which they have from
England, though barley grows there very well; but for want
of the convenience of malt-houses, the inhabitants take no
care to sow it." A little later he explains that the expense
of building a " malt house and brew house too . . . can never

[1] *Op. cit.* (ed. 1910), pp. 246–7.   [2] *History of Virginia*, p. 237.

be expected from a single family; . . ." [1] Yet in 1708
Judge Sewall makes this entry in his *Diary:* " Nov. 15, 16.
Our Malt-House by the Mill-Crick is raised."

The domestic arts of pie and tart making as well as preserving were all revived by the colonial housewives. Writing in
1671, a New England author says that the " Quinces, Cherries
and Damsins [2] set the Dames a-work. Marmalet & Preserved Damsins is to be met with in every house."

Another household task which did not fall to the lot of all
housewives, at least in New England, was the baking of bread.
Johnson mentions " Bakers " among those men who " have
left the husbandmen to follow the Plow and Cart, and they
their trades; . . ." These bakers and their bakeshops
were carefully regulated by law in most of the New England
settlements. In the New Haven colony laws of 1643 it is
ordered that " every person within this jurisdiction, who
shall bake bread for sale, shall have a distinct mark for his
bread, and keep the true assizes thereafter expressed and
appointed." The statute then provides in detail for the weight
of loaves of various prices fixed by law.[3]

But the industries connected with the production and preparation of food and drink were but a small part of a goodwife's duties in colonial times. The task of furnishing the
house with the means of light on the long winter evenings
was in her hands. Although the " Betty lamps " previously
described came into use quite early, yet most housewives
depended on candlelight. The making of candles of tallow
or bayberries was an important household industry which
required several days' work in the preparation of the
tallow, making of wicks, and tedious dipping of each candle
in turn. Some favored housewives were the owners of
candle moulds which reduced the labor of candle-making
surely one-half.

[1] *History of Virginia*, p. 261.   [2] Damson plums.
[3] Trumbull, *Blue Laws*, pp. 193-4.

Of course the industries of carding, spinning, weaving and making of housespun garments, as well as table-linen and bed-linen, were relegated wholly to the goodwives of colonial times. Yet, in the early days when hemp and flax were scarce, the spinning-wheel and the domestic loom must have been little used. So serious did this lack become that, in 1640, the Massachusetts General Court directed the towns to inquire what seeds were necessary for the growth of flax and " what men and women are skilful in the braking, spinning and weaving . . . that course may be taken for teaching the boyes and girls in all towns the spinning of the yarne." [1] A few months later a bounty of 3*d.* in a shilling for linen, woollen or cotton cloth was provided by the court on condition that the two former be spun of " wool or linen grown here." Unfortunately this bounty was withdrawn shortly after. Connecticut also took similar action in the same year. In 1656 the Massachusetts Court " fearing that it will not be so easy to import cloths as it was in past years, thereby necessitating more home manufacture," directed the selectmen in every town to encourage the women, girls and boys to spin and weave. Each family was to be assessed for one or more spinners or for a fractional part. Every person so assessed was required to " spin for 33 weeks every yeare, a pound per weeke of lining cotton or wooling and so proportionably for halfe or quarter spinners under the penalty of 12*d.* for every pound short." To encourage wool, hemp and flax production the act provided that the common lands be cleared for sheep and that hemp and flax seeds be carefully saved and sown.[2] Soon the fulling of cloth quite largely passed out of the household to the fulling-mills, the first of which in Massachusetts was licensed as early as 1655.[3] Spinning was, however, almost entirely a home industry during the colonial period. Not so with weaving. Most families had looms of

[1] *Mass. Col. Rec.*, Vol. I, p. 294.   [2] *Mass. Col. Rec.*, Vol. III, p. 396.
[3] Weeden, *op. cit.*, p. 200.

their own, but quite early weaving became, as in England, an industry carried on in large part by craftsmen. Johnson mentions weavers as plying their trade in Massachusetts as early as 1647.[1]

In the South the silk industry engrossed the attention of women as well as men; and steps were taken by Virginia in 1661 to encourage it. Beverley states that "prizes were appointed for the makers of the best pieces of linen cloth, and a reward of fifty pounds of tobacco was given for each pound of silk. All persons were enjoined to plant mulberry trees, for the food of the silkworm, according to the number of acres of land they held." It is pleasant to record that several Southern women were successful in the raising of silkworms and the manufacture of silk. Notable among these was Elizabeth Lucas Pinckney who, in 1755, "carried with her to England enough rich silk fabric, which she had raised and spun and woven herself in the vicinity of Charlestown, to make three fine silk gowns, one of which was presented to the Princess Dowager of Wales, and another to Lord Chesterfield."[2] The third is still in the possession of the family. As in New England, so in Virginia, the Assembly was early concerned about the decline of domestic cloth manufacture, and shortly after the accession of Charles II this body caused "looms and work-houses to be set up in the several counties, at the county charge. They renewed the rewards of silk, and put great penalties upon every neglect of making flax and hemp."[3] Apparently these early statutes of Virginia did not accomplish all that the framers hoped, for Beverley states in 1705 that Virginians "have all their clothing of all sorts from England; as linen, woollen, silk, hats and leather. Yet flax and hemp grow nowhere in the world better than there. Their sheep yield good increase, and bear good fleeces; but they sheer them only to cool them."[4] No doubt, the tobacco

[1] *Op. cit.*, p. 248.   [2] Earle, *Colonial Dames and Goodwives*, p. 83.
[3] Beverley, *op. cit.*, p. 58.   [4] *Ibid.*, p. 239.

industry in Virginia tended to swamp all others that might profitably have been carried on.

Certain it is that in most of the colonies the spinning wheel of the housewife and her girls was rarely idle, and the loom was often in use where the professional weaver had not established himself. The members of the family, including the servants, or " hired help," as they were called in New England, were numerous indeed and all must be clothed. When the busy goodwife was not spinning or carding or weaving, she was sitting by the evening fire knitting stockings or swiftly plying her needle, an implement " far more useful than the pen, and almost as powerful as the sword, in those days of early home-making." Mrs. Wharton cites Thomas Nelson Page's charming reference to a Virginia housewife who, when her husband complained of the gate being broken, playfully replied, " Well, my dear, if I could sew it with my needle and thread, I would mend it for you." Many of the able men who were the first framers of our constitutional government were not ashamed to wear the clothing made in their own homes by the busy fingers of their wives. In 1776 Abigail Adams writes to her husband in Philadelphia : " I feel concerned lest your clothes go to rags, having nobody to take any care of you in your long absence; . . . I have a suit of homespun for you whenever you return." [1]

In 1778 one Christopher Marshall, a well-to-do Philadelphia Quaker, left in his diary, the *Remembrances*, an eloquent tribute to his wife's tireless industry in their home. To do justice to her services, he tells us, " would take up most of my time, for this genuine reason, how that from early in the morning till late at night she is constantly employed in the affairs of the family, which for some months has been very large ; for beside the addition to our family in the house (is) a constant resort of comers and goers which seldom go away with dry lips and hungry bellies. This calls for her constant attend-

[1] *Familiar Letters*, p. 182.

ance, not only to provide but also to attend at getting prepared in the kitchen, baking our own bread and pies, meat, &c., but also on the table. Her cleanliness about the house, her attendance in the orchard, cutting and drying apples of which several bushels have been procured, add to which her making of cider without tools, for the constant drink of the family, her seeing all our washing done, and her fine clothes and my shirts, the which are all smoothed by her; add to this, her making of twenty large cheeses, and that from one cow, and daily using with milk and cream, besides her sewing, knitting &c." [1]

A vivid contrast has recently been drawn between the " Priscilla " of colonial days and the " Priscilla " of modern times with respect to the value of each as a producer of home necessities. So priceless were the services of the former maiden that she might well have been justified in taking the initiative and saying to John Alden: " John, I know you love me and I love you. Let us marry and I will help you make our home. As soon as you have built the house, with the help of our neighbors, I will furnish it. I will take the raw wool you supply me with and spin, weave and fashion it into warm blankets and homespun clothing for us both and I will knit all your worsted stockings. Then, too, I will sow hemp and flax seed, and make the fibres of the plants into linen sheets, napkins and cloths for our beds and table. I will take charge of all the work of lighting our home and will prepare the food that you bring to me from the farm and garden." [2] Surely the John Alden of colonial days was no economic loser in this experiment of marriage and setting up a new home. On the other hand one should not criticise too severely the "John " of present times who hesitates long before taking unto

[1] *Extracts from the Diary of Christopher Marshall*, 1774–81, Albany, 1877, pp. 57–8.

[2] This comparison was originally made by Mrs. Carrie Chapman Catt in a lecture given under the auspices of the Columbia University Institute of Arts and Sciences.

himself the luxury of a wife who knows little or nothing of the skilled art of homemaking.

The Colonial Home as a Training School. *Early Nurture.* — In all the colonies children were warmly welcomed and, as we have seen, families were very large. Not only was a numerous offspring a fulfilment of the divine command to " be fruitful and multiply " but children were most valuable aids to their parents in the struggle for a comfortable livelihood. We are told that Sir William Phipps, first royal Governor of Massachusetts (1692–5), was one of twenty-six children, all born of the same mother; and it is well known that Benjamin Franklin was one of a family of seventeen. Yet, as we have seen, child mortality was very high in those days when little was known of the hygienic care of infants and when homes were far from warm and comfortable in the coldest days of winter. Mrs. Earle writes: " There lies open before me an old leather-bound Bible with the record of my great-grand-father's family. He had sixteen children. When the first child was a year and a half old the second child was born. The baby was but four days old when the older child died. Five times did that mother's heart bear a similar cruel loss when she had a baby in her arms; therefore when she had been nine years married she had one living child, and five little graves bore record of her sorrow." [1] Only two children of the Puritan divine, Cotton Mather, survived their famous father, — and so the record goes. No wonder women were expected to be fruitful as an important part of their life-work!

The colonial baby was likely to be ushered into the world by a midwife, who was assisted by several nurses. A spirit of kindly helpfulness prompted busy housewives in the colonies to proffer their services to a neighbor who was about to become a mother. These friendly helpers did much of the housework during the confinement of the mother and as-

[1] *Child Life in Colonial Days*, p. 5.

sisted in caring for the new-born infant. Judge Sewall's *Diary* abounds in references to the midwives, nurses and women who attended his wife on the numerous occasions when their help was needed. He refers, also, to the custom, doubtless handed down from the Middle Ages, of entertaining these women with a plentiful dinner. In 1694, after the birth of his daughter Sarah the Judge makes this entry: " Women din'd with rost Beef and minc'd Pyes, good cheese and Tarts." [1] Again, on January 16, 1702, he writes: " My Wife Treats her Midwife and Women: Had a good Dinner, Boil'd Pork, Beef, Fowls; very good Rost Beef, Turkey-Pye, Tarts." He carefully names the *seventeen* women who partook of this bounteous spread and adds: " Comfortable, moderat wether: and with a good fire in the Stove warm'd the Room." [2]

Unfortunately there was not always a stove to warm the room, and many a baby, at least in the Middle and New England colonies, must have shivered in its cradle whenever it was not placed near the fireplace. In those days babies' little shirts were made of linen, and even the warmth of the homespun blankets in which they were wrapped could not wholly counteract the chilling effect of such garments. Then, too, helpless infants were taken to church to be christened very early in their earthly careers. At least in Massachusetts few days were allowed to pass after the birth of a child before it was brought before the minister with a view to outwitting " the old deluder Satan." Again it is Judge Sewall who furnishes us with testimony of the ruthlessness with which babies were carried out into the bitter cold of a New England winter and into the damp chill of the meeting-house to be christened. Under date of Feb. 6, 168$\frac{6}{7}$ he writes of his week-old child: "Between 3 and 4 P.M., Mr. Willard baptiseth my Son, whom I named Stephen. Day was Lowring after the storm, but not freezing. Child shrunk at the water but cry'd not." Ap-

[1] *Op. cit.* (*Mass. Hist. Soc. Coll.*, V, p. 394).　　[2] *Ibid.*, Vol. VI, p. 51.

parently poor little Stephen, despite his Stoic control, did not survive his chilly welcome into the world, for a few months later his father records that his " dear Son Stephen is carried to the Tomb. . . ."

Family Discipline. — As might be expected, the colonists brought with them to the new world the ideas of family discipline that prevailed in seventeenth century England. Everywhere children were trained to render respect and obedience to parents, and their childish offences were punished with severity as the best means of driving out " the old Adam." In a work on *Children and Their Education* written by John Robinson, the beloved pastor of the Pilgrim flock in Holland, the common belief in the inherent evil of child nature is set forth. " Surely," he declares, " there is in all children (though not alike) a stubbernes and stoutnes of minde arising from naturall pride which must in the first place be broken and beaten down that so the foundation of their education being layd in humilitie and tractablenes other virtues may in their turn be built thereon." Certain it is that the process of breaking down the child's stubborn will began early in most families and was conducted with thoroughness. Yet, for all his Puritan sternness, Judge Sewall makes very few references to the punishment of his children. Once he records chastising his little son Joseph who " threw a knop of Brass and hit his Sister Betty on the forehead so as to make it bleed and swell; upon which, and for his playing at Prayer-time and eating when Return Thanks, I whip'd him pretty smartly." [1] Little sinful, four-year old Joseph! His attempt to hide from his father " behind the head of the cradle " served forcibly to remind the latter of " Adam's carriage " after he had eaten the forbidden fruit and thus brought sin into the world! It is pleasant to know that Cotton Mather heartily disapproved of the " slavish way of education carried on with raving and kicking and scourging, in schools as well as in families. . . ."

[1] *Diary*, Vol. I, p. 369.

His son testifies of him that " He would never come to give the child a blow, except in case of obstinacy, or something very criminal. To be chased for a while out of his presence he would make to be looked upon as the sorest punishment in his family." [1]

Religious Training in the Family. — It is a truism to state that religion played a far more prominent part in the lives of the American colonists than in those of their descendants. In the Southern and Middle colonies children were carefully educated in the catechism of the Church of England and were very early familiarized with its ritual. Likewise the Society of Friends enjoined upon all parents the painstaking education of their offspring in the principles of morality and religion accepted by them. But it was in New England that religious training was most severe and, it may truthfully be added — gloomy. Family prayers were almost universal, and the daily reading of the Bible by parents and children was never overlooked in most families. Judge Sewall writes in 1689 : " It falls to my Daughter Elizabeth's Share to read the 24 of Isaiah which she doth with many Tears not being very well, and the Contents of the Chapter, and Sympathy with her draw Tears from me also." Poor Betty Sewall ! Her fear of death and punishment for sin was never far from her sensitive mind during her whole lifetime. Her father records a few months later that when he reached his home in the evening his wife told him that Betty had been dejected and sorrowful all day. A " little after dinner she burst out into an amazing cry, which caus'd all the family to cry too." Her mother's questioning at last revealed the cause, — " she was afraid she should goe to Hell, her Sins were not pardon'd." The Judge adds : " She was first wounded by my reading a Sermon of Mr. Norton's, about the 5th. of January. Text Jno. 7 . 34. Ye shall seek me and shall not find me. And those words in the Sermon, Jno. 8 . 21. Ye shall seek me and shall die in your sins, ran in

[1] Quoted in Earle, *Child Life*, p. 209.

her mind, and terrified her greatly." [1] One cannot refrain from thinking that the childhood years of many sensitive children besides Betty Sewall were darkly overshadowed by the Puritan doctrines of original sin, predestination and election, and the punishments of a fiery, material hell, so faithfully taught them by parents who sought to perform their utmost duty. Even boys were profoundly affected at times by the theological instruction they received at home. Judge Sewall tells us how he tried to arouse his son Sam to the " need he had to prepare for Death," but is forced to record that he " seem'd not much to mind, eating an Aple." Later, however, when the boy was saying the Lord's Prayer, " he burst out into a bitter Cry and said he was afraid he should die. I pray'd with him," writes the father, " and read Scriptures comforting against death, as ' O death, where is thy sting,' &c." [2]

In the better class of families the manners of children were carefully looked after. Little books of etiquette were written and widely circulated during the eighteenth century. Mrs. Earle has reproduced the title-page of one of these courtesy books published in London in 1701. It was called *The School of Manners* and contained unbending rules of behavior for children " at Church, at Home, at Table, in Company, in Discourse, at School, abroad, and among Boys." One is permitted to hope that this excellent manual was not always in evidence.

Following the custom in England, some parents did not permit their children to sit at table with them, but required them to stand through the whole meal. Of this practice Mrs. Earle writes: " Sometimes they [the children] had a standing place and plate or trencher; at other boards they stood behind the grown folk and took whatever food was handed them. This must have been in families of low social standing and meagre house-furnishings. In many homes they eat or stood

[1] *Diary*, Vol. I, pp. 419–20.   [2] *Ibid.*, pp. 308–9.

at a side-table and trencher in hand, ran over to the great table for their supplies." [1]

Notwithstanding the care and pains spent by most Puritan parents upon the moral and religious training of their children, the lawmakers of Massachusetts Bay and later of Connecticut conceived it to be an important part of their business to have oversight of the young, whether these were under family government or not. A Massachusetts Act of 1642 empowered the selectmen of every town " to take account from time to time of all parents and masters, and of the children, especially of their ability to read and understand principles of religion and the capital laws of their country, and to impose fines upon such as shall refuse to render such account to them when they shall be required. . . ." In 1654 it was ordered that " Magistrates have authority to whip divers children and servants who behave themselves disrespectfully, disobediently and disorderly toward their parents, masters and governors."

Such interference with the rights of parents seemed perfectly just and natural to our Puritan forefathers. And indeed the tendency in this and other countries has for many years been in the direction of State control of the rearing and education of children. Our statutes compelling the attendance of children at school and limiting the power of parents to chastise or abuse their offspring are encroachments upon parental privilege no less marked although more humane than those of Puritan New England.

Industrial Training in the Home. — Not many idle hours or happy playtimes fell to the lot of children in the northern colonies, at least in early times. Life was too strenuous in this new land and the struggle to wrest a livelihood from the wilderness too intense not to react upon the children. Moreover, Isaac Watts' oft-quoted lines regarding Satan's skill in finding mischief " for idle hands to do " were more popular in the eighteenth century than now. Boys and girls were very early

[1] *Child Life in Colonial Days*, pp. 216-17.

put to work both in and out of doors, although the tasks in farm and garden fell more largely to the share of boys. Yet the labor of children was not sharply divided according to sex. Boys were taught to weave garters and suspenders on the small tape-looms found in almost every family, while girls took part in the spring sowing on the farm and shared with their brothers the task of weeding flax fields and vegetable gardens. We have seen how the governments of Virginia and the New England colonies sought to encourage the raising of wool and flax. Flax manufacture was a complicated industry involving, we are told, about twenty different operations. Half of these could be carried on by children who learned to hetchel flax, comb wool, skein yarn, wind spools with newly spun thread and even fasten the warp threads to the frame of the loom. Tiny girls of six or seven began the task which was to be theirs through life — the spinning of flax and later of cotton. For this a small hand distaff was often used which was called a " rock." Some children became very dexterous in making smooth, well-twisted thread with this simple appliance. The oft-quoted Massachusetts law of 1642 enjoined it upon the selectmen to see that even the boys and girls who tended cattle . . . " be set to some other employment withal as spinning upon the rock, knitting, weaving tape, &c. . . ." Apparently the hand-looms in use could be taken to hill or meadow and the small shepherds and cattle tenders could be kept busy weaving tape and braid for use as shoe-laces, belts, hatbands, etc.

In Virginia and other colonies, where silk raising became a craze at one time or another, boys and girls were frequently set to work picking mulberry leaves from the trees which were kept low by pruning. The care of silkworms was held to be fit work for children, and it was commonly said that two boys " if their hands be not sleeping in their pockets," could care for six ounces of seed from hatching till within two weeks of spinning, when " three or four more helps, women and

2 D

children being as proper as men," were needed to feed, cleanse, air and dry the worms.[1]

In addition to tasks of cooking, sewing, spinning and weaving, girls in the colonies must learn to make samplers, not only that they might become expert needlewomen, but also in order to learn their letters. Mrs. Earle describes the eighteenth-century sampler as " a needlework hornbook, containing the alphabet, a verse indicative of good morals or industry, or a sentence from the representations of impossible birds, beasts, flowers, trees, or human beings." [2] Dutiful and virtuous were the sentiments stitched by childish fingers into the canvas of their samplers; and one wonders what were the inner feelings of the little needlewomen, pining to be out of doors, as they embroidered such verses as the following:

> " Next unto God, dear Parents, I address
> Myself to you in humble Thankfulness.
> For all your Care and Charge on me bestow'd,
> The means of learning unto me allowed.
> Go on! I pray, and let me still Pursue
> Such Golden Arts the Vulgar never knew."

Probably most boys and girls in colonial days received their industrial training in the home from their own parents. However, in poor families, girls as well as boys were apprenticed when very young. The colonial laws made early provision for binding out orphans and the children of indigent parents with suitable persons who would care for their morals and teach them various industries. The girl's indenture, however, unlike that of the boy, did not stipulate that she was to be taught a specific trade; hence she probably received a general training in spinning, weaving and household tasks. In Boston in 1720 a " Spinning School House " was established which owed its origin to the public spirit of a philanthropist who later turned over the equipment to the city " for the educa-

---

[1] Earle, *Child Life in Colonial Days*, p. 310.   [2] *Ibid.*, p. 328.

tion of the children of the poor." Later the city itself organized
several spinning schools where orphans and neglected children
were taught to be skilled spinners. We are told that the girls
sometimes plied their tasks on Boston Common surrounded, at
first, by an admiring audience of towns-people.[1] Virginia,
also, in the Act of 1646 empowered the county commissioners
to send two children from each county " at the age of eight or
seven years at the least . . ." to James City . . . " to be
employed in the public flax houses under such master and mistress as shall be there appointed in carding, knitting and spinning." The commissioners were enjoined to " have caution not
to take up any children but from such parents who by reason of
their poverty are disabled to maintain and educate them." [2]

Intellectual Education. — As we have seen, scant attention
was given to the intellectual education of girls throughout
the American colonies. Boarding -schools were established
after 1725, but they offered instruction chiefly in reading,
writing, and a smattering of music, with dancing and embroidery taught by special teachers. Such was the education
of English girls in the eighteenth century; and the English
idea of superficial " accomplishments " as constituting the
sole necessary education for " females " crossed the seas to the
colonies. Here and there a girl received serious intellectual
training at the hands of a cultivated father who refused to
accept the ideal of " female education " almost universal in
colonial days. But ordinarily girls in the Northern colonies
were sent to dame schools to learn to read, sew, spin and knit,
— the reading not always being followed by training in writing.
Therefore many colonial women were forced to " make their
mark " whenever their signature was required, as deeds and
documents of colonial times abundantly prove. In the New
England colonies, at least in Massachusetts, girls were per-

[1] Edith Abbott, *Women in Industry*, p. 21.
[2] Elsie Clews, *Educational Legislation . . . of the Colonial Governments* (New
York, 1899), p. 356; Hening, *Statutes*, Vol. I, pp. 336-7.

mitted to attend the town elementary schools only at hours
when the boys were not using the building, *i.e.*, early in the
morning and late in the afternoon.   Even this grudging privilege was restricted to the summer months and was promptly
withdrawn at the approach of winter on the ground of regard
for " female health."   Boys, however, seem to have attended
the New England town schools pretty generally and those who
intended to enter Harvard or Yale were prepared in the town
grammar schools established by law in the colonies of Massachusetts and Connecticut.

Apparently, then, the colonial family restricted its education
of the young very largely to moral, religious and industrial
training, relegating such intellectual education as was deemed
fitting to the dame school, the town, church or private school,
and, in the Southern colonies, to tutors brought in from the
mother-country.   Even Judge Sewall in his voluminous *Diary*
makes no mention of giving intellectual instruction to any of
his numerous offspring.   Occasionally such home instruction
was given, however, but it was certainly unusual.

The Plantation Family of the South. — In the Southern
colonies a type of home life developed, which was peculiar to
that region, and deserves special consideration.   Unlike the
Puritan homes built in towns or villages, the colonial " mansion " of the Southern planter was set in wide acres of tobacco,
cotton or rice fields.   These plantation homes, established in a
virgin wilderness by men of English stock and strong English
feeling, were the nurseries of a type of man and woman
peculiar to the South and differing in many respects from
their stern and more democratic Puritan cousins of the New
England colonies.   A fortunate combination of fertile soil,
mild climate and valuable indigenous products, made of
these Southern settlers, in whom the land-owning instinct
was already strong, an agricultural class, reproducing many
of the aristocratic customs and characteristics of their
English forefathers.   Along the rivers of Virginia and the

Carolinas large plantations were established, vast tracts of land were cultivated and the products shipped by natural waterways to the coast. The institution of slavery was doubtless of the greatest assistance to the settlers in maintaining manor-houses similar to those of the landed gentry of England. Early in the seventeenth century a Dutch ship brought the first cargo of slaves from Africa to Virginia and thereafter for many generations English, Dutch and New England traders kept the Southern landholders amply supplied with negro slave workers. This condition, in the words of Thomas Nelson Page, " emphasized class distinction and created a system of castes, making the social system of Virginia as strongly aristocratic as that of England." [1]

Just as the Southern planter sought to reproduce the manorial estate of the English gentleman in the wilds of America, so he transplanted the English Church to his new abode. Likewise he adopted the English system of primogeniture and entail, carefully seeing to it that his house and lands descended to his eldest son or his nearest male heir.

Several contemporary descriptions have come down to us of colonial plantation homes. In his valuable *Journal* Philip Fithian describes his year of residence as tutor in the house of Mr. Robert Carter of Virginia, and draws a vivid pen picture of his surroundings. The mansion stood on the " high, craggy banks of the River Nominy " and was known as Nomini Hall. Around it were wide stretches of fertile land worked by negro slaves. The house, our journalist tells us, " is built with Brick, but the bricks have been covered with strong lime Mortar; so that the building is now perfectly white. It is seventy-six Feet long from East to West; and forty-four wide from North to South, two Stories high; . . . " On the ground floor, in addition to dining-rooms and a study, was " a Ball-Room thirty Feet long." At equal distances from the corners of the main house stood four other buildings — the school-house

[1] *The Old South* (New York, 1900), p. 104.

(for the children of the family only), the stable, the coach-house and the work-house where the family washing was done. In the triangle made by the wash-house, stable and coach-house were placed the "Kitchen, a well built House as large as the School-House; Bake-House; Dairy; Store-House and several other small Houses: all which stand due West, and at a small distance from the Great House, and form a little handsome Street." Not far away stood the planter's mill and granary where the wheat and corn from his fertile acres were ground and stored. To the east of the mansion were "two Rows of tall, flourishing, beautiful Poplars . . . (which) form an extremely pleasant avenue, and at the Road, through them, the House appears most romantic, at the same time that it does truly elegant." [1]

So much for the plantation home at its best — and many such charming residences there were, scattered through the Southern colonies on the wooded heights overlooking quiet rivers. But the estates of some planters, especially near the Western frontiers, were far from being either so pretentious or so comfortable. Indeed, as the traveller proceeded into the interior, the stone houses gave place to wooden ones, the extensive farms to smaller holdings, the numerous retinue of slaves to half a dozen or so, until the typical log shelter of the frontiersman was reached, standing like a faithful scout at the outposts of civilization.

What was the character of the life on the great estates near the coast? In the first place every plantation of any size was well-nigh an economic unit, producing almost all the food and drink needed for its own consumption as well as some of the materials for clothing, although much of the latter was imported from England. It was an important industrial establishment, carrying on agriculture, milling, gardening, horse-raising and dairying. Within doors the lady of the mansion was probably the busiest member. Hers was the

[1] Fithian, *Journal and Letters*, 1767–74 (Princeton, 1900), pp. 128–31.

duty of overseeing the labors of a horde of household slaves, and of feeding, clothing and caring for the health of every negro-worker on the estate. On her devolved the careful oversight of all supplies, locking them up from thieving fingers and giving them out when needed. She must not only know how to spin, weave and make clothing for scores of men, women and children — her own family and the families of her slaves — but she must train ignorant, undisciplined and child-like beings to perform a multiplicity of household tasks with industry and skill. All this required enormous executive ability and almost infinite patience, firmness and tact. Thomas Nelson Page has paid enthusiastic tribute to the wife and mother of the Southern plantation.

" She was the necessary and invariable functionary, the key-stone of the domestic economy which bound all the rest of the structure and gave it its strength and beauty. From early morn till morn again the most important and delicate concerns of the plantation were her charge and care. . . . From superintending the setting of the turkeys to fighting a pestilence, there was nothing that was not her work. She was mistress, manager, doctor, nurse, counsellor, seamstress, teacher, housekeeper, slave, all at once. She was at the beck and call of every one, especially of her husband, to whom she was ' guide, philosopher and friend.' " [1]

In addition to this rather overwhelming catalogue of duties the Southern matron was expected to maintain the lavish hospitality so dear to the hearts of all colonists of the South. " Little excuse," says one writer, " was needed to bring people together where every one was social, and where the great honor was to be the host." And so it is not surprising to find Fithian's *Journal* fairly bristling with references to social doings — to dancing parties where the minuet was performed with stateliness and charm, to dinners, excursions on horseback and by boat, house-warmings and card parties. The hostess

[1] *Social Life in Old Virginia*, pp. 37–8.

who entertained at a dance well knew that most of her guests must be accommodated for a night or two, since distances were great, and all must be entertained at her generous table. Literally the lady of the Southern plantation kept open house where all her friends were welcome at all times.

Such a laborious life must have proved onerous if not exhausting to many a Southern housewife. No wonder that Thomas Nelson Page stops in the middle of a panegyric in honor of Virginia matrons to record that the lady was " often delicate in frame, and of a nervous organization so sensitive as perhaps to be a great sufferer ; . . . " [1]

The Status of a Southern Matron. — Although the wives and mothers of plantation days were treated with much courtesy and chivalrous deference by all right feeling men, their legal and economic position was entirely one of dependence. Writing of the economic status of the Southern matron Mrs. Putnam says :

" Her life was on its professional side the life of the Greek lady. . . . Each was the wife and steward of a farmer. Each was responsible for the reception in the house of the produce of the farm intended for home consumption. Each must keep order regnant among slaves and goods. A surprising amount of what the household used was in each case made under the lady's direction from raw material produced on the estate. . . . And each was responsible for the health of the household ; it was her duty to prevent sickness if possible, and when it came to tend it. Each doubtless, if not overtaxed, derived satisfaction from the performance of important work bearing directly on the welfare and happiness of those she loved best, but neither could be called a free woman." [2]

It is only fair to add that if Southern women were constrained to fill only one exacting sphere of work — home making, with all the laborious tasks implied by this word in the eighteenth century — if they had little pocket money they could

[1] *Social Life in Old Virginia*, pp. 35-6. [2] *The Lady*, p. 300.

call their own, no control of their property, and no rights with respect to contract and suit, yet their condition in this regard was that of all the women of their age, shared in equal measure by their sisters of the Northern colonies. And doubtless many women found happiness and a considerable outlet for their powers under this eighteenth century régime. One of the oldest and most energetic of Southern women, Eliza Lucas Pinckney, administered with remarkable skill and executive ability the large estate of her father in South Carolina, while he was held in the West Indian island of Antigua by his duties as Royal Governor. Apparently Governor Lucas left his talented daughter of sixteen a free hand in the management of his plantation and, as her biographer attests, her "planting was no holiday business." She early began to experiment with regard to the crops best suited to South Carolina's soil and climate and discovered that indigo might be made to yield a rich profit. In 1739 she writes: "I wrote my father a very long letter on his plantation affairs . . . on the pains I had taken to bring the Indigo, Ginger, Cotton, Lucern and Cassada to perfection, and had greater hopes of the Indigo — if I could have the seed earlier the next year from the East Indies, — than any of ye rest of ye things I had tryd . . . also concerning pitch and tarr and lime and other plantation affairs." [1]

After this managing young lady had become the wife of Colonel Charles Pinckney, her father seems to have been beset by some misgivings that she would forget her duty of obedience and respectful subordination to her husband. Apparently he wrote a warning letter on this question to his daughter, for she replied: "I am well asured the acting out of my proper province and invading his, would be an inexcusable breach of prudence; as his superior understanding; (without any other consideration), would point him to dictate, and leave me nothing but the easy task of obeying." [2]

[1] Ravenel, H. H., *Eliza Pinckney* (1896), p. 7.   [2] *Ibid.*, p. 100.

Home Training and Education. — In these charming plantation homes boys and girls were educated in the ideals of their fathers and grandfathers before them. They developed, through association and training, the same delicate breeding, the same aristocratic ideas, the same high spirited and narrow devotion to their established social structure that were conspicuous in their forbears. As we have seen, most of these Southern plantation children were taught by tutors in their own homes until the girls were sixteen or thereabouts and the boys fitted for higher study. Then the sisters entered happily into the round of social gayeties that enlivened colonial life in the South while their brothers were sent to William and Mary College or, more probably, to Oxford or Cambridge in the mother country. Thence these young men returned, more in love than ever with the life of the landed aristocracy, to perpetuate unchanged the social and economic system in which they held so favored a position. Such a life as they led was not stimulating to intellectual research or to social reconstruction. It was too agreeable, too well oiled by the labor of an enslaved class, to challenge their highest intellectual powers. In the words of Professor Trent, himself a Southern gentleman :

" Southerners lived a life which, though simple and picturesque, was nevertheless calculated to repress many of the best faculties and powers of our nature. It was a life affording few opportunities to talents that did not lie in certain beaten grooves. It was a life gaining its intellectual nourishment, just as it did its material comforts, largely from abroad, — a life that choked all thought and investigation that did not tend to conserve existing institutions and opinions, a life that rendered originality scarcely possible except under the guise of eccentricity." [1]

[1] *William Gilmore Simms* (1899), p. 37.

SELECTED BIBLIOGRAPHY

SOURCES.

Adams, Charles Francis (editor). *Familiar Letters of John Adams and his Wife Abigail Adams* . . . (1876).

Beverley, Robert. *The History of Virginia* (reprinted in 1855 from second edition of 1722), pp. 54, 58, 231-2, 235-9, 262-4.

Clews, Elsie W. *Educational Legislation* . . . *of Colonial Governments* (1899), passim.

Dunton, John. *Letters from New England* (*Pub. of Prince Soc.*, 1817), pp. 67-73.

Fithian, Philip. *Journal and Letters*, 1767-74. (Princeton, 1900), pp. 50, 51, 56-7, 62-6, 75, 87, 103, 109.

Johnson, Edward. *Wonder-working Providence of Zion's Saviour in New England*, 1628-57. (Scribner's, 1910), pp. 71, 246-7.

Kemble, Frances G. *Journal of a Residence on a Georgia Plantation.*

Sewall, Samuel. *Diary*, 1674-1729. (*Coll. of Mass. Hist. Soc.*, Vols. V-VII, Boston, 1878.) Vols. I, II, III (of series).

Trumbull, *True Blue Laws* (1876), pp. 60, 69-70, 78-9, 87, 104, 106-7, 123-4, 150-2, 156, 159, 216-19, 241-3, 261, 279.

Winthrop's Journal (Scribner's, 1908), Vol. I, pp. 120, 266-8, 285-7; Vol. II, 43-4, 161-3, 225, 330.

SECONDARY WORKS.

Adams, Charles Francis. *Some Phases of Sexual Morality* . . . *in New England*, Cambridge, 1891.

Brooks. *The Olden Time Series: The Days of the Spinning Wheel in New England* (1886).

Bruce, H. Addington. *Woman in the Making of America* (1912).

Cook, Frank G. *Marriage Celebration in the Colonies* (*Atlantic Monthly*, LXI, 1888, pp. 350 ff.).

Crawford, Mary C. *Social Life in Old New England*, chs. V, VI.

Earle, Alice Morse. *Home Life in Colonial Days* (1889).
  Colonial Dames and Goodwives.
  Child Life in Colonial Times (1889).
  Colonial Days in Old New York (1905).
  Customs and Fashions in Old New England (1894).
  Margaret Winthrop (1898), chs. I-III, VI, pp. 174-80.

Goodwin, John A. *The Pilgrim Republic* (1888).

Howard, E. G. *History of Matrimonial Institutions*, Vol. II.

Irving, Washington. *Knickerbocker History of New York*, Book III, chs. III, IV, VII.

Page, Thomas Nelson. *Description of a Virginia Plantation*, pp. 19-56, 75 ff.

Putnam, Emily. *The Lady*, pp. 282-323.

Ravenel, H. H. *Eliza Pinckney* (1896).

Weeden, W. B. *Economic and Social History of New England* (1890), pp. 170, 191-8, 200, 212-19, 227-30, 291-310, 388-99, 413, 428.

Wharton, Anne H. *Colonial Days and Dames* (1895).

Winsor, Juston (editor). *The Memorial History of Boston* (1880), Vol. I, 229-31, 303-4, 483-97, 512-18; Vol. II, 450-62, 479-80, 485.

CHAPTER XI

THE INDUSTRIAL REVOLUTION AND ITS EFFECT UPON THE FAMILY

Industrial Conditions at the Middle of the Eighteenth Century. — Until after the middle of the eighteenth century industry was almost wholly organized around the family. Hand labor was still the rule; and the plough, the loom, the distaff and spindle were quite similar to those in use in the ancient world two thousand years before. About 1725 Daniel DeFoe made a leisurely journey through England and fortunately left to future generations a vivid description of the cottage system of industry as he saw it. He writes:

The " land being divided into small Inclosures from two Acres to six or seven each, seldom more, every three or four Pieces had an House belonging to them . . . hardly an House standing out of a Speaking-distance from another; . . . We could see at every House a Tenter and on almost every Tenter a Piece of Cloth, Kersie or Shalloon which are the three Articles of this country's Labour. At every considerable House was a Manufactury. Then as every Clothier must necessarily keep one Horse, at least, to fetch home his Wool and his Provisions from the Market, to carry his Yarns to the Spinners, his Manufacture to the Fulling-mill, and, when finished, to the Market to be sold, and the like; so every one generally keeps a Cow or two for his Family. By this means the small Pieces of inclosed land about each House are occupied; . . . Tho' we met few people without Doors, yet within we saw the Houses full of lusty Fellows, some at the Dye-vat, some at the Loom, others dressing the Cloths;

the Women and Children carding or spinning; all employed from the youngest to the oldest; scarce anything above *four Years* old, but its Hands were sufficient for its own Support." [1]

From this account of an eyewitness the reader may form a pretty accurate mental picture of domestic industry as carried on in the villages and market-towns of Somersetshire, Wiltshire, Dorsetshire, Gloucestershire and Yorkshire — the cloth manufacturing counties of England. Likewise the description shows clearly enough that only the carding and spinning were handed over to the women and children; the processes of weaving, fulling, dyeing and dressing cloth so long the exclusive work of the housewife were now performed almost wholly by men who, long before, had invaded the women's field of labor. The "lusty fellows" who carried on the industry were the master and his apprentices, among whom the master's own sons were probably to be reckoned. They made use of simple implements — the spinning-wheel twisting only a single thread, the hand loom, requiring two men to throw the shuttle back and forth, and wooden cards for combing the wool and flax by hand.

It should be noted further that this cottage system of labor was pretty evenly distributed over the rural districts of England, and did not as at present demand the concentration of vast numbers of workers in urban centres where crowded tenement sections were bound to appear. At times, when the textile industry became slack, the workers in these cottages betook themselves to the fields and raised grain and vegetables for home consumption. This combination of simple agriculture with the manufacture of cloth was highly characteristic of domestic industry in rural England. Such an organization of labor made it possible for father, mother and children to ply their work at home, and, where the conditions of life were

[1] DeFoe, *A Tour Thro' the Whole Island of Great Britain.* 4th Edition, 1748; Vol. III, pp. 137–9. Quoted in part in Robinson and Beard, *Development of Modern Europe*, 1908, Vol. II, pp. 44–5.

not too hard, to develop strong family feeling and love of homestead and soil. Yet it is perhaps well to remember, in this age
of righteous discontent with industrial conditions, that domestic industry was far from an ideal system. In the first
place it tied the workers to the narrow confines of home and
village, permitting little of the free movement from place to
place enjoyed by the modern workman, — a movement bound
to be in some degree broadening in its effect upon the mental
outlook. Then, again, many a master workman was hard in
his treatment of his apprentices, exacting from them the last
ounce in labor, and dealing out food and clothing with a
niggardly hand. Even the younger sons and daughters of
the master were expected to work continuously at spindle or
cards with rare intervals for rest or play. In an earlier age
when gild organizations were numerous and powerful, a
regular supervision was exercised over every master employing apprentices. But the gilds had been steadily declining
in influence since the fifteenth century when Parliament had
begun to enact legislation governing their organization and
conduct. This decline had, of course, been enormously
hastened by the Acts passed in the reigns of Henry VIII and
Edward VI dissolving some gild organizations and confiscating
the property of others. Moreover, the cottage system of
industry in the rural districts had grown up outside the gilds
and despite the bitter opposition of the latter. In consequence it had never been subject to the oversight and direction
of gild officials.

Beginnings of the Commission System. — It must not be
supposed that Europe passed abruptly from an industrial
régime purely domestic in character to the factory system of
the present day. As early as the seventeenth century there
had appeared in England a new class of employers called
" clothiers " who were the forerunners of our modern capitalists. These men bought up a dozen or more spinning-wheels
and looms and rented them out to such workmen as were too

poor to own these implements. The thread was spun, or the yarn woven in the home and the finished product was then taken to the clothier who paid the worker by the piece. In some cases a clothier gathered together a score of workers in a town and paid them regular wages for spinning, carding, reeling the thread and weaving, fulling, bleaching or dyeing the cloth. Very often these processes were carried on by different workers and this division of labor was fairly minute. Obviously such a system of industry has some of the features of the modern. The existence of the capitalists, albeit in a small way, the centralizing of the workers, and the payment of a fixed wage for labor, are important elements in the factory system of the present day. Yet in the majority of cases, work under the commission system was given out by the clothier to be done at home, and the loom or wheel was rented by him for domestic use. The commission form of industry, then, may be said to represent a transition stage between the purely domestic system, in which goods were independently made in the home and sold independently by the master, and the factory system that followed hard upon the industrial revolution.

That English women were very early drawn into industry of the sort described above is made plain by the ballads of the seventeenth century. Doubtless the women, like the men, were attracted by the certainty of a fixed wage however small. One of the simple ballads of the period, in which a mother gives good counsel to a daughter recently married, runs as follows:

> " Maids by their trades to such a pass do bring,
>   That they can neither brew, bake, wash or wring,
>   Nor any work that's tending to good housewifery,
>   This amongst many too often I see.
>   Nay, their young children must pack off to Nurse,
>   All is not got that is put in the purse,
>   Therefore of old I this lesson have learn'd,
>   A penny well sav'd is as good as one earn'd." [1]

[1] Ashton, *A Century of Ballads* . . ., p. 9.

Thus, here and there at least, the commission system of industry tended to play havoc with " good housewifery " as did later the long hours of labor of the wife and mother in the factory.

Another seventeenth century ballad called *The Clothiers' Delight* represents these men as saying of the weavers, tuckers, combers and spinners in their employ :

" When they bring their work home unto us, they complain,
  And say that their wages will not them maintain." [1]

Truly there is nothing new under the sun ; and the small capitalist in the days of family industry was probably no less desirous of getting large returns from his investment than is his successor of modern times, although it may well be true that he was less shrewd and resourceful in accomplishing his ends.

THE INDUSTRIAL REVOLUTION

The Period of Mechanical Inventions. — While the clash of arms in the revolutions of America and France was ringing in the ears of Europe and while the struggle of these countries for political freedom was being watched with varying sympathies by thoughtful men and women, a revolution none the less dramatic and far-reaching in its effects was being enacted in England. The voyages of Prince Henry the Navigator, of Columbus, Vespucci, the Cabots and a score of others had opened vast, undiscovered lands to the knowledge of Europe. With the expansion of the known world went a corresponding expansion of commerce. New markets were opened to European merchants at the same time that a demand for the products of foreign zones was created in the home countries. In course of time cotton from the Southern colonies of America was imported in large quantities into Europe, especially into Eng-

[1] *Ibid.*, p. 65.

2 E

land. This cotton, spun, woven and stamped in the mother-country, was sent back to the New World along with stout English woollens, to serve as clothing for the colonists.

Such an expansion of commerce could produce but one result, — manufacturing was left far behind. Handwork with spinning-wheel and loom could not keep up with the ever increasing demand for cotton, linen and woollen cloth. Thus it was that the laboring men themselves set to work to bring about improvements in the implements of their trade in order to secure a larger output. The hand-loom was the first appliance to be modified for the better. As early as 1738 John Kay, a Lancashire workman, by inventing a long handle to drive the shuttle back and forth through the warp, made it possible for one weaver to do the work formerly done by two. A challenge was thus thrown out to the spinners to improve their implements in order to furnish the increased supply of yarns and thread now demanded by the weavers. But it was nearly thirty years later (1767) when James Hargreaves, a weaver and carpenter by trade, invented the spinning-jenny which drove eight spindles at once by the turning of a wheel. The machine was so simple that a child could easily operate it and thus accomplish the same results as eight spinners with the ancient wheel. As might be expected, the new invention was an instant success and within a decade thousands of spinning-jennies were in operation in various parts of England.

Curiously enough, it was a barber named Arkwright who took the next important step in advance. In 1768 he invented a roller machine for spinning which was driven by water-power. This was the first power machine ever used in the textile industry. Arkwright followed up his invention by the establishment of the earliest factories in England in which were installed machines driven by water-power. A few years later, in 1779, a material improvement in Arkwright's invention was made by one Crompton, who combined with the roller machine the best features of Hargreaves' spinning-jenny. The result was the contrivance known as " the mule " which was capable of spinning much finer thread than Arkwright's roller machine.

Spinning could now be done by water-power machines far more expeditiously than could weaving by hand. The urgent need for a loom worked by mechanical means to keep pace with the increased output of yarns and thread stimulated the inventive capacity of an English clergyman named Cartwright, who, in 1787, gave to the world the first power loom. It proved almost as immediate a success as Crompton's spinning " mule," and in a quarter of a century twenty-four hundred power looms had been set up in England.

It is noteworthy that all these machines were of English invention. France, before the close of the century, was in the throes of revolution, followed by the crushing Napoleonic wars which drained the country of its men and resources. But the new Republic of America was destined to play its part in the revolution of industry by mechanical inventions. In the Southern States, that furnished England with the bulk of its raw cotton, the need for some more expeditious method of separating the seeds from the fibre had long been pressing. At this time the seeds were removed by hand and the most rapid workers could hardly clean more than five pounds daily. In a happy moment the much-needed invention was worked out by a keen young Northerner, fresh from Yale College, Eli Whitney by name. After some experimenting he produced, in 1792, a mechanical device that was capable of cleaning a thousand pounds of cotton a day and could be operated by one man. Thus the supply of raw cotton was kept up to the enormously expanded market in England.[1]

[1] For this brief account I am largely indebted to the excellent discussion of the "Industrial Revolution" in Robinson and Beard, *The Development of Modern Europe*, II, 30–44. Good treatments may also be found in Cheyney, *Industrial and Social History of England;* Beard, *The Industrial Revolution;* Allsopp, *Introduction to English Industrial History;* and Gibbins, *Industry in England*, chs. XXI and XXIII, and pp. 336–40.

Development of the Factory System in England and America. — As a result of the invention of power machinery, great factories sprang up in those districts of England given over to textile manufacturing. In them were gathered the handworkers of the outlying country who speedily learned that they could no longer compete with machine-made goods. Gradually, and not without much distress and bitterness, the industrial system of England was completely transformed. One by one the cottages that had been the centres of home industry were abandoned; and apprentices and masters alike sought the rapidly growing towns and cities where factories were built and expensive machinery installed. This influx of working population led to the erection of cheap and ugly houses in the neighborhood of the factories. Built close together, without even a tiny patch of ground that could serve as a garden, these workingmen's homes were the forerunners of the unsightly tenements and slums of our modern cities. No longer was the worker an independent agent; on the contrary he became wholly dependent on the capitalist who owned the factory and its machinery and who was thus in a position to fix both the wages and the working hours of his employees. After ages of industrial history extending from ancient to modern times, during which the family had been the unit of industry, the household group was at last displaced by the crowded factory with its organized body of workers.

Conditions in America. — While the industrial revolution was proceeding in England, the American colonies and, later, the United States were likewise passing through a period of transition from the earlier domestic industry to the factory system of the present time. But in America the change was a more gradual one, owing largely to the fact that England carefully guarded the secret of her new mechanical inventions in the hope of becoming the industrial mistress of the world. In the words of a modern historian:

" The exportation of any machinery used in manufacturing and the emigration of work-people who had learned to operate the machines were alike prohibited. We were, therefore, cut off from profiting by the work of English inventors and we were greatly handicapped in making similar experiments for ourselves because of the lack of capital and the scarcity of skilled workmen here." [1]

Here and there, notably in the cities of New York, Boston, Philadelphia and Baltimore, so-called "manufactories" were set up. Most of these were merely rented rooms containing a number of hand-looms. The spinning of the yarn was still largely done by the women at home, whence it was brought to these establishments where the spinners were paid.

Toward the close of the eighteenth century Yankee inventiveness asserted itself and experiments were successfully carried on which resulted in the production of much of the new machinery then in use in England. In 1789 Samuel Slater, called the " father of American manufactures," established in Rhode Island the first cotton mill fully equipped with machinery for spinning. But the power loom was not used in America until 1814, about which time weaving, like spinning, became a factory occupation in the true sense of the term.

The introduction of the factory system into this country proceeded under strikingly different conditions from those prevailing in England. In America the men were very generally employed in agriculture which was so profitable that few male workers were tempted to enter the new field of manufacturing. Therefore the textile industry, when it came to be carried on in factories by modern methods, fell into the hands of the women from the first. To quote Miss Abbott again :

" So long as land remained cheap and agriculture profitable, it was taken for granted that women could be counted on to continue, in the mills, the work they had formerly done at home." [2] Our forefathers apparently had no misgivings with

[1] Edith Abbott, *Women in Industry*, p. 36.   [2] *Op. cit.*, p. 47.

respect to the employment of women and children in manufacturing. Instead rosy pictures were painted of the improved circumstances of young women, once living in miserable
hovels with their parents, and now comfortably housed,
clothed and fed by their own efforts. Enthusiastic accounts
were also written of the villages and households where the
whole family was employed in industry. Very general likewise was the approval of child labor. Those mechanical
devices were most esteemed which could be operated in part
by children from five to ten years old. In *Niles's Register* it
was held to be a fortunate circumstance that the machines for
carding, roving and spinning were separate contrivances; " the
first worked by a girl or woman and fed by a child; the second
worked by a child; the third worked by a child or girl." [1]

This being the widespread attitude of economists and
writers throughout the United States, it is not surprising to
learn that, in 1831, women over ten years of age constituted
68 per cent of all employees in the cotton industry throughout the country. In Lowell, Massachusetts, one of the most
important centres of cotton manufacturing, 80 per cent of
the workers in the mills were women, of whom the greater proportion were under twenty-five years of age. Most of these
girls were daughters of self-respecting New England farmers
and represented a distinctly superior class of workers. Lucy
Larcom worked in the Lowell mills from the time she was
eleven years old and so did her sister Emeline and other
girls of good stock and real ability. [2] But after 1850 the
places of these young women of sound New England ancestry
were gradually taken by an inferior class of immigrant workers;
and many of the mill girls turned their attention to teaching.

Effects of the Industrial Revolution on the Home. *In
England.* — As stated above, the industrial revolution
wrought a profound and fundamental change in the family
life of the small workman in England. Instead of plying

[1] Quoted in Abbott, *op. cit.*, p. 59.   [2] *Ibid.*, p. 122.

his trade in his own home, surrounded by his wife, his children and his apprentices, whose work he directed, he betook himself at the shriek of the whistle to the factory, where he labored with his fellows in crowded, unwholesome rooms until the evening. Instead of carrying through a piece of work to its end and thus experiencing the satisfaction that comes to the worker from the finished product, he carried on one simple mechanical process from morn till night, which, as division of labor became more and more minute, was but a small portion of the work necessary to a completed product. Absent from home the entire day, his influence over his children was necessarily weakened and he became distinctly less powerful a force in shaping the life and ideas of his family.

But this was not the sole effect of the industrial revolution upon family life in England. Except in a few industries where bodily strength was essential, the new machinery was so easily operated that, little by little, women and children were drawn into the busy life of the factories. Not only was their labor as effective as that of the men but they could be hired far more cheaply. Before the middle of the century the wives and children of working-men were actually taking the places of husbands and fathers in the mills. Thus Gibbins writes :

" A curious inversion of the proper order of things was seen in the domestic economy of the victims of the cheap labor system, for women and girls were superseding men in manufacturing labour, and, in consequence, their husbands had often to attend, in a shiftless, slovenly fashion, to those household duties which mothers and daughters hard at work in the factories were unable to fulfil. Worse still, mothers and fathers in some cases lived upon the killing labour of their little children, by letting them out to hire to manufacturers who found them cheaper than their parents." [1] In the half century from 1841 to 1891 the number of women in the

[1] Gibbins, *Industry in England*, p. 392.

textile factories of England increased 221 per cent, whereas the increase of men during this period was only 53 per cent.[1]

It can hardly be doubted that the efforts of women in England to increase the family income by laboring in the factories not infrequently resulted in lessening the earning power of husbands and fathers. But this was not the only harmful effect of their entrance into the field of labor. Whole families in many of the English mill towns were employed all day in the factories, from little children four or five years of age to the mother and father. Indeed, the English system of employment was known as the " family system." Grave abuses grew out of this condition. Homes were ill kept, meals were hastily prepared and unappetizing and the foundation was laid for those hard drinking habits of the English laboring class so frequently pointed out and deplored by social writers during the nineteenth century. Furthermore family discipline was gradually undermined and the old English traditions of the duty of parents with respect to the moral and religious training of their children were well-nigh forgotten. The children themselves, employed from their earliest years in feeding and tending machines in the textile factories, grew up in the densest ignorance and in moral darkness. Before two decades of the nineteenth century had passed the English nation began to awake to the tremendous social evils bred by such family conditions. Then was initiated that long course of factory legislation which was ultimately to free England of the most harmful forms of child labor. It is interesting to note that steps toward this reform had many years before been taken by the socialist Robert Owen in his mills at New Lanark, Scotland.

In America. — In the early days of the factory system in America the number of married women in the mills seems to have been relatively small. In Lawrence, for example, out of a thousand women working in the cotton factories only

[1] Robinson and Beard, *op. cit.*, Vol. II, p. 48.

thirty were married or widowed. In Lowell, about the same time, nearly all of the women mill workers were between sixteen and twenty years of age [1] and few of these were married. But such conditions changed after 1850, when foreign labor began to invade the factories of the United States. The census returns for 1900 show the conjugal condition of women in cotton mills throughout the country to have been as follows: [2]

Married	19,688
Widowed	5,381
Divorced	485
	25,554
Single or unknown	95,049
Total	120,603

These figures indicate that nearly 27 per cent of the women employees were either married, widowed or divorced and more than 20 per cent were married. This means that in 1900 one-fifth of the women employed in the cotton mills of this country who were absent from their homes the entire day were home-makers. And this represents only one of the many industries in which married women were engaged. The condition of the families, thus almost wholly deprived of the services of the home-maker, can readily be imagined and can easily be duplicated at the present time in any industrial centre.

As we have seen, child labor was very general in the United States from the first establishment of the factory system. No doubt the almost universal approval which it met from the colonists and later from a large body of thoughtful American citizens had its birth in the Puritan's horror of the sin of idleness and in his corresponding conviction that work is the worst enemy of Satan. Early in colonial history, regulations were passed in many of the colonies from Virginia to Massachusetts, urging " masters of families " to see to it that their children were busily employed.

[1] Abbott, *op. cit.*, p. 122.
[2] *Twelfth United States Census* (1900), "Occupations," p. 600.

The early poor laws likewise fairly bristled with provisions for binding out indigent children as apprentices that they might not " live idly or misspend their time in loitering." Children who were town charges were very early taught to card, spin and knit and had scant time for the enjoyment of childhood pleasures. Such customs made easy a transition to child labor in factories. As early as 1829 an Englishwoman, in a public address before an American audience, made the reproachful charge: " In your manufacturing districts you have children worked for twelve hours a day . . . and you will soon have them as in England, *worked to death.*" [1] A few years later a Report of the Committee of Education of the Massachusetts House, makes the following statements:

" According to the estimate made by an intelligent friend of manufactories . . . there were employed in 1830, in the various manufacturing establishments in the United States, no less than 200,000 females . . . most of them of young and tender years. . . . (With the increase of numerous and indigent families in manufacturing districts) there is a strong interest and an urgent motive to seek constant employment for their children at a very early age, if the wages obtained can aid them even but little in bearing the burden of their support. . . . (Causes) are operating, silently perhaps but steadily and powerfully, to deprive young females particularly, and young children of a large and increasing class in the community, of those means and opportunities of mental and moral improvement . . . essential to their becoming . . . good citizens." [2]

Since 1870 the census returns show a large increase in child labor in this country and a greater range of industries in which children are employed. Needless to say such employment of young boys and girls at mechanical labor for long hours con-

[1] Frances Wright, *Lecture on Existing Evils* (New York, 1829). Quoted in Abbott, *op. cit.*, p. 337.
[2] House Document No. 49; quoted in Abbott, *op. cit.*, pp. 342-3.

stitutes one of the crying social evils of the present age as well
as a very real menace to wholesome family life in the present
and in the generations to come.

SELECTED BIBLIOGRAPHY

Abbott, Edith. *Women in Industry* (1913), chs. II, III.

Allsopp. *Introduction to English Industrial History.*

Beard. *The Industrial Revolution.*

Cheyney. *Industrial and Social History of England*, pp. 203–12, 220–39.

DeFoe, *A Tour through the Whole Island of Great Britain* (1748), Vol. III, pp. 137–9 and *passim.*

Gibbins. *Industry in England*, chs. XXI, XXIII, and pp. 336–40.

Hobson. *Evolution of Modern Capitalism*, chs. II, III, XII.

Robinson and **Beard.** *The Development of Modern Europe*, Vol. II, ch. XVIII.

Samuelson. *The Civilization of our Day*, pp. 182–95.

CHAPTER XII

THE FAMILY DURING THE NINETEENTH CENTURY

Changes in the Economic, Legal and Social Status of Women. In England. — The political revolutions in America and France, in the closing decades of the eighteenth century, were signs of a growing spirit of democracy, a quickened perception of the nature and extent of human rights, which was bound in course of time to transform the institutions of all countries. In England, the land where ideas and customs " mellow down from precedent to precedent," the enlargement of the rights and opportunities of the common man came gradually and without violence after England's richest colonies had been lost. Little by little, first in the new American Republic and later in the mother country, the ideal of manhood suffrage was realized; and the benefits of free public education were extended to all classes. The vision of economic freedom later began to quicken the imaginations of laboring men and resulted in the organization of trades unions whose purpose quite consistently has been to secure better wages, shorter hours of labor and improved living conditions for the laboring class. These economic changes were, as truly as the political, an outgrowth of the democratic spirit; — and its harvest is by no means fully reaped.

To men first came the emancipation that was later to be extended to women. This, of course, was wholly natural. Men were still almost universally regarded as the dominant sex, — masters in private as in public life by the gifts of nature and education. Therefore political freedom, educational advantages and the right to organize in order to uphold their economic rights were first awarded to them. But the strong current of democratic feeling could not fail to draw the women into its forward movement as the generations passed. It is the purpose of the following discussion very briefly to trace the course of events leading to the partial emancipation of women in England and America.

Extension of Property Rights. — Up to the year 1857 the English law took no steps to remedy the hard position of married women with respect to their property disabilities. But in that year an Act was passed partially to protect the property of a deserted wife. The Act provided that at any time after her desertion a woman might apply to a police magistrate for a protection order. The order once granted, any property that she had acquired *after her desertion*, either by her own labor or by gift or bequest, became protected and belonged to her as completely as if she were a single woman.[1] In 1861 this Act was followed by another designed to protect the property rights of a woman whose husband had been convicted of a serious assault upon her person.[2] The Act of 1861 granted to a wife thus assaulted the right to obtain a magistrate's order exempting her from liability to cohabit with her husband and placing her in the position of a single woman with respect to her property.

Obviously these Acts were of benefit only to wives who had been deserted or abused. Yet, for many years, intelligent and reflective Englishmen had regarded the private law of England as needlessly harsh in respect to the property rights of all married women. Appeal after appeal for its amendment had been made to Parliament by both men and women with little effect. But in 1870 a Married Woman's Property Act was passed which applied equally to all married women. The provisions of this Act may be briefly summarized:

---

[1] Chitty, *Statutes at Large*, VIII, pp. 855–69; 20 and 21 Vict., c. 85.
[2] It will be remembered that as early as 1674 Chief Justice Hale had rendered the opinion that a husband had no right to inflict personal chastisement upon his wife.

1. All the earnings and savings bank deposits of a married woman were her sole and absolute property.

2. The rents and profits (only) of all landed property belonging to her were to be her own. The husband, however, was still privileged to administer this estate.

3. All personal property coming to a married woman not in excess of £200 was to be her own.

4. Any married woman or woman about to be married having £20 or more invested in certain specified banks might have this sum transferred upon the books to her name as her separate property.

5. Every married woman was allowed to insure her own or her husband's life for her separate use.[1]

Radical as this legislation was doubtless held to be in its own day, it proved unsatisfactory after a short time. Clearly an Act which left the management of a married woman's real estate and the ownership of all personal property above the value of £200 to her husband would not be permanently satisfying. Therefore in 1882 England took the final step in the emancipation of her wives and mothers from the property restrictions under which they had labored since the Norman Conquest. The Married Woman's Property Act of 1882 gave to every woman married on or subsequent to January 1st, 1883, the absolute ownership of all property belonging to her at the time of the marriage or coming to her afterwards, including earnings and property acquired by skill or labor. As a result of this Act a married woman in England can now hold and dispose of real and personal property as freely as a single woman and without the intervention of a trustee. Her husband has no legal rights over her property. Moreover, the Act of 1882 permitted a woman to enter suit, to contract, or to bring criminal action in her own name and without her husband's consent, with respect to all property belonging to her *before marriage*. Thus, after many centuries,

[1] 33 and 34 Victoria, c. 93; Chitty's *Statutes*, VIII, 709–12.

the English woman came to be recognized as a " person " in the eyes of the law. With her emancipation went the partial freeing of the husband from his ancient liabilities as to (1) his wife's ante-nuptial debts, and (2) any civil wrongs (torts) committed by her.

While granting to a married woman almost full property rights, the Act of 1882 rendered her liable to support a pauper husband out of her separate estate, as well as to maintain her children and grandchildren in a manner suitable to her station so long as the husband was unable to meet his responsibility in the matter.[1]

Although the property disabilities of married women in England have almost wholly disappeared from the statute-books, there remains the law of primogeniture which even now discriminates against the elder daughter in favor of the younger son in the inheritance of landed estates. It is doubtful whether this ancient custom, grounded in the feudal system, will easily yield to the pressure of public opinion and the attacks of progressive women against its apparent injustice. Many fair-minded persons are in favor of its continuance on the ground that, with equal division of estates, the vast landed properties of England would be divided, subdivided and alienated by sale. This would mean changing proprietors and a weakening of the tie between landlord and tenant. But these arguments hardly seem satisfactory to the thoughtful student of twentieth-century institutions. Even among the English lower middle class, which so long has cherished with pride its landed aristocracy, the retention of great estates in the little isle of England in the hands of a small group of proprietors is becoming unpopular. It would seem as if the drastic system of land and inheritance taxes, levelled through the initiative of Chancellor Lloyd George against wealthy English landowners, must in time bring about a more equitable distribution of land among a far larger number of

[1] 45 and 46 Victoria, c. 75; see Chitty's *Statutes*, VIII, pp. 713 ff.

individuals. This would mean an increase in the detached homesteads of England, and might also result in inheritance of a fair portion of the family estates by daughters.

Laws for the Protection of Working Women. — Not content with legislation that made English women free agents in the control of their possessions as well as independent legal " persons," the English Parliament passed a series of Factory Acts designed to protect the health and welfare of laboring women. These Acts cannot be discussed in detail; it must suffice to say that from the year 1842, when the employment of women in mines was declared illegal, up to the present time, Parliament has enacted laws limiting the hours of women's labor, prescribing sanitary conditions in factories and workrooms and securing to women workers suitable allotments of time for meals.[1] Most interesting for our purposes is a clause in the Act of 1891 which provides that no employer of female labor in factory or workshop shall " knowingly permit a woman to be employed therein within four weeks after she has given birth to a child." The growing sense of responsibility felt by many modern governments for the health of women wage-earners, as mothers or prospective mothers of citizens, is clearly reflected in this almost paternalistic clause. It marks the awakening of the public mind to the close correlation that exists between women's labor and the high infant mortality in manufacturing centres. Yet, although the Act of 1891 shows a distinct advance in the conservation of womanhood and childhood, it would have been improved by a further clause forbidding factory owners to employ women for a minimum period of two weeks before confinement. Some experimental evidence is at hand to show that the children of women who do not labor in factories for a period of several weeks before childbirth are heavier and more sturdy than the

[1] These Acts are ably discussed in Hutchin's and Harrison's *A History of Factory Legislation* (London, 1911). See especially chs. II, IV, VI, X. A brief discussion may be found in Gibbins, *Industry in England*, pp. 391–406.

offspring of women who work up to the last few days before confinement.[1]

Corresponding Changes in the Status of Women in America.
Removal of Property Disabilities. — In democratic America, as might be expected, the emancipation of married women from the economic and legal restrictions of English common law began earlier than in England, although the battle in the United States is not even yet wholly won. As early as 1809 Connecticut led the way by granting to married women the right to will property. Her example, however, failed to inspire followers until 1835, when Ohio also removed the age-old limitation on the right of a married woman to make a will. The action of Ohio was followed by Alabama in 1843, by Pennsylvania in 1848 and by Michigan in 1850. Until 1844, however, no State had seen fit to allow married women the absolute ownership and control of their property. But in that year Maine led her sister states in granting this right to wives; and in 1845 and 1848 respectively Florida and Pennsylvania did likewise. As we have seen, Michigan permitted married women to make a will in 1850; five years later she removed all the remaining legal restrictions with respect to their property. Massachusetts enacted similar legislation in the same year (1855). But most of the other states, while ready to concede to married women the right to will property, or to control earnings, were reluctant to go farther and grant them unhampered control of all real and personal property including earnings. Thus Virginia, while permitting her wives to make a testament as early as 1849, did not concede them the control of their earnings until fifty years later. Connecticut, despite her brave beginning in 1809, failed to grant married women the absolute ownership of all property and wages until 1877; while Florida, which had removed the

[1] See doctoral dissertation by Sigismund Peller of the University of Vienna. The conclusions, reached after careful experiments, are summarized in the *Survey*, Jan. 17, 1914.

restriction on control of property as early as 1845, hesitated to give wives command of their wages until 1891.

In those States of our Union that once formed part of the great Louisiana Purchase or were ceded by Mexico after the Mexican War, there still persists the custom of "community property." All real and personal property owned by husband or wife at marriage or obtained subsequently by gift or bequest constitutes his or her separate estate. On the other hand, all property acquired in any other way by either partner after the marriage is community property and nominally belongs to both husband and wife equally. In practice, however, the husband holds and controls all community property, including his wife's wages. Only if the wife be separated from her husband, or if he deserts her or becomes insane can she enjoy the fruits of her own labor. In Nevada, one of the States where this custom prevails, a wife may control her wages when " the husband has allowed her to appropriate them to her own use, in which case they are deemed a gift from him to her." [1] It will be seen that such a practice might easily work hardship upon the wife; and such, in fact, is sometimes the case. Not long ago, in the enlightened State of California, a married woman who for years had supported herself and an idle husband by working in a café was denied by the courts the right to hold and manage her holdings since these were community property and hence under the control of her husband. In consequence the woman was forced either to continue turning over her wages to her husband, who allowed her a niggardly sum for her support, or to separate from him.

Thus the economic emancipation of American women is even yet not completed. In three Southern States, namely, North Carolina, Tennessee and Texas, a married woman until very recently was forced to submit to the complete or partial

[1] Wilson, *The Legal and Political Status of Women in the United States* (Cedar Rapids, 1912), p. 218.

control of real and personal property, as well as wages, by her husband. By an Act of March 13, 1911, a married woman in Texas " may petition the courts to remove her disabilities and declare her a *femme sole* for mercantile and trading purposes. The husband must consent and must join in the petition." At the discretion of the court the plea may be granted and the petitioner may then " in her own name contract and be contracted with, sue and be sued. . . ."[1] In Tennessee up to a year or two ago a wife's personal property passed into the absolute control of her husband who might even dispose of it by will. If he died intestate, it remained part of his estate and was distributed in like manner as his other personal property.[2]

Such provisions, of course, hark back to the Middle Ages when property was concentrated in the hands of a family head. In those days the term household property had a very real meaning. But with the progress of individualism — that movement which seeks to free every human being from all limitations unjustly or unwisely hindering his full and free development — these restrictions will one by one be removed, and in every State property will rest on an individualistic, not a paternalistic basis. That the tendency has developed steadily in this country is evidenced by the very few States that still place limitations upon the right of married women to control property and to contract, sue or bring criminal action in the protection of that property.

Extension of Educational Opportunities to English-women. — Little by little, during the first decades of the nineteenth century, the views of Englishmen regarding women were undergoing a silent transformation. Woman, who had so

---

[1] Wilson, *op. cit.*, p. 298. The author is largely indebted to this valuable work for the statements made above.

[2] The author has been informed that the domestic codes of Tennessee and Texas have recently been revised, but has been unable to secure copies of the new statutes.

long been regarded as the handmaid and dependent of man,
was being forced by economic pressure into the field of labor.
The poorer women entered the factories; their middle-class
sisters, some years later, were driven to take up the only employment deemed not degrading for a gentlewoman — the
work of teaching. Before many years economic independence, replacing as it did the old enervating dependence upon
husband or relations, caused many women to discover and
develop strong personalities. No longer was a Mary Wollstonecraft alone in declaring that women were individuals
with minds and characters worthy of broad and thorough
training. Large numbers of young women were demanding
wider intellectual opportunities and asserting their right to
think for themselves. Yet in 1831 a book appeared in England
which vied in sickly sentimentalism with the worst produc-
tions of the eighteenth century. It emphasized, as had its
predecessors, the engaging quality of " strictly feminine
deportment " and clinging weakness in all women. " Nothing is so likely to conciliate the affection of the other sex as a
feeling that women look to them for guidance and support,"
says the author.[1] But here and there other ideas were in
the air and were being voiced with some vigor. Charlotte
Brontë in 1849 wrote with deep earnestness: " Believe me,
teachers may be hard-worked, ill-paid and despised but the
girl who stays at home doing nothing is worse off than the
hardest wrought and worst paid drudge of a school. Whenever I have seen, not merely in humble but in affluent homes,
families of daughters sitting waiting to be married, I have
pitied them from my heart." The intellectual achievements
of Mary Somerville, Harriet Martineau, George Eliot and the
Brontë sisters did much to inspire those women of the mid-
century who enthusiastically labored to improve the educational opportunities of girls. With sure insight these
leaders of a new movement perceived the intimate relation

[1] Mrs. John Sandford, *Woman: In her Social and Domestic Character* (1831).

between freeing the minds of their sex and improving their social and economic status. In consequence they threw themselves into the cause of the more thorough education of women.

The first important step in opening the doors of a sound, higher education to women was taken when Queen's College, London, was opened in 1848. This college had its origin in a Governesses' Benevolent Institution, founded in 1843, thus affording some evidence that the higher education of English-women grew out of the great need for better-trained gov-ernesses. In his inaugural address at the opening of the College, Professor Maurice, one of the Faculty of King's College, spoke in a deprecating way of the dangers attending the intellectual training of young women.[1] Such was the general view of Englishmen, and, be it added, of most English-women. Yet this sceptical timidity did not prevent the establishment of Bedford College for girls by Mrs. Reid in 1849, and of Cheltenham Ladies' College in 1854. These institutions were not colleges in our American sense of the term, but higher schools for girls modelled on the pattern of the so-called "Public Schools" for boys. It is interesting to read that the first report of Cheltenham contains a pledge that the modesty and gentleness of the female character shall be preserved.[2] When Miss Dorothea Beale was appointed principal of this school in 1858 its success was amply assured. At her death in 1906 over one thousand English girls were receiving a thorough secondary education in the " college " and many were passing thence to carry on advanced uni-versity studies at St. Hilda's Hall, established by Miss Beale in connection with the University of Oxford.

In 1862 a long step forward was taken when the University of Cambridge permitted its professors to admit women to their

[1] See Monroe, *Cyclopedia of Education*, Vol. V, p. 801; article by Elizabeth Adams on the *Higher Education of Women*.

[2] Blaese, *The Emancipation of Englishwomen*, p. 108.

examinations if they so elected. This doubtful favor was made more positive in 1865 when women were admitted to the Cambridge examinations on the same terms as men. In 1869 the first beginnings of a college for women at Cambridge were made by Miss Emily Davies and others and three years later the institution was incorporated as Girton College. In 1873 the Association of the Higher Education of Women began its honorable career in a private house near Cambridge. From this humble beginning sprang Newnham Hall, later incorporated as Newnham College, and offering to young women courses leading to the examinations of Cambridge University. From this time forward the opportunities of English girls to obtain university training have steadily multiplied. In 1878 London University opened all its examinations for degrees to women. A year later Somerville Hall and Lady Margaret Hall were established in connection with Oxford. In the new universities of Manchester, Birmingham and Bristol women were admitted to full privileges, including the reception of degrees. Scotland also, in 1892, threw open the doors of her four great universities — Edinburgh, Glasgow, St. Andrews and Aberdeen — to women, and Trinity College, Dublin, did likewise. At the present time, English girls have almost as favorable opportunities as English boys for securing broad and thorough education and developing trained and independent minds. Oxford and Cambridge, however, still refuse to women their coveted degrees, despite the fact that English girls have more than once honorably won the senior wranglership and senior classic — titles denied them merely on the ground that they were women.

The effect of the higher education of Englishwomen in developing their initiative and individuality can hardly be overestimated. Largely owing to the intelligent and persistent efforts of women, aided by a growing body of enlightened Englishmen, social legislation has been passed in England that has vastly improved the status of women in the home as well as in the world outside. The Matrimonial Causes Act of 1878, the Married Women's Property Act of 1882, the Guardianship of Infants Act of 1886, — all these and more were the direct or indirect result of the efforts of educated wives and mothers in England who sent petition after petition to Parliament. It may be said with much truth that the elevation of Englishwomen from a position of legal and economic dependence in home and society has gone *pari passu* with the training of their minds and characters.

The Higher Education of American Women. — As in England so in the American democracy the improvement in the status of women — especially of married women — has been synchronous with their higher education. In colonial days, as we have seen, the education of girls other than in household duties was not seriously considered. Even as late as 1788 the town of Northampton, Massachusetts, now the seat of Smith College, voted to be at no expense for the education of girls. And Boston, home of New England culture, in 1790 admitted girls to its public schools only in the summer months. Not until 1822 were girls in Boston freely admitted to the common schools.[1]

Yet, after the Revolutionary War, public opinion began to change with regard to the education of girls. Not only were they admitted to the summer district schools but many towns made provision for their attendance at the boys' winter schools at hours when the boys were not using the buildings. But such education as the girls received was shallow enough, consisting merely of reading, writing, spelling, sewing, knitting and making elaborate samplers. As for higher education many young women received none at all. Others attended boarding schools, where imperfectly educated teachers dispensed doubtful accomplishments. In an earnest address made to the legislature of New York in 1819 in behalf of the establishment of "a seminary for

[1] Johnson, *Old-time Schools and Schoolbooks*, p. 139.

females," Mrs. Emma Willard urged that the elevation of
the minds and characters of women would be a benefit to the
entire community. " As evidence that this statement does
not exaggerate the female influence in society," she writes,
" our sex need but be considered in the single relation of
mothers. In this character, we have charge of the whole
mass of individuals, who are to compose the succeeding
generation; during that period of youth, when the pliant
mind takes any direction, to which it is steadily guided by a
forming hand. How important a power is given by this
charge! Yet, little do many of my sex know how, either to
appreciate or improve it."

Owing to the efforts of a little band of devoted women,
ably led by Catherine Beecher, Emma Willard and Mary
Lyon, the earliest academies and seminaries for girls were
founded. Most advanced of these was Mt. Holyoke Seminary,
opened in 1837 as a result of the splendid campaign of Mary
Lyon carried on through the length and breadth of Massachusetts. In 1855 was chartered Elmira College, offering a
collegiate course of study to young women. After the Civil
War followed Vassar, chartered in 1861, Wellesley, chartered
as a Seminary in 1870 but empowered to grant degrees in
1877, Smith College, chartered in 1871, and Bryn Mawr,
chartered in 1880. Meanwhile certain men's colleges, notably
in the Middle West, threw open their hospitable doors to
women. Oberlin admitted women from its foundation in
1833 and the University of Michigan followed its example
in 1870. Since that time most of the higher institutions of
learning in the United States have either admitted women
to their courses and degrees or have established a woman's
college in connection with the University. Of the latter
type are Barnard College of Columbia University and Rad-
cliffe College affiliated with Harvard.

Thanks to this vast extension of their educational privileges,
accompanied, as it was, by the removal from the statute

books of most of the hampering economic and legal restrictions of the past, American women have developed intelligent
and vigorous personalities.   No longer confined, with almost
religious strictness, to the confines of home, church and
neighborhood, they are taking an active part in movements
for social betterment, from the securing of public playgrounds
for the city's children to the improvement of sanitary conditions in factories and slums.   With every year that passes,
more women are coming to see that their interest cannot wisely
or righteously be confined to their own homes but must
expand to include the homes of the entire community.   If
signs do not fail, the campaign to secure wholesome family
life and home surroundings for " all sorts and conditions of
men " and women will more and more challenge the attention
and receive the intelligent coöperation of American womanhood.   And with the extension of full suffrage rights to
women their influence on social legislation will be enormously
increased.

STATE INTERVENTION IN THE CONTROL OF PARENTAL RIGHTS AND PRIVILEGES

In England. — Nothing is more noteworthy in the social
legislation of England during the last seventy-five years than
the number of Acts of Parliament directly affecting the custody
and control of children by their parents.   Up to 1839 the
English Government had scarcely questioned the well-nigh
absolute power of parents over their offspring.   In only two
special cases had parental rights been curtailed.   During
the reign of George II a statute was enacted designed to
prevent the children of criminals and vagrants from being
drawn into the evil ways of their parents.   This act provided
that the children of men or women convicted of criminal
offences should be taken from their parents and apprenticed
to honest persons to learn a trade.   A further attempt to
limit the guardianship rights of unfit parents was made during

the same reign. The law in this instance declared that an infant possessed of property so as to fall under the jurisdiction of the Court of Chancery might be taken away from parents grossly unfit to rear it and be placed in the custody of some person nominated by the Court. It will be noted that in both instances where the law interfered with the time-honored rights of English parents, the incapacity of those parents to bring up children had been abundantly demonstrated.[1]

Before the middle of the last century popular sentiment in regard to the inviolable character of the father's rights of guardianship had begun to change. This change was reflected in English legislation. As early as 1839 an Act was passed amending the law with respect to the custody of minor children. The Act provided that upon petition of a mother whose children were in the exclusive custody of the father, or of a guardian appointed by him, a Judge in Equity might make an order allowing the mother to visit her children at specified times. In case the children were under seven years of age they might even be delivered over to the custody of the mother. But it was expressly declared that no mother guilty of adultery was to benefit by the Act.[2] Strictly limited as were the privileges granted to mothers by the Act of 1839, this law at least made it possible for women separated from their husbands and for mothers whose children had been taken from them by the arbitrary act of the father to see their offspring on stated occasions and even to care for them until they had reached the age of seven.

In the following year, 1840, an Act was passed empowering the Court to take any child, whether possessed of property or not, out of the control of a parent or guardian convicted of crime and to place him in charge of suitable guardians selected by the Court.[3]

[1] Cleveland, *Woman under the English Law*, pp. 200 and 211.
[2] 2 and 3 of Victoria, c. 54; summarized in Cleveland, *op. cit.*, p. 270.
[3] *Ibid.*, pp. 270–1.

Between the years 1845 and 1873 Parliament took action with regard to the custody and support of illegitimate children, such action being designed to compel a putative father to contribute to the support of his child. The Acts, briefly summarized, contain the following provisions:

1. The mother of a bastard child is entitled to its custody in preference to the father and is liable for its support up to the age of sixteen or, if it be a female, until it marries.

2. If the mother is unable to maintain her child she may make application to a Justice of the Peace, either before the child's birth or within a year thereafter, charging a person by name as the father of her child. The Justice thereupon is to bring up the party so charged and investigate the question of paternity. If the evidence of the mother is convincing to the Court, he may adjudge the person summoned to be the actual father, and order him to pay the mother a weekly sum of money until the child shall die or shall attain the age of thirteen or sixteen years, as the Court may decide.[1]

Until 1886 Parliament took no steps to secure to women any rights of guardianship over their children other than in the special cases mentioned above. But in that year the Guardianship of Infants Act was passed which granted to a mother equal rights in the custody and care of her children with any guardian appointed by the father. In the appointment of guardians by a court account is to be taken of her wishes as well as of the father's. If the father dies or is incapacitated, the mother may appoint a guardian and she may also appoint one to act jointly with the father after her death.[2]

Finally, in a series of Factory and Education Acts the English government has further curtailed the ancient rights of parents by refusing to permit them to exploit their children

[1] Cleveland, *op. cit.*, pp. 295–6.
[2] 49 and 50 Victoria, c. 29; summarized in Chapman, *The Status of Women under the English Law*, p. 65.

in order to swell the family income. This legislation, covering a long period of years from 1819, is designed to secure for boys and girls suitable working conditions, to limit hours of employment and to compel parents to keep their children in school at least until the age of thirteen.

In America. — A similar tendency to limit the authority of parents with regard to the custody and control of their offspring has gained headway in the United States. In most States of the Union outside of the South parents are compelled by law to keep their children in schools and out of factories and stores until they have attained the age of fourteen. Ruthless exploitation of young boys and girls by needy or vicious parents still goes on, however, and such will be the case for years to come, owing to the fact that each State may rule upon these matters independently and in accordance with its own selfish interests. A majority of the States have made provisions whereby children may be taken from the custody of cruel or irresponsible parents and placed with guardians appointed by the Court or in institutions for children where they can receive proper care and training. Sixteen States have refused to permit children over fourteen to work more than eight hours a day, no matter what the need of the family might be. Such encroachment upon parental privilege would not have been dreamed of fifty years ago. Yet it is probable that the tendency toward State interference in behalf of young children will go steadily forward in years to come.

Recognition of Mothers' Rights of Guardianship in America. — Unlike England, which may cut the Gordian knot of many a social difficulty or outgrown law by a single legislative act applicable to the entire country, the United States intrusts all domestic legislation to the individual States as sovereign in their own domain. Hence in a majority of the States of our free Union the mother who has borne and reared a child has no rights of guardianship in that child unless she is separated from her husband or he is deceased. In fifteen Southern States, practically the " solid South," the father is unequivocally declared to be " the natural guardian of his children," and " the mother is the guardian only if the father is dead." In nine Southern States, namely, Alabama, Florida, Georgia, Maryland, North and South Carolina, Tennessee, Virginia, and West Virginia, the father may legally will away the guardianship of his child without the' consent of the mother; and in the two Carolinas and West Virginia the father is even permitted to will away the custody of a child yet unborn.

But the South is not alone in retaining mediæval laws upon its statute books. Thirteen States of the West, namely, California, Idaho, Indiana, Michigan, Montana, Nevada, North and South Dakota, Ohio, Oklahoma, Utah, Wisconsin and Wyoming, regard the father as the natural guardian of his children and grant the mother rights of guardianship only in case of her husband's death or desertion. Such is likewise the law in four Eastern States — Vermont, Rhode Island, Delaware and New Jersey.[1]

DIVORCE LEGISLATION DURING THE NINETEENTH CENTURY

In England. — Among the English Reformers of the sixteenth century, more liberal ideas concerning divorce than those of Roman canon law undoubtedly were upheld.[2] Yet despite the impassioned pleas of the poet Milton for greater freedom in matters of divorce, England retained, with scant changes, the divorce practices sanctioned by the canon law well into the nineteenth century. In the words of Howard : " It is a striking illustration of the completeness with which in social questions the English mind was dominated by theological modes of thought that no change in the law of divorce

---

[1] Wilson, *op. cit.* See laws for different States.
[2] See Howard, *History of Matrimonial Institutions*, Vol. II, pp. 73-92.

was effected until the present century. Yet there was crying
need of reform. The rigid tightening of the bonds of wedlock
seems to have produced its natural fruit. Immorality grew
apace. The lot of the married woman became harder even
than before the Reformation." [1] This condition seems to
have been due to a conflict between the spiritual courts that,
strictly speaking, alone had the right to grant divorce, and the
temporal courts that occasionally took cognizance of divorce
cases when these involved questions of dower. During the
closing years of the seventeenth century attempts were made
by persons of influence to break their marital chains by a
special act of Parliament. But such relief was reserved for
the wealthy and powerful and a decree was granted only
after convincing evidence of the flagrant infidelity of the
guilty party. In 1798 the House of Lords limited even this
privilege by requiring that " all bills of divorce shall be
preceded by a sentence of separation *a mensa*, issuing out of
the ecclesiastical court; . . ." [2] By this act the spiritual
courts were given large powers to hinder the aggrieved party
from resorting to Parliament at all. Only in case of adultery
could an ecclesiastical court be prevailed upon to issue a
separation order; it resolutely refused to grant such relief
for malicious desertion unless this were accompanied by
cruelty. Therefore divorces *a vinculo* secured by parliamen-
tary action were rare; probably not more than two hundred were granted for the century and a half during which
Parliament took divorce under its jurisdiction. Of these,
only three or four were granted to women, even when their
wrongs were proven beyond a doubt. [3]

But by the middle of the nineteenth century even conservative Englishmen were no longer firmly convinced that
marriage was an indissoluble bond and were in favor of more
liberal legislation. In 1857, despite the most bitter opposition from the Church party, jurisdiction in matrimonial cases

[1] *Op. cit.*, Vol. II, p. 92.   [2] *Ibid.*, p. 104.   [3] *Ibid.*, p. 106.

was entirely removed from the spiritual courts and placed in the hands of a new civil " Court for Divorce and matrimonial Causes." But, unfortunately, the Matrimonial Causes Act of 1857 perpetuated the same inequality of rights in respect to divorce as had previous legislation and practice. While granting to a husband the right of absolute divorce on account of the adultery of the wife, the law granted to the woman the same relief only if the husband's adultery were aggravated by cruelty, or malicious desertion for two years and upwards. Moreover, the injured husband might unite with his petition for divorce a claim for damages against his wife's paramour; whereas no such privilege was permitted the aggrieved wife. The damages thus recovered might be " applied by the court for the benefit of the children of the marriage or for the maintenance of the wife." [1] Even in that period there were not lacking Englishmen who hotly opposed the passage of the law on the ground of its gross injustice to women. Gladstone earnestly attacked it; and the attorney-general who introduced the bill declared that if the measure " were thrown aside and the whole law of marriage and divorce made the subject of an inquiry, I should be the last man to limit the field of discussion or to refuse to consider a state of law which inflicts injustice upon women most wrongfully and without cause, and which may be considered opprobrious and wicked; . . ." [2] Doubtless the attorney-general salved his conscience by the further statement that the " present bill need not be the end-all of legislation upon the subject." Nevertheless the Act of 1857 has determined English divorce practice for fifty-eight years and still continues so to do. The law prescribes that a sentence of divorce must always be a decree *nisi;* only after a period of six months can it be made absolute. Either party to the divorce may marry again; but in order to conciliate the Anglican

---

[1] *Statutes at Large*, XCVII, 537; 20 and 21 Victoria, c. 85.
[2] Howard, *op. cit.*, p. 111.

clergy the Act provides that no clergyman of the " United Church of England and Ireland " may be compelled to solemnize the marriage of a divorced person, although he cannot legally prevent a clergyman of the same communion from using his church or chapel for such a purpose. The fact that the remarriage of divorced persons is legal in civil law but illegal in the ecclesiastical law of England has led to acrimonious debates and bitter conflicts of authority. Only three years ago the Bishop of London forbade his chancellor to issue marriage licenses without the Bishop's consent, although the chancellor was well within his legal rights in granting such licenses without consulting his superior. In cases where a clergyman of the Established Church has refused to remarry divorced persons an appeal has sometimes been made to the courts, which invariably have censured the clergyman for refusing to obey the law of the land. Yet the conflict goes on and neither side has yielded ground.

The law of 1857 provided further for a judicial separation granted to either husband or wife on the ground of adultery, cruelty or two years' desertion. After such separation order was granted, the wife had all the rights of a single woman with respect to the control of her property and the power to contract and sue.

Finally, provision was made for a third method of terminating the marriage relation by means of a " magisterial separation." A woman deserted by her husband might apply to a local magistrate instead of the divorce court in London for an order to protect her property and earnings from being seized by her husband or his creditors. Previous to the laws of 1870 and 1882, that freed a wife's earnings and property from her husband's control, such a measure must have brought genuine relief to a deserted wife.

It will readily be seen that the law of 1857, while granting judicial separations for the causes of adultery, cruelty or desertion and seeking to protect a deserted or abused wife

from the greed or brutality of her husband, hedges around
absolute divorce with difficulties and limits it to the one cause
of adultery. The mere fact that an absolute divorce can be
obtained only at considerable expense from the High Court
sitting in London puts its benefits wholly out of the reach of
the poor and renders the law inequitable. In 1909 the late
King Edward VII appointed a Royal Commission on Divorce
and Matrimonial Causes to investigate thoroughly the whole
difficult problem of divorce in England. Three years later,
after diligent inquiry and the examination of 246 witnesses,
the Commission published both a majority and a minority
report. The majority report, signed by the Chairman, Lord
Gorell, together with all the Commissioners save three, took
the following liberal positions: 1. Absolute divorce should
be granted for six causes: (*a*) adultery, (*b*) desertion for
three years and upward, (*c*) cruelty, (*d*) incurable insanity,
after five years' confinement, (*e*) habitual drunkenness, found
incurable three years after a first order of separation, and (*f*)
imprisonment under a commuted death sentence. 2. Facilities should be given for hearing divorce cases in courts
throughout the country in instances where the joint income
of husband and wife does not exceed £300 and property
£250. 3. Power should be given to the courts to declare
marriages null and void in cases of (*a*) unsound mind, (*b*)
epilepsy and recurrent insanity, (*c*) specific disease, (*d*) when
a woman is in a condition which renders marriage a fraud
upon the husband, (*e*) in case of wilful refusal to perform the
duties of marriage. 4. The Commission further recommended
that (*a*) divorce reports should not be published until the
conclusion of the case, and (*b*) that judges should hear divorce
cases without a jury.

Quite as significant as the sweeping changes in the proposed
law extending the grounds of divorce is the fact that the large
majority of the Commission were earnestly in favor of equal-
izing the rights of husband and wife in respect to obtaining

divorce. In this connection the Report declares : " The social and economic position of women has greatly changed in the last hundred and even in the last fifty years. . . . In our opinion it is impossible to maintain a different standard of morality in the marriage relation without creating the impression that justice is denied to women, an impression that must tend to lower the respect in which the marriage law is held by women." [1]

The minority report, presented by three members, of whom the Archbishop of York was one, strongly objected to the positions taken by the majority as based on " purely empirical " evidence with " not even the semblance of finality." It urgently maintained that divorce legislation should be grounded on the bed rock of changeless principle, not on the shifting sands of " present expediency."   With this preamble the minority submitted proposals that may be summarized as follows :

1. There should be equality of the sexes.
2. The grounds of divorce should emphatically *not* be extended.
3. There should be local divorce courts with facilities to the poor, but not on so large a scale as recommended by the majority.
4. Marriages should be rendered null on the grounds set forth in the majority report (see above).
5. The publication of divorce reports should be limited.
6. A man should be presumed dead after a continuous absence of seven years with no communication.

A minority of the Commission, then, favored a continuance of the present situation which renders it impossible for either partner in the marriage relation to obtain an absolute divorce on the grounds of cruelty (no matter how continuous or extreme), of habitual drunkenness, of desertion, or of hopeless

[1] Digest of Commission's Report in Magazine Section of *New York Times*, Sunday, Nov. 24, 1912.

insanity. These gentlemen, in effect, record their conviction that any marriage relation stopping short of adultery, is to be preferred to a liberal divorce policy which might open the way to frequent divorces obtained on easy grounds by mutual consent of the parties.

It is an interesting fact that the leading newspapers and journals of England sided with the minority report. The *Manchester Guardian*, an excellent Liberal paper, held up the United States as an awful example of the effects of loosening the marriage bond. It declared that even if there is a popular demand in England for more liberal divorce laws, " it would be impossible to accept solutions of the problem which would strike a deadly blow at the purity and stability of family life . . . and approximate the English law of divorce to that which obtains in the United States of the American Union, where the percentage of dissolution is forty-three times what it is in England and Wales." In this connection it might be pertinent to inquire whether the low rate in England necessarily indicates that domestic life in that country is happier or more successful than here. It seems highly probable that were the rigid restrictions upon divorce once loosened in the British Isles, the prompt increase in the number of divorces would reveal much discord and misery in family life now smouldering just beneath the surface.

Divorce Legislation in the United States. — The discussion in the previous chapter of divorce regulations in the American Colonies will make plain that our forefathers, at least in the North, adopted a rather tolerant attitude toward this question as compared with the mother-country. During the nineteenth century the whole trend of divorce legislation in the various States has been in the direction of multiplying the causes for which the marriage bond may be dissolved. Thus Massachusetts in the statute of 1786 recognized only two causes for divorce — adultery and impotency. To-day the State recognizes seven causes. As late as 1848 Virginia granted absolute divorce only for adultery; at present she has placed eight causes upon her statute-books. In 1795, the States of the Northwest Territory, from which many of the North Central States were carved, recognized only three grounds for divorce. To-day, Ohio recognizes ten causes, Indiana seven, and Illinois nine.[1] Moreover, in State after State of the Union, first in the North, then much later in the South, jurisdiction in divorce cases has been transferred from the legislative bodies to the courts. In the New England States this reform was accomplished shortly after the Revolution, except in Connecticut where, even in early colonial times, the courts had entire jurisdiction. But in the South progress was much more tardy. It was nearly fifty years after the Revolution before Virginia and Maryland granted the courts even partial jurisdiction. Not until 1851 was the Assembly in both these States deprived of all authority in divorce trials, although Maryland had given her courts jurisdiction in 1842 and Virginia in 1827.[2]

As the nineteenth century progressed, the different States concerned themselves with various questions involved in the granting of divorces. (1) Shall the parties in a divorce be permitted to remarry, or shall the guilty party be restrained? (2) What provisions shall be made concerning residence in the States where the divorce is sought and due notice to the defendant in order to prevent clandestine divorce? (3) What regulations shall be framed with respect to (*a*) alimony, (*b*) the control of property, and (*c*) the custody of children in cases where divorce is granted? The conclusions reached regarding these important matters can be summed up only very briefly. In respect to remarriage of the parties to a divorce the statutes of the States vary greatly. In New England, remarriage is generally permitted, although Massachusetts and Vermont require that a period of three years elapse before the guilty party may marry again. In New York, on the contrary, a

[1] Howard, *op. cit.*, Vol. III, pp. 5, 10, 114–20.   [2] *Ibid.*, p. 31.

State which limits the causes of divorce to adultery, the guilty party may not marry within the Commonwealth during the lifetime of the other. A marriage solemnized in another State is, however, recognized as legal. In all the Southern States severe restrictions on remarriage after divorce existed until after the middle of the nineteenth century. Later these laws were modified, and in the States of Tennessee, West Virginia, Missouri, Texas, New Mexico and Arizona, were removed.[1] In striking similarity to the law of the ancient Hebrews is the regulation in Louisiana that when divorce is granted for adultery the guilty party may not marry his or her accomplice. Very generally the Western States permit remarriage with some restrictions. Thus Kansas forbids the guilty party to marry again within five years; and California and Colorado prohibit remarriage *of either party* within one year.

In all the States of the Union a period of residence either before or after marriage is required of one of the parties. This period varies from six months in Nevada to five years in Massachusetts, if the libellant be not an inhabitant of the State at the time of the marriage.[2] Whereas Nevada has gained an unsavory notoriety because of the short term of residence required of the plaintiff and the ease with which a divorce can be obtained, Massachusetts refuses a divorce to any plaintiff who clearly has moved to the State for that purpose. In this matter as in our whole body of divorce legislation, the utmost disharmony prevails. Each Commonwealth has gone its own way without regard to its neighbors. In nearly all of the States, however, the statutes require that due notice of the pending divorce suit be given the defendant.

With regard to alimony, distribution of property and the custody of children, the regulations of the various States show greater unanimity. Very generally temporary alimony is required of the husband for the support of wife and minor children pending judgment in a divorce suit. The courts

[1] *Ibid.*, p. 82.   [2] Wilson, *op. cit.*, p. 174.

also are empowered to grant the wife, if she be the plaintiff in a successful suit, such part of the real and personal estate of her husband as seems just. Furthermore, after judgment has been rendered in her favor, the wife is entitled to immediate possession of her own personal and real estate. On the other hand she is not entitled to dower except in a few States as, *e.g.*, Missouri, where the wife, if she obtains the divorce, is regarded as in the position of a widow. In the New England States, also, a wife is entitled to dower if the cause of the divorce be the husband's infidelity or sentence to penal servitude or if the husband die before a decree *nisi* [1] granted the wife has become absolute.

Throughout the Union the divorce court is empowered to make such provisions for the care, custody and education of the minor children of the divorced couple as seem in the best interests of the offspring. In most cases the children are given to the mother, if she be the innocent party, with the provision that the father be permitted to have them for a stated period every year. But if the divorce be granted for incompatibility, or some other cause not involving moral turpitude, the custody of the children is commonly divided between the parents. [2]

And so, after many centuries of ecclesiastical regulation, following upon a barbarous period of great individual freedom, divorce has become, in most civilized countries, a matter of State concern and judicial control. Neither the individual nor the Church but the State is now commonly regarded as the proper authority to adjudicate all cases of friction arising within the marriage relation.

SELECTED BIBLIOGRAPHY

Adams, Elizabeth. *The Higher Education of Women* (in Monroe, *Cyclopedia of Education*, Vol. V, pp. 801 ff.).

[1] A decree granted upon condition that the divorce does not become absolute until such time as the court shall direct.

[2] Howard, Vol. III, pp. 28–30, 90–6, 100.

Blaese, W. L. *The Emancipation of Englishwomen* (1910), chs. III, IV, V.

Chapman. *The Status of Women under the English Law, passim.*

Chitty. *Statutes at Large,* Vol. VIII, pp. 709–13, 855–69, 880–1.

Cleveland, Arthur R. *Women under the English Law* (1896), pp. 169–82, 201–7, 211–17, 226–8, 235–6.

Gibbins. *Industry in England,* pp. 391–406.

Howard, E. G. *History of Matrimonial Institutions,* Vol. II, pp. 73–120, Vol. III, pp. 28–100.

Hutchins and Harrison. *A History of Factory Legislation* (1911), chs. II, IV, VI, X.

Wilson. *The Legal and Political Status of Women in the United States* (1912).   See various state laws.

CHAPTER XIII

THE PRESENT SITUATION

Evidences of the Maladjustment of the Modern Family to Social Conditions. The Instability of the Family. — Perhaps the characteristic of the twentieth-century family that most sharply challenges the attention of the student of family history is its instability. It is a far cry from the closely knit, highly unified family organizations of the ancient Romans or the Middle-Age Teutons to the more loosely organized household of modern times wherein each member tends to claim independence as an individual with a personality to be developed and respected. Nowadays, at least in England and America, no family head holds all the property, real and personal, of its members in his own control; nor does he represent his wife and children before the law, paying their fines for civil offences. The father is no longer the religious head of his family, offering prayers and sacrifices to household gods whose supreme function it is to maintain the unity of the family and its estates. At present it is rather rare for a single will to impose itself upon every member of the family and secure unquestioning obedience to its dictates by the exercise of physical force backed by the authority of the State. Instead the modern household not infrequently presents the phenomenon of a group of clashing wills, an association of highly individualized persons, each asserting his rights and maintaining his privileges with greater or less success. The family unity of modern times — and many homes to-day exemplify this unity in strength and beauty — is more a spiritual oneness of mutual love and consideration, of common interests and goals than a unity secured

456

by centering all authority in one head. Obviously the individualistic spirit has undermined and in part superseded the autocratic; and although the gain to humanity has been great indeed, the advance has not been made without some loss. The family of the twentieth century is markedly unstable; it would seem that in some instances it has paid for the independence of its members the costly price of its very existence or its existence in a changed and incomplete form.

The social literature of the age abounds in references to this instability of the modern family organization and foretells its extinction, at least in its present form. We are told that monogamic marriage is doomed; that it was based wholly upon economic foundations, *i.e.*, upon the desire of men to transmit property intact through legitimate issue, thus securing the perpetuation of the family name and lands. With the break up of the economic, religious and legal bonds that once made of the monogamic family a strong unit, we are assured that looser and less permanent forms of association will in all probability take its place. Writers in this strain point to certain conditions in modern family life as evidence of the truth of this contention. They call attention to the wide prevalence of divorce, the increase of family desertion and the effect of modern industry in disintegrating the family. All these conditions merit careful consideration.

The Divorce Problem. — With the exception of Japan the United States stands first among civilized lands in the number of divorces granted annually by its courts. As early as 1885 more marriages were dissolved in this country than in all the rest of the Christian world combined, the figures being as follows: United States, 23,472; Christian Europe, 20,131.[1] Quite as startling is the fact of the rapid increase in divorce in the United States during the past few decades. For example, in the ten years from 1890 to 1900 the number of divorces obtained increased 66.6 per cent over the preceding decade,

[1] Ellwood, *Sociology and Modern Social Problems*, p. 114.

whereas the population increased only 20.7 per cent. In the period from 1887 to 1906 one native marriage was dissolved for every 15.6 marriages solemnized. But in 101,827 divorce cases the courts failed to state the place of marriage. If all these were native marriages, the proportion of divorces to marriages rises to 1 in 13.9.[1] During the last decade 1900–10 the United States census shows that the number of divorces granted increased by leaps and bounds. Thus in 1900 the number of males fifteen years of age or over who were divorced was 84,230 and the number of females was 114,647. In 1910 the number of divorced males fifteen years and over was 156,-162, an increase of more than 85 per cent; whereas the number of females divorced had swelled to 185,068, an increase of more than 61 per cent.[2] Moreover, it should be remembered that the number of divorced persons reported by the last census falls short of the number of living persons who have been divorced, since many of these latter have remarried and many are reported as single or widowed.

Of the divorces granted in the period 1867–1906 66.6 per cent or two-thirds were granted to the wife as plaintiff. The most common grounds for divorce in this country are desertion, adultery and cruelty. In the four-year period 1902–6 the percentage of divorces granted for these causes is as follows:

CAUSE	PERCENTAGE
Desertion	38.5
Adultery	15.3
Cruelty	23.5

Thus it will be seen that 53.8 per cent of the divorces granted in this period were given not for light causes, but for offences which had already dissolved the marriage bond — for desertion and adultery.[3] The small percentage of divorces granted for

[1] Carroll D. Wright, *Special Census Report*, 1909, Part I, pp. 8–22.

[2] *Thirteenth Census of U. S.*, 1910; *Abstract of Census on Age and Marital Conditions*, p. 149. Percentages mine.

[3] *Special Report*, Bureau of the Census, 1909, pp. 24–6.

adultery is doubtless due to the fact that the parties concerned, especially women, are naturally desirous of concealing their dishonor and therefore substitute some other ground for the divorce whenever possible.

Professor Willcox in his careful study of divorce in the United States has shown that for the twenty-year period from 1867 to 1886 over 60 per cent of divorces were granted on the ground of adultery and desertion and over 97 per cent for grave causes, including, besides the two just mentioned, cruelty, habitual drunkenness, neglect on the husband's part to provide for his family and imprisonment for crime.[1]

These figures, carefully prepared on the basis of the Census Reports, tell a plain tale concerning the prevalence and the increase of divorce in this country. The facts can be neither denied nor ignored, although there may well be different interpretations of their import and the social lessons to be drawn from them.

Family Desertion. — Another evidence of the unstable character of modern family life is furnished by the large numbers of cases of family desertion. From 5 to 10 per cent of the cases of poverty and distress treated by the Charity Organization Societies of our large cities are due to the desertion of wives and children by the husband; and, as we have seen, desertion is one of the most frequent grounds for divorce in America. Of this social problem Miss Lilian Brandt writes in her valuable monograph published by the Charity Organization Society of New York:

" For several years this phenomenon, the desertion of wife and children by the husband and father, has been forcing itself on the attention of charitable societies. It is probable that desertion is really increasing." [2]   This statement is borne

[1] See *The Divorce Problem: A Study in Statistics* (*Columbia College Studies*, Vol. I, No. 1, New York, 1891).

[2] *Five Hundred and Seventy-four Deserters and their Families*, New York, 1905, p. 7.

out by the records of the Associated Charities of Washington.
These show that, in 1896, of 2164 families aided, only 56, or
2.6 per cent, had been deserted by the husband and father;
whereas in 1904, of 3898 families requiring assistance, 266 or
nearly 7 per cent had been deserted.[1] The prime cause of such
abandonment lies in the weakening of " the individual's sense
of responsibility for his family"; and this weakening Miss
Brandt believes to be due in part to "the restlessness of American life, the constant transfer of isolated members or parts of
families from Europe to this country and from the older parts
of this country to the newer. . . ." [2] Some husbands are
chronic deserters, leaving their wives " systematically on the
recurrence of certain conditions in the family. Some leave
just before or after the birth of a child; others after
every unusually serious quarrel; others at the beginning of
winter; others whenever they lose their job, or, more frequently, when their wives make the unreasonable demand that
they help support the family. It would be expected that frequent desertions would progressively weaken the tie that
originally bound the man to his family, until the time would
come when he would stay away altogether. In some cases
this does happen." [3]

A thorough study of five hundred seventy-four cases, taken
from the records of the charitable societies of twenty-six
American cities, convinced the writer that " while here and
there the responsibility for desertion may rest with industrial
conditions, with ill-considered marriages in early youth or
between men and women of irreconcilable differences of temperament, and somewhat more frequently, with the impossible
temper and cooking of the wife, still the most constant element in the situation is the irresponsible, ease-loving man who
acts on the theory that when hard times of any sort come he

---

[1] Baldwin, *Family Desertion and Non-Support Laws* (pub. by Charity
Organization Society of New York, 1905, p. 7).

[2] Brandt, *op. cit.*, p. 7.　　　　　　　　　　[3] *Ibid.*, p. 14.

is justified in making arrangements for his own comfort which do not include his wife and children." [1]

In forty-four of the fifty States and territories of this country there are laws making non-support (the outcome of desertion) in some form a criminal offence. On the contrary five States, namely, Iowa, Nevada, Oregon, Tennessee and Texas, fail to make non-support an offence and in three of these, Nevada, Tennessee and Texas, there is not even provision for a civil suit. Therefore in these States, as well as in Arizona, Idaho, Kentucky, Montana, South Dakota, Washington and Wyoming, where non-support is a crime only against children, the wife's sole remedy is a suit for divorce. Four States make desertion or non-support a felony, applying to wife or children in Michigan, Nebraska and Wisconsin, and to children only in Ohio.[2]

Disintegration due to Industrial Conditions. — But divorce and desertion are not the only conditions undermining the solidarity of the American family. The entire industrial situation undoubtedly contributes to the same end. In the words of a modern social writer :

" Certain aspects of our industrialism, such as the labor of women and children in factories, the growth of cities, and the loss of the home through the slum and the tenement, the higher standards of living and comfort, and the resulting higher age of marriage, — all of these have had, to a certain extent at least, a disastrous effect upon the family." [3]

The effects of modern industry upon the home are various. In the first place the low wages earned by many young men make early marriage impossible, or at the least imprudent when modern standards of living are considered. Not infrequently successful business or professional men have advised promising youths in their employ that marriage cannot be prudently considered under ten years after starting their life-work.

[1] *Ibid.*, p. 45.　　[2] Baldwin, *op. cit.*, p. 13.
[3] Ellwood, *Sociology and Modern Social Problems*, p. 136.

At the end of this period the habits of the man may very well have become fixed, and ideals of romantic affection and home-making have faded in the absorbed pursuit of material success.

Another industrial condition threatening the integrity of the home is furnished by the so-called " seasonal trades," of which farming is an example. Farm laborers often have a working year of only nine months, after which they are cast adrift to join the floating population of the unemployed. Large numbers of such men drift about the cities in winter, either unable to found homes at all or else depriving their families of their society and help for the greater part of the year. Unquestionably the " agricultural family," save among the prosperous land-owners, is no longer rooted and stable. Similar conditions prevail in the case of a growing class of sailors and railroad employees absent from home the greater part of the time. It is a dubious experiment to found a family in such circumstances, and the association is a " touch and go " one at best.[1]

Again, the invention of new machinery, the shut-down of individual plants at certain seasons, and the industrial panics which from time to time sweep the country, all threaten the foundation of new homes or the maintenance of those already established. Factories shut down for one reason or another, and thousands of men, women and children are thrown out of work. Many trades, such as building, painting, plumbing, are wholly seasonal or affected to some extent by the seasons. The United States Census Bureau in its Report on Manufactures in 1905 indicated clearly the extent to which shut-downs occur even in prosperous years. A full working year has 317 days. The census figures apply to the 216,262 industrial establishments which reported : [2]

[1] Some of these ideas were suggested by Mrs. Florence Kelley in an unpublished lecture given at Columbia University in April, 1913.

[2] *Census of Manufactures*, 1905, Part I, pp. 542–3 ; also given in Scott Nearing, *Financing the Wage Earner's Family*, p. 28.

PLANTS		DAYS IN OPERATION
11,494	(5.3%)	90 or less
22,091	(10.2%)	91 to 180
27,666	(12.8%)	191 to 270
67,492	(31.2%)	271 to 300
87,520	(40.5%)	301 to 365

These figures show that nearly 60 per cent of these industrial plants under consideration offered their employees less than a full year's work and that 28.3 per cent, or more than one-fourth, were employing men 270 days or less.

Commenting upon this industrial situation the New York State Commission on Employers' Liability and Unemployment (1910) states that " unemployment is a permanent feature of modern industrial life everywhere." What is the effect upon the families of these working-men? It means that the women and even the children of the household will seek work, when the husband and father is thrown out of a job, in an anxious effort to keep the home together. The sight of men in city parks caring for the babies while their wives and older children are at work is not uncommon. In this connection the Census Bureau reported in its *Statistics of Women at Work* that 769,477 of the *married women* of the country, or 5.6 per cent, were employed in gainful occupations in 1900. A recently published Federal inquiry into the reasons why 620 selected children in the states of Rhode Island, Pennsylvania, South Carolina and Georgia left school to go to work showed that 30 per cent were driven by pressure of starvation and another 28 per cent because their parents could not maintain the standard of living that seemed to them absolutely necessary without the assistance of their children. At this time 192 fathers of these children had been unemployed for varying periods.[1]

[1] Bruère, *Reanchoring the Home* (in *Harper's*, May, 1912, p. 92).

Another result of seasonal unemployment is the lowered standard of living in working-men's homes. Some years ago the Russell Sage Foundation concluded after investigation that a family of two adults and three children, or four adults, could not be supported decently in New York City on an income of less than nine hundred to a thousand dollars a year. The New York Commission, above referred to, agreed on seven hundred dollars as the minimum on which such a family could be maintained outside New York. In 1910 this Commission received reports from the secretaries of two hundred and eleven trade-unions to the effect that, if employment had been constant, slightly more than half their members would have had an average income of one thousand dollars. In only 4 per cent would it have fallen below seven hundred. "But because of the inconstant demand for labor, the average income actually fell below seven hundred dollars in twenty-five per cent of the membership, and reached a thousand dollars in only fourteen per cent." [1] These facts of unemployment or seasonal employment led the New York State Commission to conclude that the industrial life we have so confidently built up is responsible for the deterioration of both individuals and homes. "The merely unemployed man becomes inefficient, unreliable, good-for-nothing, unemployable. His family is demoralized. Pauperism and vagrancy result." [2]

All signs seem to indicate that the freehold homes of England and America, so numerous two generations ago, are giving place to tenements and slums; and that the integrity of these homes is seriously threatened. Divorce, family desertion, the demoralization due to modern industrial conditions, all play their part in bringing about the instability of the American family.

Causes of Disharmony within the Family. *Economic Dependence of the Wife.* — But the causes of family instability are not confined to external conditions. Within the family

[1] Bruère, *op. cit.* [2] *Ibid.*

itself one of the most fruitful sources of friction is economic in character. And this difficulty is by no means confined to the wage-earning class, but makes itself felt in the homes of the business and professional group. The problem is many-sided, yet all its phases may be traced back to a common source — to the inability or unwillingness of many intelligent persons to realize that women, like men, are *individuals*, with tastes and abilities varying widely, and with the desire, becoming every year more conscious and more urgent, to make those capacities count for something in carrying forward the world's work. This is, of course, the outcome of the individualistic movement, born in the eighteenth century, and perhaps not yet full-grown. An increasing number of women are coming to regard themselves as personalities whose sphere of activity and influence cannot justly be restricted to the personal interests of the home. This individualistic tendency is furthered by the education and professional or business training now quite generally bestowed on girls of the upper and lower middle class. Such training, cultural and utilitarian, brings to clear consciousness their peculiar gifts as well as their powers of achievement: and these are later tested and refined in the fire of practical experience. Such women, especially the more efficient of them, rarely accept with good grace the economic dependence that follows the renunciation of their career at marriage. The control of the purse strings by the husband soon grows irksome to a wife accustomed to financial independence. The situation becomes strained almost to the breaking-point in those cases, not altogether rare, where the husband is a niggardly provider or where he refuses to make the wife a regular allowance for expenses. A questionnaire on this point, sent to the married women of a single large city, would probably, if honestly answered, elicit hundreds of replies showing that the writers are closely limited in ready money by their husbands. Much oral testimony may be obtained by observers and inquirers in this field to the effect that not a few wives have pocket money

2 H

doled out to them with a very sparing hand, while they are given carte-blanche by well-to-do husbands to run up bills in stores approved by them. Such meagreness of funds frequently leads these women into humiliating situations and emphasizes in a peculiarly galling way their financial dependence.

Even when the wife receives a regular and generous allowance for household and personal expenses, the situation presents difficulties. If a married woman, once self-supporting, discovers that she has little taste and less capacity for housekeeping, if she is a poor cook, an unintelligent buyer and provider, or an inefficient director of servants, her mind will sooner or later turn to the profession outside the home in which she was reasonably or perhaps notably successful. In time, especially if she has no children, she probably will come to long for the stimulus, the challenge to her trained powers, that is furnished by an occupation in which she excels. No doubt it will become increasingly true that the sphere of the home, the church, the social group, or even the club, having broad civic and educational purposes, will be found too narrow for the developed personalities of some married women who crave opportunity for self-expression, for making themselves felt in directing the course of business or professional affairs. These wives may come to regard with envy the broader, more stimulating lives of their husbands, even if the careers of the latter be at times clouded by anxiety and burdened by heavy responsibilities. For these women know, as their husbands also know, that such careers, freely chosen and intelligently prepared for, are opportunities for the further development of personal power, talent and initiative, and thus are the means for self-realization in its best and most wholesome sense. In this way knowledge may breed discontent and discontent may, and probably will, sow the seeds of a harvest of friction and disharmony. Within the last decade or two it must have been brought home to many a husband, with a sense of shock, that his wife, albeit a true woman, was completely indifferent to domestic employments and was as little of a shining light in such pursuits as he himself. The belief that every woman worthy of the name is naturally domestic sends its roots far back into family history and deep down into human feeling. No doubt many years must pass before fair-minded men will ungrudgingly face the fact that domestic life and domesticity are not synonymous terms.

There remains another phase of the economic problem bound up with family life, and this is a very modern one. During the last fifty years or so there has appeared in increasing numbers in Europe and America the phenomenon of the parasitic wife, living more or less contentedly upon the means furnished by an overworked husband whose pride it seems to be to support her in comfortable if not luxurious idleness. This social type is described with some feeling by a recent writer :

" Men have drifted away from the happy old habit of thinking of the wife as an helpmeet to the habit of treating her as a luxury to be maintained at a certain necessary expense, just as one's yacht must be maintained. In the larger towns this condition is so prevalent that in many communities the most useful women are the unmarried ones, and for a woman to marry is to retire into the seraglio of pampered luxuries. There are whole blocks in our great cities in which the women are essentially useless creatures, outside of contributing to the joy of their husbands. . . ." And the writer adds a comment, the truth of which is too often overlooked : " Idleness in women is the beginning of trouble. It is just as bad for their morals as it is for men's — perhaps a little worse." [1]

Fortunately for wholesome family life this one-sided view of the economic responsibilities of home-making is confined chiefly to the prosperous classes, and has by no means won acceptance in other ranks of society.

[1] Warbasse, *Medical Sociology*, New York, 1910, p. 119.

Hitherto the discussion has been concerned almost solely with the wealthy and the middle-class family and the difficulties growing out of its imperfect adjustment to the present economic situation. But a word should be said of the economic problem presented by the wage-earner's family. As we have seen, low wages, seasonal trades and frequent periods of industrial depression make it impossible for many working-men to support their families without the assistance of wife and children. What becomes of the homes under such conditions? What of the children? Unlike her more favored sister of the prosperous middle class, who can engage more or less expert help to care for her house and her little ones, the woman who labors in factory or store must leave her home to take care of itself until evening, when she returns too weary to do more than prepare a hasty meal for her family. But this is not the whole story. Most persons are accustomed to the fact that the laboring class live in ugly tenements built in unsanitary slums; and therefore they tend to take such conditions for granted. Some day we may wake up to the fact that dwelling-places such as these are not homes in any true sense of the word — that family feeling cannot easily thrive in such a stifling atmosphere. It is idle to expect that a squalid tenement in the slums, sending forth in the morning all but its youngest members to labor and receiving them at night to eat and sleep without privacy or comfort, can nourish the sentiments of family loyalty, love and responsibility to their full strength and beauty. That these feelings do develop and sometimes even grow strong is evidence of the deep-rooted racial character of the instincts from which they spring.

Disharmony due to Ignorance of the Meaning of Marriage. — But the causes of friction within the family are not solely economic. A fertile source of trouble exists in the ignorance of both husband and wife concerning the nature and meaning of marriage. When we stop to consider the question impartially is it not an amazing fact that, in many instances, no instruction on the facts of sex life and sex relations is given to boys and girls, to young men and women, hereafter to be husbands and wives, fathers and mothers of the new generation? Against this unintelligent rule of silence placed upon all matters relating to sex a modern writer indignantly protests:

" That we should leave our children to pick up their information about the most sacred, the most profound and vital of all human functions from the gutter, and learn to know it first from the lips of ignorance and vice, seems almost incredible, and certainly indicates the deeply-rooted unbelief and uncleanness of our own thoughts." [1]

This taboo laid upon any discussion of sex functions as " vulgar " is a relatively modern phenomenon of our complex civilization. It is not so frequently found among simpler folk, who do not hesitate to speak of all natural functions with candor. The disastrous effects of the taboo upon the lives of our young men and women are not confined to the adolescent years, when they may " go astray " through ignorance and lack of intelligent direction, but threaten the happiness and security of marriage itself. What knowledge and guidance have most young people received concerning sex functions and sex instincts, together with their control in the interests of both physical and moral health? How many mothers have explained to their girls the physical basis of marriage, the deeper personal and social meaning of fatherhood and motherhood? How many fathers have talked frankly and above all *naturally* with their growing boys on the racial significance of their sexual natures, on the vital need of self-restraint, on the beauty and vigor of the clean life and the moral dignity of the fight for personal purity? How many young men before marriage have been taught " the possibility of deflecting physical desire to some degree into emotional and

[1] Carpenter, *Love's Coming of Age*, Chicago, 1906, p. 14.

affectional channels, and the great gain resulting " therefrom ?
This is by no means an advocacy of asceticism, but only a plea
for self-control in the interests of love itself.

Even when young people have " picked up " through conversations with their fellows, eked out by hints gained from
fiction and science, some knowledge of the facts of sex, what
responsible person has given a thought to furnishing them
with standards that will be of help when they come to the
point of choosing a life mate? To quote Mr. Carpenter
again :

" That one ought to be able to distinguish a passing sex
spell from a true comradeship and devotion is no doubt a very
sapient remark ; but since it is a thing which mature folk often
fail to do, how young things with no experience of their own
or hint from others should be expected to do it is not easy to
understand. The search for a fitting mate, especially among
the more sensitive and highly-organized types of mankind,
is a very complex affair ; and it is really monstrous that the
girl or youth should have to set out — as they mostly have to
do to-day — on this difficult quest without a word of help as
to the choice of the way or the very real doubts and per-
plexities that beset it." [1]

As matters stand, " a passing sex spell " is too often mistaken
by youths and maidens for great and enduring love ; and if
the social and financial condition of the young pair is reasonably satisfactory, and their characters pass as respectable,
their parents see little cause for interference. So the girl is
led to the altar, — many times with only the vaguest notion of
the physical rites by means of which the intimate communion
of marriage is consummated. But the ignorance does not stop
with the woman. The man, likewise, often knows little or
nothing of the marked differences in sexual nature of men and
women, and may be quite unprepared for the coldness and even
aversion with which his bride receives his advances. More

[1] *Op. cit.*, p. 78.

often than not he is " unaware that love in the female is, in a sense, more diffused than in the male, less specially sexual: that it dwells longer in caresses and embraces, and determines itself more slowly toward the reproduction system." The man and wife, then, approach the supreme hour of their wedded life in a mist of misapprehension; and not infrequently the shock of sudden knowledge destroys the joy and beauty of the first weeks of marriage and may result in permanent alienation. In spite of the delicate nature of the subject more than one physician and biologist, interested in the spread of enlightenment on sexual matters, has collected evidence to show that this rude shattering of illusions on the wedding-day is not uncommon. With many young people who truly love each other a readjustment is effected through mutual consideration, and a truer ideal of wedded happiness may thus be won. But in cases where the wife is highstrung and not oversensible and the husband is " just the ordinary thick-skinned, wholesome fellow of the world," who has been jarred into astonishment and irritation by his wife's attitude, mutual adjustment becomes difficult and mere toleration may in course of time take the place of love. And much, if not all, of this painful experience, so threatening to marital peace, might have been prevented by wise and sympathetic instruction.

Of course the ignorance of newly married couples concerning the meaning of marriage is not confined to its physical aspects. Few have gained insight into the spiritual nature of a true marriage. In the face of the growing volume of divorces in America, some of which might have been prevented by intelligent guidance before marriage, how can we much longer persist in being " blind leaders of the blind "? Surely it would be of the utmost service to both girl and youth to discuss with one or both parents some of the obstacles to happy married life that they are likely to encounter. Each should understand that any marriage relation worthy of the name is one of comradeship and mutual respect as well as one of romantic passion; each should be made fully aware of the numerous delicate adjustments of one personality to the other that must be made if wedded life is to be serene and happy. The girl should be taught that marriage can not always remain on the ecstatic heights of romance, but must be content to follow the humdrum highway of daily life, and learn to find much happiness thereon. To be thus forewarned is to be forearmed against the sharp disappointment felt by many a young wife who is convinced that her husband has lost all affection for her because he no longer dashes upstairs two steps at a time to embrace her. On his side the young man should be taught to look upon his future wife as an *individual*, as truly as he himself is, and to appreciate the logical consequences of that recognition, namely, respect for her ideas, points of view and life purposes. Such honest and whole-souled acknowledgment of the claims of his wife to consideration as an independent personality would prevent many an ugly marital jar and not a few permanent estrangements.

Perhaps the day will dawn when our youth are as carefully prepared for marriage as they are educated for culture and efficiency. When that time comes, selected reading and conversations with parents will be followed, on the part of betrothed couples, by frank talks with each other, in which many a knotty question is untangled and many a just agreement reached before the wedding-day. But it should not be forgotten that if sex instruction is to be given to young people, it must not only appeal to the intellect, but must stir the emotions and stiffen the will. And it must begin early, — for unselfishness, sexual control and devotion to a lofty monogamic ideal of marriage are not won in a day.

It is quite possible that the causes of family disharmony thus far discussed may be found in cases where the marriage was one of true love. Fortunately for the future of wedded happiness, comparatively few marriages in the middle and lower ranks of society are contracted to-day for reasons of convenience. Where such unions do occur it would seem as if the greater number must, in this age of unsettled social conditions and standards, be doomed to failure from the start. In the words of a contemporary writer : It " is time to maintain, for the good of all, that the woman who enters the bonds of matrimony for a home or because it is considered the thing to do, without being sure of the love that would illumine the way, not only degrades herself, but paves the way to the divorce court by her insincerity." [1]

The Social Evil as a Disruptive Force within the Family. — By the social evil is, of course, meant that promiscuous intercourse of the sexes which is not sanctioned by public opinion and morality although it may be licensed or tolerated by the State. One of the heaviest of the burdens that society has borne upon its shoulders, the social evil is as old as society itself. Among certain primitive tribes prostitution exists to-day; and its disastrous effects were well known to the ancient world. Hebrews, Greeks and Romans all were familiar with this social scourge and sought to regulate it in the spirit of toleration of a necessary evil. Bad as is the institution in itself, its harmful effects were vastly increased when, in the twelfth century, it became a medium for the transmission of venereal diseases of a most virulent sort. From that century to the present, prostitution and venereal disease have gone hand in hand, the former serving as the chief means for the dissemination of the latter.

Within the last decade the prevalence and awful ravages of these diseases have aroused the medical profession and scientific men to undertake a campaign against them. Statistics have been gathered by them and given to the public showing the appalling frequency of vice and the spread of disease among men in all social classes, who thus have become a menace to the health of others. In this campaign of enlightenment

---

[1] Wilkinson, *Education as a Preventive of Divorce* (in the *Craftsman*, February 1912, p. 477).

figures were freely quoted by the leaders of the movement, — earnest men such as the late Dr. Prince Morrow. These figures at least had the effect of arousing and even terrifying the men and women who became acquainted with them. For the first time in history the widespread existence of prostitution and the prevalence of the diseases which it spreads became known to the intelligent public.

No doubt this publication of statistics concerning the social evil has accomplished some good. It has acquainted men with the dangers attending vice and with the awful price paid by the large proportion who contract disease. It has opened the eyes of innocent and ignorant young women to conditions of which they had only the dimmest knowledge or none at all. But even now there is a reaction among scientists and physicians against the confident publication of figures respecting vice and venereal diseases, on the ground that previous estimates have been made after too restricted a study of conditions and the percentages thus obtained are probably too high. Moreover, many pioneers in the social hygiene movement have already discovered that information concerning the statistics of disease breeds caution in the pursuit of vice rather than develops self-control in the interests of a nobler ideal. That mere knowledge of the results of evil-doing too often leads to prudence rather than morality is, perhaps, a truism, but it is one that appears to need frequent reiteration.

But, although the number of men who have at one time in their lives yielded to temptation and sought the haunts of the prostitute has probably been exaggerated; and although the proportion of men who are or have been the victims of venereal disease has doubtless been set too high, it yet remains true that the social evil is a menace to public health and one of the surest destroyers of happy family life. So much has been written on this theme that it may be briefly treated here. The testimony of physicians leaves no doubt that many a man has taken unto himself a clean and innocent wife knowing that he was diseased and unfit to marry. Many more men believed themselves cured of the consequences of earlier vicious practices and discovered their fatal error only after months or years of married life. The taint in the husband is communicated to the wife in whom it may work with far more deadly effect. Gynecologists know only too well the awful price paid by thousands of wives for the sins of the husband. Science has illumined the problem of the " invalid wife," once a healthy girl, who has so pitifully failed to realize her own hopes of happy married life and has profoundly disappointed her husband.

But the evil does not stop with the wife. The " sins of the fathers " are visited upon their children, who are born blind, or weak in mind and body, where they do not actually develop disease in its most virulent form. Even this is not all. Venereal disease is probably responsible for a high proportion of sterile marriages. On this point Dr. Warbasse writes :

" Childless marriages were once thought to be due to certain incompatibilities, visitations of Providence and inherent defects on the part of the wife. The wife was once regarded as guilty in the sight of the law if she bore her spouse no children, and could be cast aside for sterility. Scientific knowledge has thrown light upon this dark place in the progress of women's emancipation and the culpability is now placed where it belongs." The writer then goes on to state that on the basis of " pretty full statistics " it has been computed that 75 per cent of childless marriages may be traced to the effects of venereal disease.[1] This figure may very well be too high; but this does not dispose of the theory that an important cause of our sterile marriages is the existence of the social evil in our midst.[2]

[1] Warbasse, *Medical Sociology*, p. 74.
[2] See also Dr. Prince Morrow, *Social Diseases and Marriage*, pp. 108-10.

In earlier times, when wives were almost wholly ignorant of these facts, the disastrous results of their husbands' vicious living, past or present, did not lead to permanent alienations. It is true that many married women gradually became chronic invalids whose lives were a drag upon themselves and their families. But, in a large number of cases, probably neither the wife nor her husband was aware of the true source of the trouble and so their mutual affection was not destroyed. Yet the invalidism of the wife, combined with her sterility or incapacity to bear healthy children, must have been a heavy strain upon the husband's affection and happiness, especially when he was quite ignorant of the fact that he alone was to blame. Such marriages must have been fruitful in blasted hopes if nothing worse. But nowadays, when books and journals treat these subjects with freedom and in the spirit of science, few young women are as ignorant of the facts concerning prostitution and disease as were their mothers of a generation past. Having eaten the bitter fruit of knowledge, they will, when married, better understand the ills that may attack them and their children. If these evils come upon them, who will dare to prophesy that the marriage bond will hold fast under the strain? Probably, in some cases, love will survive even this supreme wrong; but in many other instances disease and its shameful cause, once discovered, will bring about the complete disruption of the families concerned.

The roots of the trouble are several. Ignorance of the facts of sexual life and hygiene, combined with lack of firm, sympathetic and intelligent training of boys in self-restraint, will, however, account for much of the social evil. But another cause may be found in society's double standard of moral conduct that makes a venial offence in the man what it harshly condemns in the woman. Until one standard of personal purity be held up for both sexes, until *absolute monogamy* be the ideal held before our youth from their boyhood, this evil, with its disintegrating effect upon family life, will not disappear from among us.

The Normal Family. — Lest the reader may draw too gloomy conclusions from the above discussion of family evils it may be well to remind him that the nations of Europe and America contain countless homes where true affection and mutual consideration have bound families together in the strongest of human bonds. Such homes furnish cogent reasons for believing in the future of wholesome and happy family life when the present trying period of readjustment has been safely passed. Yet, even in homes where love dwells, and where the stresses and strains just considered are reduced to their lowest terms, it yet remains true that the wife and grown daughters have frequently failed to recognize their responsibility for the maintenance of the home. After the necessary planning for the day and the direction of the servant or servants have been attended to, these women have hours of vacant time upon their hands which they fill with shopping, calls, bridge or other pastimes more or less frivolous. Meanwhile the husband and father is quite possibly working long hours and carrying a heavy financial burden in order to maintain his family in comfort and relative idleness. This problem is a very real one, even in an age when women are more and more entering the various fields of gainful employment; and it raises the question whether every human being, male or female, rich or poor, should not be trained in some form of lucrative work, and, at the same time, educated to a sense of responsibility for his or her share of home maintenance.

The Problem of the Marriage Rate. — A further problem that concerns the establishment of families is furnished by the *rate of marriage* in the United States, as well as in Europe. This is regarded by many writers as a serious matter. These men point to a marked decline in the marriage rate as an ominous fact of modern life. This is accompanied, they tell us, by an equally marked increase in the age of marriage, an increase that shortens by so much the child-bearing period of the woman. So many references in contemporary social literature have been made to this state of affairs that most readers have accepted the assertions as facts. Yet these statements need drastic modification if they are not to be misleading. The *United States Census Report* for 1910, recently published, shows that there has been a steady *increase* in this country since 1890 in the percentage of married males and females *of marriageable age*, *i.e.*, fifteen years and over. The figures are as follows:[1]

	1890	1900	1910
Male	53.9	54.5	55.8
Female	56.8	57.0	58.9

Not only is this increase true for the total marriageable population, but it holds good in general for the group of native whites of native parentage wherein the decline in the marriage rate has been believed to be most marked. The figures follow:[2]

NATIVE WHITES OF NATIVE PARENTAGE	PERCENTAGE		
	1890	1900	1910
Male	55.4	55.0	56.3
Female	58.2	57.7	59.4

It will be noted that there was a slight falling off in the proportion of marriages of native white males and females in 1900, but this was more than made up in 1910.

Now turning to the question of the age of males and females at marriage. Is this age progressively rising? The census

[1] *Abstract of the Thirteenth U. S. Census. Age and Marital Condition*, p. 151.
[2] *Ibid.*

returns for 1910 give the percentage of males and females married, widowed or divorced in different age periods from 1890 to 1910. The figures speak for themselves.

AGE GROUP	MALE			FEMALE		
	1890	1900	1910	1890	1900	1910
15 to 19 years . .	0.5	1.0	1.2	9.7	11.2	11.6
20 to 24 years . .	19.2	22.1	24.6	48.1	48.3	51.4

Clearly, then, the percentage of both males and females who were married before the age of twenty-four years is higher in 1910 than in either of the two preceding decades. And the increase is as true of the native-born white population as of the foreign-born. Commenting on these figures the *Census Report* concludes:

" This would indicate that in all classes of the population a larger proportion are marrying in the earlier ages than was the case 10 or 20 years ago. *The falling off in the natural rate of increase of population in this country would therefore seem not in any way due to the postponement of marriage.*" [1]

May we then conclude that there *is* no problem with respect to the marriage rate in this country? — that social writers are wholly mistaken in maintaining that such a problem does exist? Probably not. For, although the marriage rate for the total marriageable population is undoubtedly higher than in 1890 and the age of marriage has not advanced in general, yet it is unquestionably true that, in certain sections of the country and in certain groups, there has been a progressive decline in the marriage rate. The Special Census Report on Marriage and Divorce, published in 1909 and covering the period from 1867 to 1906, indicates that there was an actual decrease in the rate

[1] *Ibid.*, p. 152. Italics mine.

of marriages in the North Atlantic States in the decade 1890–1900. Whereas in 1890 there were eighty-four marriages in this division for every ten thousand of the adult population, in 1900 there were only eighty-two. Moreover, of the five states and the District of Columbia which alone have complete records of marriage during the thirty years 1870–1900, only one state (Vermont) shows an increase in the marriage rate. All the others indicate a decrease. The figures are as follows:[1]

ANNUAL AVERAGE NUMBER OF MARRIAGES PER 10,000 POPULATION

STATE	1870[2]	1900[2]
Connecticut	91	77
District of Columbia	113	112
Massachusetts	103	86
Ohio	96	91
Rhode Island	109	87
Vermont	85	87

It is noteworthy that with the exception of Ohio and the District of Columbia all the states in the above group belong to the New England division; and three of the four latter states showed a very marked decrease in the rate of marriage. This is especially striking in the case of Rhode Island, where the average number of marriages per 10,000 population actually fell off 22 in the period under consideration.

It is worth noting, also, that, with the exception of the District of Columbia (in which the decrease was very slight), all the states showing a decline in the number of marriages are industrial centres. This suggests that there is probably a close connection between advanced industrial development and the marriage rate. In colonial days, when productive domestic industry played a most important rôle, a wife had great

[1] *Op. cit.*, p. 9.
[2] For the five-year period of which 1870 and 1900 are the medians.

economic value, as we have seen. In the vigorous language of a modern writer :

" The colonial gentleman had to have his soap kettles and his candle molds and looms and smoke-houses and salting tubs and spinning wheels and other industrial machines operated for him by somebody, if he was going to get his food and clothes and other necessaries cheap. He lost money if he wasn't domestic. He was domestic." [1]

But nowadays, when so many occupations have been taken away from the housewife, her economic value has enormously declined. Now that the industries of lighting, textile manufacture, making of clothing and household furnishings, food preparation and preservation are largely extra-household pursuits, it has been seriously suggested that the training of a housewife should emphasize her responsibilities *as a consumer* rather than as a producer. For a producer she no longer is in any important sense.

In an age when the standard of living in all classes is steadily rising, a man thinks twice before he marries a woman accustomed to the comforts and a few, at least, of the luxuries of life, especially when he knows that she is quite untrained and perhaps uninterested in home-keeping. The woman also stops to think before she resigns a lucrative position, industrial or professional, which guarantees her economic independence and, with reasonable thrift, an assured future. In many instances marriage is postponed beyond the age when it appears romantic and desirable, and finally, when life-habits become fixed, is given up entirely. This means, of course, a decline in the marriage rate ; and it is precisely in the large industrial centres, where women are most frequently found working outside the home, that this condition prevails.

The responsiveness of the marriage rate to the economic conditions of particular sections of the country has not failed to attract the notice of social observers. One writer calls

[1] Hard, *The Woman of To-morrow*, New York, 1911, p. 7.

2 I

attention to the fact that between the ages of twenty-five and thirty there are 279 single persons in every 1000 in the state of Vermont; whereas in New York there are 430 single persons in every 1000. He argues that the real reason lies in the fact "that New York, with its large cities, is farther removed than Vermont, with no large cities, from the primitive industrial conditions of colonial times." [1] The census figures for 1910 tend to support this position. They show that the percentage of single women 25 to 34 years of age in New York State was 27.6, whereas in Vermont it was only 21.8. If we look at the age group 35 to 44 years we find 15.5 per cent of the women single in New York and only 12.2 per cent in Vermont. When these percentage differences are translated into figures they mount up to many thousands.

The problem, then, is a real one. In sections where industries are numerous and important the women as well as the men are valuable as producers. But when the woman marries " she leaves most of her economic value behind." Her labor within the home, if she be thrifty and efficient, will, in some measure, make up for the financial loss that follows her withdrawal from industrial or professional life. But it will by no means compensate wholly for that loss. In the many instances where the wages of the man are small it becomes a serious question whether he is at all justified in marrying the woman of his choice. It is hardly a solution of the difficulty to suggest that the standard of living upheld by the couple should be materially lowered until the man's earning capacity has increased. Men and women alike have a rooted objection to living on a much lower plane of comfort and convenience than that in which they have been reared; and their objection increases in proportion to their initiative and ambition. Then, too, they are genuinely averse to bringing up their children with fewer of the comforts and opportunities of life than they themselves have enjoyed. This feeling must be

[1] Hard, *op. cit.*, p. 20.

reckoned with. What, then, shall be done? Shall society accept philosophically a steadily decreasing marriage rate in those sections where both sexes are engaged in gainful occupations and console itself with the thought that "we may be approaching a new social adjustment like that of the ant-colony, where, in certain members of both sexes, the reproductive function will be subordinated to other forms of efficiency?"[1] Such a society would resemble that of the bees in which the workers are sterile, leaving the entire function of maintaining the species to the queens and drones. Or, shall society squarely face the facts and accept the alternative that the wife shall, if she chooses, continue to labor outside the home until her husband's income warrants her in withdrawing from gainful pursuits to concentrate her interest upon household and children? We shall return to this question later.

Not only is it true that the marriage rate in certain sections of the country is affected by normal economic conditions, it is also true that in periods of industrial depression or panic, when the price of food-stuffs rises, the marriage rate goes down. The census reports make this plain enough. For example, in 1893, a "panic year," the increase in the number of marriages was only 803; and in the following year, when the effects of the industrial crisis were more fully felt, there was a *decrease* of 12,512.[2] Doubtless it is the more well-to-do classes that hesitate longest to incur the responsibility of founding new homes in a period of industrial depression. On this point a political economist wrote forty years ago:

"The middle and upper classes do not often marry unless they have reasonable prospect of being able to bring up a family in a state of social comfort. . . . But the laborers, who form the majority of the population, are but slightly

---

[1] Coolidge, *Why Women are So*, New York, 1912, p. 303. The author cites Professor Woodworth, the entomologist of the University of California, as offering this suggestion.

[2] Wright, Carroll D., *Special Census Report on Marriage and Divorce*, 1909, p. 7.

influenced by such cautious foresight. Even a trifling temporary improvement in their material prosperity acts as a powerful impulse to induce them to marry; for it is a demonstrated statistical fact that the number of marriages invariably increases with the decline in the price of bread." [1]

War is, of course, one of the prime causes of a decrease in the rate of marriage. Not only does warfare draw into the field of battle men who, under normal conditions, would be "marrying and giving in marriage," but it plays havoc with all forms of industry, and thus indirectly exercises a most unfavorable influence on the marriage rate. The terrible carnage and destruction now going forward in Europe will have disastrous effects upon all phases of the civilization so painfully built up in the past; and nowhere will the blight fall more heavily than upon family life for generations to come. The young and vigorous sons of the warring nations are being cut down; families are desolated daily; and in every land the women so outnumber the men that marriage and the founding of homes of their own will forever be denied thousands of girls just growing into full womanhood. Moreover, it is the older and the very young males, together with the weaklings, who will be left to continue the race.

The Problem of the Birth-rate. — During the latter third of the nineteenth century the birth-rate in many civilized countries has decreased markedly. At the same time the death-rate in these countries likewise shows an even more notable decline and thus the population has been maintained with increase. In France, however, there has been a struggle for many years to keep the birth-rate above the mortality rate. According to the French *Journal Officiel* of 1910, the net excess of births over deaths in France, a country having a population of over 39,000,000, was 70,581, whereas in 1909 this excess was only 13,424.[2] In some years, as in 1907, the birth-rate

---

[1] Fawcett, *Manual of Political Economy*, London, 1874, p. 143.
[2] *World Almanac*, 1914, p. 253.

actually fell below the death-rate. England and Germany make a better showing, although the decline in the number of births per thousand of the population in those countries has been very evident since 1870. In 1904 the three leading European nations showed the following rate of deaths and births (per 1000 of the population).[1]

	BIRTH-RATE	DEATH-RATE
England	28.0	16.2
Germany	35.2	19.6
France	20.9	19.4

It will be seen that Germany in 1904 had an excess of the birth-rate over the death-rate of 15.6, and England an excess of 11.8, while France could show a surplus of only 1.5. But this marked advantage of Germany over France is rather rapidly disappearing. The *Deutsche Tageszeitung* gives statistics for the Empire which show that the number of births per 1000 declined from 37 in 1901 to 30.7 in 1910. The figures for the larger cities of Germany are even less favorable. Thus Berlin in 1910 showed a birth-rate of only 22.3 and Hamburg one of 23.9 — both revealing a striking decrease since 1901.[2] In like manner the birth-rate in England and Wales had sunk to 25.1 in 1910.

The decline in the birth-rate among the native-born whites of native parentage in the United States is also very noteworthy and has been the subject of frequent pessimistic criticism by social writers. Unfortunately statistics are not available, as in European countries, owing to the fact that registration of births in the United States is absent or defective. But the size of the average family in the United States is stated to have

[1] See Ellwood, *Sociology and Modern Social Problems*, p. 143.
[2] Figures quoted from *Deutsche Tageszeitung* by *New York Times*, Aug. 26, 1913.

declined from 5.6 in 1850 to 4.7 in 1900 — a decrease of almost one person per family.[1] The rate of increase in the native white stock of certain sections of this country is pitifully small when compared with the rate among whites of foreign parentage and among the foreign born. The census returns for 1910 show that in New England the native whites of native parentage increased only 4.1 per cent in the decade from 1900 to 1910, while the native whites of foreign or mixed parentage increased 30 per cent. In New Hampshire there was an actual decrease of native whites of native parentage and in Maine and Vermont the increase was very slight. The Middle Atlantic division also revealed a much higher rate of increase for native-born whites of foreign parentage than for those of native parentage, the former rate being 27 per cent and the latter 14.3 per cent. In other sections of the United States, however, the percentage of increase of native whites of native parentage was materially higher than that for native whites of foreign or mixed parentage. It is only in the New England and Middle Atlantic divisions, then, that the native white stock of several generations back is not holding its own.[2] This condition is much more marked in the urban than in the rural population. Hardly two-fifths of the population of the cities of the United States are at present composed of native whites of native parentage, whereas more than three-fifths of the rural population are thus composed.[3] In 1900 the cities of Boston and Providence showed a birth-rate among native-born parents of 18.2 and 16.0 respectively, while the corresponding birth-rate among foreign-born parents was 31.1 in both cities.[4]

But a decline in the proportion of births is not necessarily a cause for alarm, at least not until the birth-rate more closely

[1] Ellwood, *op. cit.*, p. 144.
[2] *Abstract of the Census for 1910, Section on Population*, pp. 90 and 91.
[3] *Ibid.*, p. 93.
[4] Newsholme, *The Declining Birth Rate*, New York, 1911, p. 27.

approaches the death-rate. On this point Ellwood writes:
" On the whole, this [the decrease in the rate of births] is a
good thing. The birth rate should decrease with the death
rate! This leaves more energy to be used in other things;
but when the birth rate falls more rapidly than the death rate
or falls beyond a certain point, it is evident that the normal
growth of a nation is hindered, and even its extinction may be
threatened. While an excessively high birth rate is a sign
of a low culture on the whole, on the other hand an excessively
low birth rate is a sign of physical and probably moral degeneracy in the population." [1] It is quite possible that biologists
and sociologists alike might take issue with the last clause of
this statement as not borne out by a closer analysis of the
facts. This leads us to a consideration of the causes for the
declining birth-rate.

Causes of Decline. — Many and various are the reasons
assigned for this social phenomenon. Newsholme has examined some of them with impartiality and has estimated
their cogency in the light of the facts and figures. A favorite
theory in the nineteenth century was that of Doubleday, who,
in his work on the *True Law of Population*, published in 1841,
stated that throughout the animal and vegetable kingdoms
" over-feeding checks increase; whilst, on the other hand,
a limited or deficient nutriment stimulates and adds to it."
Commenting on this hypothesis, Newsholme says: " It is
highly improbable . . . that the average nutrition of French
wives is so much higher than that of Irish wives as to account
for a difference in corrected birth-rates of 21.6 and 36.1 per
1000 of population; or to account for a difference between
28.4 and 35.7 in England and Prussia respectively." [2] The
theory also fails to explain the small birth-rate in urban
communities.

Another hypothesis has been furnished by Herbert Spencer,
who held that as the intellectual and moral development of the

[1] *Sociology and Modern Social Problems*, p. 142.   [2] *Op. cit.*, p. 31.

race advances fertility decreases. Or, in other words, the higher the intellectual development, the lower the fertility among civilized peoples. Whetham [1] has collected data bearing on this question from among the long-established families of English nobility who " possess a large proportion of the selected and inherited capacity of the country " and receive all the advantages of cultured home surroundings. A hundred fertile marriages for each decade from 1831 to 1890 were considered. The results obtained are as follows:

PERIOD	AVERAGE BIRTHS TO EACH FERTILE COUPLE
1831–40	7.1
1841–60	6.1 (about)
1871–80	4.4
1881–90	3.1

Now, on the basis of Spencer's hypothesis, are we willing to infer that the degree of culture and intellectual capacity in these families was so vastly inferior in 1840 to what it was in 1890 as to account for a decline in the average births per family of more than one-half? Put in this concrete form, the Spencerian theory seems hardly adequate to explain the problem, even while it may be admitted that " increasing individuation " in the human species is probably associated to some extent with decreasing fertility.

Rejecting the hypothesis discussed above, Newsholme comes to the important conclusion that " *volitional limitation of the family* is the chief and vastly predominant cause of the decline in the birth-rate which is taking place in so many countries." The author cites in support of his contention the testimony of experienced medical men which shows how widespread is the practice of voluntary restriction of families. He quotes from

[1] *The Family and the Nation*, 1909, pp. 138–9; also cited in Newsholme, *op. cit.*, p. 32.

the results of a " confidential census among a class of ' intel-
lectuals ' " which was published in the London *Times* of
Oct. 16, 1906, by Mr. Sidney Webb. The results showed
that of 120 married couples, 107 had voluntarily limited the
number of their offspring and 13 had not. The average
number of children *in each group* was under two.[1]

There are many causes at work which might well produce
voluntary limitation of families. Of these, the economic is
probably the most important. The cost of living has steadily
risen in most countries at a more rapid rate than wages have
advanced. When this increased cost of maintaining a family
is considered in relation to the higher standards of living that
prevail at present, in all but the poorest classes, we find one of
the chief reasons why the size of families has been deliberately
limited. Nor is such restriction fairly open to the charge of
selfishness. On the contrary it would seem that a growing
regard for decent and comfortable living conditions were a
mark of civilization. When this is combined with a heightened
sense of the obligations of parenthood, of the duties owed to the
child, not alone to provide for his physical well-being, but for
his moral and intellectual education and his efficient training
for life work, the motives leading to restriction of families seem
both prudent and unselfish. It is only among undeveloped
peoples that procreation goes on with little or no thought for
the future of the offspring thus carelessly brought into the
world. Indeed it is a matter for some concern that the
poorest half of the wage-earning class is the more prolific,
" that the careful artisan is beginning to adopt the policy of a
restricted family, and that the unskilled labourer is not doing
so. . . ." [2] Biologists assure us, however, that if there is
cause for apprehension in this fact, the reason lies chiefly in the
unwholesome conditions in which the children of the poor
are brought up. If these are very bad, from the standpoint
of nutrition and sanitation, the youth reared in such circum-

[1] Newsholme, *op. cit.*, pp. 33–4.   [2] *Ibid.*, p. 45.

stances can hardly grow to efficient maturity. Of course there are social writers who maintain that the poorest classes, who so largely recruit the ranks of each generation, are inferior physically and mentally to the higher artisan and professional classes now tending to limit the size of their families. But few sociologists are terrified by this bogey. They point out that the " wage-earning classes have always formed a large majority of the total population; and their birth-rate in the future as in the past, must determine the composition of the people." [1] So far as physical fitness is concerned, the children of the poor *at birth* appear not to have suffered from the bodily deterioration which has taken place in the parents. This does not dispose of the question whether or not the poorest classes come up to the standard of intellectual ability of their more favored countrymen. But here, again, unfavorable life conditions may account largely for inferiority of achievement. Only a few individuals in each generation are so gifted as to rise superior to all hampering circumstances. May not the small advances in economic and social status made by a proportion of the very poor in each generation represent quite as high ability as the more rapid and striking progress of individuals in the favored classes? The efforts of social workers, and legislators then, might well be even more earnestly and consistently devoted to securing better living conditions for society's most prolific group.

To return to the question of the economic causes leading to voluntary limitation of families. It is quite possible, as Newsholme points out, that, in certain factory centres where young children's labor in the past was a valuable asset but is so no longer until after the age of thirteen or fourteen, families have become smaller because the child is no longer " his parents' savings bank, from which savings could be drawn as soon as the child could go to the mill as a half-timer." [2] Certainly in those English textile towns, where the *corrected* birth-rate

[1] Newsholme, *op. cit.*, pp. 44–5. [2] *Ibid.*, p. 38.

shows a decline, between 1881 and 1903, from 22 to 32 per cent, some such cause would appear to have been at work.

It is probable that another cause of the limitation of families may be found in the congested conditions in our large cities. Apartment houses and tenements, housing scores and even hundreds of people, have taken the place of detached homes, to the profound loss of family life. No family can develop life-long associations and a feeling of permanency in an apartment or " flat." Some of the essential conditions of a home are lacking here. Moreover, in such tenement life, with few rooms all on one floor, the family are more closely thrown together than in a detached home, — they cannot escape each other, so to speak. In such circumstances children would be constantly " under foot." When to this disadvantage is added the fact that many managers of apartment houses object to families with more than one child, or to any children, we have a situation highly unfavorable to the rearing of even moderate-sized families. Recently the manager of a large and expensive apartment house in New York proudly boasted to one of his tenants that he had got rid of every family in his house that had a baby.

The Restriction of Families among the Educated Classes. — It has been suggested in the above discussion that the decline in the birth-rate among the intellectual and prosperous classes is more marked than in any other social group. This fact has sometimes been used as an argument against the higher education of women on the ground that the woman of collegiate training is less inclined than her sisters of the same social class to assume the cares of motherhood. But this contention is hardly borne out by the facts. A valuable study was made some years ago of the proportion of marriages among college and non-college women and of the number of children per marriage in each group. For the purposes of the study 343 college-bred women, graduates of Smith College, were compared with 313 non-college women *of the same social class and age*. It was discovered that the mean age of marriage of the college women (Class A) was 26.3 years, whereas the mean age of marriage of non-college women (Class B) was 24.3 years. Class A had a total of 566 children as against 584 children in Class B. Absolutely, then, the non-college group had the larger number of children; but if comparisons be made on the basis of *the number of years of married life* in each group Class A had the advantage, having borne 9 per cent more children. The English statistics collected by Mrs. Sidgwick show the same results. The author sums up the facts as follows:

"In both English and American statistics the number of children born to *each year of marriage* is slightly larger for the college women than for the non-college women; in both cases, also, the number of *children per woman* is slightly less for the college women than for the non-college women."[1]

When the matter of childlessness is considered 25.4 per cent of the marriages in Class A were sterile as against 17.9 per cent in Class B. But if all the women married less than two years be subtracted from each group the results are not so unfavorable to Class A. They show 19.2 per cent of childless marriages in Class A as against 15.3 per cent in Class B.[2]

It seems pretty clear from the above figures that this selected group of college women was fulfilling its obligations to the race about as satisfactorily as the group of less highly educated sisters, and that the slightly lower birth-rate in the former was due to the more advanced age at which they married.

Yet dark prophecies are frequently made concerning the increasing number of sterile marriages in the intellectual class. At a recent Conference for Race Betterment held at Battle

[1] Smith, Mary R. *Statistics of College and non-College Women*, in *Publications of the American Statistical Association*, VII, pp. 11–12.

[2] Smith, *op. cit.*, pp. 13–14.

Creek, Michigan, Dr. J. McKeen Cattell made the following rather startling statements:

"The completed family of contemporary scientific man, is about 2, the surviving family about 1.8 and the number of surviving children for each scientific man about 1.6. Twenty-two per cent of the families are childless; only one family in seventy-five is larger than six. The same conditions obtain for other college graduates.

"If the size of family of college graduates should continue to decrease as it did during the nineteenth century, students graduating in 1925 would have no children at all . . . .

"Answers from 461 leading scientific men giving the causes which led to the limitation in the size of their families show that 176 were not voluntarily limited, while 285 were so limited. The cause of voluntary limitation was health in 133 cases, expense in 98 cases and various causes in 54 cases."[1]

These figures are certainly suggestive and illuminating. They show that more than 59 per cent of this selected group of scientific men were voluntarily restricting the size of their families and that nearly 50 per cent of the latter group were doing so because the health of one or both parents did not justify them in having offspring. More than 34 per cent of the men who limited their families were actuated by economic motives — the question of expense. When it is remembered that the standard of living among professional men is notoriously high and, except in rare instances, the salaries of such men are relatively low, the motive is seen to be not a merely mercenary one. In the intelligent class, more than any other, we have the right to expect that foresight and a sense of responsibility for the upbringing and education of children shall regulate the procreation of offspring.

However, it is quite probable that prudential and moral motives do not always actuate parents who keep down their

[1] Quoted in *New York Times*, Jan. 13, 1914.

families to one child or none at all. When the birth-rate is markedly low among the prosperous class economic excuses cannot be urged. Undoubtedly selfishness is at the root of this condition, — the unwillingness of fashionable wives to give up some of their pleasures in order to bear and rear children, and the unwillingness of husbands to limit their expenditure for luxuries in order to clothe and educate a family. Selfish motives were responsible for an enormous decrease in the birth-rate among the wealthy class in Imperial Rome, and they probably are at work among the luxury-loving class in our own day.[1]

Summary. — In the foregoing chapter the maladjustment of the modern family to economic and social conditions has been discussed with no attempt, at this stage, to suggest remedies for the evils that undoubtedly exist. The instability of the twentieth century family, as revealed in the frequency of divorce and family desertion, has been indicated; and the part played by modern industrialism in breaking up home life has also been described. Another striking feature of family life at present is the decline of the marriage rate in groups where the standard of living is high as compared with the income, and where women are largely represented in industry and the professions. Here again is an illustration of the unsatisfactory adjustment of marriage to the modern economic situation.

When we turn to the family institution of the present we find numerous evidences of friction within itself. One fertile source of trouble is the reluctance of many men to recognize frankly and unreservedly that their wives are independent personalities like themselves, and therefore are entitled to a wide range of opportunity as regards their interests and life-work. When this reluctance on the husband's part is accompanied by an aggressive assertion of her personal ideas and

[1] For this whole question of the decreasing birth-rate see Drysdale, C. V., *The Small Family System* (New York, 1914).

rights by the wife the train is laid for an ultimate explosion. Another cause of family friction is the financial one, growing out of the unwillingness of many husbands to make their wives such a regular allowance as accords with their income and to do it as a matter of course in recognition of the wife's valuable services within the household. Quite a different problem is bound up with the entrance of the wives and mothers of the poor into industrial life to the immense disadvantage of the home.

Another source of family disharmony is found in the ignorance of most young women and many men concerning either the nature or the mutual obligations of the marriage relation. It follows from this ignorance that marriages are lightly contracted only to be lightly broken. The crying need for intelligent instruction and training of young people for marriage has long been appreciated by reflective men and women interested in the reconstruction of the family. The lack of guidance and moral inspiration is in large measure responsible for the social evil in our midst with all its disrupting effects upon family life. To the prevalence of prostitution and the diseases that it propagates may be traced a large proportion of the sterile marriages so characteristic of modern times.

But the declining birth-rate has other causes than the one just mentioned. Quite possibly the increasing individuation characteristic of cultured societies is accompanied by a decrease in fertility, although no adequate statistics are at hand to establish this contention. On the other hand it appears to be true that the declining birth-rate in most countries is due in a marked degree to voluntary restriction of families. This limitation, in turn, is caused by economic pressure, by questions of health, by the unfavorable conditions of modern city life and by the selfishness of one or both parents. Each of these four causes plays its part, large or small, in bringing about a serious decrease in the birth-rate among most civilized peoples.

SELECTED BIBLIOGRAPHY

Bosanquet, Helen. *The Family*, chs. VIII–XV.

Bruère, Robert W. *Reanchoring the Home* (*Harper's*, May, 1912).

Dealey. *The Family in its Sociological Aspects* (1912).

Devine, Edward T. *The Economic Place of Women* (in *Report of Assoc. of Coll. Alum.*, Jan. 1905).

Dike, Rev. Samuel W. *Problems of the Family* (*Century*, XXXIX, 385–95).

Drysdale, C. V. *The Small Family System* (1914).

Ellis, H. *The Problem of Race Regeneration* (1911).

Ellwood. *Sociology and Modern Social Problems*, pp. 136 ff.

Finot, Jean. *The Problem of the Sexes* (1912).

Geddes and **Thompson.** *The Evolution of Sex*, ch. XX.

Hagar, F. N. *The American Family*, chs. XIII, XIV, XVI, XVIII, XXI–XXIV.

Howard, E. G. *History of Matrimonial Institutions*, Vol. III, pp. 185–259.

Newsholme. *The Declining Birth-Rate* (1911) entire.

Parsons, Elsie Clews. *The Family.* (See especially last chapter.)

Patten, S. N. *The New Basis of Civilization*, chs. III, IX, X.

Sumner, Wm. G. *War and other Essays.* (See chapters on *The Family and Social Change* and *The Status of Woman*.)

Thwing, C. F. *The Family* (1887).

United States Census, Report for 1910. (See *Abstract*, Sections on *Population* and *Age* and *Marital Condition*.)

Wilkinson, M. V. B. *Education a Preventive of Divorce* (in the *Craftsman*, Vol. 21, Feb. 1912, 473–90).

Willcox. *The Divorce Problem: A Study in Statistics.* (*Columbia College Studies*, Vol. I, No. 1, 1891.)

Wright, Carroll D. United States Census, *Special Report on Marriage and Divorce*, 1909, Part I, pp. 8–22.

CHAPTER XIV

CURRENT THEORIES OF REFORM

The Variety in Points of View. — While the modern family institution remains so unsatisfactorily adjusted to twentieth century conditions, voices are not lacking, either to point out the evils of our present marriage system or to preach, with greater or less confidence, their special gospel of reform. The variety and contradictory character of the views upheld by one group or another are merely signs of the great complexity of the problem and the different temperaments and experience of the champions engaged. Nothing is more important, in the education of young men and women, than an understanding of the theories of these would-be reformers and the ability to estimate their social philosophy in a liberal and impartial spirit. This suggests the necessity for some standard of judgment. The author submits that custom of itself affords no satisfactory criterion, even when it masks as "the good, old ways of our ancestors" in an age when family relations were wholesome. The trite saying with regard to the impossibility of turning the hands of civilization's clock backward needs repetition now and again. We cannot return to the old ways of our fathers. What, then, can serve as a touchstone for determining the worth of new schemes? Perhaps the only standard that can be accepted by all thinking persons is the ideal of the common good, the community welfare, with explicit recognition that this good cannot be attained by the arbitrary suppression of the individuals who compose the group. If society exists to secure "the good life" for individuals, manifestly its conventions and its laws must be progressively reshaped to secure the best and fullest life, not for one class but so far as possible for every member of the community. With this standard in mind we may venture to consider a few of the widely variant schemes for the reform of sex relations and family life now so freely set forth in the literature of our day. The preachers of these conflicting theories of family regeneration fall into three groups which may be termed the Radicals, the Conservatives and the Moderate Progressives.

THE THEORIES OF THE RADICALS

Socialistic Views of Family Relations. — The comment has frequently been made by students of society that the Socialist party has given special attention to the family institution because this organization was an outgrowth of private property and because it admirably illustrates in their eyes the evils inseparable from such an economic system. Doubtless this is one explanation of the universal interest taken by Socialists in the reconstruction of the family. Thus the German socialistic leader Bebel writes: " Bourgeois marriage . . . is the result of bourgeois property relations. This marriage, which is intimately related with private property and the right of inheritance — demands ' legitimate ' children as heirs: it is entered into for the purpose of acquiring these: under the pressure of social conditions it is forced even upon those who have nothing to bequeath: it becomes a social law, the violation of which the State punishes by imprisoning for a term of years the men and women who live in adultery and have been divorced." [1]

Other socialistic writers inveigh against the monogamic family as at present constituted for binding together two persons, congenial or uncongenial, for the period of their natural lives in an exclusive association which sometimes shuts out other intimate and broadening human relationships. Writing

[1] *Woman under Socialism* (ed. 1904), p. 346.

on this question Mr. Edward Carpenter criticises " the harshness of the line, the kind of ' ring-fence,' which social opinion
(at any rate in this country) draws around the married pair
with respect to their relations to outsiders." He adds with
some feeling: " However appropriate the union may be in
itself it cannot be good that it should degenerate — as it tends
to degenerate so often . . . into a mere *égosime à deux*.
And right enough no doubt as a great number of such unions
actually are, it must be confessed that the bourgeois marriage
as a rule, and just in its most successful and pious and respectable form, carries with it an odious sense of stuffiness and
narrowness, moral and intellectual: and that the type of
Family which it provides is too often like that which is dis-
closed when, on turning over a large stone we disturb an in-
sect Home that seldom sees the light." [1]

What, then, are the constructive principles of the radical
Socialists so far as marriage and family relations are concerned?
Mr. Carpenter would answer: (1) The complete freedom of
the woman so that she is *treated without question* as the equal
of the man; (2) Freedom in marriage.

With regard to the first point all Socialists are united in
upholding the necessity for according to women the full
measure of personal, economic and political independence and
privilege enjoyed by men. Thus Mr. H. G. Wells, the English
Socialist, boldly declares:

" Essentially the Socialist position is a denial of property
in human beings; not only must land and the means of production be liberated from the multitude of little monarchs among
whom they are distributed . . . but women and children,
just as much as men and things, must cease to be chattels.
Socialism indeed proposes to abolish altogether the patriarchal
family amidst whose disintegrating ruins we live, and to raise
women to equal citizenship with men." [2]

[1] Carpenter, *Love's Coming of Age* (1906), pp. 85, 87.
[2] *Socialism and the Family*, London (1908), p. 56.

Likewise Bebel, in his sketch of *Women in the Future* declares:

" The woman of future society is socially and economically independent; she is no longer subject to even a vestige of dominion and exploitation; she is free, the peer of man, mistress of her lot. Her education is the same as that of man, with such exceptions as the difference of sex and sexual functions demand. . . . She chooses her occupation on such field as corresponds with her wishes, inclinations and natural abilities, and she works *under conditions identical with man's.*" [1]

In similar strain writes Mr. George Bernard Shaw. After criticising with his accustomed pungency the insistence of romantic idealists " on self-surrender as an indispensable element in true womanly love," Mr. Shaw fearlessly proclaims a doctrine of sheer individualism.

" The sum of the matter is that unless Woman repudiates her womanliness, her duty to her husband, to her children, to society, to the law, and to everyone but herself, she cannot emancipate herself. But her duty to herself is no duty at all, since a debt is cancelled when the debtor and creditor are the same person. Its payment is simply a fulfilment of the individual will, upon which all duty is a restriction, founded on the conception of the will as naturally malign and devilish. Therefore, Woman has to repudiate duty altogether. In that repudiation lies her freedom; for it is false to say that Woman is now directly the slave of Man: she is the immediate slave of duty; and as man's path to freedom is strewn with the wreckage of duties and ideals he has trampled on, so must hers be. . . . A whole basketful of ideals of the most sacred quality will be smashed by the achievement of equality for women and men. Those who shrink from such a clatter and breakage may comfort themselves with the reflection that the replacement of the broken goods will be prompt and

[1] *Woman under Socialism,* p. 343. Italics mine.

certain. It is always a case of 'The ideal is dead; long live the ideal!'"[1]

So much for woman's equality with man in the ideal socialist society of the future. What views are championed by Socialists concerning the other knotty question of freedom in marriage? On this point no such harmonious agreement exists among them; indeed quite contrary theories are maintained by writers each of whom proclaims his sympathy with socialism. The most radical views are confidently advanced by Mr. Carpenter, who asserts:

"The more people come to recognize the sacredness and naturalness of the real union, the less will they be willing to bar themselves from this by a life-long and artificial contract made in their salad days. Hitherto the great bulwark of the existing institution has been the dependence of Women, which has given each woman a direct and most material interest in keeping up the supposed sanctity of the bond — and which has prevented a man of any generosity from proposing an alteration which would have the appearance of freeing himself at the cost of the woman; but as this fact of the dependence of women gradually dissolves out, and as the great fact of the spiritual nature of the true Marriage crystallizes into more clearness — so will the former bonds which bar the formation of the latter break away and become of small import. . . . Ideally speaking it is plain that anything like a perfect union must have perfect freedom for its condition; and while it is quite supposable that a lover might out of the fullness of his heart make promises and give pledges, it is really almost inconceivable that anyone having that delicate and proud sense which marks deep feeling, could possibly demand a promise from his loved one. As there is undoubtedly a certain natural reticence in sex, so perhaps the most decent thing in true Marriage would be to say nothing, make no promises — either for a year or a lifetime. Promises

[1] *The Quintessence of Ibsenism* (New York, 1912), pp. 44-5.

are bad at any time, and when the heart is full silence befits it best." [1]

Obviously, we have here a theory of free marriage in its unmodified form. The reader will no doubt be acutely aware of certain very concrete difficulties in the way of its realization, at any rate in our present stage of civilization. (1) Can men and women be depended upon to form " spiritual marriages " which have the element of permanence without some external pressure on the part of State or Church? If marriage could be freely entered into and terminated by private agreement would not the tendency be to contract marriages even more lightly than at present with the consciousness that the union could be terminated at pleasure? If so, what would prevent a return to at least partial promiscuity in sex relations, — a sort of serial polygamy? (2) Then, too, what would become of the offspring of these temporary marriages?

It is only fair to Mr. Carpenter to say that he attempts to meet these objections. He freely concedes that " Love is doubtless the last and most difficult lesson that humanity has to learn; in a sense it underlies all the others." [2] Therefore, since comparatively few men and women know how to love nobly and unselfishly and *with freedom* granted each to the other, " and since the partial dependence and slavery of Woman must yet for a while continue, it is likely for such a period that formal contracts of some kind will still be made; only these (it may be hoped) will lose their irrevocable and rigid character, and become in some degree adapted to the needs of the contracting parties." Such contracts, the author holds, might be concerned with conjugal rights, conditions of termination of the union, responsibility for offspring, etc. They might even be " preliminary to a later and more permanent alliance . . . " — a sort of " trial marriage." However, the author feels that " rather than adopt any new system of contracts, public opinion in this country would tend to a

[1] *Love's Coming of Age*, pp. 105–6.   [2] *Op. cit.*, p. 111.

simple facilitation of Divorce, and if the latter were made (with due provision for the children) to depend on mutual consent, it would become little more than an affair of registration, and the scandals of the proceeding would be avoided. In any case we think that marriage-contracts, if existing at all, must tend more and more to become matters of private arrangement as far as the relations of husband and wife are concerned, and that this is likely to happen in proportion as woman becomes more free, and therefore more competent to act in her own right. It would be felt intolerable, in any decently constituted society, that the old blunderbuss of the Law should interfere in the delicate relations of wedded life." [1]

So in Mr. Carpenter's scheme private contracts are to bridge the gulf between our present public marriage celebration and a condition in which marriage is so spiritualized and free that formal agreements are not only unnecessary but offensive to the fine feeling of the men and women concerned. So, too, divorce is to be treated once more as a private matter, as it was in the ancient world, with but few limitations. But what is to prevent such private contracts from being thoughtlessly made and lightly broken? Moreover, they are confessedly a makeshift, spanning the gap between our present methods and free marriage. This leads us to our second question. Would not free marriage result in more or less promiscuity in sex relationships? Carpenter thinks not. He reminds us " that the responsibility for the rearing and maintenance of children must give serious pause to such a career; and . . . to suppose that any great mass of the people would find their good in a kind of matrimonial game of General Post is to suppose that the mass of the people have really never acquired or been taught the rudiments of common sense in such matters — is to suppose a case for which there would hardly be a parallel in the customs of any nation or tribe that we know of." [2]

[1] *Ibid.*, pp. 106–7.   [2] *Ibid.*, p. 109.

But do these statements dispose of the difficulty? In the first place the constant decline in the proportion of births to the married population justifies us in concluding that the limitation of families is, in many instances, voluntary and deliberate. Why should the man and woman held solely by love (or passing attraction mistaken for love) have children at all? Doubtless some couples would desire offspring, but would there not be at least as many barren marriages as there are now? In such unions the curb which children afford to free experiments in mating would, of course, not exist. Then, again, even though large numbers of intelligent and disciplined people, who had been educated to an appreciation of true marriage, would doubtless turn in disgust from a " matrimonial game of General Post," would such a game be repulsive to the considerable body of untrained and frivolous persons who at present, even with the help of our religious and state sanctions, are not inclined to regard either marriage or divorce with too much seriousness? Doubtless Mr. Carpenter would emphasize the supreme importance of training and preparation for the right use of the freedom that he extols. And here we are in hearty agreement with him. But does he duly appreciate the herculean nature of the task he sets humanity? To make over the ideals, customs and attitudes of the masses of the people toward the marriage relation, to prepare them to enter responsibly into true alliances of the spirit as of the flesh, unions wherein they strive, with no compulsion from public opinion, law or Church, to make their intimate relationship life-long, is to accomplish a magnificent reconstruction of human nature and human convention which must remain, it would seem, a vision for many generations to come. To be sure, there is reason to believe, as Mr. Carpenter points out, that " as the spiritual and emotional sides of man develop in relation to the physical, there is probably a tendency for our deeper alliances to become more unitary. Though it might be said that the growing complexity of man's nature would be likely to lead him into more rather than fewer relationships, yet on the other hand it is obvious that as the depth and subtlety of any attachment that will really hold him increases, so does such attachment become more permanent and durable, and less likely to be realized in a number of persons." [1] But does this monogamic tendency express itself in the greater or the lesser number of mankind? Divorces, not one but several granted to the same applicant, desertions of wife and children to form connections with new charmers, above all the existence of the social evil in our midst, all point to tendencies the reverse of monogamic.

Let not the above criticisms be interpreted to mean that the ideal of free spiritual marriage, so enthusiastically proclaimed by certain radical socialists, is merely visionary and forever impossible of realization. To many reflective men and women, who have learned to govern passion by an enlightened reason and sensitive regard for the rights of others, such a conception of free marriage, entered into with the hope and purpose of making it permanent, no doubt makes a moving appeal. And who shall say that when our girls and boys are one and all intelligently trained from early childhood in self-control and are inspired with the ideal of a true marriage that the vision of the socialists may not descend to earth?

But while conceding that the ideal in its purest form is not without beauty, we must recognize that there is in it, as usually presented, elements of undeniable dross. Mr. Carpenter does not hesitate to recognize that some natures will not be satisfied with a life-long union with one mate. Not content to make an urgent and, on the whole, sensible plea that married couples " come out of their secluded haven to reach a hand to others, or even to give some boon of affection to those who need it more than themselves," he goes on to declare that because of the variety of modes of loving " it does remain possible, in some cases for married persons to have in-

[1] *Love's Coming of Age,* p. 96.

timacies with outsiders and yet continue perfectly true to each other and in rare instances, *for triune and other such relations to be permanently maintained*." [1] And again, referring to " the enormous diversity of practice which has existed over the world in this matter of the relations of the sexes," the author suggests that we cannot venture " to put our finger down finally on any one custom or institution, and say, Here alone is the right way." Even polygamy, " supposing it really did spontaneously and naturally arise in a society which gave perfect freedom and independence to women in their relation to men, would be completely different in character from the old-world polygamy, and would cease to act as a degrading influence on women, since it would be the spontaneous expression of their attachment to each other and to a common husband; Monogamy, under similar circumstances, would lose its narrowness and stuffiness; and the life of the Hetaira, that is, of the woman who chooses to be the companion of more than one man, might not be without dignity, honor, and sincere attachment." [2]

It is conceivable that an age may dawn when such ideas will convey no sense of shock and outrage. But in this present era they offend not only our finer feeling, but also our intelligence. To the women and men the world over who have deeply loved, the notion that such love can maintain itself side by side with other similar loves for other men and women appears monstrous and absurd. Their own deepest experiences are its utter refutation. Nor does history furnish evidence to support such a conception. The supremely satisfying and ennobling marriages recorded in literature have been monogamous, not polyandrous or polygamous. Moreover society has, it would appear, pretty thoroughly learned its lesson that monogamic unions are best designed to secure the highest welfare of offspring by insuring the undivided love and care of the parents.

[1] *Love's Coming of Age*, p. 104. Italics mine.   [2] *Ibid.*, pp. 114–15.

The Views of Radical Feminists. *The Social Philosophy of Mr. George.* — In close sympathy with the Socialists on many issues affecting marriage and family life are the advanced leaders of the feminist propaganda. Of these, perhaps the Englishman, Mr. W. L. George, is as influential an exponent as any writer of the day. In a vigorous article entitled *Feminist Intentions* in the *Atlantic Monthly* for December, 1913, Mr. George boldly throws down the glove and enters the thick of the combat. " Convention," he says, " which is nothing but petrified habit, has lain upon woman perhaps more heavily than any law. . . . While the Suffragists wish to alter the law, the Feminists wish to alter also the conventions." And their first attack is upon the economic side, proceeding on two lines:

" 1. They intend to open occupations to women.

" 2. They intend to level the wages of women and men."

This economic change Mr. George does not hesitate in the least to aver " will be brought about by revolutionary methods, by sex strikes and sex wars." Indeed, he proclaims his " full sympathy " with such militant tactics on the ground (which is unfortunately solid enough) that " the sweated trades are almost entirely in the hands of women, — laundry, box-making, toys, artificial flowers and the like." So, likewise, " the underpaid trades are women's trades." Hence war on male monopoly of lucrative industries!

But the economic attack is only one aspect of the feminist war. Mr. George goes on to declare in no uncertain words that " the Feminists have designs upon the most fundamental of human institutions, marriage and motherhood." With all earnestness these radicals have set about the task of " training women's reason, to place her beyond the scope of mere emotion and mere prejudice, to enable her to judge, to select a mate for herself and a father for her children, — a double and necessary process." Now entire freedom of choice in marriage implies economic independence. Therefore the Feminists have adopted, as temporary measures, " the endowment of motherhood and the lien on wages." They lay down the principle " that a woman being incapacitated from work for a period of weeks or months while she is giving birth to a child, her liberty can be secured only if the fact of the birth gives her a call upon the state. Failing in that, she must have a male protector in whose favor she must abdicate her rights because he is her protector." Until women have achieved complete economic independence, feminists demand that every married woman who serves as a housekeeper " should be entitled to a proportion of the man's income or salary. . . ."

The above measures, however, are to be regarded as purely transitory makeshifts. It is in his statement of the ultimate aims of the feminists that Mr. George allies himself with the advanced radicals and parts company with his more moderate brethren. After declaring that the leaders of the feminist movement desire to " loosen the marriage tie," he goes on to explain that, as a temporary expedient they would " accept a partial extension of divorce facilities, subject to an adequate provision for all children." But quite frankly he states as his personal conviction " that the ultimate aim of Feminism with regard to marriage is the practical suppression of marriage and the institution of free alliance." However, Mr. George concedes that this end " will be attained only when socialization shall have been so complete that the human being will no longer require the law, but will be able to obey some obscure but noble categorical imperative; when men and women can associate voluntarily without thrall of the State, for the production and enjoyment of the goods of life." Many struggles will no doubt be necessary before this golden age of marital freedom shall be ushered in; and Mr. George believes that one of these struggles will have to do with " the ennobling of the nature of the male."

Free marriage, then, is one of the far-off goals toward which, in the view of our author, feminism is advancing. Another goal is the development on earth of " a new kind of matriarchate, that is to say . . . a state of society where man will not figure in the life of woman except as the father of her child." Already, he holds, certain radical women have come to " consider that the child is the expression of the feminine personality, while after the child's birth, the husband becomes a mere excrescence. They believe that the ' Wife ' should die in childbirth, and the ' Mother ' rise from her ashes." While Mr. George expressly disclaims anything utopian about this point of view, provided every woman can secure for herself an independent living, yet he attempts to reassure us by saying that he does not believe " it will be carried to extreme "; the reason being that " the association of human beings in couples appears to respond to some deep need." [1]

It is this last position that will, no doubt, evoke the sharpest criticism from moderate progressives as well as from dyed-in-the-wool conservatives. Instinctively they shrink with repugnance from such a one-sided view of the marriage relation as glorifies motherhood at the expense of the husband and father. Indeed, a telling criticism of this clause of the advanced feminist creed was not long in coming from the camp of the more cautious progressives. The writer says of Mr. George's view:

" This is bewildering. For many of us have supposed that the development of fatherhood has been one of the main lines of social progress: that the goal which society has been working toward is the equal comradeship of man and woman. If it is important to achieve this as regards all other aspects of life, why should we deliberately throw it away in the one that touches us most deeply? It is worth any price, it is what spiritualizes passion and makes of marriage something a thought more wonderful than friendship. And now to forget, to be blind to the infinite desirability of men and women

[1] W. L. George, *Feminist Intentions*, in *Atlantic Monthly*, Vol. 112, No. 6, pp. 721-32.

standing together as regards the most precious thing they can create and possess, the child, — any one who can do this would seem to have strayed so far as to have forfeited all claim to be listened to." [1]

The Theories of Ellen Key. — Let it not be supposed that all feminists are in entire agreement with Mr. George. Among this group may be found all shades of belief and of selective emphasis with respect to the various planks of the feminist social platform. Foremost among the prophets of a new order in which Love shall come to his own is Ellen Key, the gifted Swedish author. Quite simply and naturally she proclaims her creed: Love is the supreme enhancement of life: and the enhancement of life is a religion in itself. " Love . . . has now become a great spiritual power, a form of genius comparable with any other creative force in the domain of culture, and its production in that region is just as important as in the so-called natural field. Just as we now recognize the right of the artist to shape his work, or of the scientific man to carry out his investigations as it seems good to him, so must we allow love the right to employ its creative force in its own way provided only that in one way or another it finally conduces to the general good." [2] The only standard of morality Love can accept is the enhancement of life. " The new conception of morality grows out of the hope of the gradual ascent of the race towards greater perfection." Believing, as the writer ardently does believe, in the power of love to heighten all other human values she accords ideal passion highest place in the great work of perfecting life. But to accomplish its supreme mission the unity of love and marriage must be maintained; and this implies Love's freedom. " It is true that the idea of unity involves the right of every person to shape his sexual life in accordance with his individual needs, but only

[1] Elizabeth Woodbridge, *The Unknown Quantity in the Woman Problem,* in *Atlantic Monthly*, April, 1914, p. 520.
[2] *Love and Marriage* (New York, 1911), p. 46.

on condition that he does not prejudice unity or the rights of the beings to whom his love gives life. *Love thus becomes more and more a private affair of the individual, while children are more and more the business of society. . . ."* [1] When the young have been educated to a pure and intense appreciation of the enhancement of life that springs from a great love, then coercive marriage and prostitution will alike disappear as no longer meeting the needs of humanity.

No doubt there arises in the reader's mind a question concerning the possibility of loving more than once where love is quite free from external control. The author attacks this problem with entire frankness. Great souls can doubtless " love several times without becoming erotically depreciated, . . . But this is not the spiritual soil or climate of humanity at large." [2] Nevertheless, since love is a gracious gift to life's elect, " *There can be no other standard of morality for him who loves more than once than for him who loves once only:* that of the enhancement of life. He who . . . is prompted anew to magnanimity and truth, to gentleness and generosity, he who finds strength as well as intoxication in his new love, nourishment, as well as a feast — that man has a right to the experience." [3]

But once more questions arise and will not down. Suppose the person who loves again — and again — is already bound to one who was gladly and freely chosen? And suppose that there are children of the union? Undaunted by these possibilities Ellen Key upholds the doctrine of freedom in divorce, as in marriage, both matters being held to be personal and outside the control of the state. She believes that " those who thoughtlessly separated . . . would be the same class of people who now, in coercive marriage, secretly deceive one another "; whereas to " the serious, divorce will always be serious. Before a person of feeling and thought consciously hurts another who has loved or loves him, he himself has

---

[1] *Ibid.*, p. 24. [2] *Ibid.*, p. 38. [3] *Ibid.*, p. 39.

suffered terrible pain. Gratitude for a great devotion in a free connection has often proved more powerfully binding than the law could have been." [1] As for the children, surely loveless homes or homes in which bickering and antagonism are uppermost are not good nurseries for the young. However, the author freely concedes that children must be considered when a new union is contemplated. If the divorce is sought because a new love has come into the life of one of the pair, " then this father or mother must be prepared one day — when the children can understand them — to justify the step by showing them how the new love has made him or her a richer and greater personality. The children have a full right not to be sacrificed to the degradation of their parents." But, the reader may well ask: Who will enforce this right? On this point the author remains silent. If love is wholly free to bind or to loose, then the right of the offspring " not to be sacrificed " rests solely on the nobility and strength of their parents' characters. Should these be neither strong nor noble, there is no help for the children. Clearly the social theory of Ellen Key is open to the same objections brought forward in the case of Socialists and other radicals. Its success is wholly dependent upon a far completer moralization of mankind than exists at present.

Because she believes in " the simultaneous enhancement of the feeling of love and the racial sense " Ellen Key becomes the apostle of a new sexual morality " where the light as in Correggio's *Night*, will radiate from the child. . . ." The perfect marriage is the union of souls and bodies of which children are the living symbols. Yet the author condemns unsparingly " all irresponsible parentage " and " all parentage of immature or degenerate persons," and calls for " limitation of the freedom not of love, but of procreation, when the conditions are unfavorable to the race." While she does not deny the right of man and woman " to enter upon their union with

[1] *Love and Marriage*, p. 328.

the resolve not to become parents" when such resolve makes for social betterment, she stamps as immoral "all voluntary sterility of married people fitted for the increase of the race." Very earnestly the author urges upon all who use "Love's Freedom" that they measure the genuineness of their love by the degree in which it "finally conduces to the common good. From this point of view, then, we cannot extend the proposition that love is an end in itself so far as to say that *it may remain unfruitful*. It must give life; if not new living beings then new values; it must enrich the lovers themselves and through them mankind." [1] Scant sympathy has Ellen Key with those "cerebral, amaternal women [who] must obviously be accorded the freedom of finding the domestic life, with its limited but intensive exercise of power, meagre beside the feeling of power which they enjoy as public personalities, as consummate women of the world, as talented professionals." Let them go their misguided way provided they do not "*falsify life values in their own favor* so that they shall represent the highest form of life, the 'human personality,' in comparison with which the 'instinctive feminine' signifies a lower stage of development, a poorer type of life." [2] To Ellen Key the domestic sphere of the wife and mother who loves greatly is surpassing rich beside that of her loveless professional sister. It is just at this point that she breaks company with radical feminists. Hers is the Gospel of Love, not the stirring war-cry of equal rights. While demanding for her sex ample social and educational opportunities, she yet feels that for most women, no matter how cultured and capable, the Home, in which Love dwells and children call for the intelligent care of the mother, will provide a sphere of work both varied and stimulating, especially if it be in close touch with the larger life of the community.

The Doctrine of Economic Freedom for Married Women. — There is another group of feminists whose chief interest it is

[1] *Ibid.*, p. 47. [2] *The Woman Movement.*

2 L

to minimize the importance of woman's sex attributes and to emphasize her mission as a social worker, laboring shoulder to shoulder with man in every field of human endeavor. This school deprecates such doctrines as are preached by Ellen Key, and urges that women have too long been regarded from the single viewpoint of their functions as wives and mothers. It is time, they declare, to admit frankly and without reservation that women have an important, nay an indispensable, part to perform in the vast sum of the world's work. The functions of a man as husband and father by no means absorb all his energy and interest: why should the correlative functions of the woman occupy all her time and thought? Perhaps the ablest exponent of the evils of an over-emphasis upon the sex characteristics of woman and an under-emphasis upon her capacities as a creator and a worker is Mrs. Charlotte Perkins Gilman. Attacking the age-old economic dependence of women upon men she writes: " For, in her position of chronic dependence in the sex-relation, sex-distinction is with her not only a means of attracting a mate, but a means of getting her livelihood; as is the case with no other creature under heaven. Because of the economic dependence of the human female on her mate, she is modified to sex in an excessive degree." [1]

Life, Mrs. Gilman holds, is largely made up of action along the two main lines of race-preservation and self-preservation. Now, whereas in race-preservation the sexes have different organs and functions, in self-preservation " male and female have the same organs, the same functions, the same lines of action." All " the varied activities of economic production and distribution, all our arts and industries, crafts and trades, all our growth in science, discovery, government, religion, — these are along the line of self-preservation: these are or should be common to both sexes. To teach, to rule, to make, to decorate, to distribute, — these are not sex functions:

[1] *Women and Economics*, pp. 38–9.

they are race functions. Yet so inordinate is the sex distinction of the human race that the whole field of human progress has been considered a masculine prerogative." [1] In consequence of their narrow restriction to the home with its individual interests women are " more personal than men, more personally sensitive, less willing to ' stand in line ' and ' take turns,' less able to see why a general restriction is just when it touches them or their children." [2]

But nowadays all this is gradually changing for the better. Women are demanding work outside the home not only that they may attain financial independence but for the sake of self-expression. And, in the opinion of the author, this is wholly good. She believes that such free participation in the work of society does not prevent woman from fulfilling her functions of motherhood. Indeed, the " over-development of sex caused by her economic dependence on the male reacts unfavorably upon her essential duties. She is too female for perfect motherhood. Her excessive specialization in the secondary sexual characteristics is a detrimental element in heredity." [3] Over-specialization in sex attributes is chiefly responsible for the " small, weak, soft, ill-proportioned women " of whom there are too many. Furthermore, in Mrs. Gilman's view, when we consider " the few admittedly able mothers " and the " many painfully unable ones " we are driven to the conclusion that " there is nothing in the achievements of human motherhood to prove that it is for the advantage of the race to have women give all their time to it. Giving all their time to it does not improve it either in quantity or quality. The woman who works is usually a better reproducer than the woman who does not. And the woman who does not work is not proportionately a better educator." [4]

Having thus demolished, to her satisfaction, the theory of the superior fitness of the human mother when compared

[1] *Ibid.*, p. 52.   [2] *Ibid.*, pp. 83–4.   [3] *Ibid.*, p. 182.   [4] *Ibid.*, pp. 190–1.

with the mother among the lower animals, Mrs. Gilman goes on to make her final points. If women are, at the same time, to be wives and mothers on the one hand and independent workers outside the home on the other, there must be " a change in the home and family relation. . . . This will, of course, require the introduction of some other form of living than that which now obtains. It will render impossible the present method of feeding the world by means of millions of private servants, and bringing up children by the same hand." [1] The " segregation of an entire sex " to the function of food preparation has not been an unmitigated success. " The art and science of cooking involve a large and thorough knowledge of nutritive value and of the laws of physiology and hygiene." Few women have received the necessary training which would make them skilful food providers and cooks. The same holds true of housekeeping and the expert work of rearing and educating children. Such large tasks should be performed by specialists, leaving the woman free " for full individual expression in her economic activities and in her social relations. . . ." At this point Mrs. Gilman paints a glowing picture of the apartment-house home of the future.

" The apartments would be without kitchens; but there would be a kitchen belonging to the house from which meals could be served to families in their rooms, or in a common dining room as preferred. It would be a home where the cleaning was done by efficient workers, not hired separately by the families, but engaged by the manager of the establishment; and a roof-garden, day nursery, and kindergarten, under well-trained professional nurses and teachers, would insure proper care of the children." [2] If " housekeeping " were taken out of our homes, "the union of individuals in marriage would not compel the jumbling together of all the external machinery of their lives, — a process in which much of the delicacy and freshness of love, to say nothing of the

[1] *Women and Economics*, pp. 210-11.   [2] *Ibid.*, p. 242.

power of mutual rest and refreshment, is constantly lost." [1] Then, too, when children are not so exclusively under the fond care of their mothers, but are brought up in nurseries and kindergartens by experts they will learn " peaceful lessons of equality and common interest instead of the feverish personality of the isolated one-baby household, or the innumerable tyrannies and exactions, the forced submissions and exclusions, of the nursery full of brothers and sisters of widely differing ages and powers." [2]

It is only fair to say that any impartial critic of these feminist views must concede at the outset that they embody a large amount of truth and common sense. Unquestionably sex distinctions have been overemphasized by both men and women in the past with distinctly harmful results. It is equally true that economic dependence has been largely responsible for the subordination of women in the past and their relative lack of influence in the present. Again, it may freely be granted that the qualities necessary " to teach, to rule, to make, to decorate, to distribute " are not sex qualities, but human qualities shared by women as well as men. But *is it true* that women would be better wives and mothers, especially the latter, if they devoted from six to eight hours daily to the exacting and often exhausting demands of some business or profession? Is it true that the " woman who works is usually a better reproducer than the woman who does not? " Certainly it is not if the large body of women workers in factories be considered. The evidence here goes to show that exacting labor under pressure carried on to within a few days of confinement is distinctly harmful to both mother and offspring. Has Mrs. Gilman collected evidence to establish her position with reference to other lines of work or is her statement the uncritical pronouncement of a partisan? This is no idle question. Much hinges upon our accurate knowledge of the effects of industrial or professional work,

[1] *Ibid.*, p. 299.　　　　　　[2] *Ibid.*, p. 288.

with its usual accompaniment of nervous strain and long hours, upon the health of prospective mothers.

Again, is Mrs. Gilman justified in discounting almost to zero the value of mothers both as the nurses and first teachers of their children? Can any expert nurse and kindergartner make up to a little child for the loss of his mother's loving personal services, her sympathetic insight into his individual nature with its peculiar weaknesses and strengths and needs? It is in no spirit of weak sentimentality or tradition worship that psychologists and social writers tell us no substitute has yet been found for the intelligent mother as a developer of the personality, the individual qualities, of her offspring. Can this fact be ignored in any fair-minded discussion of this vexed question? When we read the feminist's enthusiastic praise of experts as the best rearers of the nation's children and the best home-makers, we may, perhaps, come to somewhat the same conclusion as a contemporary writer who says: " It does not require much scrutiny to discover that if we want any particular thing done in the best way we must go to the expert. The question is, whether this is the best way for society to do things. It is rather generally assumed that it is. And yet there is another theory which casts doubt upon this : the theory that it is better for anyone to do many things for himself, even if he does them rather badly, than for him to have them done — even better done — for him. . . . It all depends on whether your eyes are fixed on the people who are doing the things or on the things they are doing. If it is the things, go to the expert. If it is the people, don't." [1] From this point of view women grow into better mothers and home-makers, not by turning over these duties to others, but by performing them with what skill and intelligence they may and learning from experience what home-making and motherhood mean.

[1] Elizabeth Woodbridge, *The Unknown Quantity in the Woman Problem* (in *Atlantic Monthly*, April 19, 1914 , p. 519).

But, you may ask, do not home and children suffer far more from these loving but ill-directed efforts than from the efficient services of trained specialists, however much these latter may be deficient in personal interest and affection for those they serve? It is probable that in some instances, where the woman shows little aptitude for household affairs or for mother tasks, the home would profit by her extra-domestic labor, the proceeds of which would secure the services of a good cook and nurse-maid. But can we lump all wives and mothers together and say of them that they would better turn over their housekeeping affairs to skilled cooks and cleaners and their children to trained nurses and kinder-gartners? There is a wholesale and indiscriminate quality about such a programme that should render us cautious of accepting it. Married women engaged in gainful occupations outside the home are still a small minority of all married women, although they are steadily on the increase. Surely it is quite practicable for married women not inclined toward professional or business life to receive such just recognition of their economic value as home-makers and their social value as nurses and educators of the rising generation that their financial independence may be assured.

There is another and more powerful argument against withdrawing completely from the housewife and mother the tasks which she has so long performed. Will not a certain spiritual satisfaction that is born of loving personal services freely rendered to make home a better and happier place to live in be irrevocably lost to the woman who employs specialists to care for house and children? It is this idea that Elizabeth Woodbridge emphasizes in criticising Mr. W. L. George's description of a feminist home. " I imagine the Feminist home," writes Mr. George, " rather as a large block of flats in a garden over a common restaurant: the staff is directed by an elected manageress and her deputy . . . a competent kitchen staff under a well-paid chef, prepares *table-d'hote* meals for the lazy and a lengthy *à la carte* bill for the fastidious. . . . Everything that can be done to throw the business of the household upon a salaried staff is done." [1]

This picture Miss Woodbridge does not hesitate to characterize as " bleak "; and perhaps many readers who have not forgotten what real homes are like may be inclined to agree with her. " The home," says our critic, " if it is anything, is a spiritual reality. But we are so constituted that we have to get at the spiritual through the physical. . . . The things we most care for . . . the spiritual rewards — seem to come always as by-products. . . . And so, in the case of the home, if, in one extreme there is danger of submerging its significance in the mass of its physical expressions, there is at the other extreme the danger of dissipating significance through a paucity of physical expression. . . . Detail is stultifying only if it is not vitalized. . . . Concretely, the detail of home management is not to be despised and evaded, it is to be valued and seized upon and made vital. Mr. George considers it an obstacle. I consider it both a means and an end." [2]

Yet, even if the meaning of " home " in its full blessedness come only to the wife and mother who, working through the medium of material things, is rewarded with rare spiritual values, it must be admitted that the trend is away from home management by unskilled housewives and toward centralizing all these processes in the hands of experts. The family " apartments " of Mrs. Gilman with their " roof-garden, day nursery and kindergarten " may as yet be visions rather than realities, but who can say that they will not be widely established before many years? Already the labor of women has been greatly lessened by the economic movements that have carried one industry after another out of the

---

[1] Quoted in Miss Woodbridge's article, *The Unknown Quantity in the Woman Problem, op. cit.*, pp. 517-18. [2] *Ibid.*, pp. 517-18.

kitchen and the home. Even now a growing band of women are electing to continue after marriage the vocation for which they are specially trained. We must reckon with the facts. Nor can we decide offhand whether the home will be greatly the loser if these tendencies continue. To quote Miss Woodbridge once more: " How this is affecting the home, whether it is helping it or destroying it, whether it is developing some group-form of social life other than the family form, and whether this would be a good thing or a bad thing — these are questions which we cannot help debating even though we have as yet few data to go on."

This much, perhaps, we can safely say, — that, in view of the complexity of the whole question, each case involving the regular labor of married women outside the home must be decided individually on its merits.[1]

Views of the Conservative Group. — In the camp of the conservatists fewer differences of opinion on vital issues may be discovered than is the case among their radical opponents, the reason being that the conservative party is chiefly concerned in maintaining the *status quo*. Yet in defence of their position they make use of arguments drawn from such diverse sources as religion and biology. Indeed the rich field of biological science has been as eagerly and confidently drawn upon by conservatives as by radicals, thus furnishing one more proof of the theory that any complex body of knowledge may be made to serve quite opposite points of view, if only the principle of selection be discriminately used. The theories of both the theological and the bio-sociological groups deserve further consideration.

The Religious Conservatives. — This party, of course, plants itself squarely on the ground that monogamous marriage is a divine institution and therefore is indissoluble or at least (as in the theory of Anglicans and Episcopalians)

[1] See the excellent discussion of this question in Mrs. Anna Garlin Spencer's book, *Woman's Share in Social Culture*, ch. VI.

is dissoluble only for the cause of adultery. Perhaps the sanest presentment of the pro-Catholic point of view is furnished by Dr. Foerster, Professor of Education in the University of Vienna, in his temperate study of *Marriage and the Sex Problem*.[1] At the outset the author declares his belief that individual reason and conscience " are in need of training, purification and liberation, and of constant intercourse with a higher wisdom before the direction of our life can be entrusted to them. Faith in God, emancipation through Christ, and guidance by a great tradition, show our reason the way to the widest knowledge and save it from the bypaths and precipices of subjective folly and mere individual speculation." [2] This is, beyond question, the traditional position of Christianity. Only when the individual approaches any difficult world question with certain theological preconceptions can he find truth. It is hardly necessary to point out that this attitude is opposed to that of science which enjoins upon the seekers after knowledge the cultivation of an open mind, stripped of all bias or preference.

Having stated his general attitude toward his problem, Professor Foerster makes an eloquent plea for the retention of the " old ethics " so bitterly attacked by Ellen Key. He declares that religious ethics " does not despise the sensuous feelings . . . its sole object is the complete subordination of the sensuous and natural man to the needs of the spiritual man! As a necessary consequence of this position it demands the absolute rejection of all sex relationships outside marriage." Monogamous marriage as at present contracted and solemnized is a sacred form " and follows from the essential nature of Christianity, because its earnestness and its solemn dedication possess the greatest educational value for human nature and afford the greatest outward protection against the impulses of the sensuous world and the glamour of irresponsible feeling." [3] Those radical leaders who pro-

[1] New York, 1912.   [2] *Op. cit.*, p. 10.   [3] *Ibid.*, pp. 23–4.

claim freedom in love and marriage " are obsessed by a great illusion due to their remoteness from real life ; they believe that men will bow to the moral necessities of social life with no motive other than an enlightened sense of social interest." Only after the doctrine of " the right to sex life " has borne terrible fruit in a complete departure from " the old moral grooves " will the abstract reformers " understand that they had overestimated human nature, and that the moral discipline and social education of man is an infinitely more difficult task than they have been wont to believe." [1] A rigid form of marriage is essential to mankind ; it represents his " firm and lasting ego." " It deprives the individual of his freedom of action and hampers him most strongly precisely in that region of life where he is most in danger of making momentous decisions profoundly affecting another life, at a time when he is not in his most responsible condition."

Free love is not a healthy doctrine, since it would emancipate the erotic impulses of the individual at the expense of other powers and demands of his nature, thus destroying the unity of his inner life and rendering it difficult, if not impossible, for him to view his life as a whole consisting of many needs, many responsibilities. " *He who breaks away from the whole and resigns his responsibilities himself ceases to be a whole :* the economy of his own personality goes to pieces : . . ." [2] Far is it from being true that " free love emancipates us from cramping and outworn restraints." If all religious bonds were removed from sexual relations, numbers of weak people " who are to-day saved by the rigid and sacred form from the tyranny of the lower powers within themselves, and constantly reminded of their better selves, will then come to curse the freedom which has made them slaves." [3]

Then, too, the whole question should be looked at from the child's point of view. It is a fundamental right of childhood to possess a mother and a father. Here the exponents of

[1] *Ibid.*, pp. 29–30.   [2] *Ibid.*, p. 35.   [3] *Ibid.*, p. 37.

free love are guilty of gross inconsistency. " That is to say, for the parents they demand individualism and the free development of personality; while for the children they advocate a governmental upbringing which would tend in the highest degree towards uniformity and impersonal development, thus injuring in the deepest possible way, the very cause in the name of which all their theories are advanced." [1] Moreover, the child brought up in a state institution loses that valuable social training in " responsibility, sympathy, self-control, mental toleration and mental education " which it has been the supreme social function of the monogamic family to give. " And it fills this central place precisely because it is lifelong and indissoluble, and because, through its performance, the community of life in the family becomes deeper, firmer and more manifold than in any other human relationship." [2]

The author then turns to a discussion of the widespread tendency toward the voluntary restriction of families. He boldly declares that even " the most excessive production of children could not endanger women so greatly or so deeply undermine the true necessities of their existence as will the artificial restriction of the family. For such methods unleash the male sex passion by relieving it of all sense of responsibility for the results of its indulgence. The true cure for the evils of excessive childbirth is to be found in man's mastery of his sexual nature which will ensure the liberation of the woman from every species of sexual slavery." [3]

There is much high ethical idealism as well as wholesome sense in Dr. Foerster's philosophy of marriage. The author is probably right when he says that the " earnestness and solemn dedication " of the Christian marriage service " possess the greatest educational value for human nature and afford the greatest outward protection against the impulses of the sensuous world and the glamour of irresponsible feeling."

[1] *Op. cit.*, p. 47.   [2] *Ibid.*, p. 50.   [3] *Ibid.*, pp. 92–101.

Men and women, ill-trained in self-restraint and only dully responsive to the call of personal obligation and social duty — and we know there are many such — need the support that is furnished by the public marriage service with its solemn religious ritual. For such persons the doctrine of " the right to sex life " is a dangerous one; and its general acceptance at this stage of moral development would probably have immeasurably harmful social consequences. Until mankind has learned to govern erotic impulses — powerful and compelling as they are — by an enlightened regard for personal and public good, " free love " might easily result in that division of the soul life, that pulling of other impulses and moral demands against the controlling love passion which, carried to extremes, means the disintegration of personality. This is one of the strongest arguments advanced by Dr. Foerster. Since man's nature is many-sided, no one impulse can be enthroned at the expense of others without a disastrous crumbling of the inner self.

Again, the argument from the child's point of view is a forceful one. If " free love " means that " individualism and the free development of personality " are restricted to adults while children are reared in public institutions, admirably designed to discourage individuality, and to produce uniformity, then " free love " is a profoundly insincere and mistaken doctrine. But *does* the theory involve this? Certainly not, in the view of Ellen Key, whose social philosophy is a very apotheosis of motherhood, proclaiming, as it does, that to cherish the sacred individuality of her child is the noblest task of every mother. But Dr. Foerster, to strengthen his own case, has turned from the Swedish advocate of free love to other exponents who do not hesitate thus to sacrifice the offspring for the sake of the parents.

Two other sound theories of our author may be briefly touched upon : First, it can hardly be disputed that permanent marriage alone makes possible that " community of life in

526 The Family as a Social and Educational Institution

the family" which "becomes deeper, firmer and more manifold than in any other human relationship." And this community of life, if wisely directed by parents worthy of their responsible mission, may make of the family the most far-reaching educative influence that society has yet developed. More than this — although the author does not make this point — is not the persistent continuity of family life strongly to be recommended on the ground that, amid the multiplicity of interests and demands so characteristic of life in modern society, men and women need to find permanence somewhere, to know that *home abides* — a haven of refuge from the flux of things? With the possibility of repeated changes in family personnel and relations (and its actuality in many cases) what enduring element other than religion remains to which our divided lives may be securely anchored? The second point made by the author that women be released from " sexual slavery," not by artificial restraints upon conception, but solely by the method of increased self-control, seems a sound one in principle although no doubt admitting exceptions.

But when full recognition of the sanity of many of Dr. Foerster's positions has been accorded, it is probable that the reader will feel dissatisfied with his solution of the problems of sex and marriage. In the first place few educated men and women of the present day will be willing to surrender their individual judgment, trained more or less to unbiassed conclusions, into the keeping of the Church, and to return to the religious idea of marriage as a sacrament whose form is a sacred symbol. Imbued, as they are, with the Lutheran conception of marriage as a social institution and a social contract, they are disposed to criticise its workings as impartially as those of any other institution of society that is out of gear. Nothing is plainer in the history of the family than the drift of marriage and divorce from the custody of religion to the custody of the State, and the accompanying tendency on the part of individuals to consider its problems in the light of reason and experience rather than in the light of theological dogmas.

But this is not all. Dr. Foerster's greatest strength lies in his attack upon the advocates of greater freedom in love and marriage. He criticises them, justly, it appears, for failing to take account of the weakness of human nature, of its proneness to throw off all moral bonds under the influence of sex passion. But does not the conservative critic fail quite as conspicuously as his radical opponents to take note of actual conditions when he proclaims his theory of indissoluble marriage? No idealistic sentiment, no preaching of the doctrine of the sacredness of marriage as a divine institution will purify or dignify many ill-mated unions. In the interests of morality itself, of a fine erotic idealism, marriages that have brought little but constant misunderstandings and bitter alienations should be terminated. Nor does mere separation meet the needs of the case. Why should a couple who have made, perhaps in entire good faith, a disastrous mistake in marriage, be forever prevented from forming another and perhaps worthier union in the light of their hard-won experience? Again, why should one loyal partner pay to the end of life in single loneliness for the disloyalty of the other? Indissoluble marriage has been tried for centuries and its failure to meet present conditions and standards is evident, not only by the increased facilities for divorce offered in most civilized countries but in the growth of an overwhelming sentiment, among reflective men and women, in favor of dissolving permanently unsuccessful marriages under limitations fixed by the State. Nor can the argument of the harm done to children by divorce be allowed too much weight. No one will deny that children are best reared by both father and mother in homes where love is. But when love gives place to indifference, and in some cases to an antagonism which at last, under the strain of daily friction, breaks down the barriers of decent reserve and restraint, children are made vastly better off by the separation of their parents. In such an atmosphere of bitterness and recrimination no child can be brought up without grave risk that his ideas of marriage and family life will be permanently distorted and degraded. Better divorce and the care of one parent than " continuity of family life " where strife and not love prevails.

The Conservatives of the Bio-sociological School.—One of the leading representatives of this group is the Englishman, Mr. Grant Allen. His position, grounded in biology, can be briefly summed up. As an opening gun the writer quite confidently declares that if " every woman married and every woman had four children, the population would remain just stationary." [1] Death, infertility or incapacity for marriage will account for two out of every four children, leaving two to replace their parents and reproduce at the same rate. Obviously, if this be true, and if " some women shirk their natural duties, then a heavier task must be laid upon the remainder." But this is an unjust burden for the faithful to have to carry. Moreover, many marriages and smaller families mean, on the average, healthier, better fed and better reared children. Therefore the author urges that many women should marry and raise families if society is to prosper. A little farther on Mr. Allen rather surprisingly announces himself as in sympathy with the demand of the modern woman for emancipation. " Only," he quickly adds, " her emancipation must not be of a sort that interferes in any way with this prime natural necessity. To the end of all time, it is mathematically demonstrable that most women must become the mothers of at least four children or else the race must cease to exist. Any supposed solution of the woman problem, therefore, which fails to look this fact straight in the face, is a false solution. It cries ' Peace, Peace ! ' where there is no peace." [2]

[1] *Plain Words on the Woman Question* (in *Fortnightly Review*, October, 1889, pp. 448–58).   [2] *Ibid.*, p. 450.

Now if a woman performs her paramount social duty and
bears four or five children, she must give up at least ten or
twelve of the best years of her life to this work.   During this
period "women can't conveniently earn their own livelihood";
therefore, in the opinion of Mr. Grant Allen, " they must
be provided for by the labour of the men — under existing
circumstances (in favour of which I have no Philistine prejudice) by their own husbands."   Indeed the author is inclined
to think that " in consideration of the special burden [women]
have to bear in connection with reproduction all the rest of life
should be made as light and easy and free for them as possible."[1]
On their part women should see to it " that their training and
education should fit them above everything else for this their
main function in life ; . . ."   A profound mistake was made a
generation ago when the need for the reform of women's education was generally felt.   Instead of " educating them like
men — giving a like training for totally unlike functions,"
women should have been educated " to suckle strong and intelligent children and to order well a wholesome, beautiful,
reasonable household." [2]

After reflection upon this strenuous plea to women to
marry and rear a goodly family of children it may occur to
some reader to suggest that the disparity in numbers between
males and females in England and in sections of America makes
it impossible for many women to find mates unless polygamy
once more come into good repute.   But Mr. Allen has considered this situation and assures us that it is a passing one,
due to the emigration of men in eastern America to the West
and the withdrawal of Englishmen into the army, the navy
and the colonies.   The author holds it to be a most unlucky
fact that the Woman's Rights movement should have coin-
cided with a dearth of men in the middle and upper classes.
This condition has led advanced feminists to take the view that
it is possible and desirable for the mass of women to be " self-

[1] *Ibid.*, pp. 451–2.   [2] *Ibid.*, p. 453.

2 м

supporting spinsters." Such a woman the author elects to regard as " an abnormality," to be reckoned with, of course, and accorded fair play, but still "a deplorable accident of the passing moment." [1]

Perhaps the first criticism of the above views which suggests itself is concerned with Mr. Allen's statement that to " the end of all time it is mathematically demonstrable that most women must become the mothers of at least four children or else the race must cease to exist." Is this " mathematically demonstrable," we may ask, or is the enormous decrease in child mortality within the past decade, when taken in connection with the lower adult death rate in many civilized countries, even now a partial refutation of the theory? Again, while conceding that individual preference should yield, where it is clearly necessary, to the public good *does* the welfare of society require that the great majority of married women be once more strictly relegated to the domestic sphere — to the task of maintaining households and rearing children? Certainly the tendency is rather toward broadening and deepening the social interests and activities of wives. Gradually the idea is dawning upon the world that no woman can represent the highest ideal of wife and mother who does not concern herself with the problems of municipal and national economy, with questions concerning sanitation, pure food supply, adequate police protection and education in its Protean aspects. Moreover, why should it be assumed, as it so often is by men and women alike, that household management is or should be attractive to all women — that it is the " natural " sphere of women? Granted that a well-conducted home requires wide knowledge of hygiene, sanitation, food values, textile values, household decoration, the arts of buying and consuming wisely, yet it hardly follows that this field of work, however broad, will appeal to every daughter of Eve. Would it not be as reasonable to descant on the social value of the pro-

[1] *Op. cit.*, p. 455.

fessions of law, medicine, engineering or what you will and then insist that a majority of men choose that sphere? Of course it may be said that society is in urgent need of home-makers, whereas the other vocations can safely be left to individual choice. But might not society itself profit more from the intelligent extra-home labor of a trained woman who can afford to pay specialists to do her household tasks, than from her half-reluctant and inefficient work within the home?

But the matter does not end here. Is it not a little unintelligent to urge that the education of all women be determined wholly to the one end of enabling them " to suckle strong and intelligent children and to order well a wholesome, beautiful, reasonable household . . ."? Might it not be profitable and enlightening to inquire how many young men and women will, in all probability, remain unmarried if the future may be foretold in terms of the present, and to recognize that social conditions themselves are largely responsible for the undue proportion of bachelors and spinsters in our midst? So long as salaries and wages are low and increase slowly while the standards of living remain relatively high; so long as young men, ambitious to attain distinction in their chosen field of work, can be comfortably provided for in "bachelor quarters"; so long as young women are trained to think, to work, to be financially independent and self-reliant at all times; and so long as our present social scheme affords relatively few opportunities for self-supporting young men and women to meet and know each other; just so long will there be a large and perhaps increasing number of unmarried men and women in society. Is this group of women a negligible factor, a passing " abnormality "? Time will show; but it seems highly inadvisable at present to mould the education of girls solely with a view to their work in homes which many will never enjoy.

Beyond doubt the doctrines in Mr. Allen's frankly stated social philosophy that will arouse the most hostile criticism are those which appear to undermine the economic independence of women, so newly won and as yet so incomplete. Active hostility will certainly be aroused among all women who have attained any sense of personal power and initiative by the author's statement that, in consideration of the burden of reproduction they have to bear, " all the rest of life should be made as light and easy and free for them as possible." Such a theory seems to push women back into the Oriental position of pampered weaklings, kept in luxury and ease, so far as is practicable, in order that they may perform their sole function of bearing and bearing again to replenish the race. In a day and generation when girls are educated to think straight and act efficiently in many walks of life, a doctrine such as this, framed solely, and even then, narrowly, from the standpoint of social need, sounds strange and not a little offensive.

Even more unwelcome to the modern woman will be the outspoken views of Mr. Ferrero, the talented Italian historian, who also aligns himself with the bio-sociological conservatives. Setting for himself the problem of discovering the " natural " conditions of a woman's life, Mr. Ferrero turns to biology for an answer. He finds that " the physiological prosperity of species depends on division of labor between the sexes, for in exact ratio to this is the duration of life." [1] Among insects, where division of labor rarely exists, the duration of life is short. Ants, bees and wasps, on the contrary, among which division of labor is very marked, live long. Likewise, among birds and the higher animals, such as monkeys, gorillas and apes, where the task of defending the female and young and providing them with food falls to the male, the duration of life is relatively long. But, on passing upward in the scale of life to primitive man, the author is confronted with a serious difficulty in the application of his theory. Nothing is better established than the fact that, among savages, women are ruthlessly exploited and their labor as tillers of the soil, burden

[1] *The Problem of Women from a Bio-Sociological Point of View* (in the *Monist*, IV, No. 2, pp. 262-3).

bearers, food preparers, makers of leather, pottery, clothing, etc., is indispensable to the maintenance of primitive society. Here is division of labor, to be sure, but a division which assigns to women by far the more burdensome tasks. However, Mr. Ferrero gets around this contradictory fact by the assertion that " this is merely a passing phase, a very dangerous aberration, produced by the excessive selfishness of man, which does not and cannot last long." [1] Where such division of labor does continue the group remains in a savage state.

In civilized society the writer grants that it " is a more difficult matter to prove that the labor of women . . . is unnatural; for it is so recent a phenomenon that the harmful results which all unnatural conditions of life produce are in its case difficult to demonstrate." Nevertheless the author does not hesitate to stamp female labor as " pathological," unnecessary for the production of sufficient wealth to supply human wants, and serving to lower the marketable value of male labor. Clearly Mr. Ferrero means by " female labor " the work of women outside the home, for he can hardly be ignorant of the very strenuous industries of a productive sort carried on by housewives for scores of centuries. That he ignores this phase of woman's labor and confines his strictures to extra-domestic work is shown by his statements respecting the strain of factory life upon women and the increase of mortality among those women and children pressed into the ranks of industrial workers.

But the reader is tempted to think that the most moving reason for Mr. Ferrero's objection to the labor of women outside the home is neither biological nor social, but personal and masculine. This reason he frankly states to be that men wish a woman " to be to us beautiful and attractive, her whole person, her dress, manners, her ideas and words filled with exquisite grace. . . . A perfect woman should be a *chef d'œuvre* of grace and refinement, and to this end she must be exempt

[1] *Ibid.*, pp. 266–7.

from toil. . . . The working woman grows ugly and loses her feminine characteristics, she loses what is most exquisite and æsthetic in woman." [1] Moreover, if the "lady," though working far less than man, " still benefits more than he from the effects of civilization, this should alone suffice to demonstrate the unreasonableness of labor. Nature's great aim is the economy of forces. How absurd is it, then, that a human being should expend painful energy in attaining a certain point when he can get to precisely the same point without expenditure of labor at all." [2] Only " women of genius, possessing unusual intellectual qualities, have the right to labor like men."

It would be hard to find in modern literature a more frank and naïve exposition of the long-lived masculine theory that women are made primarily for the pleasure and satisfaction of men. Be it granted that Mr. Ferrero stresses the æsthetic aspect of the pleasure that a graceful, attractive woman may afford to masculine admirers. None the less the underlying assumption that this woman is an instrument and not an independent person is unmistakable. It is hardly necessary to point out the further unjustified assumption that women can attain the finest fruits of civilization by a sort of absorption, without the stimulus of productive effort. If a rich measure of man's highest satisfactions spring from the exercise of his developed powers in labor that he knows to have real and perhaps lasting value, why should the trained woman be denied that stimulus and joy? And can she be truly educated without this active experience? To deny the right of productive work to all women save geniuses is to hedge in their lives far more narrowly than has been the case in any previous period of human history.

The German Steinmetz attacks the economic independence of women on other grounds.[3] He believes that if women at-

[1] *Op. cit.*, pp. 268–9.   [2] *Ibid.*, p. 272.
[3] See his *Feminismus und Rasse* (in *Zeitschrift für Socialwissenschaft*, VII, 1904, pp. 751–8).

tain complete financial independence, the result will be smaller families or none at all. In support of his view he points to Australia and New South Wales where the number of independent women workers, especially in the liberal professions, is extraordinary, and where, in consequence, women marry so much later as seriously to curtail the period of child-bearing. Accordingly such marriages are less fruitful. Furthermore, the author firmly believes that, with feminine economic independence, will go a disinclination on the part of women to submit to the restrictions of married life. In consequence the doctrine of " free love " will find many adherents among self-supporting women. Already Steinmetz notes a tendency among young girls who earn their own money to dally with this dangerous theory. He reminds us that the freeing of women will mean the freeing of man from the obligations of family support and loyalty. Therefore, with free love and the loss of family ties will go a decrease in the number of children; for the woman, not being able to look to the man for support, will find it impossible to have more than one child if she is to carry on her work successfully and rear her offspring in accordance with the best standards of her age. After these dark prophecies, Herr Steinmetz concludes that, since humanity needs as numerous as possible a rising generation born of capable women, feminism, in striving against these essential needs, must be condemned.

Perhaps there are thoughtful men and women who will be impressed by these arguments and will see much reason to fear that feminism and free love may enter into a permanent alliance. But, while granting that certain natures in both sexes may prove hospitable to the doctrine of complete freedom in love and may even favor sexual unions that resemble " serial polygamy," yet will not the deep-seated craving of men and women alike for a permanent, ideal love — of comradeship as well as of passion — together with their appreciation of the service rendered by pure and lasting family life to the social body, render such an association between feminism and sexual freedom highly improbable? The genuine concern felt by not a few students of society lest woman's emancipation " go to her head " and lead to ill-regulated sex relations, seems hardly justified by the feminine nature which is, and long will be, far more attracted by those modes of life which are firmly established and amply justified by experience than by those which seem radical and dangerous. For, as psychologists and biologists have not failed to indicate, women in physical structure and in mental life hold closer to the norm than do men.

The Views of the Moderate Progressives. — There remain to be discussed the views of a considerable body of educated men and women who may be termed the moderate progressives. It is probable that this group is composed of a majority of the enlightened and reflective minds in the community. As their name implies, the moderate progressives are sincerely in favor of a gradual solution of the perplexing questions involved in modern family life in the light of reason, good will and social experience. They believe that thorough and impartial study of the social conditions which menace family life should be followed by attempts to reform those conditions through (1) legislation, (2) education. By these two means they earnestly believe that a far more wholesome and satisfying form of family life may be secured to the coming generations than exists in any large measure at present. Let us consider these remedies in some detail.

Legislation as a Remedy. I. The Revision of Domestic Codes. — It should clearly be understood at the outset that the moderate progressives, in favoring reform of the domestic relations codes of the various nations are not unduly optimistic with regard to the happy results to be secured by such methods. Every thoughtful social observer must realize soon or late that good laws do not guarantee good societies, good homes or good characters. The most that enlightened legislation can accomplish is to furnish certain external conditions and influences favorable to wholesome social life in one or more of its multiform phases. Beyond this it can do little. But to secure wise and equitable conditions of life is one of the most essential functions of government. Only a very cursory study of the marriage laws of the various states and territories of our Union is needed to reveal the lack of uniformity as well as the laxity in matters of procedure that characterize them. Despite the fact that most states have enacted statutes governing the procedure necessary to a legal marriage, viz., the obtaining of a license, public celebration of the marriage by a designated civil officer or by a clergyman in good standing, and proper registration of the union, yet these statutes are too often taken to be merely directive instead of mandatory and hence self-marriages, innocent of legal or religious forms, still take place in our own country. " In short," to quote Professor Howard, "the vicious mediæval distinction between validity and legality is retained as an element of common matrimonial law in the United States." [1]   That is to say, irregular or " common law " marriages, in which the couples take each other for husband and wife without the assistance of any properly constituted official, and often without witnesses, are recognized as valid and binding (although not legally solemnized) in twenty-three states of the Union. In only eighteen states have such informal marriages been expressly repudiated by statutes or by the courts.[2] Is it not an amazing fact that, in a matter which so profoundly affects the dignity and stability of the family institution, society should be so slow to take enlightened action? Surely no legislative reform is more needed than clear and positive statutes declaring such loosely contracted unions null and void.

When this initial step has been taken, much remains to be done. Until a vigorous campaign of education has broken down the strong feeling in many sections of our country in

[1] *History of Matrimonial Institutions*, Vol. III, p. 170.   [2] *Ibid.*, p. 182.

favor of States' rights in all matters originally left to the States, it is probable that no federal marriage code, uniform for the entire country, can be secured. And this work of education may be the work of years. In the interval many States may well devote time and thought to the revision of their matrimonial laws. The age at which minors may marry without the consent of parents is still too low in some States. For example, in Tennessee both boys and girls may contract a legal marriage without parental consent at sixteen years of age, and in Idaho and North Carolina both sexes may marry at eighteen with no obligation to secure parental consent.[1] Again, there is not a State in the Union, with the exception of Wisconsin and Maine, which demands an interval of several days after the marriage license has been secured in order that objections to the union may be filed and examined. Such a delay, together with publication of the intention of the parties to marry, should be obligatory in every State in order that illegal marriages or those contrary to the best interests of the individuals or of society may be prevented. Under the present State laws, which permit the marriage ceremony to follow immediately upon the securing of the license, it is difficult to see how objections to a marriage can be made without an actual interruption of the nuptial service. Finally, although an advance has been made in this respect during the last fifteen years, the various State laws requiring the registration of marriages are either extremely lax or are carelessly executed. Howard urges the division of every county into matrimonial districts in each of which " a registrar should be authorized to license, solemnize and register all marriages civilly contracted therein ; and to license, register, and attend religious celebrations. His authority should be carefully restricted to the district and no other person should be permitted to share his functions. The district registrars should report at short intervals to the county registrar, who in turn

[1] *World Almanac*, 1915, p. 284.

should annually submit a summary of statistics to the registrar-general for the state, by whom the local registrars should be commissioned." [1] It is probable that such an organization for the intelligent administration of matrimonial law would drive home to the public mind the importance attached by the State to the institution of marriage and thus would lend it an added dignity and seriousness. In any case matrimonial statistics, thus carefully collected and revised, would be of the utmost value to sociologists and students of social institutions.

Any discussion of the reform of State domestic codes would manifestly be incomplete which did not refer to the question of our divorce laws. But when revision of these codes is contemplated the whole problem of divorce, with its causes and its cure, is thrust into the forefront of discussion. What is the attitude of the so-called moderate progressives on this difficult question? Certainly it is not in sympathy with the conservatives who would wholly abolish this relief from domestic misery or would rigidly restrict its causes to the scriptural ground. Very justly the progressives argue that an arbitrary refusal of the remedy of divorce may be as immoral, as opposed to the well-being of the community, as the laxest system of divorce procedure could be. To quote Professor Howard once more: "Divorce is a remedy not the disease. It is not a virtue in a divorce law, as appears to be often assumed, to restrict the application of the remedy at all hazards, regardless of the sufferings of the social body. If it were always the essential purpose of a good law to diminish directly the numbers of *bona fide* divorces, the more rational course would be to imitate South Carolina and prohibit divorce entirely. Divorce is not immoral. . . . The most enlightened judgment of the age heartily approves of the policy of some states in extending the causes so as to include intoxication from habitual use of strong drinks or narcotics as being . . . de-

[1] *Ibid.*, p. 194.

structive of connubial happiness and family well-being. Indeed, considering the needs of each particular society, the promotion of happiness is the only safe criterion to guide the lawmaker in either widening or narrowing the door of escape from the marriage bond." [1]

At the same time the moderate progressives are by no means in accord with those radical theorists who would abolish all State control of marriage and divorce and place in the hands of individuals full power to contract and terminate sexual unions. Such a course they regard as giving sanction to the sheerest individualism, and an abandonment by society of its authority over an institution in which its well-being is closely bound up. Rather would the moderate school of social philosophers desire to see a thorough overhauling of the divorce laws of our various States with a view to securing greater uniformity than at present prevails. A reform of this sort would render impossible such scandals as, now and then, disgrace the annals of our divorce courts. More specifically it would result in a saner interpretation of certain highly general causes for divorce such as " cruelty," " non-support," and " gross neglect of duty." It is the lax interpretation of these clauses that is partly responsible for the unsavory reputation of places such as Reno, Nevada, and Sioux Falls, South Dakota. Again, such a standardizing of divorce codes would prevent couples living in States where immediate remarriage after divorce is forbidden (as in California), or where the causes of divorce are few or none (as in New York and South Carolina respectively), from evading the laws of their own States by seeking relief in neighboring commonwealths where the divorce laws are more liberal. In this connection Howard cites the fact that Reno, Nevada, is the " Mecca of newly divorced people from California " who hasten across the border with the object of immediate remarriage ; and Greenwich, Connecticut, serves the same purpose for divorced couples living in New York State

[1] *Op. cit.*, p. 220.

where the laws forbid remarriage of the guilty defendant until after the death of the plaintiff, except in special cases of good behavior for a period of five years.[1]

But, even when the divorce laws of the various States have been brought more nearly into harmony, too much must not be expected from this reform. It is improbable that the current of divorces in the United States will be stemmed in any marked degree by such means. Indeed so important an authority as Rev. Samuel Dike, for many years Secretary of the National Divorce Reform League, records it as his opinion that the " establishment of uniform laws is not the central point of the problem." [2] The evil lies deeper than the arm of the law can reach, its roots being laid in the irresponsible attitude of individuals toward the marriage relation, an attitude leading to unions contracted thoughtlessly and ignorantly or under the spell of a sex passion, too easily mistaken for abiding love. From this point of view, an ounce of prevention by means of education is worth a pound of cure in good divorce laws.

II. Reforms through new Social Legislation. — But the moderate progressives are not satisfied with the mere revision of existing domestic relations laws. The more socially minded of this group are urging the passage of new laws which shall make it possible to hold together the homes of the poor and to preserve the health of their members. To this end they are interested to secure legislation providing for widows' pensions and shorter working days for women, and prohibiting child labor and the labor of women immediately before or after childbirth. A smaller group, perhaps, are advocates of State eugenics laws, more or less drastic in character.

The movement to secure pensions for mothers either widowed, deserted or deprived of support by the disablement of their husbands has been actively carried forward since the White House Conference on Children held in January, 1909,

[1] *Ibid.*, p. 205.
[2] *Statistics of Marriage and Divorce* (in *Pol. Sci. Quarterly*, IV, 602–12).

The social philosophy behind such legislation has been briefly expressed as follows :

" We cannot reasonably hope for any upward trend in families we would help ; we cannot hope for results by way of stronger, more resolute bodies and minds which shall in the children's later years mean a larger initiative, efficiency and productiveness, unless we remove from their lives to-day that constant crushing anxiety that not only deadens hope and aspiration in the mother's life, but also gradually lays its withering, paralyzing hand on the lives of the children, creating a downward pressure on life instead of an upward energy, sapping and undermining the vigor and hope of every member of the family." [1]

If this paralyzing pressure is not to dwarf lives and bring about the break-up of families, mothers with dependent children and little or no means of support must be given a minimum income which, after careful investigation of the circumstances, may fairly be said to be indispensable. At least fifteen States have taken action within the last few years providing for motherhood or widows' pensions. These are Massachusetts, Illinois, Missouri, Colorado, Washington, Oregon, Utah, South Dakota, Idaho, Minnesota, Iowa, Nebraska, Ohio, New Jersey, New York and Pennsylvania. Since the Massachusetts act became effective Sept. 1, 1913, it is estimated that about $460,000 have been expended in aiding 2967 mothers to hold their homes together.

The protection of the womanhood of the nation against overwork in the various industries where women are employed has not proceeded very far. The District of Columbia and the States of Washington, California and Colorado have enacted an eight-hour law applying to women in all industries except household work and trained nursing. When it is remembered that 26.3 per cent of all females in the United

[1] Wm. H. Matthews, *Widows' Families, Pensioned and Otherwise.* Reprinted from the *Survey*, June 6, 1914.

States between the ages of twenty-one and forty are employed in gainful occupations and when it is further known that " matrimony has had little effect in decreasing the number of workers "[1] the beneficent effect of such eight-hour laws in preserving a portion of the mother's time and strength for the home is better appreciated. A few States have taken action looking to the conservation of mothers and children by passing laws forbidding women to work in factories or stores for a specified period before and after childbirth. But in such legislation the United States lags far behind the progressive nations of Europe.

In the households of the poor the scanty income furnished by the labor of father or mother has forced the children under fourteen years into a wide variety of gainful pursuits. The United States *Census* returns show that 1,990,225 children of both sexes between the ages of ten and fifteen years — 18.4 per cent of the total number of the nation's children — were employed in gainful occupations in 1910. This is an advance of .2 per cent over the proportion employed in 1900. Such exploitation of the country's youth is not only a detriment to the health and general intelligence of the children themselves, but may well exercise an adverse influence on family life, since children who thus early become self-supporting, or nearly so, show a tendency to submit with an ill grace to the counsel and discipline of their parents. Too soon they assert their independence, seek the street or the " movies " for excitement after their day's toil, and thus push the individualistic spirit to its limit in their own family life. The Palmer-Owen bill before Congress at this writing (January, 1915) is designed to " prevent interstate commerce in the products of Child Labor." It provides that no persons or corporations employing children under 16 in mines or quarries, and no mill, cannery, workshop or factory in which children under 14 are employed or in which children between 14 and 16 years are permitted to

[1] *World Almanac*, 1915, p. 230; taken from *Census Report*.

work more than eight hours daily or more than six days a week " shall ship or offer for shipment (their) products in interstate commerce." [1] Such a Federal Act should be supported by every progressive citizen, not only because it conserves childhood, but also because, by protecting the health and extending the period of education of children, it will exert a beneficent influence on the parents of the future and on the homes they will establish.

When the question of eugenics comes up for consideration the group that we have elected to call the " moderate progressives " finds itself divided. The more advanced favor rather drastic legislation by the state to prevent the marriage of tubercular and epileptic persons as well as the feebleminded and criminally degenerate. They even go further and hope for great things from the wisely directed mating of men and women of pronounced intellectual and moral gifts. Such unions, guided by intelligence and knowledge, and thus controlled during several generations, they believe will progressively elevate the culture and character of the race. But unfortunately for these optimistic plans, there is already a reaction on the part of scientists against the large claims made by too enthusiastic eugenists. These experts are pointing out that " conscious selection has no creative power whatever "; in other words we have *no guarantee* that the most reflective and intelligent selection of a mate would result in offspring superior or even equal to their parents. The germ cells of the parents are almost infinitely complex and the characters transmitted to their children are not always the desirable ones. Moreover, the effect of the varied environment of man in developing the potentialities of his original nature can hardly be too vigorously emphasized. The most gifted mind can be stunted in wholly bad surroundings and the dullest will admit of marked improvement in a stimulating environment. For these reasons Professor Conklin of Princeton University has recently urged great caution upon the advocates of state

[1] Pamphlet of National Child Labor Committee, February, 1914.

control of marriage and the scientific breeding of the race. Writing of eugenics he says:

" Undoubtedly it represents an important application of biological discoveries to human welfare, but it seems to me that it cannot wisely go farther at this time than to attempt to eliminate from reproduction the most unfit members of society. Giving advice regarding matrimony is proverbially a hazardous performance, and it is not much safer for the biologist than for others." [1]

The United States has probably accomplished more in the direction of eliminating the unfit from reproduction than most of the nations of Europe. The states of Oregon, California, Indiana, Wisconsin, New Jersey and Connecticut have passed laws providing for sterilization of persons in state institutions, in cases where procreation on their part would, in the judgment of a competent examining board, be likely " to produce children with an inherited tendency to crime, insanity, feeblemindedness, idiocy, or imbecility. . . ." [2] Commenting on this legislation Professor Kellicott says:

" These states are to be commended in the highest possible terms for their enlightened action in this direction. Who can say how many families of Jukes and Zeros [3] have already been inhibited by this simple and humane means? Could such a law be enforced in the whole United States, less than four generations would eliminate nine-tenths of the crime, insanity and sickness of the present generation in our land. Asylums, prisons and hospitals would decrease, and the problems of the unemployed, the indigent old, and the hopelessly degenerate would cease to trouble civilization." [4]

It is rather a pity in any way to detract from the effect of

[1] Article in *Science*, Vol. 37, 1913.

[2] Quoted from Connecticut Statute, enacted in 1909.

[3] Reference to two historic families, one in New York State and one in Europe, in which tainted heredity was responsible for hundreds of criminals, prostitutes and imbeciles.

[4] Kellicott, *Social Direction of Human Evolution*, p. 222.

such rosy prophecies. Yet two facts should be remembered by the careful student. (1) Whereas the operation of vesectomy which secures the sterilization of males is simple and attended with no harmful results, the operation of oöphorotomy that produces sterility in females is a much more serious matter and should be performed with the utmost care and circumspection and only in cases of real necessity. (2) Even when society has taken steps to prevent the manifestly " unfit " of our generation from propagating, it has no assurance that the work will not have to be repeated in the next and the next generation, since the germ cells contain a vast number of harmful potentialities that have never developed in the adults who transmit them. In the words of Dr. T. Claye Shaw of London: " We may assist nature [in the elimination of the unfit] by placing under lock and key every degenerate of the country; but it would only be a respite, the condition would soon reassert itself, because, however we try to eliminate it, the measures cannot touch the elements which are present in many of the lives which would be passed by the eugenists as sound, though they may only declare their existence too late and when the danger by transmission has been effected. . . ." [1] Such statements are calculated to dampen the enthusiasm of certain over-optimistic leaders in the eugenics campaign.

Despite these discouraging declarations many moderate progressives would go a step farther than the sterilization of the degenerates in our State institutions. They would favor the enactment of laws to prevent the marriage of the unfit in society at large. A few States have already passed bills providing that a health certificate be issued with every marriage license as a guarantee that the applicants are not afflicted with epilepsy, tuberculosis or venereal disease and that they are of sound mind. Massachusetts, Pennsylvania, Wisconsin and several other States have enacted such laws and a similar bill was recently presented to the legis-

[1] Quoted in *Current Opinion*, September, 1914, p. 180.

lature of New York but failed of passage. The Pennsylvania measure is the most radical, since it not only requires the health certificate, but prohibits the granting of a marriage license to any male person who has been within five years an inmate of a county asylum or home for indigent persons unless it appears that he is able to support a family.

Such legislation is indicative of the growing sense of responsibility felt by all progressive communities for the quality of the stock that is to carry forward the work of civilization. It is probable that in increasing numbers the States in our Union will enact laws to prevent marriages among those clearly unfit to propagate. The difficulty, of course, centres about the determination of unfitness. Already physicians are advising the public that tuberculosis is not directly transmissible — only the tendency to succumb to the germs of the disease (which we all carry about with us) being inherited; and that if children of tubercular persons are carefully brought up and given plenty of fresh air and nourishing food, they have a good chance of becoming healthy and useful citizens. Other physicians point out that the tests prescribed by State laws for determining the presence of venereal disease are not sufficiently searching to be of much value. Only the Wasserman test is reliable and that is both difficult and expensive. Certain doctors in Wisconsin are opposed to the eugenics law of that State, passed in 1913, partly on the above ground. The validity of the act has recently been subjected to a legal test by a determined group of citizens who are hostile to it.

A Campaign of Education. — When legislation has done its utmost to provide conditions favorable to the growth of wholesome, happy and permanent family life, there still remains the problem of fitting men and women to found such families. And this education of individuals the moderate progressives believe to be the *crux* of the whole matter. How can youths and maidens be given ideals of marriage and home-making that shall be sincere and dynamic and shall control their choice of a mate? How can they be led better to understand that the union of man and woman and the establishment of a new family is a matter, not alone of profound interest to themselves, but of vital concern to the society of which they are members? How can they most wisely be acquainted with the dangers that surround warm-blooded, inexperienced youth, — dangers not only of sexual immorality, but of unwise marriage choices governed almost solely by sex attraction and little or not at all by real knowledge on the part of each of the other's nature. How can they be instructed in the responsibilities of parents, alike to the offspring they bring into the world and to the society in which these children must play their parts as workers and citizens?

Knowledge, of course, must do its share in this great work of fitting the young men and women of a nation for marriage and family life. It has been suggested in the preceding chapter that scientific instruction should be given in the facts of reproduction and in sex hygiene. But who should impart such knowledge and when should it be given? It would be a courageous person who would answer these queries dogmatically. Yet is there not a considerable consensus of opinion in favor of leaving the more intimate and personal facts of sex life to be imparted by parents to their children, at least until the high school age? At once there arises the question whether parents are fitted to give such instruction — fitted either with respect to sound knowledge or insight into their children's needs. So much may be accomplished by wise choice of the time, place and manner of imparting such facts as are really needed, and so much harm may be done by artificiality and insincerity. Probably a large proportion of parents are not at present in a position to teach their own children much that they need to know. Not only is their own information inaccurate and incomplete, but their attitude toward the whole question is neither enlightened nor sympathetic. Plainly, many of them see no urgent need of giving their girls and boys any more knowledge than they themselves received from their parents. Both the ignorance and the unsympathetic attitude might be overcome by a campaign of education of fathers and mothers through public school lectures and mothers' meetings. But this means that leaders must arise among us to organize this work and inspire others with their own animating ideals.

To the schools could then be left the task of imparting knowledge concerned with the general laws of reproduction in courses in biology and nature study. These facts could be introduced quite naturally from the lower grades to the higher as occasion arose. At the high school stage boys and girls probably need more specialized knowledge than the average parent can give them; and here the sexes might be divided into groups for the study of sex functions and sex health. As the work advanced it might well include simple lessons on the social meaning of marriage and the family and the degree in which the welfare of society is intimately bound up with the welfare of the families that compose it.

But this educational effort on the part of parents and schools will be largely wasted if the instruction is not shot through and through with a fine spirit of idealism. Knowledge is good as far as it goes, but it is proverbially barren of moral effects unless it is so imparted as to stir the emotions and stiffen the will. It is *better and more dynamic ideals* that we want rather than more facts; and although sound knowledge may beyond doubt be an aid to virtue, it will prove a sterile thing in the hands of teachers not inspired with a high and flaming ethical purpose and endowed with tact and understanding of the nature of youth. It would be a most hopeful sign for the uplift of humanity if a growing number of teachers properly endowed with sympathy, ideals and knowledge, should fit themselves for this work as for a great mission. But the specialists need not work alone. As Stanley Hall so wisely insists, every teacher who arouses in youth, in the insurgent period of puberty and adolescence, enthusiasms and living interests — be they in literature, art, science, sports, what you will — is helping to draw off sex feeling into channels of worthy achievement. He is really illustrating in his own teaching the principles of the Aristotelian *Katharsis*. Every teacher shares in this great work of transmuting sex impulse into ideal effort whenever he awakens enthusiasm for things worth while.[1]

And so this chapter would close with a plea that parents and teachers bend their efforts to secure sounder knowledge, truer idealism, a firmer self-control for the young men and women of our land who are to be the husbands and wives, the fathers and mothers of the coming generation. Only thus can we get at the root of the disease that is sapping the vigor of married life; only thus can we combat the tendencies that are making still further for the disintegration of the family. And when we recall what this institution has accomplished for the good of the social body in the past, we may well put forth our best efforts to preserve it. For what substitute for the monogamic family as the nursery of individuality has society yet evolved? What other form of organization so completely secures the proper maintenance and training of the young? What other type of sex relationship has done so much to nourish the more spiritual phases of sex passion? In an age of domestic unrest every thoughtful man and woman should inform himself or herself on questions concerned with the family institution and exercise such influence as he or she may possess to deepen the respect in which it is held by the public in general, as well as to bring about needed reforms in its operation.

SELECTED BIBLIOGRAPHY

Allen, Grant. *Plain Words on the Woman Question* (in *Fort. Rev.*, October, 1889, pp. 448–58).

[1] In an address delivered by Dr. G. Stanley Hall before the American Association for Social Hygiene, in the fall of 1914.

Bebel, August. *Woman under Socialism* (1904), pp. 343 ff.

Carpenter, Edward. *Love's Coming of Age*, pp. 85 ff.

Coolidge, Mary R. *Why Women are So* (1913).

Creighton, Louise. *The Social Disease and how to Fight It* (1914).

Ferrero, G. *The Problem of Woman from a Bio-Sociological Point of View* (in *Monist*, IV, No. 2).

Galton, Francis. *Eugenics: its Definition, Scope and Aims* (*Amer. Jour. of Soc.*, July, 1904).

George, W. F. *Feminist Intentions* (*Atlantic Monthly*, Vol. 112, pp. 721–32).

Gillette, John M. *The Family and Society* (1914). See last two chapters.

Howard, E. G. *History of Matrimonial Institutions*, Vol. III, pp. 239–59.

Kellicott, W. E. *Social Direction of Human Evolution* (1911), pp. 180 ff.

Key, Ellen. *Love and Marriage.*

Nearing, Scott. *Woman and Social Progress.*

Saleeby, C. W. *Parenthood and Race Culture* (1909).

Schreiner, Olive. *Woman and Labor* (1911).

Spencer, Anna Garlin. *Woman's Share in Social Culture.*

Tarbell, Ida M. *The Business of Being a Woman* (1912).

Wells, H. G. *Socialism and the Family* (1908).

Woodbridge, Elizabeth. *The Unknown Quantity in the Woman Problem* (in *Atlantic Monthly*, Vol. 13, April, 1914).

INDEX

Abacus, in English nurseries, 334–35.

Abbott, Edith, quoted, on transitional industrial conditions in America, 421; on female labor in factories, 421–22.

Aberdeen, University of, doors opened to women, 438.

Abipones, divorce among, 29.

Abortion, in early Roman empire, 138; in Middle Ages, 212; attitude of early church toward, 168–69; motives for, in pagan times, 169.

Abraham, marriage with half-sister Sarah, 22; nomadic life, 49.

Acceptance of child by father, primitive, 37, 39; Greek, 82; Roman, 126; in Middle Ages, 183, 185.

Accipiam vs. *accipio*, 247.

Achilles, deprived of his concubine, 95.

Acolytes, service of Roman boys and girls, 128.

Acts of Legislature, extending property rights of women, 435; limiting authority of parents over children, 444–45. *See also* Laws; Ordinances.

Acts of Parliament, concerning apprentices, 294; guardians and wards, 298; property of intestate man or wife, 299; marriage licenses, 320; penalizing performance of illegal marriage, 321; restricting time and place of marriage, 321; dissolving gilds, 415; extending property rights of women, 429–33, 439; affecting parental control of children, 439, 441–44; concerning divorce, 446–52. *See also* Laws; Ordinances.

Adams, Abigail, quoted concerning care of husband's clothing, 393.

Addison, quotation from *Clarinda's Journal*, 308.

Adoption, of slave as heir, 53; among Greeks, 81; among Romans, 114, 139; into kin of European barbarians, 182.

Adultery, as ground for divorce, among primitive peoples, 29–30; Hebrews, 68; Greeks, 97; Romans, 122; Talmudic treatise on adultery, 48; in Christ's view, 160; in the medieval church, 205; during Renaissance, 248–49, 250. — Adultery gave power of life and death to Hebrew husband, 52; prevented remarriage, 60; condoned in Hebrew husband as in modern Occidental, 69; in Ionia,

91; punishment, 97; relative frequency in Athens and Sparta, 97–98; of Roman wife, punishable by death, 115; unchastity of betrothed girl considered adultery, 119; views of early Christian church, 167–68; engaged girl's infidelity considered as adultery in Middle Ages, 191; distinction between husband's and wife's, 202, 203; during Renaissance, quotation from *Of Spousals*, 249–50; wife's adultery sometimes punished with death, 268; even men's sometimes penalized, 270; death penalty in New England, 354, both offenders punished, 354; in American colonies, 377–78, 379, 381; in nineteenth century, 446, 447, 448, 450, 451, 452, 453; at present, 458, 459, 522; debarred English mother from visiting child, 442; reason for punishing, Socialist theory, 498. *See also* Double standard of morals; Sexual intercourse.

Æmilia, her divorce, remarriage and death, 141.

Æmilius, reasons for divorcing Papiria, 140.

Æschylus, quoted on single parentage, 79–80.

Æthelbert, laws concerning wife purchase, 189.

Æthgift, joint-owner of her husband's lands, 201.

Affection, conjugal, in primitive times, 23–25; in polygamy, 26; in Greece, 86, 91; in Middle Ages, 189; during Renaissance, 265–67; at present, 477. *See also* Love.

Affection, parental, in primitive family, 36–39; in early Rome, 126; in England, 287–88.

Africa, divorce in, 29; life from hand to mouth, 32; status of primitive child in, 36, 37, 38, 39; charms in nurture of infants, 40. *See also*, Bushmans; Gold Coast negroes; Hottentots; Kafirs.

Agamemnon and his concubines, 94, 95.

Agde, Council of, on divorce, 203.

Age, legal, for Hebrew marriage, 60–61; for Roman, 139; alleged increase in age at present, 477–78, 478–79; statistics proving contrary, 479, except in certain groups or regions, 481–82. *See also* Child betrothals; Child marriages.

Agnates, definition, 117.

Agnation, definition, 10; in Greece, 82; in Rome, 182.

Agni, Aryan god of fire, 80–81.

Printed in the United States of America.